WITHDRAWN
FROM THE LIBRARY OF
UNIVERSITY OF ULSTER

D1320930

COMPUTATIONAL AND PSYCHOPHYSICAL MECHANISMS OF VISUAL CODING

COMPUTATIONAL AND PSYCHOPHYSICAL MECHANISMS OF VISUAL CODING

Edited by
MICHAEL JENKIN
York University

LAURENCE HARRIS
York University

CAMBRIDGE
UNIVERSITY PRESS

407390

612.84
COM
xx1

Published by the Press Syndicate of the University of Cambridge
The Pitt Building, Trumpington Street, Cambridge CB2 1RP
40 West 20th Street, New York, NY 10011-4211, USA
10 Stamford Road, Oakleigh, Melbourne 3166, Australia

© Cambridge University Press 1997

First published 1997

Printed in the United States of America

Computational and psychophysical mechanisms of visual coding / edited
by Michael Jenkin, Laurence Harris.
        p. cm.
     Based on a conference.
     Includes bibliographical references and index.
     ISBN 0-521-57104-9
     1. Vision—Congresses.   2. Computer vision—Congresses.   3. Visual
perception—Congresses.   I. Jenkin, Michael (Michael Richard
MacLean), 1959–   .   II. Harris, Laurence (Laurence Roy), 1953–   .
QP474.C63   1997
612,8′4—dc21   96-52594
                                                               CIP

A catalog record for this book is available from the British Library

ISBN 0-521-57104-9 hardback

To HLM and CMO.

Contents

Contributors

Stuart Anstis
Dept. of Psychology, University of California at San Diego, San Diego, CA.

Martin Arguin
Dept. de Psychologie, Univ. de Montrèal, Montreal, Canada H3A 2B4.

Daniel Bub
Montreal Neurological Inst., McGill University, Montreal, Canada H3A 2A7.

J. Douglas Crawford
Department of Psychology, York University, North York, Ontario, Canada, M3J 1P3.

Peter Dayan
Department of Computer Science, University of Toronto, Toronto, Ontario, Canada, M5S 1A4.

Sven Dickinson
Center for Cognitive Science and Department of Computer Science, Rutgers University, New Brunswick, NJ 08903.

Michael Dixon
Psychosocial Research Unit, Douglas Hospital, Montreal, Canada H4H lR3.

Gregory Dudek
McGill Centre for Research in Intelligent Machines, McGill University, Montreal, Quebec, Canada.

David J. Fleet
Department of Computing and Information Science and Department of Psychology, Queen's University, Kingston, Ontario, Canada.

Brendan J. Frey
Department of Computer Science, University of Toronto, Toronto, Ontario, Canada, M5S 1A4.

Laurence Harris
Department of Psychology, York University, North York, Ontario, Canada, M3J 1P3.

David J. Heeger
Department of Psychology, Stanford University, Stanford, California, 94305.

Geoffrey E. Hinton
Department of Computer Science, University of Toronto, Toronto, Ontario, Canada, M5S 1A4.

Heather Jenkin
Department of Psychology, York University, North York, Ontario, Canada, M3J 1P3.

Michael Jenkin
Department of Computer Science, York University, North York, Ontario, Canada, M3J 1P3.

Dennis M. Levi
University of Houston, College of Optometry, Houston, Texas, 77204-6052.

Dimitri Metaxas
Department of Computer and Information Science, University of Pennsylvania, Philadelphia, PA, 19104-6389.

Hans-Christoph Nothdurft
Visual Perception Laboratory, Goettingen, Germany, and Max Planck Institute for Biophysical Chemistry, Goettingen, Germany.

Edmund T. Rolls
Oxford University, Department of Experimental Psychology, South Parks Road, Oxford, OX1 3UD, England.

Christopher Tyler
Smith-Kettlewell Eye Research Institute, San Francisco, CA.

Herman Wagner
Department of Zoology, Aachen University, Germany.

Preface

This book is based on a conference on Visual Coding, the third conference of the York Centre for Vision Research organized by I. P. Howard, D. M. Regan and B. J. Rogers in June 1995 and sponsored by the Human Performance Laboratory of the Institute for Space and Terrestrial Science at York University. Operating from the theory that biological and computational researchers have much to learn from each other, speakers at these conferences have been invited from both the biological and computational communities. The resulting presentations and papers illustrate the similarities in the problems that are considered by the biological and computational worlds, and the common models and algorithms that are proposed to solve them.

The York Vision Conference, and this book, would not have been possible without the advise and support of Ian P. Howard, David Martin Regan and the Human Performance in Space Laboratory of the Institute of Space and Terrestrial Science (ISTS). Behind any successful endeavour is the person who really runs things, and none of this would have been possible without Teresa Manini.

Finally we would like to thank Lisa Manini who helped us track down all those references and Lauren Cowles at CUP for letting us do it again.

1

Computational and psychophysical mechanisms of visual coding

Laurence R. Harris

Department of Psychology, York University,
North York, Ontario, Canada

Michael R. M. Jenkin

Department of Computer Science, York University,
North York, Ontario, Canada

This chapter discusses the relationship between codes and tasks. As incoming energy cannot be directed or channelled into performing a task directly, some intermediate steps must be involved: light cannot directly move an eye nor cause a finger to wag. The incoming energy must be filtered or converted into an appropriate form or series of forms. And that is what a code is, a representation of information. This does not imply that a sensory code only codes sensory information. This is far from being the case in either a machine or an organism! The content of the code will derive from a combination of sensory input (so called bottom-up) and top-down processes. The enormous influence of the latter is only just coming to be recognized (see Chapter 12).

We distinguish between two levels of coding; a trivial level in which information is coded as an undiscriminating representation of as much of the original information as possible. Decoding a trivial code is not normally useful because all that is retrieved is an arbitrarily-filtered version of the original signal. More interesting are profound codes which extract specific elements of information related to specific tasks. Whereas decoding or breaking a trivial code does not necessarily reveal anything about the underlying computational process, breaking profound codes reveals specific task-related information.

After an examination of trivial and profound codes, this chapter considers mechanisms of implementation of profound codes in biological and computational worlds. Lastly we compare biological and computational implementations and show that although each community may have helpful things to share with the other, there is in fact very little cross-fertilization. We discuss some reasons as to why this might be the case.

1.1 The representation of knowledge

The representation of knowledge is fundamental to human cognition and machine understanding. From the simplest computer program that captures an image and displays it on the screen, to the most complex biological visual processes, an underlying representation of the information is required. The structure or *coding* of this representation provides the framework within which any and all processing of the information can occur. Tasks which may be impossible or impractical based on one encoding strategy, may be trivial based on another.

Both the biological and computational communities have had to address the task of designing or inferring visual coding strategies. Some representations appear very similar in both the biological and computational communities. For example, neural networks, which are discussed in Chapter 13, are common representations in both the biological and computational communities. Although the details may be open to debate, there are obvious similarities between a computational 'neural net' and biological structures. Other representations are common in terms of the intent of the representation but which very different in the two fields. Disparity coding, which is discussed in Chapter 6, is described using similar concepts in both the biological and computational literatures but the respective implementations may be very different. Yet other representations, such as superquadrics (see Chapter 10), are unique to one or other research community.

The biological and computational communities have very different mediums within which to represent information. The computational community typically deals with digital machines with fixed and finite resolutions, standard and fixed clock and bus rates, etc. Within the biological community, the underlying biological structures require representations such as impulse, cell-type, or topographic codings (see Uttal, 1973, Howard, 1982). Biological systems and machines obviously use very different media but this does not restrict what is to be represented nor its format or code.

The representation of knowledge or information can be broken down into discrete facets. Various schemes have been devised for such a division (eg. Gibson, 1966; Gregory, 1969; Marr, 1982; Glasss *et a.*, 1979). Essentially there are three stages: (1) the *content*, what is to be represented, (2) the *medium*, the physical realization of the information, and (3) the *code*, the format of the representation. But this is not enough to define a code. A fourth stage, a *retrieval* stage demonstrably able to recover or decode the information, is needed. Otherwise it is meaningless to describe the information as being represented. This is a restatement of the old schoolyard, philosophical question "if a tree falls in a forest and there is no one there to hear, does it make a sound?". Here we are only interested in sounds that are heard: those sounds that *maybe* heard have not yet been coded in the profound sense (see below).

1.2 Codes and tasks

There is a fundamental relationship between the code of a representation and the task for which the information is required. Certain encodings of information are better suited for certain tasks. Finding a particular card (say the queen of hearts) in a pack of cards is much easier if the pack is sorted than if the order of the cards is randomized. The nature of specific visual tasks suggests a certain form of knowledge representation in order to optimize the solving of the task. As an example from visual information processing, consider the problem of performing local stereo matching. What is a good mechanism for representing the intensity information that must be used for the matching? Based on a considerable body of psychophysical and neurological evidence, biological models which combine sets of spatial-frequency, orientation and phase-tuned filters have emerged (see Chapters 6 and 11). In these models the monocular images are represented by the output of a large number of filter operators applied to each image. The computational community has experimented with various representations; from using the raw intensity values through complex monocular image representations based on edges, to representations based on the output of a large number of filter operators applied to the image. This filter-output representation has emerged because it simplifies the task of combining the monocular images. It also permits algorithms which would not be possible with less sophisticated representations. For example, representations which do not describe images at different spatial scales are susceptible to noise localized in a different frequency band or orientation.

1.3 Levels of coding

As a task becomes more and more specific, the algorithms and representations that are applicable to the task become more and more tuned. Specific tasks may permit special solutions which are prohibited by more general versions of the task. There is an intimate relationship between task and

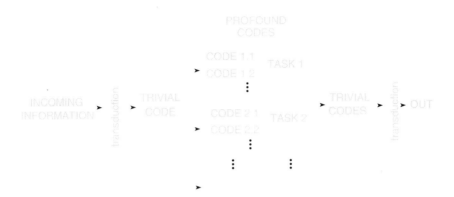

Fig. 1.1. A diagrammatic scheme of the levels of codes, showing task-related profound codes extracting information from the literal "re-presentation" of the trivial codes generated by the transduction process. Trivial codes are also used at the output stage to convert the task-outputs to motor actions.

the set of possible codes that can be used in the task's solution. Given this intimate relationship between representational code and task it is useful to recognize two different classes of codes or encodings The first is a simple, essentially *trivial* code created as part of a transduction or simple transformational process. The second is a task-related, *profound* code. Our scheme is described in Fig. 1.1.

1.3.1 Trivial coding

A defining feature of a trivial coding is that it does not extract any particular piece of information from the input. It is not a goal-directed or task-directed code. The goal is merely to represent or carry all the information, not to process or extract particular features. Transduction represents a trivial coding operation. The process of transduction converts energy from one form to another. Sensory transduction converts external energy such as light, into neural energy. Transduction always involves some kind of filtering process but it can be regarded as a trivial coding operation because it effectively preserves as much of the original information as possible. Trivial codes correspond to the null or empty task. The task associated with the coding is simply to present the information to some later task which will introduce its own code.

Another defining feature of a trivial code is that, at least in biology, there is no decoding process that attempts to recover the coded information: the next stage is always further coding, that is, extracting some higher-level aspect of the information and re-coding it in an appropriate format.

Many examples of trivial encodings exist. Digitization, photo transduction by the photoreceptors of the retina, Fourier transforms and wavelet transforms can be treated as simple transformations of an input which generate trivial codes. If the goal of a coding procedure is simply to transform the input and not to extract specific items, then the code can be considered trivial. Trivial codes do not aid in the process of reasoning about the information being represented. A particular transformation may generate trivial code in one context but that very same transformation may generate profound code in other contexts. As an example, consider the Fourier transform of an image. The Fourier transform may act as a trivial encoding if it is only being used to package up the image in an efficient manner for transmission and the original image will be recovered via an inverse Fourier transform on receipt. However a Fourier transform may be used in a less trivial manner. For example, one way to determine if an image is in focus is to examine the power distribution of the Fourier transform of a set of images. A sensor might continually adjust its focus based on the information represented in the 'trivial' Fourier transform. In this case the Fourier encoding is 'non-trivial'.

Trivial codes are as ambiguous as the original information that arrived at the subject and are certainly not uniquely interpretable. Consider the state of the silver granules in a photograph or the state of CCD pixels in a TV image or the membrane potentials of a set of photoreceptors in the retina. Each of these image representations can be affected in the same way by a variety of stimuli. The states could be created by bright light for a short time or dimmer light for a longer time within the system's integration time. These states could even be created by the application of some other stimuli altogether such as chemical, electrical or mechanical pressure. They could be created by light reflected from a moving object, a coloured object or from light emitted from a light source involving no object at all. Any interpretation of the visual image has to be applied to this trivial code but it is not helped along by this code. From an information perspective it is the same as working with the original stimulus.

1.3.2 Profound codes

The second level of 'code' is a profound code. . Profound codes represent the extraction of specific, useful information from the incoming bombardment with a view to a particular task. That task may be perceptual (Chapter (2), for example recognizing your grandmother, or may be motor, such as guiding an arm or eye movement (Chapter 5). And the task does not have to be a high-level one: detecting and representing motion (Chapter 4) requires profound coding.

A defining characteristic of a profound code is that it is uniquely interpretable. Identifying and counting people's faces in an image and then representing that as a number (eg. 6) is a fundamentally different type of coding from the trivial digitization 'code' of a picture of six people taken by a CCD camera. If the aim of taking a picture is to identify the presence or absence of a particular person in a scene, then the profound code would be 'YES' or 'NO' as opposed to the trivial code of the state of the pixels in the CCD array. That is, it must be possible to extract a coded variable unambiguously from the signal if the signal is to be regarded as a genuine, profound code. This does not mean that a signal needs to contain only a single code. Codes can be multiplexed (more than one piece of information can be handled by a single carrier) in biological (Van Essen & Anderson, 1990; Brotchie et al., 1995) as well as computational systems. Although each multiplexed code still needs to satisfy the defining conditions of a profound code, especially that it can be demonstrably and unambiguously decoded.

A profound code, in which specific information has been extracted from the output of the transducers, does not have to be high-up in the nervous system or in a computer algorithm. Rabbit retinal ganglion cells, for example, encode details of visual movement (see Chapter 4), which involves integration over the output of many individual transducers (Oyster et al., 1972) or trivial codes.

1.4 Requirements of any code

For trivial codes there are no rules. That is there is no unique key for extracting any particular type of information. The codes are as rich (apart from the filtering) as the original stimulus. They are general and unfocussed and, at least in biological systems, there is nothing to be gained by breaking these codes. For a real, profound, goal-directed code, certain rules are required. These rules define the coding process and in a sense, paradoxically, are not really applied so much to the coding as to the decoding process. For a profound code to be decodable there has to be a known reference frame and a known coordinate system. These concepts are defined and explored in the context of coding self motion, where the concepts are readily graspable, in the chapter by Harris on the coding of self motion (see Chapter 8). Here these terms are expanded to embrace more general applications. Coordinate systems and reference frames are often confused. But they should not be since they are entirely independent aspects of a code.

1.4.1 Reference frames

A coding system has to be relative to something. The anchor points to which a code is relative forms its reference frame. A reference frame thus defines the *meaning* of the code. The reference frame for a head movement, for example, might be external space. In this case then the code *means* space. This is a natural concept when talking about movement since it is intuitive to realize that motion is a relative term and *has* to be defined relative to something to be meaningful. But what would the 'reference frame' look like for a coding system that was representing a human face, for example? What is the face being coded relative to?

One possible approach is to suggest that the face is coded relative to all of the other objects or patterns that could be present. This is to use a reference frame as part of the definition of groups of categories. This is consistent with equating a reference frame with meaning. It is not a reference frame problem to decide whether the thing being coded is to be represented as discontinuous categories or a continuous variable, that is the problem of defining the coordinate system (see below). The detection of a face, for example, precludes that pattern of light falling on the retina from being simultaneously identified as anything else. So the reference frame is "recognizable, exclusive, outside items". Notice that recognizing something as a face does *not* interfere with the coding of other attributes such as motion, colour, size, distance etc.. Those would be coded in *other* separate, parallel reference frames.

1.4.2 Coordinate systems

A coordinate system is the rules by which the code is implemented within a reference frame. That is, once the meaning has been established, the coordinate system is the mapping rules between the code value and the attribute being coded. A coordinate system may be linear, logarithmic, polar, vectorial or any number of non-linear schemes including categorization: a reference frame does not imply or define a particular coordinate system.

1.4.3 Decoding rules

A functional profound code thus needs both a reference frame and a coordinate system. And in order to decode the information it is necessary to know what these are. The information about the reference frame and the coordinate system cannot be present in the code itself. These are things that have to brought to the code in order to extract the information. If the wrong reference frame or coordinate system is applied, then errors will occur. Reference frame errors would be errors of meaning - interpreting the code as representing colour when it was actually representing sound. Coordinate systems errors would be of quantity - mistaking your spouse for a hat (in the single reference frame of 'outside objects'), for example (Sacks, 1985) or less dramatically, misjudging values eg. speed or direction of movement. Experimentally, coordinate system errors can be introduced eg. by adaptation (see Chapter 4).

How are profound codes realized? In the following sections we describe some biological and computational realization of coding systems.

1.5 Biological codes

The biological representation of information is a central theme of this book. A basic principle is that the brain appears to divide up or channel information into a number of sub-modalities eg. visual motion and colour, each of which is processed individually. These channels have been labelled sub-modality processing (SuMP) channels (see Chapter 8). This leads to a modular functional organization (see Chapter 9). Within each of these modules, various coding systems are potentially available. If the sub-modality is defined closely enough, then the definition can actually include the reference frame. The question then becomes what coordinate system or coding system to adopt within a SuMP channel?

1.5.1 Labelled line coding

The simplest coding system would be a sub-modality defined so closely that it became one dimensional. Then a simple monotonic meter could carry the code. This is the essence of a labelled line: a cell or system whose activity always means one thing. An example close to such a pure system is found in the pain channels of the somatosensory system (Mountcastle & Powell, 1959; Willis, 1985; Kandel *et al.*, 1994) and might also apply to other aspects of somatosensory processing (Vallbo, 1989). Such a system is vulnerable to ambiguity: the end organ has to be so selective that it is only activated by the relevant stimulus and then responds proportionally to the only coded attribute of that stimulus. Normally a stage has to intervene between the end organ and the coding channel to provide such robustness.

One method of providing protection from ambiguity is by passing the information through several overlapping filters, often, confusingly called channels (see Chapter 8).

1.5.2 Channel coding within a sub-modality

Since end-organs are not usually specific to the attribute in question, their response is inherently ambiguous. For example, a cone might alter its activity in response to changes in either colour or luminance, or a semicircular canal hair cell might alter its activity in response to changes in either acceleration or direction of head rotation. A SuMP system that uses within-sub-modality-processing (WiSuMP) channels achieves its robustness in coding a particular attribute because all the WiSuMP channels are affected equally by irrelevant factors whose influence can therefore be removed by a comparative process. This is a well-known idea, sometimes called common mode rejection (see for example, (Regan, 1982; Regan, 1989; Campbell & Tedeger, 1991)). For example, cones are all affected the same way (eg. doubling their responses) by a change in luminance, but each cone type is affected differently by a change in wavelength. This makes cones able to extract wavelength information. But an individual cone type cannot carry wavelength information: the wavelength information can *only* be extracted by comparison. This method of coding has been successfully applied to the coding of spatial frequency, orientation and the direction of full-field motion (see Chapters 7, 8 and 11). The WiSuMP method of coding a parameter is thus one example of population coding, where the information is not carried by any individual cells but by the population.

1.5.3 Population coding

In its most general form, a population coding system is any system in which information is coded with appropriate resolution and accuracy not by an individual neuron but by the whole population. WiSuMP channels are an example of a population coding method. For some examples of population codes, although no individual contributor carries the whole message, each cell shows a strong correlation with the parameter in question. Other methods of coding information within a population or cell assembly (Hebb, 1949) can be less approachable. When information is coded in a distributed way

(Rumelhart & McClelland, 1986) it can be all but impossible to reconstruct the message experimentally from the activity of the cells which carry it.

An example of an approachable population code is a system of several labelled cells tuned to all possible values of the parameter. As such this hardly differs from the channel system already described. The difference comes not so much in the coding, which is essentially also by a set, albeit usually a much larger set, of WiSuMP channels, but in the decoding method. Decoding of a population coded attribute is achieved simply by identifying the most active cell at any one time: the value of the parameter can be found by simply reading off the label of that cell (see Fig. 1.2). This coding method still requires a comparison mechanism to determine which cell is the most active, but instead of *deducing* the hypothetical parameter value of most activity from the activity levels of a small set of contributing channels, this system involves the much less sophisticated process of simply looking up the answer. This kind of coding is postulated to be used in the coding of movements in the motor cortex (Georgopolous *et al.*, 1986; Georgopolous, 1990; Heeger, 1987) and the superior colliculus (Sparks *et al.*, 1990) and also in the coding of visual movement in the MT region of the cortex (Albright *et al.*, 1984; Malonek *et al.*, 1994) and in the coding of faces (Baylis *et al.*, 1985; Young & Yamane, 1992).

1.5.4 Population and channel combination

A modification of a population coding system is to combine the principles of both channel and population systems and have the movement coded in a large number of labelled lines, tuned to cover the range. But the activity between the highly active lines could be extrapolated to deduce the value of a stimulus parameter which fell between the 'lines'. With this modification, the two systems start to merge since we are now again dealing with a multiple-channel system. We can enjoy the advantages of higher resolution (from the channel system) with the simplicity of using the maximum firing rate as an indication of vector amplitude. Evidence that such an extrapolation system is actually used has been provided by Sparks *et al.* (1990). They showed that small focal lesions of the areas of peak activity in the colliculus had no effect on the saccade, demonstrating that information about saccade direction is distributed across many cells.

The population code putatively carrying information about the direction of visual movement in the MT region of primate cortex seems to be decodable in two different ways: either by detecting the most active contributor or by averaging, depending on the task. That is, there seem to be two independent, task-related codes present in MT. For each area in the visual field there are collections of cells in MT that each respond best to a particular direction of visual movement such that a large number of directions are represented (Albright *et al.*, 1984; Malonek *et al.*, 1994). When two groups of these cells, signalling different directions, are unusually arranged to be active at the same time by combining electrical microstimulation with natural stimulation, the coding method can be revealed. When the task is to judge direction of movement, a perceptual task, animals behave as if the most active contributor determines the response: judgements intermediate between the electrically and naturally signalled directions are not found (Salzman & Newsome, 1994). But when the task is to move the eyes, intermediate directions are observed, suggesting averaging or a channel system (Born *et al.*, 1995; Groh *et al.*, 1995).

The implementation of channels and other population codes raises questions. When a code is distributed and many codes are present at once (corresponding, for example to many objects present in the image at once), how is the system to know which component goes with which? This is the binding problem (Von der Marlsburg & Schneider, 1986; Singer, 1993). And even having identified the components of a single code, how are the cells involved labelled such that their activity can be interpreted?

1.5.5 Map coding

In a neurally-mapped coding system, the meaning of the cells' activity (that is the reference frame in which they are defined) is coded by their geographical location in the nervous system (Konishi, 1986). This is a method of labelling the cells. As such, mapping is thus compatible with either channel or population coding. Geographical maps are widespread throughout the nervous system. Examples include area 17 (Van Essen & Zeki, 1978) and the superior colliculus with their spatial maps (Berman & Cynader, 1972) and also the auditory cortex with its map of sound frequencies (Merzenich & Brugge, 1993; Imig & Morel, 1983; Phillips, 1989).

Simply demonstrating that an orderly, topographical arrangement exists, however, does not prove that this arrangement is in any way part of the code. It might be merely an anatomical convenience with no functional consequences. A map as such is just an example of a trivial code from which information may or may not be extracted by another level of coding process. Convincing demonstrations of such extraction rules, and thus interpretation of the meaning of cells' activity deduced from their location in the map, have been made for motor maps (Knudsen *et al.*, 1987; Sparks & Mays,

1990). But the functional significance of other maps, such as the orderly arrangement of the visual field to area 17 is unknown.

1.5.6 Comparison of channels, population codes, maps and labelled lines

The difference between a population code and a channel system for coding the value of a coordinate lies in the level of flexibility and in how the information is retrieved. To decode information from a channel coding system requires a comparison between the activity in all the channels involved whereas the activity of a labelled line is interpretable in splendid isolation as always meaning the same thing. This means that a channel system can give only a single answer. For many, exclusive variables - for example the head can only have one linear velocity and be moving in only one direction at a time - this may represent a positive advantage. A population code, on the other hand, can signal several different values at the same time. This is shown in Fig. 1.2 which compares the multiple hills of a population code with the smoothed profile of the WiSuMP channels system. The output of the channel system is a single value, the output of the population code is the whole bundle (Georgopolous *et al.*, 1986; Georgopolous, 1990). An example of a parameter coded by a population code is target location which is coded in the profile of single cell activity over the surface of the superior colliculus. The cells are labelled as corresponding to particular target locations (Schiller & Koerner, 1971; Schiller & Stryker, 1972). It would be inappropriate to combine the processing of these labelled lines by a spatial channel system to encode position because such a system would provide only a single answer and one that represented a misleading and useless average of all the possible selections. A population code is far more suitable, with multiple hills of activity corresponding to the location of different potential targets The process of enhancement (Wurtz & Albano, 1980; Wurtz & Mohler, 1976) helps to pull out the peak of the population and so guide orientation movements (Sparks *et al.*, 1990).

A population code also has another advantage over a WiSuMP channel system. The robustness of the channels comes from throwing away the absolute activity levels, but in a population code, having identified the most active cell, the firing rate of that cell can then be taken as being proportional to the amplitude of the coded attribute.

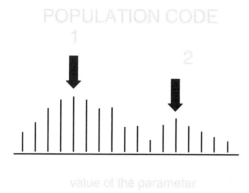

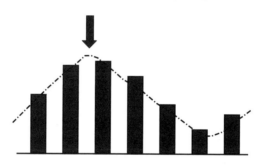

Fig. 1.2. This diagram shows a parameter being coded by a population code (top) or a WiSuMP channel system (below). Population code: The vertical lines represent the activity of each of an arbitrary number of labelled lines that make up the population of coders. The position of each of the vertical lines on the parameter axis corresponds to their label. The value of the coded parameter is found by finding the most active member of the population and reading off its label. Multiple peaks might be present in the activity profile (here shown as 1 and 2). Channel code: The bars represent the activity of a small number of channels that make up a typical channel system. The position on the 'parameter' axis at which each bar is plotted represents the parameter value to which each channel is tuned. This is the preferred value of each channel. The value of the parameter is found by comparing the activity in the different channels and extrapolating the position of the peak onto the parameter axis. This usually falls between the preferred values of the channels.

1.5.7 *Multiple inputs to a single, goal-directed profound coding system*

SuMP channels or modules are *functionally* defined: they do not carry information about the source of their information which might arise from many sources, including top-down processes. For example, head velocity or target location can be signalled by several different sensory systems that combine together to represent a single attribute. This is a potentially useful strategy but also represents a complication. Ian Howard has distinguished between *nested* sources of information and *parallel* sources of information concerning some particular attribute (Howard, 1996). In some cases, to obtain a given attribute, it is necessary to combine or nest information from several sources, no one of which can provide the information alone. In other cases, different sensory inputs duplicate each other and provide redundant or parallel versions of the same, relevant information.

An example where nested information is required is provided by generating the attribute of knowing the position of a visual target in the reference frame of the body. Since the eye can adopt various poses with respect to the body, and the visual information is in the reference frame of the retina, other information has to be added (eye-in-head position; head-on-body position) to obtain the required attribute.

An example of redundant, parallel information comes from locating a target by sound and vision simultaneously (Stein & Meredith, 1993). Either system could provide the attribute ('target direction') alone. Examples of these redundant sources of information concerning a single attribute highlight the nature of knowledge itself. This redundancy underscores the frail connection between our consciousness and the world of which we are conscious. If more than one sense provides the information and they disagree, which, if either, is right?

Experiments can be designed to separate the two sources, for example using prisms to separate auditory and visual sources of target localization (Harris, 1965). They show that when the senses disagree, vision tends to dominate and 'capture' the other sense . But it is not always vision that dominates.

Information from many sources contributes to the assessment of self motion, most obviously visual and vestibular cues (Howard, 1982). During active movements a further source of information comes from the efferent copy of the motor command (Bridgeman, 1995). The different sources of information have different reference frames and different coordinate systems. For example, retinal motion is encoded with respect to retinal reference points whereas vestibular information is encoded in the reference frame of the head. The efferent copy will be encoded in the reference frame and co-ordinate system of the system that is being instructed to move. If the head movement comes about as part of locomotion for example, then the efferent copy of the motor command will be in body coordinates. If more than one source is to be used to code self motion, then they need to be brought into a common system or perhaps several parallel systems.

We have carried out experiments to look at the combination rules for visual and non-visual cues to linear self motion (Harris & Jenkin, 1996). Visual and non-visual system, including the otoliths and top-down, high-level cognitive processes underlying expectancies, comprise redundant systems for at least certain linear motion stimuli in which many systems are well stimulated, for example, during periods of linear acceleration. We separated visual and non-visual cues to movement by providing visual cues through a virtual reality helmet during physical movement on a cart. During these conditions, we demonstrated non-visual capture over visual dominance!

So in summary, biological processes extract particular attributes and code them in a way that protects them from the vagaries of other unrelated attributes: the codes are maintained as invariant. Invariant, profound codes can be achieved in a number of ways in biological systems. In computational systems, some of the problems facing biological systems can be engineered out. For example sensors can be designed that respond in an extremely selective manner to the attribute in question. Let us first review some of the coding systems used in engineering and then review the merits of reinventing perhaps not the wheel, but the sensors attached to it.

1.6 Computational codes

Within the computational community 'code' and 'representation' are so tightly bound that they are almost synonymous. Codes are so fundamental that instructions on how to code, encode, and decode information accompany new processors as they are developed. Standard codes have emerged for characters, integers, and floating point numbers. Programs using different codes must explicitly translate between their codes if they are to communicate with each other at all.

A primitive code standardization for integers and other basic data types exists and extends partially into the computational vision community. Although not very far. Even for trivial codes, such as raw image data, hundreds of representations (coding schemes) exist and the task of importing a foreign representation is never as trivial as it should be. A digitizer might be described as providing a 640x480 unsigned 16 bit intensity image and this code identification is reasonably well understood †. But this image code is trivial. It may make later codes possible but very few, if any, tasks are based on this code alone.

Given the tight coupling between tasks and profound codes, there are almost as many codes within the computational community as there are tasks. Some of these codes are considered in this volume (e.g. Chapter 10), but rather than trying to enumerate the various representations here, consider the oft-studied task of attempting to obtain a line-based description of a scene given a single digitized image of it.

Many different approaches to this classic computational problem have been proposed (Marr & Hildreth, 1980; Canny, 1986). Many involve convolving the image with one or more filters and then combining the output of these convolutions in order to postulate the existence of edge elements (edgels) at locations and orientations and scales in the image. Computationally the task is often expressed as the convolution of the image im with one or more operators op and then examining the output of $op * im$ in order to identify edgels. This simple and straightforward task can identify edgels in various ways including

- An edgel could be postulated wherever $op * im$ exceeds or falls below a threshold value, or whenever an individual unit of $op * im$ has a specific value.
- An edgel could be postulated whenever the local derivative of $op * im$ has a particular value or falls below a particular value.
- An edgel could be postulated whenever $op * im$ has a local maximum in at least one direction.
- An edgel could be postulated whenever the local structure of $op*im$ meets a particular criteria.
- An edgel could be postulated whenever the local structure of $op * im$ over a number of different scales and orientations meets a particular criteria.

Different representations of $op * im$ are possible for each of the above. For some edgel computations the determination can be made based on only a single value of $op * im$. For others larger neighbourhoods of $op * im$ must be examined, while for others, larger neighbourhoods of $op * im$ over families of filters. Each of these edgel computations require different image codings. Each of these rules provides a different coding of the image. They

---

† Leaving aside issues such as does zero represent black or white, is the digitizer linear or logarithmic, does the digitizer provide automatic gain correction, etc..

all represent 'edgels', they all construct and use a map as the medium of representation, but the image codes are different.

As a second example of how computational codes are carefully and intentionally linked to the task in hand, take the case of programming a robot to reach and grab something. Controlling such a system needs feedback to make fast, accurate movements. What are the codes used to process and use the various *sensor* outputs?

The signals from the transducers reporting about the positions of the various robot joints are in a much higher-level code than the trivial codes arriving from biological transducers because of the very high degree of filtering and control engineered into the design of the transducer.

At first glance, it would seem that to use the signal effectively requires external information about the transduction rules (the encoder resolution) and also the mounting of the encoder, its orientation etc. But if the programmer does *not* have access to this information, the joint transducer's signal can still be used if there is feedback about the overall effectiveness of the arm. By optimizing the *use* of a given encoder's information, the information can be used without knowing what its signal actually means, only that it correlates with some aspect of the task at hand. This is, of course, the problem facing biological systems: not how to interpret the activity of various transducers, but how to achieve a particular task.

1.7 Computational versus biological coding

In the evolution of species or the development of an individual, the use of various profound codes is refined in ignorance of what each is reporting. Performance in particular tasks provides the feedback that regulates the use and weighting of the various coding stages. In contrast, when an engineer builds a computational system, the comprising codes are directed by the system design and usually calibrated and established separately with a very clear idea of the reference frame and coordinate system of each code.

By engineering task-specific filtering characteristics into the design of transducers, computational systems can generate profound codes (task-related stimulus feature extracts) at the transducer level which are not available in biological systems which can never afford to devote a whole sensory system to a single task.

The consequences of the dominance of flexibility in animals in a comparison of animals and machines was introduced in our introductory chapter to our previous book (Harris & Jenkin, 1993a). Now we extend this point to the microlevel: getting information into an organism has to be done in the most comprehensive way feasible. This is achieved by making the initial codes no codes at all - simply transductions with minimal, essential filtering. Subsequent stages can now extract sophisticated processed information that is related to each task performed. But if the task changes, new later stages (new profound coding systems) can be added without altering the core architecture.

In a machine, such exhaustiveness and flexibility is just counter-productive. It is usually better to build the whole machine in a task-oriented way from the transducers up and to focus or attend to *only* and *exactly* the information that is related to the task at hand. Information that is not related to the task in hand is intentionally filtered out of the system as early as possible. And if the task changes, there is no need to rely on gradual evolution: just replace the system!

Biological systems are often redundant or over-specified. For example both vision and non-visual information contribute to knowledge about self motion and both visual and auditory cues assist in object localization. Computationally, dealing with redundant systems can be awkward. In machine control, redundant systems are used to improve reliability when failure would be disastrous for example in controlling the space shuttle. There the computations are carried out by three machines which must agree. If the super-system which assesses disagreement detects a problem, the entire system is shut down. There is a parallel to this protection in the biological processing. If visual and vestibular cues to self motion are found to disagree, motion sickness results (Reason, 1978; Oman, 1990).

1.8 Where do we go from here?

Biological codes are very general. They are redundant and general. Robotic codes are very specific. They have very limited inputs and are very task specific. It is these differences that have lead to the lack of common coding strategies between the biological and computational communities, rather than the different media within which the communities operate.

Although specific codes for specific tasks may make the design and implementation of a computer algorithm easier, the tight link between code and task leads to systems which are very fragile. In general they cannot be easily modified to integrate different sources nor to deal with more general versions of the task. As computer vision and robot tasks become more complex, and more closely similar to the tasks and problems that biological systems must solve, we can expect more similarities to emerge between coding mechanisms in machines and organisms. The computational community continues to have considerable interest in the representations identified within biological vision systems (see Harris & Jenkin 1993b). Although biological representations may be more general than are currently required in computation applications, they do suggest potential directions and approaches for the more limited applications that currently exist.

From the biological point of view, computational tasks and codes provide limited versions of the more complex tasks that biological systems must deal with. But many of these limited tasks are similar to the tasks considered in specific experimental conditions. The York Vision Conferences attempt to bring these two communities together. They and this book, attempt to expose each community to the approaches and philosophies of the other. As the biological community comes to understand the workings of biological vision processing and its codes better, these models will be more and more applicable in the machine vision community. Likewise, computational models for complex visual tasks may find provide hints in the hunt for profound, biological codes.

2

Different approaches to the coding of visual segmentation

Hans-Christoph Nothdurft

Visual Perception Laboratory, Goettingen, Germany
and
Max Planck Institute for Biophysical Chemistry,
Goettingen, Germany

The paper is divided in four sections. In the first section, I present a view of texture segmentation, and visual segmentation in general, as it has developed from a series of experiments in our laboratory. This overview is given along five statements each of which is illustrated and briefly discussed. In the three remaining sections, new data are reviewed that were obtained from different approaches into studying visual segmentation, (i) a physiological investigation of single cell responses in the primary visual cortex, (ii) psychophysical experiments on the performance of human subjects in detecting texture boundaries that are masked by luminance modulation, and (iii) the exploration of properties of neuronal interactions simulated in a simple computer model.

2.1 Introduction

Visual segmentation is a compelling perceptual phenomenon. Beside the detection of luminance contours, borders between higher-order differences of visual information can also be seen. Such differences are differences in the motion of, e.g., camouflaged objects which are not seen when they stand still but immediately pop out when moving against background. Also certain differences in the visual structure of object surfaces (i.e., in visual texture) can be easily seen and allow to segregate different objects from each other. This phenomenon is particularly interesting if surface structures do not differ in mean luminance and segmentation can only be achieved from analysis and comparison of texture properties.

Understanding the coding of visual segmentation is interesting in several aspects. First, a complete description of neuronal processes that explains the perceptual organization obtained with complex patterns will improve our understanding of vision and may perhaps even help to improve the treatment of occasional dysfunctions. Secondly, the implementation of texture segmentation into machine vision would require a thorough understanding of underlying neuronal processes. Although a relatively good performance is achieved with algorithms that are merely ignorant of biological processes, further improvement and, in particular, human-like performance with sophisticated patterns seems to require implementation of algorithms borrowed from biological systems.

There have been, in principle, two approaches to complex visual segmentation (the term 'complex' is used here to distinguish segmentation of structural differences from the 'simple' segmentation based on physical cues such as differences in luminance or colour). One approach going back to the grouping experiments of Gestalt psychologists investigates the ability of the visual system to combine single elements to new perceptual entities. The presumably underlying process is the perceptual linking of features, or objects; segmentation occurs where elements cannot be linked. The other approach looks at visual segmentation as the detection of feature discontinuities. Objects are seen as compact if discontinuities in texture, or texture motion are smaller within regions than at the region boundary, which then is seen to provide segregation. While the role of borders in visual segmentation seems to have been underestimated for some time, I will stress this aspect in the following contribution. There is, however, evidence that the human visual system is also capable to perform perceptual grouping of elements on the basis of feature similarity, provided the features to be linked are sufficiently distinct from other features not to be included in the group.

The following presentation will first give an overview of recent findings in visual segmentation, mainly texture segmentation. The aim of this overview is to present, and illustrate, our view of how texture segmentation, and visual segmentation in general, may be encoded in the visual system and what predictions can be made from such a model. The presentation is, therefore, biased towards findings from our laboratory; the numerous data from other labs will only partially be reviewed here. The interested reader is referred to the review by Bergen (1991) which gives an excellent, and much wider overview of the work on texture segmentation before 1990, and to several other reviews on specific aspects of it (e.g., computational models, Bergen & Landy 1991; machine vision, Caelli 1995; early vision, Julesz 1991; perceptual organization, Beck 1982; psychophysics, Sagi 1995). Some parts of the following overview have already been described (e.g., Nothdurft 1994a,b) and will only briefly be summarized here.

In three sections following this overview, I will then pick up certain aspects in more detail and will present new information achieved from recent experi-

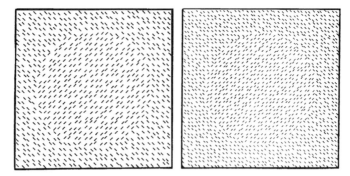

Fig. 2.1. Segregation is not the same as discrimination. With increasing line length and element spacing, lines can be discriminated by their orientation before perceptual segregation of texture regions occurs. This impression may be strengthened by varying the viewing distance. Reprinted from Nothdurft (1985a), Copyright (1985) with kind permission of Elsevier Science Ltd., The Boulevard, Langford Lane, Kidlington, OX5 1GB, UK.

ments. These sections concentrate on different approaches to the analysis of visual segmentation, (a) a physiological approach studying responses of single cells in cat striate cortex (Kastner, *et al.*, 1995, and in prep.), (b) a series of psychophysical experiments that investigated limitations and properties of human perceptual performance when segmentation of orientation differences was gradually disturbed by superimposed luminance variation (Nothdurft, in prep.), and (c) a computer simulation of neuronal interaction that was meant to explore the properties of certain neuronal interactions (Nothdurft, in prep.).The combination of these three experimental techniques - physiology, psychophysics, and computer simulation - provides a thorough approach to the understanding, and encoding of visual segmentation.

2.2 Five notions on visual segmentation

Three decades of interesting work on texture segmentation (e.g., Beck 1967; Olson & Attneave 1970; Julesz 1975) have made it clear that perceived segregation is restricted to certain visual properties while others though visible under careful inspection do not give rise to the spontaneous segregation of regions and the percept of boundaries between. However, even feature properties that potentially segregate do not do so in every condition. As is seen in Fig. 2.1, for example, clearly visible differences in the orientation of line elements do not produce the percept of a texture border unless stimulus magnification and (not shown here) line contrast are sufficient. So, let us start the overview of texture-based segmentation with this notion:

[Notion 1.] *Segregation of texture regions is not strictly related to their discriminability.*

Rather, texture regions made of clearly distinct elements may appear to merge. This is, of course, part of an old story. Texture elements, in general, do not, at least not readily segregate from the same texture elements upside-down (Julesz, 1975; Rentschler *et al.*, 1988) although these often look quite different. On the other hand, an only slight tilt of otherwise identical elements may provide strong segregation (Beck, 1967). The texton concept of Julesz and coworkers (Julesz & Bergen, 1983) is based on this distinction of features that provide, and features that do not provide segregation. It is not the discriminability of texture features that defines their texton quality, but it is their property to segregate; segregation and discrimination are not related. However, even texton differences fail to segregate under certain circumstances, which underlines that there is more than just the texton property that matters. A wide spacing of line elements, for example, reduces both segregation (Nothdurft, 1985b) and pop out (Sagi & Julesz, 1987) of orientation differences which, in denser arrangement, would produce strong percepts of such phenomena.

This suggests that the neuronal mechanism providing texture segmentation is not identical (although perhaps related) to the encoding of information about relevant features and feature differences. It would be interesting to see what this mechanism could be.

[Notion 2.] *Segmentation of texture (and luminance) differences requires sufficiently strong texture (or luminance) gradients.*

For luminance, this has, in fact, been shown in several studies and has given rise to compelling illusions (Craik, 1966; O'Brien, 1958; Cornsweet, 1970). This is also the case for differences in orientation or other texture cues; the local gradient is essential for segregation and pop out (Nothdurft, 1985b; Nothdurft, 1990; Julesz, 1986; Sagi & Julesz, 1987). The same (minor) differences in global statistics between two texture regions segregate, or remain invisible depending on whether texture variation across the boundary is sufficient or not. For the evaluation of object boundaries, the visual system ignores small and constant variations in texture or luminance. There is an interesting difference in the encoding of absolute feature properties themselves. While certain texture properties are identified and distinguished even when they do not give rise to the percept of a texture boundary, this is not the case for small variations in luminance. While a small luminance shift may remain undetected thus giving rise to incorrect brightness estimates

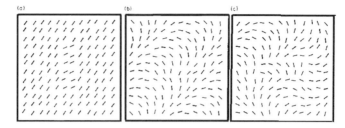

Fig. 2.2. Segregation from locally increased orientation contrast. For texture regions made of identical line elements (a), a local orientation contrast of 30 deg is sufficient to provide segregation. With increased overall variation (b and c, 20 deg orientation shift between neighbouring lines) orientation contrast at the texture border must be increased in order to segregate (b, 30 deg; c, 90 deg). Reprinted from Nothdurft 1991, copyright (1991) with kind permission of Elsevier Science Ltd, The Boulevard, Langford Lane, Kidlington, OX5, 1GB, UK.

(Craik-O'Brien-Cornsweet illusion; Craik 1966; O'Brien 1958; Cornsweet 1970), a continuous shift in line orientation even when not affecting the percept of a homogeneous texture region may be visible - another illustration of notion 1.

When this observation is investigated further, it turns out that the gradient required is not fixed but that the local feature difference needed for segregation depends on the strength of texture variations nearby.

[Notion 3.] *For segregation, texture variation across region boundaries must be significantly increased over the overall variation within regions.*

That is, for segregation of orientation differences, for example, region boundaries are seen where the local orientation contrast is well above the overall variation in line orientation. This is demonstrated in Fig. 2.2. For uniform texture regions (no variation in line orientation; Fig. 2.2a), an orientation difference of 30 deg across the texture border is certainly enough to make regions segregate. If orientation variation within regions is increased, the same orientation contrast is not sufficient (Fig. 2.2b) but larger differences are required to obtain segregation (Fig. 2.2c). It is interesting to note that segregation in the latter case is not related to the perceptual combination of identical features (e.g., lines at the same orientation) but even figures and backgrounds of virtually identical sets of line elements may segregate. This is illustrated in Fig. 2.3. Segmentation is obtained at local discontinuities or, using another formulation, at points of locally increased feature (orientation) contrast (Nothdurft 1992, 1993b, 1994a).

Response modulation by feature contrast is a well settled neuronal phenomenon. In several studies, orientation contrast between a driving stimulus

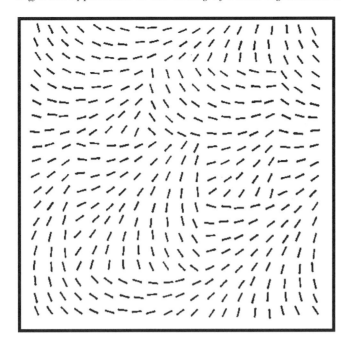

Fig. 2.3. Segregation of virtually identical texture regions. Two squares are seen to segregate although regions and background are made of virtually identical elements. Segregation is obtained from locally increased orientation contrast, or from discontinuities in orientation flow.

and stimuli applied to regions outside the classical receptive field was found to modulate the responses of cells in cat striate cortex (Blakemore & Tobin, 1972; Fries *et al.*, 1977; Nelson & Frost, 1978; Gilbert & Wiesel, 1990). Similar observations have been made for cells in monkey area V1 with line textures similar to those shown here (Knierim & Van Essen, 1992). The major effect seen in about one third of the cells in V1 is a stronger suppression by 'texture surround' when lines are identical to the actual stimulus over the receptive field than by lines at the orthogonal orientation. This "differential suppression" results in a response modulation by feature (orientation) contrast which lets these neurons respond more strongly to line elements at texture borders than to line elements within homogeneous texture regions (Gallant *et al.*, 1995).

Response modulation by feature contrast helps in the encoding of texture boundaries but alone is not sufficient to provide a representation of perceived borders when texture regions are composed of different line elements. This is illustrated in Fig. 2.4.

[Notion 4.] *In order to encode texture borders between regions each made of different elements, responses from different filters (cells) must be pooled.*

Except from modelling, there is only little evidence that such a pooling mechanism should indeed exist. In monkey V1 (Knierim & Van Essen, 1992), for example, as well as in cat striate cortex (Kastner, *et al.*, in prep.) a number of cells were found to prefer orientation contrast for textures around both an optimal and non-optimal centre line. The proposal is also based on indirect evidence. Inspection of Fig. 2.3, for example, shows that segregation of texture regions is not revealed by the identity of line elements; such information is rather ignored for segregation. Also in fast, presumably pre-attentive grouping, the information on absolute line orientations is not only ignored but seems not even to be available to the observer (Nothdurft, 1992). Non-specific pooling of filter outputs was also proposed by other authors (Sagi, 1995) and provides a plausible explanation of several phenomena in texture segmentation.

Note that the schematic model given in Fig. 2.4 predicts the observation made in Fig. 2.2. While texture boundaries in patterns with homogeneous texture regions (Fig. 2.4A) are encoded with a high signal- to-noise ratio, representation of the same texture boundaries in the case of overall variations (Fig. 2.4B) is much more noisy, because every single line element itself displays some orientation contrast. This implies that a given orientation difference at the texture border should appear to be more salient for homogeneous texture backgrounds than for backgrounds with an overall variation in line orientation. Also, for segregation to occur, homogeneous regions should require a smaller orientation contrast at the texture border than inhomogeneous ones. These predictions, illustrated in Fig. 2.2, were experimentally confirmed (Nothdurft 1992, 1993b).

An interesting aspect comes from the comparison of these above findings with properties of other segmentation phenomena in vision. As is well known, not only texture differences but also differences in motion (direction or velocity) or differences in disparity may give rise to strong perceptual segregation, beside, of course, such basic keys as differences in luminance or colour. When the same tests used to estimate the role of feature (orientation) contrast in texture segmentation were applied to other segmentation phenomena, it turned out that properties were very similar. Also for the segmentation of textures that move in different directions, or for the segregation of colour differences and other properties, local feature contrast against overall variation was found to be a critical parameter (Nothdurft, 1993b). This suggests that feature contrast plays a particularly important role in all visual segmentation tasks.

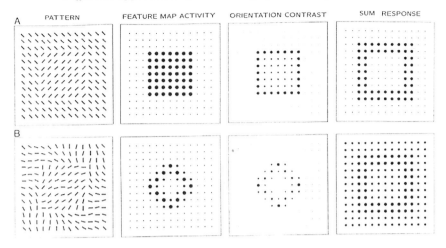

Fig. 2.4. Schematic drawing of response maps to different texture stimuli. Stimulus patterns (left-hand column) and presumed responses of cells with preference for oblique line orientation (middle columns). Only for homogeneous texture regions (A) can orientation tuned cells represent the perceived square. Responses fail to reveal the percept for texture regions with a continuous shift in line orientation (B) even when modulated by local orientation contrast. Only when responses from cells with different orientation preference are pooled (right-hand column) the sum reveals the perceived square. Reprinted from Nothdurft (1994b). Used with permission.

[Notion 5.] *Segmentation, in general, can be obtained from locally increased feature contrast in any of at least five different visual dimensions: texture (orientation), direction of motion, colour, luminance, and stereo disparity.*

While there is increasing evidence that would support such a notion (e.g., Nothdurft 1993b, 1994a, 1995), it would be interesting to test the validity of such a generalization with respect to the other notions above. The important role of contrast for the detection of luminance contours (notion 2) is obvious; it is also clear that the perceived distinction of luminance levels does not automatically gives rise to the percept of segregated regions (notion 1). The validity of notions 1 and 2 for differences in the direction of movement are less obvious. However, even in motion, segregation is not obtained without a local gradient that is larger than the overall variation in movement direction (Nothdurft, 1993b). Waves on a lake, for example, do not produce the impression of segregating regions but look like a continuum that only segregates where the wave structure abruptly changes.

A particularly interesting aspect is the pooling of information from different filters (notion 4). While observations similar to those which have

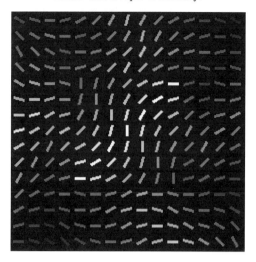

Fig. 2.5. Pooling across visual dimensions. Notice that outlines of the square are defined by local orientation or local luminance contrast depending on which corner of the square you are looking at. Despite these differences, the square itself appears as continuous. For segregation of the complete figure, information from different boundary mechanisms must be pooled. Reprinted from Nothdurft (1994a). Used with permission.

suggested the existence of pooling for the segregation of orientation differences, also suggest pooling for the segregation of either motion, luminance, or colour differences, it would be interesting to see whether even information from different such visual dimensions is combined. The square in Fig. 2.5 shows that information about luminance and orientation gradients is indeed pooled for visual segmentation.

After this brief overview of contrast-based segmentation, I will now analyze certain aspects of this concept in more detail. Three issues will be addressed, two of which arise from the idea of generalized feature contrast in different dimensions. First, I will summarize recent experiments in which response modulation by feature contrast was investigated in the motion domain using stimuli like those used in psychophysical experiments. For individual cells in the cat striate cortex, the effect of motion contrast was compared with the effect of orientation contrast. These experiments have been performed together with Sabine Kastner and Ivan Pigarev. It was found that the influence of feature contrast in the motion domain was qualitatively similar to, and quantitatively at least as effective, as feature contrast in orientation. Second, I will address the question of pooling of information across dimensions in more detail. If information about feature contrast is pooled over dimensions, noise in one dimension, for example luminance, should affect segmentation in another dimension, e.g. from orientation contrast. While such distortions are, in general, not strong enough to mask segregation completely, in particular not under prolonged viewing conditions, specific masking effects from luminance variations are found for short stimulus presentations. In a third section, finally, I will review work that explores the requirements of interactive processes in the orientation domain in order to obtain saliency and segregation properties similar to those observed in psychophysical experiments.

2.3 Response modulation by feature contrast in cat striate cortex

There have been several reports of contextual modulation of response properties of cells in cat striate cortex. Until recently, however, this modulation has not been related to texture segmentation. Knierim and Van Essen (1992) have shown that contextual influences from stimuli applied to regions outside the classical receptive field could explain the particular saliency of targets in pop-out configurations. Responses to a line over the receptive field were, in average, smaller when this line was surrounded by identical lines (Fig. 2.6A) than when surrounded by orthogonal lines so that it 'pops out' (Fig. 2.6B; Treisman 1985; Nothdurft 1992). It is tempting to speculate about the role of such effects for visual segmentation (Nothdurft 1991, 1994b, 1994a). Recent experiments have confirmed that response modulation by feature (orientation) contrast may indeed explain perceived segmentation of orientational differences (Gallant *et al.*, 1995; Nothdurft *et al.*, 1992). Since cats appear to be capable of segmenting textures in a similar way as humans do (Wilkinson, 1986; DeWeerd *et al.*, 1992), we wondered whether response modulation by orientation contrast were also found in cat striate cortex with stimuli that correspond to the patterns usually tested in psychophysical or behavioural tasks. In addition, we were interested to see whether response modulation by feature contrast could also be seen for differences in the direction of movement, another effective key for visual segmentation. Contrast dependence in the motion domain has been found in area MT of the owl monkey (Allman *et al.*, 1985) and later also in area V1 (Allman *et al.*, 1991), and there have also been reports that cells in cat striate cortex may be sensitive to relative motion (Hammond & Smith, 1982; Orban *et al.*, 1987). None of these studies, however, used stimuli similar to those applied in psychophysical experiments. Thus, the aim of our study was threefold. We wanted to establish whether responses were modulated by (1) orientation or (2) directional contrast, and whether (3) possible contrast effects in either dimension were comparable.

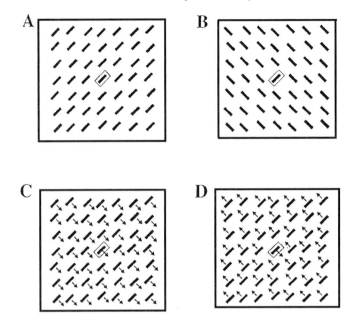

Fig. 2.6. Texture stimuli for testing orientation and motion contrast. The central line element located within the receptive field of a neuron (schematic outlines) was presented with texture surrounds made of same (A, C) or different elements (B, D). For orientation tests, lines in the surround were stationary and either parallel (A) or orthogonal (B) to the central line element. For motion tests, lines moved in the same (C) or opposite (D) direction. Stimulus patterns displayed uniform texture fields (A, C) or patterns with orientation (B) or motion contrast (D). After Kastner, Nothdurft, and Pigarev (submitted).

Extracellular recordings were made from single cells in anaesthetized and paralyzed animals in a technique described elsewhere (Nothdurft & Li, 1985; Kastner *et al.*, 1995). For each dimension (orientation, direction of motion), responses to different stimulus conditions were compared in order to calculate general and specific (i.e., differential) effects from texture surround. We tested the same stimulus conditions that had been used by Knierim and Van Essen (1992) and applied the same computational analysis to the data as they did. Responses to the centre stimulus alone (presented over the receptive field of a single neuron) were compared with responses to the same stimulus shown together with similar or different surrounds (uniform texture and contrast conditions, respectively; cf. Fig. 2.6B, D vs. Fig. 2.6A, C). For control, surrounds were also shown alone. In order to analyze the general response properties of a cell, responses to patterns around an optimal centre line stimulus were compared with those to a non- optimal centre line stimulus (orthogonal to the cell's preferred orientation, for orientation tests; movement in the non-preferred direction, for motion tests). Texture elements were individually adjusted to the response properties of each neuron by adjusting length, width, and orientation of texture lines. In full texture patterns, lines were arranged in such a way that only the central line was presented within the receptive field; all other lines were applied to regions outside the classical receptive field and did themselves not activate the cell (cf. the schematic drawings in Fig. 2.6).

Following the work of Knierim and Van Essen, we classified response properties along different categories, two of which were found to occur more frequently than the others. These categories refer to general (i.e., non-specific) suppression and preference for orientation, or motion contrast. Responses were classified to resemble general suppression, when both texture surrounds significantly suppressed the center line response. Responses were classified to resemble preference for orientation, or motion contrast when responses were significantly stronger for patterns with the contrast condition (Fig. 2.6B, D) than for uniform texture stimuli (Fig. 2.6A, C). (Response differences were taken as significant if the means differed by at least two standard errors.) Examples of preference for feature contrast are shown in Fig. 2.7. Also responses from other categories (e.g., preference for uniform texture patterns; cf. Knierim & Van Essen 1992) were found but these were relatively rare. About one third of the cells failed to reveal significant response modulation by texture surround. As far as orientation is concerned, the data in the cat closely resemble the data obtained in the awake (Knierim & Van Essen, 1992) or anaesthetized monkey (Nothdurft, Gallant, & Van Essen, in prep.).

Interestingly, the same variation of response properties seen for differences in line orientation was also found for differences in the direction of motion, and we could not see any general difference between encoding of orientation or motion contrast in single cells of area 17. Preference for directional contrast was, on average, as frequently observed as preference for orientational contrast. That is, responses of cortical cells though encoding the specific information about the features to which a cell is tuned (e.g., a certain orientation, or movement in a certain direction) are also strongly modulated by feature contrast whether this is obtained from differences in line orientation or the direction of movement. This implies that visual borders do not need to be extracted from (specific) combinations of (specific) responses in area 17 but are rather encoded in the mean response of such neurons itself, as shown for orientation contrast in monkey V1 (Gallant *et al.*, 1995). The only requirement in order to make use of this response modulation is that

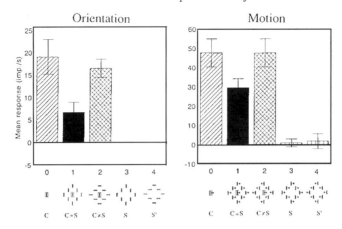

Fig. 2.7. Response modulation by orientation or motion contrast in striate cells of the cat. Histograms give mean responses of two neurons (left and right hand histograms) to the stimulus conditions sketched underneath. The neuron on the left responded better to orientation contrast than to uniform texture; the neuron on the right responded better to motion contrast than to full field motion in the preferred direction. Preference for orientation, and motion contrast was one of the most frequently encountered response properties of striate cells (22-35%). After Kastner, Nothdurft, and Pigarev (submitted).

information from different feature detectors must by pooled in such a way that the feature specificity itself is not a distinguishing property anymore.

2.4 Interaction of luminance and orientation contrast

Pooling of information represented in different filters is a central property of the above model on visual segmentation. As Fig. 2.5 illustrates, even information from different visual dimensions can be pooled so that texture boundaries are seen from a combination of orientation and luminance differences; texture regions appear as homogeneous as long as differences remain relatively small within an area. This view implies, however, that segmentation should also be disturbed by variations in another feature dimension. Like the increased overall variation in orientation reduces the saliency of an orientation-defined texture boundary, also an increased overall variation in luminance should render segregation of orientation differences more difficult if information from different dimensions is pooled in a non-specific way.

There have been incidental reports of such an interaction. Morgan *et al.* (1992) have found evidence for an interference between orientation and colour. Also, weak texture boundaries or boundaries between texture elements that were presumably distinguished from associated differences in

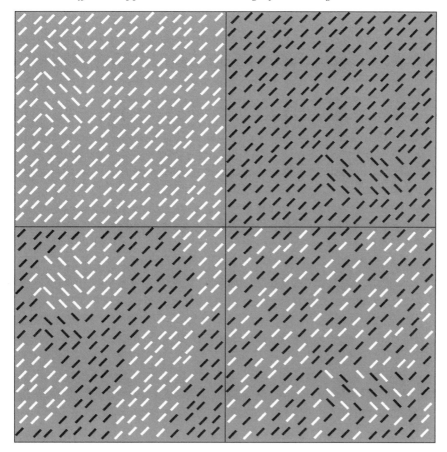

Fig. 2.8. Difficult segregation of orientation differences under luminance variation. A texture bar defined by orientation contrast is more difficult to identify when luminance modulation of texture elements gives rise to segregation of areas of similar size (bottom left). The bar is, however, readily recognized if luminance contrast of line elements is either constant (top) or random (bottom right).

spatial frequency or mean luminance have been found to disappear when texture elements were varied in luminance contrast or contrast polarity (e.g., Nothdurft 1990, Fig.14). For orientation, however, such an interference was much smaller and hence assumed to merely not exist (Nothdurft, 1990).

In order to investigate the interference between luminance and orientation (or motion) defined segmentation, a series of experiments was performed (Nothdurft, in prep) some of which will briefly be summarized in this section. Does luminance modulation of a texture pattern (e.g., an array of differently oriented lines) affect the visibility of texture (orientation) differences?

Stimulus patterns (similar to those shown in Fig. 2.8) contained a regular arrangement of bright and dark lines at two orientations. The subjects' task was to detect or discriminate figures defined by orientation contrast (large bars in Fig. 2.8) when the luminance contrast of line elements had the same (Fig. 2.8, upper row) or different (Fig. 2.8, lower row) polarity. The design of these experiments was based on the assumption that interference might be stronger if regions defined by luminance variations had similar size as regions defined by orientation contrast. This is suggested from Fig. 2.8; identification of the orientation-defined bar is more difficult when luminance borders define regions of the same size (Fig. 2.8, bottom left) than if luminance variations only resemble a finer spatial frequency noise all over the pattern (Fig. 2.8, bottom right).

Patterns were shown for 83-150 ms (and sometimes masked with a pattern of randomly oriented lines of randomly assigned luminance contrast). Subjects were asked to indicate the orientation of a global bar which could be either vertical or horizontal.

As Fig. 2.9 shows, performance was strongly affected by contrast variations superimposed onto the texture pattern. Interference was strongest when luminance borders defined regions of approximately the same size as those of the (orientation defined) regions to be detected. This indicates that information from an (irrelevant) visual dimension (here, luminance) may indeed contaminate the information on texture boundaries obtained in another dimension (here, orientation) but that this contamination can be more easily ignored when the spatial frequency bands used for the task are not affected.

Note that this finding is not in complete agreement with the model proposed above. The overall variation in orientation was seen to affect segmentation from this dimension irrespective of the spatial frequency bands in which texture borders or background variations were defined (Fig. 2.2). The observation here that noise in a different frequency band can quite effectively be ignored seems to be in disagreement with the idea of nonspecific encoding of texture borders. Further, when Fig. 2.8 is viewed for a long enough time, the segmentation task based on orientation contrast can be performed correctly; this is less so with Fig. 2.2b.

There may be two reasons for such a difference. First, the signal-to-noise ratio in Fig. 2.2b is certainly smaller than that in Fig. 2.8c; if the signal-to-noise ratio is increased (as in Fig. 2.2c), performance improves. A second possible solution to this problem is given in Fig. 2.10. In this task, subjects were asked to detect a single target (at orthogonal orientation) and to indicate its position (left or right from fixation point). Performance is plotted against presentation time and is seen to increase with longer presentation of

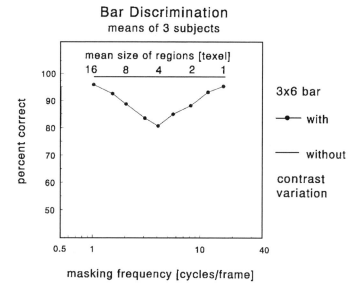

Fig. 2.9. Disturbed segregation of orientation defined regions in the presence of luminance variation. Subjects were asked to identify a vertical bar (3 by 6 elements) within a texture field of 32 by 32 line elements ('texels'); elements within and outside the bar were oblique lines at orthogonal orientations (similar to Fig. 2.8) which were displayed at either contrast polarity (dark or bright lines). Performance (thick curve) was measured as a function of the size of regions that were given the same contrast polarity (cf. Fig. 2.8c, large regions; Fig. 2.8d, small regions) and was compared with subjects' performance under absent contrast variation (thin line; cf. Fig. 2.8a,b). Identification of the global bar is disturbed when luminance variations form regions of comparable size as those to be detected from orientation differences.

the stimulus. Two different conditions were intermixed; line textures were either shown at one luminance contrast (dark or bright; data from these conditions were averaged) with no interference from luminance-based segregation (continuous curves), or were shown with a random assignment of positive or negative luminance contrast to each individual element, thus producing a high-frequency contrast modulation all over the pattern (dashed curves). Although luminance variation does not completely disturb target detection, the two curves are shifted indicating that subjects needed additional time (about 50 ms) to sort out and possibly ignore overall variation in luminance contrast.

One possible conclusion from these experiments is that information from different channels though initially pooled can quickly be sorted out by the visual system. This is also suggested from work on "guided" search for certain conjunctions (Wolfe *et al.*, 1989; Zohary & Hochstein, 1989).

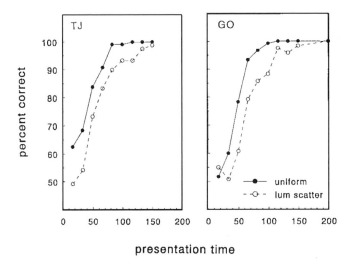

Fig. 2.10. Detection of popout of orientation in the presence and absence of luminance noise. In a 16x16 array of oblique line elements, subjects were asked to detect an orthogonal target when lines (dark or bright, on grey background) displayed same (continuous curve) or random luminance polarity (dashed curve). In the presence of random luminance variations, target detection is delayed.

2.5 Requirements for encoding feature (orientation) contrast

The last section brings us to a different topic. Which neuronal elements would be necessary to encode segmentation of orientation differences as proposed above? There have been quite powerful models on visual texture segmentation (e.g., Malik & Perona 1990) and this section does not intend to compete with them. Rather the topic of interest here is what sort of interaction of orientational filters is needed to explain certain psychophysical phenomena in perceived segmentation.

I will concentrate on two such phenomena. One is the nonlinear increase of saliency of a texture border, or a single popout target, with increasing feature contrast at the texture boundary, or target position. The other one refers to an observation made with sparse line textures that underlines the role of orientation contrast and of pooling information from different channels for visual segmentation.

2.5.1 The model

Our central interest in the following simulation was the possible interaction of oriented filters at the level of primary visual cortex. We do not care here about how orientation specificity is obtained; the input level of our model already contains orientation selective cells with filter properties that resemble properties of cells in area 17, or V1. There is a second simplification. The set of filters in the model is reduced to one per line element of the texture pattern. This does, of course, not resemble reality, as every texture patterns is encoded in a dense array of cortical filters with partially overlapping receptive fields. For the purpose here, however, this restriction is not considered to be harmful. The best way of looking at it would be to assume that all positions between such sample cells are filled with series of cells with similar response properties. Provided the receptive fields are large enough so that any cell is activated by the nearest texture element, the responses of our model would just resemble a discrete sample of the complete and continuous response distribution.

The important element of the model is a 18-fold grid of orientation selective filters (Fig. 2.11); each of these grids is tuned to another orientation (10 deg difference between grids). Orientation sensitivity is modelled by a Gaussian profile with a half-width of 30 deg, which resembles tuning profiles of striate simple cells. Activity of these filters is controlled by the actual line orientation at that and neighbouring positions (convolved with the orientation sensitivity profile of the according elements in each grid).

Response modulation by orientation contrast is achieved from local interaction by inhibitory units. Every input element in the model has an accompanying inhibitory cell which itself is activated by this and neighbouring input elements. Spatial summation was weighted according to a Gaussian weighting function; in order to obtain response modulation by stimuli "outside the receptive field", the range of spatial summation had to include next and even farther line elements. This would be consistent with the considerable spatial extent of contextual influences found in macaque and cat striate cortex (Gilbert & Wiesel, 1990; Knierim & Van Essen, 1992; Nothdurft *et al.*, in prep.; Kastner *et al.*, in prep.). Inhibitory units suppress the activity of associated elements in the input level, which by this operation become "response cells" of the model. Although the number of inhibitory units equals that of input elements, it should be stressed that similar results would be obtained with a smaller sample of inhibitory units. As the input to inhibitory units is summed over an extended area of input cells, there

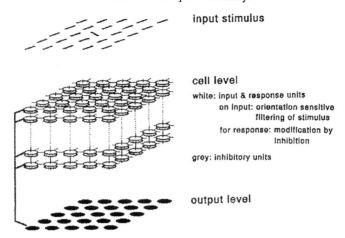

Fig. 2.11. A simple model of cortical interaction for texture segmentation. Line arrays, on input, activate 18 sets of orientation specific filters; for simplicity, the model contains only one cell per line element, in each orientation plane. The response of each cell is modulated by an accompanying inhibitory unit, the activity of which is controlled by the (stimulus-dependent) input to this and neighbouring cells. Orientation specificity, at input, together with the spatially weighted inhibition from cells within the same orientation plane produce context modulated responses similar to those experimentally observed. Activity of cells in different orientation planes is pooled in output cells (filled). Activity distribution within this output layer is compared with human performance in certain texture segmentation tasks.

is considerable overlap in the spatial summation profiles of neighbouring elements.

After these steps of computation, responses of the original input cells are modulated by local feature contrast but are still orientation specific; units respond to optimal but not to non-optimal orientation. The assumed pooling of responses was obtained in a last step. Activity from different grids (with different orientation preference) was summed into output cells which were as numerous and located at the same positions as the original input cells. Pooling was performed over all orientations at that particular position.

One aspect of this model should be stressed. It is important that interaction is nonlinear; strictly linear summation would not produce the response properties shown below. The nonlinearities implemented to the model are simple (and plausible) threshold mechanisms introduced at two levels: (i) inhibitory effects are thresholded before being applied to input/response cells, and (ii) responses of response cells are thresholded before being accumulated into output units.

2.5.2 Saliency

The perceived segmentation of line textures is not a linear function of the orientation difference at the texture boundary (Nothdurft, 1985b). When the orientation contrast of a target among distractors is increased, the target becomes more and more salient but the increase in saliency is highly nonlinear (Nothdurft, 1993a). For targets on an inhomogeneous background, similar curves are obtained but saliency, in general, is reduced (cf. Fig. 2.12a).

Fig. 2.12b shows the performance of the model in such a task. Simulation was restricted to an array of 21 by 21 texture elements, corresponding to sets of 21 by 21 input, inhibitory, and output units. Target saliency was defined as the difference of output activity at the target's position minus mean activity elsewhere (within a central region of 15 by 15 cells). As is seen in Fig. 2.12b, the computations resemble the psychophysical data when saliency is computed from the pooled activity of cells modulated by feature (i.e., orientation) contrast; curves for either specific orientation contrast, or specific responses without modulation by orientation contrast fail to reproduce the experimental data.

2.5.3 Sparse textures

An example that illustrates the role of the local orientation gradient in segregation is given in Fig. 2.13. While a bar made of homogeneous regions (at two orthogonal orientations) is easily seen (Fig. 2.13a), the same bar fails to segregate when line orientation is made inhomogeneous (but homogeneous within rows; Fig. 2.13b) likely because local differences in orientation are pronounced all over the pattern. Reduction of line element density along the vertical axis improves visibility of the (vertical) bar (Fig. 2.13c) although the percept of segregation is not very strong. Note that this bar can be seen despite the fact that it is composed of lines at different orientations, as is also the background of the figure. Reduction of line density along the horizontal axis again reduces the visibility of the bar (Fig. 2.13d). The "performance" of the model is shown in Fig. 2.13e; histograms plot the elevation of mean activity of output cells along the texture boundary over the mean activity within and outside the global bar. The values resemble the observations of strong (Fig. 2.13a), modest (Fig. 2.13c), or no segregation (Fig. 2.13b,d).

Altogether, the different properties of texture segregation were nicely mimicked by the simple model presented above. This indicates that (plausible) interaction of cells in striate cortex might be a central key to produce the observed phenomena of texture segmentation.

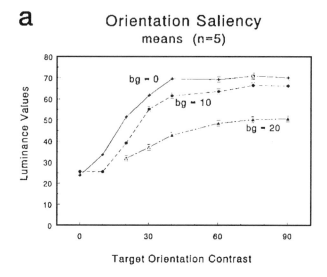

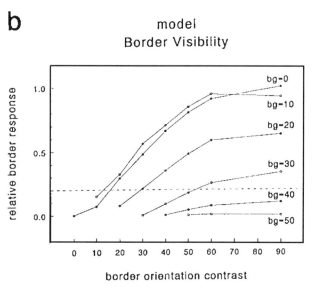

Fig. 2.12. Nonlinearities in saliency. For human subjects, the conspicuousness, or saliency, of an orientation target increases nonlinearly with increasing orientation contrast; an increase in the overall variation in line orientation reduces target salience (a) (from Nothdurft 1993b). The model of Fig. 2.11 reveals similar properties (b) if the locally increased activity of output cells at target position is measured.

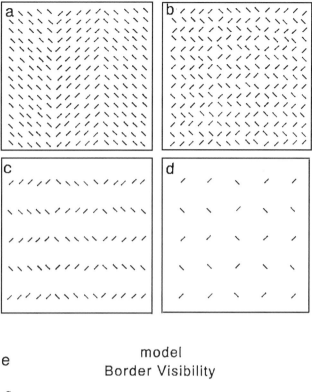

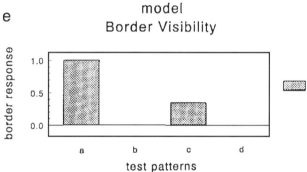

Fig. 2.13. The role of local orientation contrast for texture border detection. In line arrays, a bar of line elements at orthogonal orientation readily segregates (a) but segregation becomes difficult when orientation is switched from row to row and high orientation contrast is introduced everywhere in the pattern (b). Removal of some rows again reduces the overall orientation contrast and leaves high contrast only at the borders of the global vertical bar (c) which then appears to be seen (though less vividly than in (a)). Note that line orientation is still switched between rows in (c) but with a less disturbing effect than in (b). Local orientation contrast, now particularly high at the texture border, provides (mild) segregation despite line elements within a region display different orientations. Further removal of line elements makes the borders disappear (d). The model qualitatively resemble the perceived strength of segregation in these conditions, when responses in the output plane are analyzed and response modulation across texture borders is taken as the relevant signal (e).

2.6 Discussion and conclusion

I have introduced a model of visual segmentation that is based on the detection of locally increased feature contrast, and have completed this presentation with additional data from physiology, psychophysics, and computer simulations. Although these data support the view that segmentation is represented in the response modulation of striate cells and that texture borders merely reflect response maxima, alternative explanations or models cannot be excluded.

One such an alternative model is that of feature linking. It assumes that similar (or nearly similar) features are perceptually linked; the detection of texture boundaries then would correspond to the failure of such linking processes. There has been experimental evidence against similarity grouping as the exclusive basis of visual segmentation (e.g., Beck 1967). But there is also good evidence that line continuation odes provide a particularly salient cue for the detection of global figures (Beck *et al.*, 1989; Field *et al.*, 1993; Moulden, 1994). However, this view and the view given above cannot be easily distinguished in the patterns shown here. Segregation in Fig. 2.2a and 2.2c, for example, could be explained by either model. Regions may segregate because of the detection of locally increased differences; the smaller (and homogeneous) variations within texture regions do not give rise to segregation. This is what was proposed here. When arguing in favour of the linking model, one could also assume that the smaller differences within texture regions (e.g., those in Fig. 2.2c) are still linked, while the strong differences at texture boundaries are not, and hence segregate. In this case, however, one would need to explain why the ability to link lines differing by only 20 deg, in Fig. 2.2c, would not also provide linking in figures like that of Fig. 2.2a where such a small difference in line orientation is seen to segregate. Also, there is evidence that certain proposed mechanisms of feature linking (e.g., the synchronization of responses of different cells) would unlikely provide visual segmentation (Fahle *et al.*, 1993; Fahle & Koch, 1995) or pop-out (Ziebell & Nothdurft, 1995).

Another open question is, of course, how feature contrast is implemented in detail, and whether the true spatial properties of striate cells (that are ignored in our explanatory model) could indeed explain all observations obtained with texture segmentation. For example, texture boundaries often appear to be very sharp, while response modulation by feature contrast would produce a spatially distributed elevation of responses.

Texture segmentation and visual segmentation, in general, are still active fields in vision research. Although researchers have been approaching a better understanding throughout the last years and are about to begin to understand some of the underlying mechanism, the area has still retained a number of yet unanswered questions which will provide a good ground for future discoveries.

3

Coding simple shapes for recognition and the integration of shape descriptors

Gregory Dudek

Center for Intelligent Machines,
McGill University, Montreal, Canada H3A 2A7

Martin Arguin

Dept. de Psychologie,
Univ. de Montrèal, Montreal, Canada H3A 2B4

Michael Dixon

Psychosocial Research Unit,
Douglas Hospital, Montreal, Canada H4H lR3

Daniel Bub

Montreal Neurological Inst.
McGill University, Montreal, Canada H3A 2A7

The shape recognition deficit of a human subject (ELM) with a lesion in his inferior temporal cortex is examined and is apparently related the the global shape properties of the objects to be recognized.

For both face and blob stimuli, ELM confuses exemplars that share values of diagnostic features. Such a finding reinforces our assertion that objects are not stored as "pictures in the head" but rather are encoded using separable features which in turn are encoded using separable shape dimensions.

A model of shape coding is developed that is based on a description of simple shapes in terms of a set of global parametric equations. In this patient, shape recognition appears to be impaired by an inability to integrate or focus on multiple attributes of a shape at the same time.

3.1 Introduction

How do humans internally represent and recognize the shapes of visual objects? In some sense speculation concerning this subject dates back to Plato. The very power of the human shape recognition system and the multiple computations apparently involved have made it difficult to decompose these mechanisms functionally (Koenderink & van Doorn, 1986; Leyton, 1988).

In this paper we describe an approach to uncovering the mechanisms underlying human shape recognition by looking at the precise deficits that arise as a result of localized damage to the human visual system. By observing the functional changes that occur in the shape recognition system as a result of localized brain damage, we believe that important characteristics of the involved computations can be elucidated. In particular, although the specific deficit that we have examined occurs in only a small number of patients, the fact that similar functional deficits may be associated with different types of brain lesion suggests that the presence of the shape-processing characteristics we have discovered may have far-reaching implications.

Our work suggests that a key component of shape representation for recognition is the description of objects (or at least their sub-parts) using something akin to global parametric models – an approach with an evocative similarity to the use of Platonic solids.

Brain-damaged subjects with different types of high-level shape processing deficit are shown to be impaired in the integration of multiple shape primitives that appear to be used in object identification. We will focus primarily on the object recognition deficits of the patient ELM who presents with a rare form of category-specific visual agnosia. We will also comment on a second patient who has optic aphasia (suffers from a deficit in labelling visual objects, but who retains the ability to recognize objects if tested non-verbally).

Both patients can perform a wide range of visual tasks if the objects involved are perceptually present: that is, if the shapes are visible to them. It is only when the object shape must be *remembered* and recalled that ELM'S deficit becomes apparent. A such it appears to be the encoding of (visual) shape in memory that we are explicitly dealing with. This deficit appears to be intimately associated with specific shape attributes of the objects which he attempts to remember. We refer to these shape attributes as *dimensions* of a multi-dimensional descriptive space for shape. It seems, under certain circumstances, that when ELM consults his memories concerning the appearance of objects, he can only recover information about a single shape dimension at a time. ELM would know, for example, that a banana is elongated but does not seem to remember that it is also bent. Thus objects like carrots and cucumbers were accepted by ELM as being perfectly good examples of bananas because they had the same elongation.

This patient's ability only to partially recover object shape information from memory following brain-damage suggests that the representation of shape knowledge about objects in neurologically intact individuals is also based on a decomposition into discrete parameters (i.e. it is not an integral or template-like representation). Normal object recognition therefore requires these discretely stored shape primitives be re-associated together via an integration mechanism.

3.2 Global Parametric Shape

In October of 1987 ELM underwent neuropsychological testing which revealed normal IQ (93 WAIS-R verbal, 91 WAIS-R performance) but residual impairments in the delayed recall of both verbal (WMS verbal = 10.5) and pictorial material (WMS recall of geometric forms = 1). As well, he showed impairment in visual object recognition (Wingfield Object Naming 11/26) and face recognition (Benton Facial Recognition Task = 33). In clinical testing his object recognition deficit seemed to be attributable to an impairment in identifying *pictures of animals.*

ELM's perception is intact. He is able to draw copies of pictures of both complex geometric forms (Rey's Figure copy = 21) as well as pictures of animals. He was normal in naming photographs of household objects taken from both standard canonical viewpoints (26/27) as well as non-canonical views (25/27). He could also match canonical and non-canonical views of animals (7/7) and artifacts (18/19). He shows normal global to local interference for Navon Stimuli, and has no problem identifying overlapping objects.

ELM shows no significant language impairment, no visual field deficit no evidence for a perceptual encoding deficit, and no hemispatial neglect. On the other hand his ability to name and recognize line drawings of certain objects (for example many classes of biological objects) is severely impaired yet performance is markedly higher for other groups of objects, for example man-made artifacts (Table 3.1 a and b). While the recovery of encyclopedic (i.e. factual) information about biological objects from their names is largely spared, his ability to recover information from memory regarding their visual properties is impaired (Table 3.1c). Stored knowledge of visual properties of objects that cannot be named (eg. biological objects) is not entirely inaccessible or compromised however, since word-to-picture matching errors for fruits and vegetables are shown to be determined by visual similarity (Table 3.1d).

In addition to the agnosic symptoms described above, ELM shows a colour recognition deficit. His reading and spelling show signs of surface alexia and surface agraphia, respectively. These latter disorders are generally attributed to damage to the system responsible for the representation of the orthographic forms of words.

We have attempted to characterize the properties of the objects and object-classes that ELM has difficulty recognizing: why are some object classes difficult while others are easy? Superficially, a semantic characterization of the objects in terms on man-made as opposed natural seems appealing, but on more detailed examination it appears that, rather, the *shapes* of the objects that play a major role in his ability or inability to recognize them. On the other hand, semantics seems to play an important role for certain classes of objects, as we will see.

The morphologically simplest class of real objects for which ELM exhibits impaired recognition is fruits and vegetables (59 per cent errors in naming, as opposed to near-perfect scores for normal observers). These can be described as a single component or part objects (in the sense of Hoffman and Richards 1984).

One way to describe the shapes of such objects is with respect to progressive deformations of a circle, first through elongation into an ellipsoid (or an ellipse, in the case of the silhouette), and then by additional transformations.

An analysis of the identification errors made by ELM and other subjects (using multi-dimensional scaling analysis) leads to the hypothesis that three simple shape dimensions (or parameters) can explain much of human shape vision.

These shape parameters describe global deformations of an initial shape and can be used to deform an initial prototype (such as a circle) into one of a wide variety of forms. The three dimensions are:

(i) change of elongation (ratio of minor to major axes for a bounding ellipsoid),

(ii) tapering along the major axis of the ellipsoid,

(iii) global curvature (bending) of the ellipsoid along the major axis.

These parameters were defined using sequential global transformations of the coordinate plane $(x,y)' = \vec{p'} = \hat{\Omega}(\vec{p})\vec{p} + \hat{T}(\vec{p})$. where $\vec{p}$ and $\vec{p'}$ are the initial and transformed points and $\hat{\Omega}()$ and $\hat{T}()$ are the rotation and translation matrices.

The transformation are specified as follows (deformations are given below with respect to the y axis, with full generality). For elongation by a factor α we have

$$\hat{\Omega}(\vec{p}) = \begin{bmatrix} 1 & 0 \\ 0 & \alpha \end{bmatrix}, \ \hat{T}(\vec{p}) = [0,0]. \tag{3.1}$$

Stimulus category		
	Natural objects	Artifacts
Controls	6%	7%
ELM	61%	12%

a) Naming

Stimulus category		
	Natural objects	Artifacts
ELM	41%	7%

b) Object decision (ELM)

	Category of probe question	
	Encyclopedic	Visual
Control subjects	2%	3%
ELM	15%	45%

c) Recovery (recall) of factual (encyclopedic) versus visual or structural knowledge from animal names

Word	Picture					
	Banana	Carrot	Eggplant	Apple	Orange	Pumpkin
Cucumber	80%	60%	40%	0%	0%	0%
Tomato	0%	0%	0%	80%	60%	40%

d) Samples of ELM's performance on word-to-picture matching.

a) Error rates shown by ELM and 10 matched controls in naming line drawings presented for an unlimited duration. These results represent performance on 66 pictures of natural forms (animals, birds, insects, and fruits and vegetables) and 80 pictures of artifacts. b) ELM's error rate in deciding whether pictures were of real or unreal animals (n=70) or artifacts (n=41). Items were displayed for an unlimited duration. Unreal biological items were constructed by replacing the head of a real animal with that of another. Unreal pictures of artifacts were made by replacing one part of a real object by a functionally equivalent part from another object. c) Error rates shown by ELM and 10 matched controls on two-alternative forced-choice probe questions about animals given their names. Encyclopedic questions (n=60) probed verbal knowledge about animals. (e.g. is it domestic or wild?). Visual probe questions (n=78) concerned visual properties of the items. (e.g. does it have body markings or not?). d) Representative subset of ELM's error rates in matching pictures of fruits and vegetables to names. The subject was visually shown a picture and a word (unlimited duration) and decided whether they referred to the same object. The experiment used line drawings of 15 different fruits and vegetables and their names. Each possible word/picture pairing was tested 10 times. All data are reported as percentage errors.

Table 3.1. *Summary of ELM's agnosia.*

For tapering by a factor of γ we have:

$$\hat{\Omega}(\vec{p}) = \left[\begin{array}{cc} \gamma/(K-y) & 0 \\ 0 & 1 \end{array} \right], \quad \hat{T}(\vec{p}) = [0,0] \qquad (3.2)$$

where K is a constant larger that the maximum y value of any shape of interest. For bending by a factor β, we have:

$$\hat{\Omega}(\vec{p}) = \left[\begin{array}{cc} 1 & 0 \\ 0 & 1 \end{array} \right], \quad T = [0, \beta|y|] \qquad (3.3)$$

Note that these deformations, particularly tapering and bending, can be expressed in a variety of alternative forms. Some sample shapes generated by deforming a circle using along these dimensions are shown in Figure 3.1.

By parametrically combining deformations to a circle using only these three shape dimensions a surprisingly wide variety of alternative shapes an be generated. In particular, combinations of these three shape dimensions can define a wide variety of shapes resembling fruits and vegetables. This has allowed us to examine the shape perception deficit of ELM, as observed in terms of simple biological forms, in the context of parametrically variable synthetic shapes. It is interesting to observe that these deformations are closely related to the "intuitive" parametric deformations typically associated with synthetic solid modelling (for example using Platonic solids or superquadrics) (Barr, 1981a; Brooks, 1981; Pentland, 1985; Biederman, 1987; Pentland, 1988) as well as to the Lie groups often associated with motion processing.

The stimuli used in the present experiments were filled blobs whose shapes were generated in terms of this three dimensional parameter space. In all experiments, orientation of the items on the picture plane was constantly varied and object length was held constant (we also considered, but rejected, holding other attributes such as object area constant).

3.3 Perception, recall and recognition

The experimental approach used was based on the synthesis of artificial shapes from this three dimensional parameter space. The experiments focussed on the ability of a subject to recognize one of these shapes with respect to an ensemble of objects seen previously. By associating these objects with familiar biological forms, a version of the experiment could be carried out that directly related to a pre-existing recognition deficit (as well as being a readily accessible and comprehensible task for naive subjects).

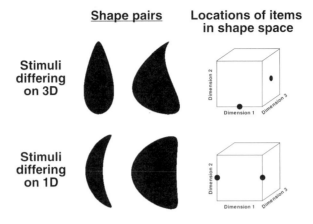

Test	Examples of test shapes	Perceptual (errors)	Conceptual (errors)
Positive trial		9%	23%
Shares 0/3 primitives with target		0%	8%
Share 1/3 primitives with target		3%	25%
Share 2/3 primitives with target		10%	44%

Fig. 3.1. Sample shapes. Several of the sample shapes in the three-dimensional shape space and their layout in the 3D shape space. The lower part of the figure illustrates the test pictures used when the target stimulus (picture or word) was 'banana'.

For unique identification of an arbitrary target shape defined within this space, the simultaneous consideration of multiple shape dimensions (in the sense described above) is required. The exposition to this point does not preclude the possibility that the actual measurement dimensions for shape used by humans are quite different from these three and hence the number of dimensions spanned by these target objects may be less than three. As it happens, there is a direct relationship between dimensionality of the ensemble in terms of the specific shape dimensions described above and the performance of our subjects.

Consider a simple shape recognition tasks with shapes labelled with respect to similar-looking fruits. Analysis of the elongation of an object may establish that it should be labelled as either a banana or a cucumber. Determining which of these two alternatives is the correct one, however, involves the evaluation of the shape along one dimension: the global curvature of the object). Note that this does not necessarily occur in a conscious or deliberative manner.

3.3.1 Experiment 1

Picture-to-word matching was one of the experiments used to examine the relationship of dimensionality to shape recognition. In this experiment a word and a black-filled 2-dimensional shape were simultaneously presented to the subject. The task was to indicate whether the word and the shape referred to the same object. For the set of shapes we used, this task was extremely easy for normal observers.

Our recognition-impaired subject ELM consistently accepted pictures that only partially matched the shape primitives corresponding to the target words (Fig. 3.1). In the perceptual and conceptual matching experiments, target stimuli were used that were either filled blobs (perceptual matching) that could unambiguously be identified by normal observers as 'banana', 'carrot', 'cucumber', or 'eggplant', or the visually-presented names of these items (conceptual matching). On each perceptual matching trial, a target picture was presented for 2 sec. followed by a blank 1 sec. interval and then by a test picture which remained visible until the subject responded. In conceptual matching, the target word and the test picture were presented simultaneously and remained on until the response. In both experiments, ELM indicated whether the test picture matched the target (yes/no).

ELM would accept word-picture matches that were correct with respect to *at least one shape dimension* while ignoring the inconsistency in the other dimension(s). This suggested that ELM's visual inability to recognize ob-

University of Ulster LIBRARY

jects may be determined by a failure to integrate or select specific shape properties such that his responses are based on only partial shape information.

To examine precisely the distinction between perceptual and conceptual shape recognition as a function of the number of shape dimensions, we developed a more refined experiment, as follows.

3.3.2 Experiment 2

We compared subject's capacity for a) *perceptually encoding* shapes defined by combinations of shape dimensions (perceptual integration) *without* having to remember them except for a very brief delay, and b) recovering shapes (as a function of multiple properties) from memorized (i.e. stored) representations of objects that were previously viewed (*conceptual integration*). These tasks were based on the subject indicating whether or not a sample shape matched a target shape using either simultaneously-presented stimuli or remembered stimuli. The two experiments used the same design. Each included both positive trials where the target and stimulus matched, as well as negative trials where the target and stimulus differed.

On negative trials, the number of shape primitives the test picture shared with either a previously presented target picture (perceptual matching) or the shape corresponding to a simultaneously-presented target word (conceptual matching) was varied. If a match is performed on partial shape information, error rates on negative trials will increase with the number of shared primitives between the test picture and the target. This effect occurred only in conceptual matching and ELM's error rates were notably greater in this task than in perceptual matching. This dissociation indicates a selective impairment for the conceptual integration of shape primitives.

On negative trials, the test picture had either zero, one, or two shape primitives in common with the target. If only a subset of the relevant shape primitives (elongation, curvature, and tapering) is considered to perform the match, error rates on negative trials will increase with the number of primitives the test-picture shares with the target. For instance, if only curvature is considered, the error rates on negative trials would be 0%, 33%, and 66% with zero, one, and two shared primitives, respectively. Overall, the error rate was much higher on conceptual than on perceptual matching [$c2(1) = 52.2$; $p < 0.001$]. On negative trials the effect of number of shape primitives by which the test- picture differed from the target was highly significant in conceptual matching [$c2(2) = 18.5$; $p < 0.001$] but not in perceptual matching [$c2(2) = 5.1$; n.s.].

This integration impairment for shape primitives dissociates from both verbal and semantic processing. Thus the experiment required no verbal mediation and did not refer to any semantic category. It therefore appears that ELM's impairment involves either

    i) the acquisition of shape information from the visual image or
    ii) the recovery of shape knowledge from memory.

The learning of arbitrary shape-to-location associations was tested to determine whether ELM's recognition errors reflect a deficit in the integration or combination of a shape measurements. Shape contrasts between the items to be learned were defined over a single dimension (elongation or tapering) or over a conjunction of these dimensions (Fig. 3.2). The subject had to memorize the positions of four target shapes located at the corners of a rectangular layout. These targets were then removed and the subject had to point to the appropriate reference location for the corresponding target when a sample shape was presented (i.e. the corresponding corner of the now-invisible rectangular layout of targets). An increased error rate on the two-dimensional conjunction cases relative to the single-dimension sets would indicate a separable analysis of shape properties. This was exactly the case for ELM.

Three sets of items differing from one another on a single dimension were constructed. The conjunction sets required the simultaneous consideration of two shape dimensions for unique identification. For example, for any item in the conjunction set there was another that had the same degree of elongation and yet another that had the same degree of tapering. Differences in elongation or tapering between items were *greater* in the conjunction condition than in the single-dimension conditions. Each stimulus set was tested in 10 consecutive blocks. Each block started with a learning trial where all items in a set were displayed simultaneously, each at its assigned location (corners of an imaginary square). Assignments of locations for each shape were random and constant. Each shape was then shown twice individually and in a random order and the task was to point to its assigned location.

ELM's problem in combining individually-solvable dimensions in a stimulus suggests that the computational process involved in recognizing these shapes is sensitive specifically to these dimensions. Further, it implies that because increased difficulty arises only when such stimulus dimensions must be extracted *simultaneously*, there must be some degree of separation in the way these individual shape parameters are extracted. We believe that the increased severity of ELM's visual agnosia when the contrast between items was defined over a *conjunction* of multiple shape dimensions indicates a deficit in the *integration* or *selection* of independent shape measurements. Perhaps most striking was the nature of the errors on the multi-dimensional stimuli: errors corresponded to an incorrect estimate of one of the shape parameters involved in the decision, but almost never two parameters simultaneously. In the conjunction condition only 4 per cent of his errors involved confusions between items that differed on *both* elongation and tapering.

A non-agnosic brain-damaged control with a left-hemisphere lesion that includes area V4 showed *more* errors on *single-dimension* sets. Normals also find these single-dimension cases *more difficult* although their error rates are very low. In general having additional shape characteristics available makes the task easier. In contrast, subject ELM was dramatically impaired on the conjunction set (Fig. 3.2)†.

In recent experiments, a second patient with with a left-hemisphere lesion that includes area V4 as well as lower visual areas unilaterally who suffers from a deficit related to naming objects has also shown a performance deficit that is directly related to the dimensionality of the task described above. This patient can correctly localize shapes independently of their shape dimensions (unlike ELM) but his reaction time for uttering their names is reduced when the task involves multiple shape dimensions. The apparent significance of these shape dimensions suggest they may play a significant role in human shape processing.

3.3.3 Experiment 3

Acquisition of structural information from the image was tested in a third experiment to rule out a deficit in the early vision system. It used the same stimuli as experiment 2 (i.e. the blob/learning/pointing experiment) in a paradigm that emphasized a perceptual load as opposed to the memory load emphasized in the previous experiment, i.e. a perceptual matching task. A single shape (target) was presented for 1 sec. and the subject was asked to remember it. After a delay of 1 sec., the four shapes tested in a particular condition (conditions were tested in a single block and were presented in a random order) were shown simultaneously and the subject was asked to point to the target. In this experiment, both the brain-damaged control and ELM showed a better performance with the conjunction set of stimuli than with the single-dimension sets. Thus, with the conjunction set of stimuli,

---

† Note that the dimensional parameterization of the shapes was not made explicit to the patient – this is an implicit characteristics of the ensemble of objects.

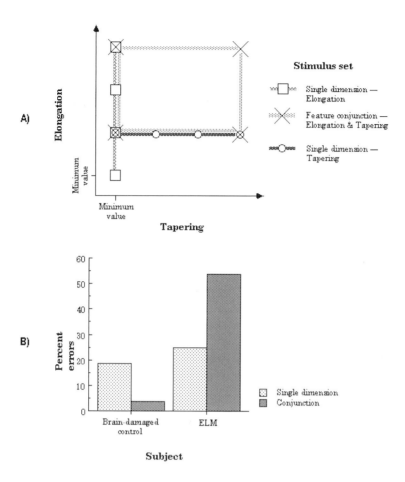

Fig. 3.2. Results for shape identification task by pointing. **A)** Positions in two dimensions of the shape used for testing the learning of shape-to-location association. Each axis represents values on a particular shape dimension. Each point represents a specific stimulus used in testing. For any item in the conjunction set there was another that had the same degree of elongation and yet another that had the same degree of tapering. **B)** Error rates shown by ELM and by a brain-damaged (left occipital lesion) non-agnosic control in the learning of arbitrary shape/location associations with single-dimension and conjunction sets. The control subject made fewer errors with the conjunction stimuli than with the single-dimension sets. The opposite result was found in ELM who committed about twice as many errors with the conjunction set than in the single-dimension conditions [$c2(1) = 19.5$; $p < 0.001$]. ELM's errors with the conjunction set were evenly distributed across items.

neither of the patients made a single error. In contrast, with the single-dimension sets, the control subject made 6.9% errors and ELM made 11.5% errors. In the case of ELM, the results indicate a cross-over interaction between experiments 2 and 3. In experiment 2, his error rate was markedly higher with conjunction stimuli whereas, in experiment 3, he showed more errors with the single-dimension sets. This, despite the fact that the perceptual discriminations that had to be performed in each experiment were identical. The perceptual matching results of experiment 3 therefore indicate that ELM's impairment with conjunction stimuli in a recognition task (experiment 2) cannot be due to a perceptual (early vision) failure. It is argued that ELM's visual recognition deficit can be attributed to an impairment in maintaining and/or retrieving shape knowledge about objects in memory. Furthermore, given that his impairment in shape-knowledge retrieval is specific to a task involving a conjunction set of stimuli, it can be concluded that this impairment is characterized by partial retrieval of shape information from memory.

Our investigations using simple stimuli conclusively demonstrate that ELM fails adequately to specify objects in terms of multiple shape dimensions. We conclude that ELM encounters recognition problems whenever he must simultaneously extract from memory the values of two or more shape dimensions and would confuse objects that had the same value on at least one of these diagnostic dimensions.

An interesting line of enquiry was whether this sharing of visual features would lead to confusions with compound as well as simple stimuli. To see if this were indeed the case, in Experiment 4 we looked at the types of confusions ELM made when attempting to identify faces.

3.3.4 *Experiment 4*

ELM is profoundly prosopagnosic. In a corpus of 48 famous faces whose identities were well known to him, he failed to identify a single face. He cannot discriminate familiar from unfamiliar faces or previously viewed from novel, unfamiliar faces. He also cannot identify emotional expressions (13/42).

In order to maintain empirical control over the stimuli presented to ELM we used 13 by 10 cm synthetic faces that varied in eye, nose, and mouth size. These faces are shown in Fig. 3.3. The Faces were presented to ELM one at a time. On learning trials faces were accompanied by a digitized recording of a name familiar to ELM (e.g. figure skaters "Nancy Kerrigan", "Tonya Harding", and "Josee Chouinard"). On test trials, shapes were presented alone and ELM had to "name" the face. Six learning trials (two of each face) were followed by six test trials. This pattern of six learning followed by six test trials was repeated 24 times for a total of 144 learning and 144 test trials per condition. A second set was administered three weeks later.

Of interest were the patterns of errors made by ELM. In each set of faces there are 3 pairs. Two pairs share two features: one pair shares the same sized nose and eyes, the second pair the same sized nose and mouth. A third shares only a single non-diagnostic feature (nose size).

The profound nature of ELM's face-recognition deficit is highlighted by the number of errors that ELM made on this relatively easy task (60/144 and 41/144 on the two sets respectively).

Of interest were the relative percentages of confusions among the pairs of faces. If faces were stored as complete integral objects, then any given face would be equally confuseable with any other face, irrespective of the features making up that face. Thus one would expect each pair of faces to account for 33% of all errors. For the first set the two pairs of faces in which there were two shared features (nose and eye size, and nose and mouth size) accounted for 90% of the errors. The faces sharing only the single non-diagnostic feature accounted for only 10% of the errors-a percentage significantly below the expected value of 33% ($c2=7.53$, p<.01). For the second set ELM never confused the two faces sharing only the single non-diagnostic feature. All of the errors were confusions among the pairs sharing two features.

The pattern of confusions made with faces is very reminiscent of the pattern of confusions ELM makes with simple shapes used in experiments 1-3. For both face and blob stimuli, ELM confuses exemplars that share values on diagnostic features. Such a finding reinforces our assertion that objects are not stored as "pictures in the head" but rather are encoded using separable features. For complex stimuli such as faces, these features are those which make up the face- features such as eyes, nose, and mouth, which may in turn be decomposed into integral shape dimensions such as curvature, elongation and tapering.

3.4 Discussion and conclusions

To summarize, an impairment specifically affecting the capacity of a subject to consider multiple shape primitives for object recognition is described. This impairment dissociates verbal and semantic processes from the perceptual integration of shape primitives in the image. The recognition deficit can therefore be attributed to a failure in the recovery of multiple proper-

SET 1

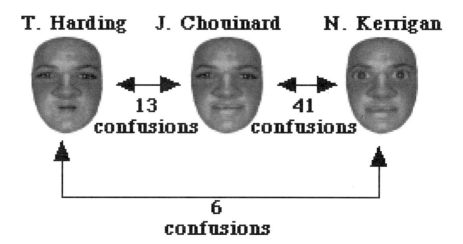

T. Harding J. Chouinard N. Kerrigan

13
confusions

41
confusions

6
confusions

SET 2

Chouinard Kerrigan Chouinard

3
confusions

38
confusions

0
confusions

Fig. 3.3. ELM's confusions for the two face sets used in experiment 4.

ties from stored representations of structural knowledge, a process we call conceptual integration.

The effect of inferior temporal cortical brain-damage on a process of conceptual integration of shape features indicates that this operation contributes to object recognition in neurologically intact individuals. The requirement of conceptual integration in visual recognition has two related implications. First, it suggests that visual knowledge about object shapes is decomposed into discrete features or attributes which may be individually accessed, rather than as integral representations. In addition, it implies that visual recognition cannot merely be defined as a process by which perceptual information is mapped to stored structural representations. The present observations rather demonstrate that visual recognition also involves an assembly operation by which discretely stored primitives are conjoined. This appears to be analogous to the manner in which spatially disparate components of a scene must be assembled by looking around to construct a complete representation. In short, recognition may involve an attention-like process that is applied across different shape properties of even a very simple object.

The link between the role of inferior temporal cortex and spatial visual attention has been previously established(Moran & Desimone, 1985; Chelazzi *et al.*, 1993). Likewise, it is well acknowledged that attention refers to a control of processing that can be applied to domains other than simply the spatial one (for example specific colours or sound pitches). It may be that the impairment in object recognition we have observed as a result of inferior temporal cortex damage in patient ELM relates to a form of attentional control in the *feature* or *shape dimension* domain: that is, the inferior temporal cortex serves to direct a non-spatial aspect of attention to the correct shape attributes to be used in recognition and access to memory. This idea has interesting implications for the design of computational vision systems (Tsotsos, 1990).

Although ELM's agnosic symptoms are category specific (see above), the underlying impairment extends to the visual classification of arbitrary shapes that have no referential content. This raises the possibility that biological and man-made objects differ in the requirements they impose in shape-knowledge recovery for unique identification.

These results suggest that human object representation involves the analysis of object shape with respect of distinct shape attributes. More surprisingly, it also implies that shape recognition involves the use of an *incomplete subset* of the available shape dimensions. This is analogous to the manner in which an incomplete analysis of a scene may lead to its recognition while failing to notice that a significant landmark has changed. Further, the subset of shape dimensions used for a given recognition task appears to be context and task dependent. This may suggest that computational vision systems can also profit from such strategies. In that context, while the notion of a collect of task-specific *visual routines* had been developed, when and how to select specific routines, and when and how to selected shape dimensions of interest, remains to be fully resolved.

Acknowledgments

This research was supported by a fellowship from the Medical Research Council of Canada (MRC), the Natural Sciences and Engineering Research Council of Canada to Gregory Dudek, and the Alzheimer Society of Canada.

4

Experiments on motion aftereffects

Stuart Anstis

Dept of Psychology,
University of California at San Diego

4.1 Introduction

How are we able to see moving objects? One might think we see them because they really are moving. But the images projected on to the retina by such moving objects are only patches of light and colour that change over space and time, so how do we proceed from retinal spatiotemporal changes in luminance to seeing movement? A single receptor, looking through its own "keyhole" or receptive field at only one point in the world, could not possibly see movement. As an object passed by, the receptor would be able to sense changes over time but it could not assess the direction from which its keyhole was being covered and uncovered. It is necessary to compare signals from at least two points in time and in space, and this is exactly the function of a Reichardt motion detector (Reichardt, 1961). Two receptors with adjacent or overlapping receptive fields feed into a comparator (Figure 4.1a). The receptor outputs are filtered with the output of one receptor being delayed. The undelayed output from one receptor is correlated with the delayed output of the other, in this case by multiplication. If the time taken for the spot to move between the two receptors is equal to the internal delay there will be a maximum signal out of the correlator. An alternative scheme proposed by Barlow and Levick (1965) uses subtractive inhibition instead of multiplicative correlation. The advantage of multiplication is that it can handle two successive inputs that are of different contrasts. In practice, two motion units are wired up back to back, so that (say) leftward motion is subtracted from rightward motion (Figure 4.1b). Reichardt's original work was on insects, and electrophysiologists have since found motion-selective neural units in nearly every vertebrate species. See reviews by Berkley (1982), Mather (1994) and Snowden (1994).

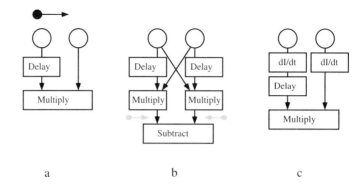

Fig. 4.1. a, Half a Reichardt motion detector. This responds only to a stimulus moving to the right. b, A Reichardt motion detector. This responds to motion to the left or to the right. c, A Reichardt detector must include a temporal filter that responds to change in luminance over time (see Experiment 1).

Adaptation to motion (say, downwards) alters the appearance of a subsequently viewed test motion in three different ways.

(i) Contrast threshold elevation. Downwards test motion is more difficult to see and must be increased in contrast to become visible. After prolonged inspection of a moving grating, Sekuler and Ganz (1963) found that the contrast threshold for a test grating moving in the same direction as the adapting grating was raised much more than for a grating moving in the opposite direction. This directionally selective adaptation was strong evidence that the moving target was detected by a motion-specific channel.

(ii) Motion aftereffect (MAE). This classic phenomenon was first reported by Aristotle (see Verstraten's review, 1996). First one adapts to a moving stimulus, say a waterfall. After 30 s of adaptation one transfers one's gaze to a stationary textured test field, which now appears to move upwards. This is attributed to adaptation of the downward branch of an up-down opponent Reichardt unit (Sutherland, 1961). A stationary field normally excites the upward and downward branches equally, so an opponent mechanism would signal no motion. However, exposure to downward motion adapts the downward branch, meaning that post-adaptation observation of stationary test field leads to an imbalance in which the up branch predominates. Consequently one sees the static test field apparently moving upwards. Barlow and Hill (1963) showed that a motion-sensitive neuron in the rabbit retina responded to motion less briskly after being exposed to prolonged motion in the cell's preferred direction.

(iii) Direction-selective adaptation. The direction of a test motion can be repelled away from the adapting motion. After adapting to downwards motion that moves toward 6 o'clock, a test field that actually moves toward 7 o'clock will appear to be moving toward 8 o'clock (Sekuler *et al.*, 1978). They concluded that the channels had broad petal-shaped receptive fields on a polar motion plot.

There are also two spatial interactions between motion pathways, which are spatial analogues to the temporal adaptation processes ii. and iii. just described:

(i) Simultaneous mutual repulsion of motion. Marshak and Sekuler (1979) and Mather and Moulden (1980) presented two overlapping sheets of sparse random dots. One set of dots moved (say) downwards, towards 6 o'clock, and the other set moved towards 7 o'clock. Subjects reported that the two directions appeared to repel each other so that the dots appeared to move towards 5 o'clock and 8 o'clock. The authors varied the angle between the two directions of motion and found a maximum repulsion effect of about 20° when the two directions differed by 22.5^o. This 'motion contrast' is analogous to simultaneous brightness contrast, and has been explained as mutual inhibition between motion-sensitive pathways.

(ii) Induced motion. A static test field surrounded by downward motion appears to drift upwards. This is the classic induced motion effect (Duncker, 1929).

Muller and Greenlee (1994) examined the effects of adaptation to a drifting grating. They found three effects:

(i) It increased the lower velocity threshold of motion, that is, reduced sensitivity to very slow movement.

(ii) It shifted the point of subjective stationarity towards higher velocities of motion in the adapted direction. This confirms a result obtained by Sachtler and Zaidi (1993).

(iii) It increased the speed discrimination threshold for test contrasts below 0.1, having a maximal effect for adapting drift rates between 8 and 16 Hz.

4.2 My experiments

I shall describe six of my experiments on adaptation to motion which tell us a little more about the motion-sensitive pathways.

4.2.1 Motion aftereffects from ramp aftereffects

If one gazes steadily at a spatially uniform gray patch which grows gradually brighter [or dimmer], with its luminance modulated by a ramp or sawtooth waveform, then a subsequently viewed steady gray patch appears to be growing gradually dimmer [or brighter] (Anstis, 1967; Arnold & Anstis, 1993). This "ramp aftereffect" reveals the presence of adaptable visual pathways that respond selectively to gradual changes of luminance. This ramp aftereffect can be made to yield a motion aftereffect from motionless stimuli (Anstis, 1990), and this will show us that Reichardt motion detectors are also able to respond to gradual luminance change. First, notice that slow apparent motion can be produced from a stationary arrangement of two gray squares with a black line running down the border where they touch. If the left square gradually brightens while the right square gradually dims, the black line appears to move slowly to the right. Why? If the luminance profile is blurred, there is a gradual rightward shift in its peak. So any low-frequency visual pathways with large receptive fields will extract this luminance change over space and time, suggesting that motion can be sensed by very low-spatial-frequency pathways. The next step is to replace the physical luminance changes in the two squares with illusory changes produced by ramp aftereffects. The subject adapted to a dimming square on the left and a brightening square on the right. The two squares abutted but there was no black line along their join, so no apparent movement was seen. The squares were then set to steady gray and in the aftereffect the left square seemed to be dimming and the right square seemed to be brightening – but no motion was seen. Part way through the aftereffect, a black [or white] line was added along the join, and immediately it seemed to move to the right [or left] in an aftereffect of motion. So although there was no motion at any time in the adapting stimulus, a motion aftereffect was seen.

We do not even need the black line. Our next display was a mass of irregular blobs, half of them brightening and the remaining half dimming. All blobs abutted so there were no gaps between them. After 30 s of adaptation to this luminance change, the display was switched to steady blobs. If fixation was strictly maintained, ramp aftereffects were seen, with the previously brightening [dimming] blobs now apparently dimming [brightening]. But if fixation was shifted by a few min arc, the regions of aftereffect were now slightly displaced on the test stimulus. This had the same effect as drawing a contour a few min arc wide around the edges of the blobs. Subjects saw a clear aftereffect of motion – and if they changed their point of fixation, which displaced the slight offset between regions of aftereffect and the test blob, the motion aftereffect promptly changed its direction.

Since ramp aftereffects can be interpreted as motion aftereffects, we conclude that motion detectors include a filter to detect gradual change of luminance, dI/dT (Figure 4.1c).

4.2.2 Adaptation to back and forth apparent motion

Usually a motion aftereffect is produced by inspecting steady motion in one direction. This upsets the balance of an opponent motion detector. However, Debbie Giaschi, Alex Cogan and I (1985) have measured adaptation to back and forth apparent motion. A single spot that jumped back and forth in apparent motion between two positions in 'ping-pong' mode (Figure 4.2a) was at first seen as moving, but after a period of time the sensation of motion adapted out and was replaced by the impression of two dots flickering in place (Kolers, 1972). Some kind of phase or sequence information in the motion system has adapted out. The percept fluctuated irregularly over time between flicker and motion, but when we time- averaged over ten runs we found that the probability of seeing motion decayed exponentially over time. The faster the alternation rate, the weaker the motion signal and the more rapidly it degraded into apparent flicker. After an inspection of 30 s, a 3 Hz alternation still looked like motion for 44.4% of the time but a 4 Hz alternation for only 8.5% (Figure 4.2c).

This situation is really an adaptation experiment in which the adapting and test motions are identical. There are two reasons why a rapidly alternating spot might lose its motion quality faster than a slower one. It might provide a stronger signal which produced more adaptation during the induction phase, or it might provide a weaker signal which gave less visible motion during the test phase. Experiments in which we adapted to one alternation rate and tested on another showed that slow alternations (2.5 or 3 Hz) gave stronger motion signals than faster alternations (3.5 or 4 Hz).

Only motion could weaken apparent motion. The adapting spot had to traverse the same motion path as the test spot, and flicker alone produced little adaptation. If one adapted to two spots flickering in phase, and then tested on a single spot jumping back and forth, the motion percept was unimpaired. More surprisingly, an alternating dot had little adapting effect unless its motion was perceived along the adapting path. When the original

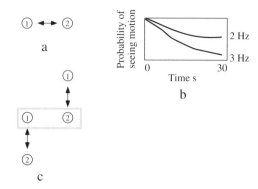

Fig. 4.2. a, A dot that alternates between two positions is first seen in apparent motion, but after a while the motion effect adapts out and the spots appear to flicker in place. b, Probability of seeing motion declines over time (Anstis *et al.*, 1985). c, Adaptation does not occur if the adapting and test dots have congruent positions but different perceived motion paths.

dot still flashed in alternation in the two usual positions, but two dots were added to the adapting display that caused two vertical motions to be seen with no perceived horizontal motion (Figure 4.2b), then again there was little adaptation.

4.2.3 Adaptation to random dynamic noise

Dynamic visual noise (DVN) is a snowstorm of randomly twinkling dots such as one can see on a detuned TV receiver. These dots jump around incoherently in apparent motion in random directions. Richard Gregory and I have found (in unpublished results) that adaptation to dynamic visual noise reduces motion sensitivity in all directions, like an omnidirectional motion aftereffect (Figure 4.3). Specifically, inspection of a twinkling field virtually halved the subjective speed of a subsequently viewed moving field. We measured this subjective slowdown by a matching method. Two adapting fields of dense random dots were presented side by side, a static field on the left and dots twinkling in random dynamic noise on the right. We used a 'topping-up' method in which the observers first adapted to this for 30 s, then alternately viewed this same adapting field for 4 s, alternating with 1 s views of a test field. The test field consisted of a random-dot field drifting downwards at 2.5^o/s on the left, and a variable-speed drifting field, under the subject's control, on the right.

We found that following adaptation to the static dots the test velocity

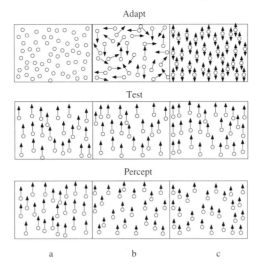

Fig. 4.3. a, Adaptation to a static noise field does not alter the perceived velocity of a drifting test field. b, Adaptation to a dynamic noise field slows it down, and so does c, adaptation to a random-dot field that moves up and down alternately.

was perceived accurately to within a few percent, as one would expect. However, adaptation to noise dramatically slowed the perceived test velocity (Figure 4.3b). Dots that drifted down at 2.5^o/s in the noise-adapted half of the field were matched to unadapted dots that drifted down at only 1.4^o/s – a 43% apparent slowdown.

4.2.4 Adaptation to opposed motions

Adaptation to downward motion generally makes a downward test motion look slower, because it unbalances the opponent-motion pathways that normally balance upward against downward motion (Sutherland, 1961; Sekuler & Levinson, 1974). Any stimulus that affects both opponent halves equally should cancel out and produce no motion aftereffect. This is so. Richard Gregory and I (unpublished results) adapted to dense random dots that moved alternately up and down at 2.5^o/s. We then looked for a motion aftereffect on a test field of dense random dots that was either stationary, or else drifted up [or down].

Adaptation to a field that moved back and forth produced no motion aftereffect on the stationary test pattern. This is not surprising, since the alternating motion clearly adapted upward and downward motion pathways equally, so the opponent motion detector would remain balanced and any equal but opposite motion aftereffects would cancel out. However, adaptation to the same alternating-motion field did produce a marked apparent slowing in a field of dense random dots that drifted up [or down]. (Figure 4.3c). We also observed apparent slowing during prolonged inspection of two superimposed sheets of random dots that drifted transparently over each other, one moving up, the other down.

The symmetrical adaptation from the double motion can produce this kind of asymmetrical aftereffect. Suppose that adaptation depressed the upward and downward gains to 80%. If the motion signals from a stationary test field were normally:

$$50U - 50D = 0 \qquad \text{(zero = stationary)}$$

then the double-motion adaptation would change this to:

$$40U - 40D = 0,$$

yielding no change in a stationary test field. If an upward moving test grating were normally signaled as:

$$100U - 10D = 90$$

then following adaptation its signal would be:

$$80U - 8D = 72$$

so the drifting grating would appear to be slowed down, as we found.

So this perceived reduction in following adaptation to up-and-down motion may be slowing down the perceived vertical test speed by reducing the strength of the motion signal. The Left/Right comparison model extracts motion from cells whose response can be altered in many other ways as well. Thus the Left cells could be firing because they saw something moving left or that it was the right spatial frequency or that it was the right orientation or high contrast etc. But the Right one would be affected by all those things too, so the comparison would bring out their only difference, direction. The absolute firing rates must be irrelevant here: it is only the Left/Right ratio that matters. Now adapting stimuli in which all directions get adapted would not affect the ratio. So it could not affect the comparison, that is, the motion information. If stimuli that affected all channels had an effect on velocity perception, then everything that affected all channels would have an effect, and high contrast patterns would appear to move faster. This has been demonstrated by Stone and Thompson (1992), who found that human speed perception is contrast dependent. They reported that when two parallel gratings moving at the same speed were presented simultaneously, the lower-contrast grating appeared slower. On average, a 70% contrast grating

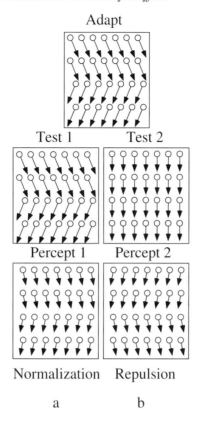

Fig. 4.4. An adapting field of sparse random dots moved downwards in a shallow V or chevron facing to the right. a, During prolonged inspection the dots appeared to slow down and their motion paths gradually shifted toward the vertical (motion normalization). b, a test field of dots that moved vertically appeared deviated into a motion path like a left-facing chevron (motion repulsion).

had to be be slowed by 35% to match a 10% contrast grating moving at 2°/sec. The misperception of relative speed was reduced when the two gratings were presented sequentially. In their latest paper (Thompson *et al.*, 1996) they do greatly modify their conclusions but they do not abandon them.

4.2.5 Motion aftereffects of normalization and repulsion

I found it easy to confirm Marshak and Sekuler's directionally selective adaptation, in which adaptation to a downward motion toward 5 o'clock

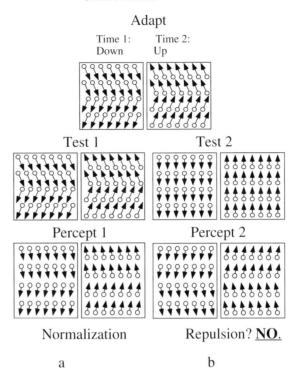

Fig. 4.5. As in Figure 4.4, except that the dots moved back and forth, reversing every 5 s. Result: some normalization occurred, but no repulsion aftereffect.

subjectively repelled a vertical test motion that drifts towards 6 o'clock by making it appear to drift toward 7 o'clock (Figure 4.4b). I used a field of sparse white dots on a black background drifting at 3°/sec. The very same adapting field also produced an aftereffect of apparent normalization of motion. During the inspection period the random dots appeared to slow down markedly and in addition their trajectory seemed to shift gradually toward the vertical (Figure 4.4a). This is analogous to Gibson's (1937a, 1937b) discovery that a tilted line appears to regress toward the vertical during prolonged inspection.

Results were less clear cut when the adapting pattern reversed in direction every 5 s (Figure 4.5). The directions of adapting motion were approximately towards 11 o'clock and 5 o'clock, actually at 30° from the vertical.

The direction alternated every 5 sec for a total adapting time of 10 minutes. The test field then moved alternately up and down vertically (toward 12 and 6 o'clock), reversing every 5 sec. Results: The moving dots still appeared to slow down during prolonged inspection, and they also normalized toward the vertical (Figure 4.5a). Following a 10 minute adapting period the observers viewed test dots that moved vertically up and down. Although these dots did appear somewhat slowed, their perceived motion paths were still correctly seen as vertical, with no angular deviation away from the vertical (Figure 4.5b).

4.2.6 Adaptation to expansion or to spatial-frequency change?

Adaptation to an expanding pattern yields a contracting motion aftereffect. Imagine a random-dot pattern, like a photograph of a sheet of sandpaper, which is electronically zoomed on a computer screen. After inspection of this pattern for about 30 s, a stationary test pattern will appear to be shrinking.

During the zoom, the contours that move outwards from the centre of the screen should suffice to stimulate motion sensors. But another way of looking at it is to say that the frequency spectrum of the pattern is zooming downwards. Since the Fourier transform that translates from space into spatial frequency is reversible in a linear system, both descriptions sound equally apt. Since we already know of visual pathways selective for gradual change of luminance (Anstis, 1967; Arnold & Anstis, 1993), Brian Rogers and I looked for hypothetical visual pathways that might respond to gradual change of spatial frequency. We attempted to adapt them by presenting a zooming display that lacked smoothly moving contours. Instead of zooming a static random-dot display, we zoomed a twinkling, dynamic random-dot noise display. This contained no smoothly moving contours but its frequency spectrum did zoom. Result: no motion aftereffect.

The spectrum of a random dot display is rather broad, so we narrowed it down with two sinusoidal gratings of the same spatial frequency (1 cpd). Both gratings expanded at the same rate (0.5 octaves/s), but whereas one simply expanded from its centre the other was jittered in phase, so that it translated randomly back and forth at right angles to its bars (Figure 4.6). Result: The smoothly expanding grating, which contained moving contours, did give a contracting motion aftereffect, but the jittered grating, which had a zooming spectrum but had no smoothly moving contours, showed no motion aftereffect.

Thus we were unable to find evidence for any phase-blind visual pathway that might be sensitive to gradual change of spatial frequency over time.

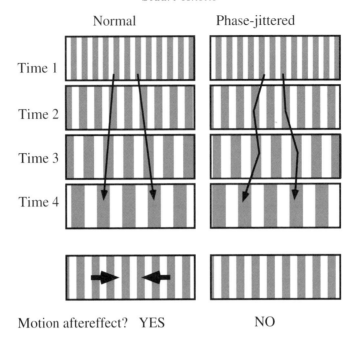

Fig. 4.6. An expanding grating gives a motion aftereffect of apparent contraction. However, a phase-jittered expanding grating does fall in spatial frequency over time, but it has no steadily moving contours, and it gives no motion aftereffect. Hence the aftereffect depends upon moving contours, not upon changes in spatial frequency.

4.3 Discussion

It is no accident that the visual system uses opponent pathways to code motion and colour. Opponency is widely used in electronic differential amplifiers, which receive two inputs and transmit only the difference between them. Respects in which the two inputs are the same are subtracted out and disappear. The higher the 'common mode rejection ratio' the better the amplifier.

All adaptation experiments are designed so that exposure to the adapting stimulus alters the appearance of the test stimulus. The test stimulus may become less visible, or may shift away from the adapting stimulus along some visual dimension (such as colour, motion, depth, etc.) A central assumption of all adaptation experiments is that such a change can only occur if the adapting and test patterns stimulate the same visual pathways. Therefore, if adaptation to motion makes a stationary pattern appear to move in the opposite direction, there must be some visual pathways that respond to both the moving and the stationary stimulus. This makes a clear physiological prediction that each opponent half of a motion detector must have a non-zero firing rate when confronted with stationary patterns. The firing rates are presumably identical in the two halves and cancel out exactly so that they do not appear at the output – any output signal would make stationary patterns appear to drift even in the absence of a motion aftereffect. A similar arrangement is known to exist for the semicircular canals (reviewed by Howard, 1982). Corresponding canals on each side of the head converge on an opponent pathway. Both canals have a resting output level, which cancel out. However, if one canal is destroyed or surgically removed, the remaining canal puts out a continuous unopposed resting level and the unfortunate patient feels the whole world constantly swimming around. The resulting vertigo is highly disabling and often there is nothing for it but to remove the other canal, a procedure which partially restores the status quo. The vertigo mercifully vanishes and the patient can maintain his balance reasonably well.

To summarize, all these results are consistent with the existence of opponent motion sensors, and they suggest several testable predictions. The sensors must contain temporal filters which respond to gradual change of luminance ($+ \, dI/dT$), and their velocity tuning curves must respond to stationary as well as to moving objects, such that the opponent halves, but not the final output path, produce a non-zero response to stationary stimuli. Adaptation to motion must reduce their gain rather than shift their zero point.

Acknowledgements Supported by NEI Grant EY 10241-4. Thanks to Laurence Harris and Dave Smith for comments on the manuscript.

5

Visuomotor codes for three-dimensional saccades

J. Douglas Crawford

Department of Psychology and Biology
York University
North York
Canada

The way that the brain codes visual space must largely be dictated by the spatial requirements of downstream motor systems. Nowhere is this more clear than in the three-dimensional (3-D) properties of orienting movements of the eyes, head, and arm toward visual stimuli. To select a unique 3-D orientation for each 2-D pointing direction (Donders' law), these systems have developed behavioural constraints such as Listing's law (of the eye) and the Fick Gimbal strategy (of the head and arm). These strategies each have their own particular perceptual consequences, but they all dictate that the correct interpretation of visual information for movement depends on initial body position. As a result (contrary to some views of spatial coding) the brain must construct internal representations of both target direction and desired body position and compare these with internal representations of current body position to generate accurate movements. We are probably closest to identifying these spatial transformations in the neural mechanisms for saccades, but the general implications for visual coding are relevant even for the most complex aspects of spatial perception and navigation.

5.1 Introduction

The way that the brain codes visual signals must largely be dictated by the requirements of behaviour and downstream motor systems. This is particularly true of the spatial aspects of vision, to the extent that some have suggested that the dorsal "where" stream of visual analysis through the posterior parietal cortex (Ungerleider & Mishkin, 1982) should really be called the "how" stream of analysis (Goodale & Milner, 1992). The point of this distinction is that our perception of the location of objects in visual space is so tightly coupled with our need to physically acquire them and manipulate them, that spatial perception is more correctly thought of as visuomotor, rather than visual alone. Thus, to understand the spatial aspects of visual codes, it is critical to study the constraints placed on this process by the informational requirements of motor control.

Often the complexity of these requirements is intimidating. Therefore, it is useful to break them down into certain fundamental computational problems (e.g. the degrees of freedom problem, the reference frame problem and the problems of matching velocity to position and handling rotational kinematics, to name a few that will be dealt with in detail below). Since various forms of all of these problems emerge in all motor systems, even the simplest, easiest to study system can potentially shed light on the general neural mechanisms of coding visuomotor space.

To this end, the study of saccades (which for the purposes of this chapter can be defined as voluntary rapid eye movements toward visual targets) has been invaluable, just as the study of smooth pursuit eye movements has been invaluable for studying the output of visual motion processing (e.g. Newsome *et al.*, 1985). Of the various goal-directed visuomotor behaviours, saccades are perhaps the most spatially accurate and yet the simplest, being remarkably accessible to both behavioural and neurophysiological study. Furthermore, this behaviour is intimately tied to the visual system because eye movements are clearly both subservient to our visual needs, and have direct consequences for vision.

Although numerous studies have capitalized on this relationship to explore visuomotor transformations, most have ignored one aspect of obvious importance for moving in real space: the three-dimensional (3-D) aspects of eye orientation and axes of rotation. This, however, was not always the case. In the nineteenth century some of the founding fathers of visual neuroscience, Donders (1847), Helmholtz (1867), and Hering (1868), were fascinated by behavioural constraints on 3-D eye rotations. Nevertheless, much of their penetrating analysis into this area lay all but forgotten for a century, kept alive by only a faithful few (i.e. Westheimer 1957; Nakayama 1975, 1983).

Fortunately, there has been a recent renaissance of research on this topic, spurred by new technologies for recording three-dimensional eye rotations (Ferman *et al.*, 1987a; Tweed *et al.*, 1990), and a better understanding among neuroscientists of the unique rules that govern rotational kinematics (Tweed & Vilis, 1987). In the present chapter we will attempt to capitalize on these advances from the perspective of their implications for vision. We will begin with a review of the behavioural and perceptual aspects of orienting movements in 3-D (with emphasis on saccades), continue with the neural mechanisms for 3-D saccades, and end by exploring their general implications for the neural coding of visual space. Our theme will be focused on the general computational issues mentioned above, and our goal will be to identify the geometric transformations and spatial representations necessary for the generation of accurate and kinematically correct movements.

5.2 Behavioural and perceptual aspects of 3-D orienting movements

5.2.1 The degrees of freedom problem and Listing's law.

Usually motor systems have more degrees of freedom than are necessary to accomplish the sensory requirements of a spatial task. This is called kinematic redundancy, and the resulting degrees of freedom problem is a central computational challenge for neural control (Bernstein, 1967). The oculomotor system provides a simple example of kinematic redundancy. Clearly the eye can rotate horizontally and vertically during saccades to foveate targets. However, the eye is a 3-D object, and is fully capable of rotating about the visual axis (i.e. the line of sight). Such rotations are often called cyclotorsion or torsion (i.e intorsion and extorsion relative to the nose), but for reasons that will become more clear below I will use a slightly different definition of torsion: clockwise (CW) or counterclockwise (CCW) rotations (from the subject's point of view) about a head-fixed axis orthogonal to the face. For example, clockwise rotation implies that the upper pole of the right eye is rotating temporally, while the upper pole of the left eye rotates nasally. Whereas each eye has a pair of horizontal recti muscles that rotate it leftward and rightward, the other four muscles (superior and inferior recti and obliques) rotate the eye up-CW, down-CW, up-CCW, and down-CCW respectively, with approximately equal torsional and vertical actions. This musculature can and does (under some circumstances) rotate the eye about the line of sight without changing the direction of gaze. Thus, the saccadic generator can choose amongst an infinite number of orientations to achieve any one gaze direction (which can be defined as the line of light rays that fall on the fovea).

This choice arises every time we decide to foveate a peripheral target because stimulation of each retinal point only specifies a desired gaze direction, not the orientation of the retina about that gaze axis (Crawford & Guitton, 1994). One might envision a complex visuomotor system that uses perceived orientation of the target to choose the final 3-D orientation of the eye (e.g. so that the horizontal meridian of the retina aligns with prominent lines on the stimulus), but as we shall see, this is simply not the way it is done. Another appealing possibility is that the eye would take the shortest possible path to foveate the target, i.e. rotating about an axis orthogonal to the plane containing current and desired gaze direction. A potential problem with this scheme is that the eye would reach different final orientations for each desired gaze direction, depending on initial position (Tweed & Vilis, 1990b). Moreover, a sequence of "round-the-clock" eye movements (where the shortest path axis would always tilt in one direction towards the head-fixed torsional axis) would cause torsional position to accumulate until the eye was jammed against its mechanical limit. Apparently these are important drawbacks, because the system did not choose this option either. So what does it do?

Despite the potentially redundant third degree of freedom, Donders (1847) found that for any one gaze direction the eye always assumes a unique three-dimensional orientation, irrespective of previous positions and movements (Donders' law). Furthermore, these orientations can be specified, as first predicted theoretically by Johann Benedict Listing, a German mathematician and student of von Helmholtz (1867). The description of Listing's theory (now called Listing's law) is simplest when eye position vectors are used. Like all other measures of position, these vectors give orientation relative to a reference position, but in this case the position vector is parallel to the axis of the rotation that would take the eye from the reference position to the current position (Fig. 5.1). When one examines the axes used to rotate the eye from a central reference position to several eccentric positions (e.g. to positions 1, 2, 3, and 4 in Fig. 5.1A) one finds that they are confined to a plane (Fig. 5.1B). For one particular reference position the direction of gaze is orthogonal to the associated plane of position vectors. This reference position was defined as primary position (von Helmholtz, 1867), and this particular plane is now called Listing's plane. Thus, "primary position" has a very specific definition (which has largely been ignored by 20th century investigators). If torsion is defined as rotation about the visual axis at primary position i.e. the axis perpendicular to Listing's plane, then Listing's law simply states that saccades only allow eye positions with zero torsion (Westheimer, 1957).

Listing's law was first confirmed indirectly with the use of visual afterimage studies (von Helmholtz, 1867), thus beginning a long (and hopefully venerable) tradition of interplay between theory and experiment in this field. Recently, Listing's plane has been measured more directly (Fig. 5.1C) using the three-dimensional search coil technique (Ferman *et al.*, 1987b; Tweed *et al.*, 1990). The thickness of Listing's plane has been quantified by mathematically fitting an ideal plane to the measured eye positions, and then determining the standard deviation of torsional positions about this plane. These measurements showed that Listing's plane has a finite, relatively uni-

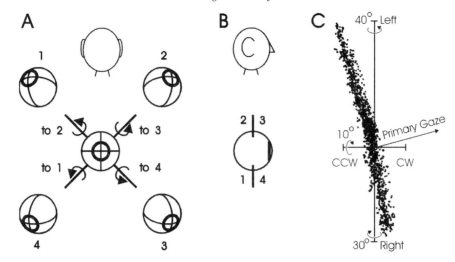

Fig. 5.1. Eye position vectors and Listing's law. **A** During head-fixed saccades, the eye reaches eccentric eye positions (e.g. 1, 2, 3, or 4) from the central primary position by rotating about the axes indicated. These axes lay in the plane of the page. **B** The axes are viewed edge-on from the side view, showing their planar configuration. Such axes are used to describe three-dimensional (3-D) eye position, by replacing them with a parallel vector whose length is proportional to the magnitude of rotation from primary position. Unlike actual axes of rotation, position vectors are always measured relative to primary position. (Based on Crawford & Vilis, 1995). **C** Actual eye position vectors recorded while a monkey made saccades with the head fixed. Only the tips of these vectors are shown. They form a Listing's plane which is viewed edge on, orthogonal to gaze direction at primary position. This data is plotted in arbitrary earth-vertical coordinates, to remind us that Listing's plane tends to tilt back in the head by variable amounts (Crawford, 1994). CW: Clockwise position relative to the animal, CCW: Counterclockwise.

form thickness of 1-2° throughout the oculomotor range (Ferman *et al.*, 1987b; Tweed & Vilis, 1990a; Straumann *et al.*, 1991). The torsional thickness is similar during steady fixations and during saccades (Ferman *et al.*, 1987c; Tweed & Vilis, 1990a), even for saccades whose direction changes (curves) during the movement (Van Gisbergen *et al.*, 1990; Minken *et al.*, 1995). Thus Listing's law is important during the generation of saccades and not just for determining final eye position.

Given the fact that eye position is confined to a plane, it is tempting to think that saccade generation is two-dimensional. However, this intuition is based on the familiar concepts of translational motion. In the case of rotations, there is an inherently non-linear relationship between angular velocity (the instantaneous axis of rotation) and position, so that similar rotations will produce different changes in position depending on the initial position

(Tweed & Vilis, 1987). One corollary of this relationship is that rotations about different axes do not commute, i.e. rotation A followed by rotation B gives a different final position than B followed by A. A second corollary is that Listing's law is only consistent with rotation of the eye about an axis (velocity vector) in Listing's plane (of position vectors) if the movement is towards or from primary position (Tweed & Vilis, 1990a; Crawford & Vilis, 1991), as in Figure 5.1A. In all other cases saccade velocity axes must tilt torsionally out of Listing's plane in a systematic, position-dependent fashion in order to keep eye position in Listing's plane (von Helmholtz, 1867; Tweed & Vilis, 1990a). Specifically, the eye must rotate about an axis that is the intersection line between the two planes orthogonal, respectively, to (1) the bisector of the angle between primary gaze direction and initial gaze direction, and (2) the bisector between primary gaze and final gaze direction (von Helmholtz, 1867; Tweed & Vilis, 1990a).

If the saccade does not have a component towards or away from primary position, this relationship can be described by the simpler "half angle rule" For example, to take the eye from position 1 to 2 (Fig. 5.1A) while maintaining zero torsion, a saccade must rotate the eye about a vertical axis tilted counterclockwise out of Listing's plane, by half the angle of gaze elevation. Without this tilt, eye position would end up deviated clockwise out of Listing's plane, which has been observed to occur during slow vestibular driven eye movements (Crawford & Vilis, 1991). The technology to measure such axes in behaving humans and animals has only recently been developed Tweed *et al.*, 1990). Such measurements have confirmed that saccade axes use the correct pattern of torsional tilts to maintain Listing's law during and after the movement (Tweed & Vilis, 1990a). Thus, even to control horizontal and vertical eye position in a 2-D plane, the oculomotor system must control the specific torsional components required in its saccade axes.

5.2.2 Does Listing's law apply to other oculomotor and visuomotor behaviours?

From a three-dimensional perspective, there are two broad strategies of eye movement. Saccades exemplify the first, i.e. redirection or maintenance of gaze direction with the head still. As reviewed above this involves a 2-D to 3-D sensorimotor transformation with one dimension of kinematic redundancy. Smooth pursuit movements, which allow us to follow a slowly moving target visually, follow the same sort of strategy, and thus show the same kinematic redundancy. It appears that, like saccades, the pursuit system uses Listing's law to define the third, initially unspecified, dimension of eye rotation (Haslwanter *et al.*, 1992; Tweed *et al.*, 1992). For some time, converging movements of the eyes towards a near target were thought to violate Listing's law because they change torsional eye position (Nakayama, 1983). However more recent studies showed that converged eye positions are still confined to a plane, but one that is rotated outward from the normal Listing's plane (Mok *et al.*, 1992; Van Rijn & Van den Berg, 1993; Minken *et al.*, 1995).

The second eye movement strategy involves stabilization of the retinal image during head movement (a 3-D to 3-D transformation with no kinematic redundancy). During head rotations vestibulo-ocular reflex (VOR) slow phases achieve this by rotating the eyes around the same axis as the head but in the opposite direction, which precludes Listing's law (Collewijn *et al.*, 1985; Ferman *et al.*, 1987a; Crawford & Vilis, 1991). Although the most recent studies suggest that slow phase axes show a tendency to tilt with eye position by about half the amount required by Listing's law (Misslisch *et al.*, 1994), it was still clear that eye position is no longer confined to Listing's plane. The optokinetic system uses visual information to assist the VOR, and thus it also violates Listing's law (Fetter *et al.*, 1982; Tan *et al.*, 1993). However, the saccade-like quick phases that interrupt compensatory VOR and OKN movements prevent large torsional violations of Listing's law both anticipating and resetting the resulting torsion (Crawford & Vilis, 1991; Guitton & Crawford, 1994). Thus Listing's law is the oculomotor system's unique behavioural solution to its degrees of freedom problem; where this problem does not arise, Listing's law does not apply.

Clearly, visuomotor behaviours produced by multi-joint systems like the arm encounter much more complex degrees of freedom problems than the eye. Can simple rules like Listing's law be applied to these complicated systems? The first logical extension from the purely oculomotor studies was to measure eye rotations in space produced by a combination of eye and head motion movements between visual targets. Initial studies suggested that in such movements eye position in space is also confined to a plane (Straumann *et al.*, 1991). However when reexamined over a wider range of movements eye position in space was found to be confined to a surface that was twisted (Glenn & Vilis, 1992; Guitton & Crawford, 1994). Up-left and down-right pointing positions have clockwise components and the down-left and up-right positions have counterclockwise components that increase with pointing eccentricity (Fig. 5.2B), where the torsional axis is now defined as a forward-pointing axis fixed in the body or space. This twist is similar to that produced by Fick nested gimbals (Fig. 5.2A), which utilize a fixed vertical axis and a horizontal axis that rotates with the pointing direction

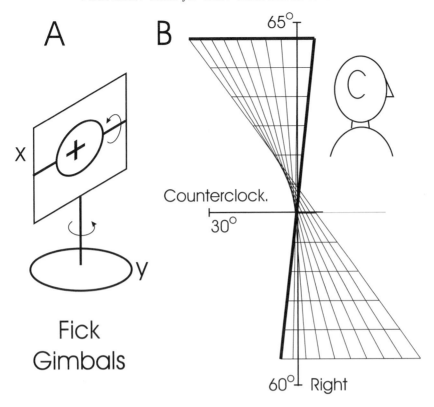

Fig. 5.2. Fick Gimbals and the range of positions that they produce. **A** A schematic drawing of a typical set of Fick Gimbals, with a horizontal axis fixed to a frame that rotates about a vertical axis fixed to a base. **B** "Twisted" range of position vectors produced by Fick Gimbals. The drawing is made from a computer fit to actual primate eye-in-space position vectors during large gaze shifts (Guitton & Crawford, 1994), plotted in a space-fixed orthogonal coordinate system. Unlike Listing's law, the amount of torsional eye position in such a coordinate system is dependent on both vertical and horizontal eye position. In contrast, if plotted in Fick coordinates such as those in part A, eye-in-space torsion would always be zero, and the eye-in-head would show "false torsion".

(e.g. like the common telescope mount). The reason for this Fick-like twist might originate from the fact that during oblique gaze shifts the eye and head do not contribute equally to the movement. The head performs the bulk of the horizontal rotation while the eye the bulk of the vertical. Since the eye is mounted in the head, the system may be inherently Fick-like.

What of systems that are not inherently Fick-like? The technology developed for measuring three-dimensional eye positions and rotation axes has now been applied both to the head and to the various segments of the arm-hand system. Surprisingly, head orientation itself, which is produced by a complex combination of spinal joint articulations, also followed the Fick-like rule during gaze shifts between visual targets (Glenn & Vilis, 1992). Furthermore, recent measurements of arm segment orientations during pointing toward visual targets showed a similar constraint (Hore *et al.*, 1992a; Miller *et al.*, 1992), and these Fick-like properties also emerged during visually-guided throwing (Hore *et al.*, 1992a) and grasping movements (Straumann *et al.*, 1991). Thus, even the segmental behaviour of complex multi-joint systems can be described in terms of a simple orientation constraint, the Fick strategy.

5.2.3 Perceptual and motor consequences of Listing's law and the Fick strategy.

To understand these strategies, it is useful to view Listing's law and the Fick Gimbal strategy as part of a continuum of constraints that uphold analogues to Donders' law. Listing's law is in the middle of the continuum with Fick gimbals and Helmholtz gimbals (which use a fixed horizontal axis and a mobile vertical axis) at either extreme. Each point along this continuum can be specified by a single computational variable (the so-called Fick score; Glen and Vilis 1993) defining a particular position-dependent rule for generating movement commands that obey Donders' law. The brain appears to select the rule along this continuum that is best suited to a particular task and skeleto-muscular structure: The eye adopts the Listing's law strategy, while the head and arm are farther along the continuum. To be precise, the head and arm actually use a strategy that is about midway between Listing's law and the ideal Fick strategy (Glenn & Vilis, 1992; Hore *et al.*, 1992b). Support for this continuum idea comes from the recent observation that the head strategy could be shifted along the continuum from the Fick end towards (and sometimes even past) the Listing's law point by altering the functional range of eye movement to a single head-fixed point, thus forcing the head to act more like an eye (Crawford & Guitton, 1995)

In choosing amongst the options on this continuum, evolution or development would presumably be guided by the behavioural and perceptual consequences of this choice. From a motor point of view, one would select the strategy that gives movements and positions that are advantageously matched to the skeleto-muscular structures it acts upon. For example, Listing's law keeps the action of the eye muscles near the centre of their torsional range, and chooses the shortest path for eye rotations towards and away from primary position (von Helmholtz, 1867). In contrast, the Fick strategy maximizes uses the most direct path about a mobile axis for vertical rotation, but at the cost of using a fixed, usually non-optimal axis for horizontal rotations. It has been speculated that this is advantageous for work against gravity (Glenn & Vilis, 1992; Hore *et al.*, 1992b).

Each point on the Listing-Fick continuum also has several perceptual consequences. Hering (1868) argued that the purpose of Listing's law is to maintain the constancy of radial lines on the retina, while looking at a asterisk-like pattern with its point of convergence in the primary gaze direction. Listings law may also be important for binocular viewing, because cyclotorsion (about the visual axis) changes the correspondence of retinal images between the two eyes. For example, the strong tilt observed in the vertical horoptor (Nakayama, 1983) requires binocular convergence between 2 non-parallel retinal lines. Geometry dictates that this horoptor will degrade when the eyes rotates torsionally, even if the movement is conjugate (Crawford & Vilis, 1991; Howard & Zacher, 1991). However, Listing's law is not the ideal solution for this problem, because it does produce small amounts of so-called "false torsion" (torsion about the visual axis) at oblique eye positions. Tweed (1994) has suggested that (taking divergence of Listing's planes during convergence into account) Listing's law is more likely a compromise, between the need for binocular alignment of images, and minimizing angular displacement of the eyes from primary position. Another factor of possible importance is that Listing's law (and its cousins in the Donders' law family) simplify the spatial interpretation of signals from the retinal map by maintaining a constant orientation of the retina for each gaze direction. Nevertheless, certain reference frame problems still result. This refers to the problem of using visual signals that (defined relative to the eye-fixed retina) to move segments relative to a different body parts (note that the eye itself moves relative to the head, not relative to itself!). For example, stimulation of a point on the horizontal meridian of the eye may correctly indicate a horizontally-displaced target when the eye looks straight ahead, but the same "horizontal" retinal error indicates an obliquely displaced target relative to the head when initial eye position is deviated vertically (Fig. 5.3). This would not be a problem if the stimulation of a given point on the retina could always be mapped onto an axis of rotation that is fixed with respect to the eye (i.e. defining both the visual and motor aspects of the task relative to the eye), but recall that Listing's law will only allow saccade axes to tilt (with respect to the head) by only half the angle of eye position. Thus there is no trivial solution to the problem of mapping points of stimulation on the retinal map onto displacements in eye position. Since this is an important problem for both the generation of saccades and the perception of spatial

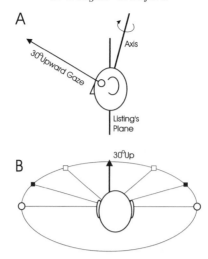

Fig. 5.3. The oculomotor visuomotor reference frame problem. **A** The head is viewed from the side, with gaze at 30° up from a theoretical primary gaze direction that is exactly straight ahead. The horizontal retinal meridian (defined as the retinal arc that is aligned horizontally when the eye is at primary position) is also tilted 30° up with the eye. If the eye is to rotate horizontally from this position about a vertical axis with zero horizontal components, Listing's law states that this axis must tilt backwards out Listing's plane by 15° ($30^o/2$) in order to keep eye position vectors in Listing's plane (Tweed & Vilis, 1990a). **B** A circle of targets that stimulates only the tilted horizontal retinal meridian of the eye is viewed from behind the head. Note from this head-fixed perspective, these targets are displaced obliquely from current gaze direction (This effect increases with target displacement, and would also increase with initial vertical gaze elevation). This poses a problem for mapping (horizontal) retinal signals onto (oblique) saccade commands for eye displacement relative to the head.

locations in general, we will return to this topic when we consider models of the visuomotor transformation for saccades.

In some respects, since the head is normally free to move when we scan the visual world, one should be more concerned with the perceptual consequences of the Fick Gimbal strategy (followed by the eye-in-space) than Listing's law. Rather than a following radial lines, the Fick strategy (Fig. 5.2) maintains the constancy of lines relative to the horizon (Glenn & Vilis, 1992; Hore *et al.*, 1992b). This is the ideal strategy for maintaining the horoptor because it keeps the vertical meridian of the eye orthogonal to the ground. Moreover, since the head also obeys this strategy, the line between the two eyes is kept horizontal to the ground (and similarly the otolith organs are consistently oriented with respect to the direction of gravity; Misslisch *et al.* 1994). Finally, the reference-frame problem occurs again for interpreting eye-fixed retinal signals for eye-in-space displacement commands, but it is slightly different from the head-fixed case. Compared to Listing's law, the Fick Gimbal strategy encounters a smaller reference-frame effect for vertical rotations (where the axis is roughly eye-fixed) but a greater problem for horizontal rotations (where the axis is body-fixed). As a result, a target that is horizontally displaced in retinal coordinates can be displaced in an entirely different direction in motor gaze coordinates, particularly when initial gaze is upwards or downwards.

Finally, it has been suggested that the use of these similar constraints in the eye, head, and arm is important for coordinating their behaviours in visual space. For example, Straumann *et al.* (1991) found that the 2-D position subspaces of the eye-in-space, head-in-space, and arm-in-space remained in close register during visually-guided pointing movements in various directions. This effect appears to emerge from the choices of constraints in the individual systems. When looking and pointing in any given direction, the Fick-gimbal strategy keeps the horizontal axes for both arm and head rotation orthogonal to that direction (equal angle rule), whereas their fixed vertical axes are automatically aligned. Since Listing's plane is essentially head-fixed (Crawford & Vilis, 1991), it remains in register with the Fick coordinate axes by rotating with the head. Since the body rotates about a purely vertical axis for the largest of these orienting movements (Radau *et al.*, 1994) the position (3-D orientation) ranges of each system is thus automatically aligned with the visual work-space (Hore *et al.*, 1992b; Miller *et al.*, 1992), and probably the gravity vector (Misslisch *et al.*, 1994). It remains to be proven if this alignment is simply a matter of strategy, or if it really signifies an attempt by the brain to represent visual signals and visuomotor commands for the eyes, head, and arms in a common coordinate system (Straumann *et al.*, 1991).

5.3 Neural implementation

Our ultimate challenge is to explain the mechanisms and algorithm used by the brain to generate these behaviours. We will examine two approaches to this problem: First, invasive physiological investigations, and second, investigations that attempt to infer the possible set of neural solutions from the geometric and behavioural constraints described. As mentioned above, the focus will be on saccade generation, since this has been the most intensely studied aspect of 3-D gaze control, and since it incorporates basic computational problems common to all visuomotor behaviours.

5.3.1 *Physiological implementation of saccade-velocity axes*

During saccades ocular motoneuron activity is driven by reticular formation burst neurons whose activity correlates with one-dimensional eye velocity in their "on direction". Thus, each burst neuron appears to encode the speed of eye rotation about a constant head-fixed axis, although this assumption has not been rigorously confirmed. Burst neurons that drive horizontal saccades are located in the pons, in the region of the paramedian pontine reticular formation (PPRF) (Cohen & Bender, 1968; Luschei & Fuchs, 1972). Primate experiments have shown that the corresponding vertical components appear to originate in the midbrain. Burst neurons for generation of upward saccades and burst neurons for downward saccades have been recorded in both sides of the rostral interstitial nucleus of the medial longitudinal fasciculus (riMLF) (Büttner *et al.*, 1977; King & Fuchs, 1979). The difference between the two sides is in their control of ocular torsion (Henn *et al.*, 1989; Vilis *et al.*, 1989; Crawford & Vilis, 1992). Stimulation of the right riMLF produces a conjugate CW rotation of both eyes, and left riMLF stimulation produces CCW rotation (Crawford & Vilis, 1992). Similarly, pharmacological inactivation of cell bodies in the right riMLF abolishes CW saccade components, whereas left riMLF inactivation abolished CCW components (Henn *et al.*, 1989; Crawford & Vilis, 1992).

Thus, the premotor saccade-generator has a three-dimensional organization similar to that of the eye muscles (Fig. 5.4A-C). The right mesencephalon contains intermingled up and down saccade generating neurons, and these same neurons also generate CW components. In contrast the left mesencephalon contains up and down neurons with CCW components. At one extreme, pure vertical saccades are generated by co-activating the up or down populations on both sides. This results in a cancellation of the CW and CCW components. At the other extreme, pure torsional rapid eye movements (which may be observed when the head rotates in the torsional, or roll direction; Crawford & Vilis 1991) appear to be generated by co-activating the up and down populations on one side (Crawford & Vilis, 1992).

How then are the torsional axis tilts observed in Listing's law encoded? If burst neurons encode angular velocity of the eye, then the torsional components of these tilts would have to be explicitly coded at this level, i.e. by specific pattern of burst neuron activity intermediate between these two extremes mentioned above. However, several pieces of evidence suggest that burst neurons may not encode angular velocity, (Crawford, 1994). For example, although torsional burst neuron activity correlates to movements

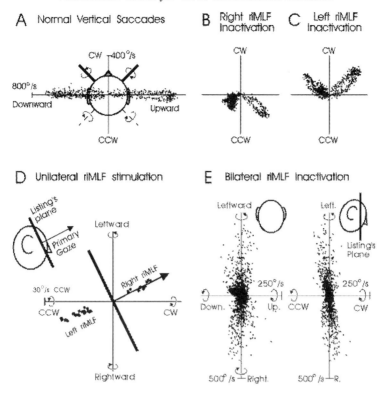

Fig. 5.4. Burst neurons utilize a head-fixed coordinate system that resembles that of the vestibular canals or eye muscles, but aligns with Listing's plane. Top Row: The canal / eye muscle-like nature of burst coordinates. **A**. Instantaneous angular velocity "loops" during normal upward and downward saccades in a trained monkey, as viewed from above the head. Purely horizontal axes (for vertical rotation) are presumably generated by combining on of the clockwise-horizontal axes controlled by the right riMLF burst neuron populations (solid axes) with one of the counterclockwise-horizontal axes controlled by the left riMLF, such that the torsion cancels out. **B, C** The intact axes controlled by the opposite side are revealed when the neurons on the other side are pharmacologically inactivated and the animal attempts to make vertical saccades (Crawford, 1994). These remaining axes are very similar to the axes of rotation sensed by the vertical semicircular canals, and those controlled by the vertical eye muscles. Lower Row: Alignment with Listing's plane. **D** During unilateral riMLF stimulation, axes of eye rotation (shown as points representing average angular velocities) align orthogonally to Listing's plane, independent of anatomic coordinates. **E** Similarly, following bilateral inactivation of the riMLF the remaining burst neurons (presumably those located in the PPRF) are essentially only able to generate a vertical axes of eye rotation aligned in Listing's plane (Crawford & Vilis, 1992).

away from or towards Listing's plane (Henn *et al.*, 1989), by and large, it does not seem to correlate well with the torsional components of angular velocity during saccades in Listing's plane (Hepp *et al.*, 1994). This evidence suggests that burst neurons instead code for rate-of-eye-position-change (the time derivative of eye position). Since torsional eye position does not change during saccades with the head fixed, this code would require zero activation of torsional burst neurons, or more correctly, symmetric activation between the left and right riMLF, similar to the early suggestion of Robinson and Zee (1981). In this case, the position-dependent torsional axis tilts would have to be implemented downstream from the burst neurons, either by interactions between burst and position inputs to the motoneurons, or by a position dependency in the eye muscles themselves (Crawford, 1994; Demer *et al.*, 1995), and net torsional burst activity would only be necessary for movements involving changes in torsional eye position.

Whatever the precise coding the burst neurons turn out to use, clearly the ratio of activity between the burst neuron populations must be tightly constrained in order to uphold Listing's law. Might this constraint have a developmental influence on the synaptic organization of burst neurons? This influence is apparent in the recent finding that, despite its resemblance to muscle anatomy, the burst neuron coordinate system appears to align best with Listing's plane (Crawford & Vilis, 1992). For example, the vertical axis for horizontal eye rotation that remains after riMLF inactivation (presumably generated by the PPRF) aligns with Listing's plane, which varied with respect to anatomical landmarks (Fig. 5.4E). Furthermore, the mainly torsional axes of eye rotation produced by unilateral riMLF stimulation were contained in the horizontal plane orthogonal to Listing's plane (Fig. 5.4D). This suggests that burst neuron coordinates are head-fixed and are aligned with / symmetric about Listing's plane (Crawford and Vilis 1992). Note that in retrospect, this is a necessary condition if symmetric co-activation of CW and CCW burst neurons is to encode movements with zero torsion relative to Listing's plane, and for isolated activation of pontine burst neurons to produce movements that obey Listing's law.

5.3.2 Holding eye position in three-dimensions

In addition to the direct velocity command from burst neurons to motoneurons, saccade generation requires a position command to hold the eye in its final orientation. The position command is thought to be derived from eye velocity commands in a parallel pathway, using a process equivalent to mathematical integration (Robinson, 1975). This theory is supported by the finding that lesions in the nucleus prepositus hypoglossi / medial vestibular nucleus disrupt holding of horizontal eye position, without abolishing horizontal saccades (Cannon & Robinson, 1987; Cheron & Godaux, 1987).

In 3-D, the non-commutative laws of rotational kinematics show do not allow simple integration to transform angular velocity into angular position. For example, integrating the torsional components of saccade angular velocity vectors during movements that obey Listing's law would yield torsional position signals that do correspond to actual position. As a result, another computational step is required to compensate for the position-dependent relationship between eye velocity and changes in eye position. For signals from the semicircular canals (which clearly encode angular velocity) this step must be accomplished by in effect multiplying an eye velocity command from burst neurons by a feedback copy of the three-dimensional eye position command, before the integrating (Tweed & Vilis, 1987). Without such a non-linearity in the oculomotor system, a mismatch would occur between eye velocity and position, resulting in torsional drift. The lack of any such torsional drift at the end of vestibular-driven slow phases (Crawford & Vilis, 1991) clearly shows that the brain utilizes the correct principles of rotational kinematics and a 3-D neural integrator, contrary to the suggestions of some (Schnabolk & Raphan, 1994). The case is less clear in the case of the saccade generator, since if burst neurons encode rate-of-position-change, this can be input directly to a neural integrator (Crawford, 1994). In any case, the neural integrator must include a torsional circuit as well as vertical and horizontal circuits in order to hold the torsional eye positions that have been observed experimentally (e.g. Crawford *et al.* 1991; Crawford & Vilis 1991, 1992).

Where then are the vertical and torsional integrators? The most likely neural substrate for the vertical integrator is the mesencephalic interstitial nucleus of Cajal (INC) (Fukushima & Fukushima, 1992). Recent experiments have confirmed this hypothesis, and showed that this nucleus also maintains torsional eye position (Crawford *et al.*, 1991; Crawford & Vilis, 1993). Single unit recordings and microstimulations have revealed a similar combination of vertical and torsional signals to that found in the eye muscles and riMLF (Crawford *et al.*, 1991; Fukushima *et al.*, 1990). Consistent with this, and the integrator hypothesis, unilateral stimulation of the INC produces mainly torsional eye movements that hold their final position, as if the input had been integrated (Crawford *et al.*, 1991). Moreover, pharmacological inactivation of the INC does not abolish saccades, but rather abolishes holding of post-saccadic vertical and torsional eye positions (Crawford *et al.*, 1991; Crawford & Vilis, 1993; Crawford, 1994). Therefore the INC appears to be the neural substrate for both the vertical and torsional components of the oculomotor integrator Since this integrator normally holds eye position at zero torsion in Listing's plane, it might not be surprising if, like burst neurons coordinates, integrator coordinates show an alignment with Listing's plane. Consistent with this idea, during INC inactivation the direction of torsional drift was orthogonal to Listing's plane, whereas this drift settled towards a line of horizontal positions parallel to Listing's plane (Crawford, 1994). Both data sets were independent of anatomically measured coordinates. These results suggest that the intrinsic vertical coordinate axis (controlled by the horizontal integrator in the nucleus prepositus hypoglossi) is parallel to Listing's plane, and the intrinsic coordinate axes for vertical and torsional positions (controlled by the INC) are contained in the horizontal plane that is orthogonal to Listing's plane. Thus, the premature coordinate systems for both the "move" and "hold" commands for saccades are symmetric about Listing's plane. In more general terms, this suggests that visuomotor commands are coded in population coordinate systems that are defined behaviourally (independent of sensory or muscular geometries) even down to the lowest premature levels (Crawford & Vilis, 1992; Crawford, 1994). The observation that these particular oculomotor coordinate systems are fixed relative to the head will have important consequences when we consider the higher levels of the visuomotor transformation.

5.3.3 The visuomotor transformation for 3-D saccades

The most pressing question in this field is what does Listing's law tell us about the visuomotor transformations and codes for saccades? To address this question, it is important to understand the geometries of both the inputs and outputs of this system. Despite overwhelming evidence to the contrary, some investigators are still attracted to the old idea that the eye muscles themselves constrain eye position to Listing's plane (e.g. Demer *et al.* 1995; Schnabolk & Raphan, 1994). The confusion over this issue seems to arise from the serious possibility that the eye muscles might generate all or part of the position-dependent axis tilts required by Listing's law (Crawford, 1994; Demer *et al.*, 1995). However, even if this is true, several observations demonstrate that the eye muscles cannot possibly constrain eye position to two-dimensions, let alone determine the orientation or torsional offset of Listing's plane.

First, the observation that certain non-saccadic eye movements (such as slow phases of the VOR), which act through the same muscles as saccades, are not constrained by Listing's law (Crawford & Vilis, 1991). Contrary to some statements (Demer *et al.*, 1995), these torsional deviations can be quite large (up to 15°), depending on the precise behavioural paradigm, and would accumulate indefinitely if it were not for goal-directed torsional quick phases (Crawford & Vilis, 1991; Guitton & Crawford, 1994). Moreover, even larger torsional shifts can be observed during stimulation and damage to the brainstem saccade generator (e.g. Crawford & Vilis 1992). Second, the orientation of Listing's plane varies with respect to anatomic landmarks (Tweed & Vilis, 1990a; Crawford & Vilis, 1992), even within one subject (Ferman *et al.*, 1987b). Finally, Listing's plane has been observed to shift or tilt during rotations of the head (Crawford & Vilis, 1991), static head tilts (Crawford & Vilis, 1991; Haslwanter *et al.*, 1992), and vergence movements (e.g. Mok *et al.* 1992). These results show clearly that the choice of Listing's plane as the normal range of eye positions for saccades is made neurally.

Where then are the neural circuits that make this choice? It is clear that the ocular motoneurons and their immediately premature burst neurons can generate eye rotations about any three-dimensional axis, and have been observed to do so during rotations of the head (Henn *et al.*, 1989; Crawford & Vilis, 1991). It is equally clear that the initial signal for saccades is a two-dimensional retinal signal specifying a desired shift in gaze direction (this should not be confused with three-dimensional depth information from binocular disparity, which is not relevant for determining monocular eye orientation). Thus, a 2-D to 3-D transformation must take place between these two points. This is the point where the degrees of freedom problem must be resolved, and hence, this transformation is the fundamental neural implementation of Listing's law. The precise anatomic location of this transformation has been the subject of extensive debate (e.g. Tweed & Vilis, 1990b; Crawford & Vilis, 1991; Van Opstal *et al.*, 1991; Van Gisbergen *et al.*, 1990). One scheme was inspired by the idea that neurons in superficial layers of the superior colliculus encode a sensory retinal error signal, whereas the deeper layers of the superior colliculus encode a saccadic motor error signal that appears to drive the reticular formation burst neurons during saccades (Wurtz & Albano, 1980) This lead to the suggestion that the Listing's law operator is implemented between these two layers (Tweed & Vilis, 1990b; Crawford & Vilis, 1991). In this scheme, Tweed and Vilis (1990b) proposed a neural Listing's law operator that takes in desired gaze direction and computes the unique three-dimensional eye position in Listing's plane that satisfies this condition (Tweed & Vilis, 1990b), before computing motor error.

In this initial scheme, the motor map of the deep superior colliculus was viewed as a map of different eye rotation axes that were used to drive the downstream burst neurons. The axis required by Listing's law, for a given eye position and saccade direction, was computed by dividing the desired eye position (from the Listing's law operator) by a neural representation of current eye position (Tweed & Vilis, 1990b). This scheme suggested that stimulation of a site in the deep superior colliculus would result in saccades with the same axis, independent of eye position, a result that would generally violate Listing's Law (Tweed & Vilis, 1990b). However, such stimulations did not violate Listing's law (Van Opstal *et al.*, 1991). Instead, the colliculus appeared to have a 2-D organization: stimulation produced constant changes in eye position within Listing's plane, independent of initial eye position. Based on this finding, Van Opstal *et al.* (1991) concluded that Listing's law is implemented downstream from the superior colliculus. Upon closer examination, what the experiment of Van Opstal *et al.* (1991) did clearly show, is that the torsional axis tilts are implemented downstream from the colliculus (which now seems less surprising, since as we have seen some think that this may occur as low as the muscles themselves). However, this experiment did not directly address the location of the Listing's law operator (which some have more recently called the Donders' box; Hepp 1994). In other words, we still don't know where the choice of eye positions on Listing's plane is made, and (perhaps surprisingly) this may still be above the level of the collicular motor map. The reason, we don't know is that although the best experiments available (Van Opstal *et al.*, 1991; Hepp *et al.*, 1993) suggest that the collicular map does not encode axes, they did not distinguish between retinal error (the eye displacement encoded by stimulation of one point on the retinal map) and change-in-eye-position (the authors interpreted these two be essentially indistinguishable). In fact these codes are qualitatively different in two ways, and these differences have important consequences for visuomotor coding (Crawford & Guitton, 1994).

First, whereas retinal error is fundamentally 2-D (i.e. torsional retinal error is meaningless), change in eye position, derived by subtracting initial 3-D position from final 3-D position, is fundamentally 3-D (i.e. its torsional component, even if zero, must be specified). Thus, if the brain uses both of these codes for saccades generation, the degrees of freedom problem (and therefore the Listing's law operator) would occur between these two levels. Second, since the retinal points are fixed in the eye, retinal error signals are defined in the oculocentric reference frame, whereas the change in eye position vector (like the eye position vectors it is derived from) is defined in the craniotopic (head-fixed) reference frame (This may come as a surprise to those who have assumed that all saccade-related displacements codes are "retinocentric" by definition.). Thus, the reference frame problem illustrated in Figure 5.3 arises. As a result of this problem, a trivial mapping from the retinal error to the change-in-position command will result in position-dependent errors in final saccade direction. Since some kind of 3-D craniotopic code, whatever its form, is required to drive the 3-D craniotopic coordinate systems of the brainstem burst neurons (Crawford & Vilis, 1992), this poses a new problem for the visuomotor transformation that has not previously been addressed.

5.3.4 New model of the saccade generator

To address the geometric problems outlined above and fill in the gap left with the partial demise of the Tweed-Vilis model (1990b), my colleagues and I have proposed a new model of the saccade generator (Crawford, 1994; Crawford & Guitton, 1994). Since the most recent version of this model addresses, for the first time, all of the major geometric transformations necessary for accurate and kinematically correct saccades, right from the level of retinal stimulation down to muscular contraction and eye movement, it incorporates most of the concepts that have been discussed in this chapter. The basic workings of the visuomotor parts of this model are shown schematically in Figure 5.5.

The model begins by treating the horizontal and vertical position of stimulation on the retina as the horizontal and vertical components of a vector pointing at the target (desired gaze direction, Fig. 5.5A). Since this direction is initially defined relative to the eye, it is then rotated by an internal estimate of 3-D eye position to give desired gaze direction relative to the head (Fig. 5.5B), thus accomplishing the eye-to-head reference frame transformation. This estimate of eye position is derived from a signal fed back from the downstream neural integrator that holds eye position in the model, but it could just as well be derived from proprioceptive inputs (e.g. Buisseret 1995). Desired gaze relative to the head is then input to the Listing's law operator proposed by Tweed and Vilis (1990b), which computes the unique corresponding 3-D eye position on Listing's plane (Fig. 5.5C), thus accomplishing the 2-D to 3-D transformation. Finally, the visuomotor transformation is completed by subtracting the internal estimate of current eye position from the desired 3-D eye position command, thus yielding the 3-D craniotopic change in eye position command (Fig. 5.5D) that serves as the initial "motor error" command in this model. To reflect the use of internal representations of body positions and target directions in space in this visuomotor transformation (similar to the classic 1-D model of Robinson, 1975) I have dubbed this the "3-D spatial model".

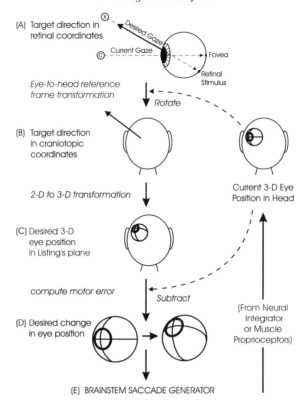

Fig. 5.5. Schematic representation of the visual-motor transformation for saccades (Crawford & Guitton, 1994). **A** Target direction is initially represented (on the retina, visual cortex, and probably the superficial superior colliculus) as target direction relative to current gaze in oculocentric coordinates. (In the illustration, the desired target is upward relative to the eye, as viewed from the side) This is then rotated by an internal representation of current 3-D eye position (which here is rotated to the subject's right) to give (**B**) target direction (i.e. up-right) relative to the head, thus effecting an eye-to-head reference frame transformation. Used as "desired gaze direction" this is then input to an operator which computes (**C**) the unique corresponding desired 3-D eye position on Listing's plane, thus performing a 2-D to 3-D transformation and solving the degrees of freedom problem. Finally, initial 3-D position is this time subtracted from the latter representation to give (**D**) desired change in eye position, which in this case will have a zero torsional component, a large vertical component, and surprisingly, a smaller horizontal component (due to the reference frame effect on displacement vectors). This may be the code used in the collicular motor error command (Van Opstal *et al.*, 1991) that drives the brainstem saccade generator (**E**). The position-dependent transformations in this scheme are probably accomplished by distributed eye position "gain-fields" in cortical and sub-cortical visuomotor structures (Andersen *et al.*, 1985).

From thereon the model resembles a 3-D version of the classic 1-D displacement- feedback model (Jürgens *et al.*, 1981). When the saccade is initiated, initial motor error drives the burst neurons, but their output (in addition to driving motoneurons and the neural integrator) is used to derive the cumulative position displacement of the eye (with the use of a second neural integrator). Since this latter is subtracted from the initial change-in-position command, the saccade is automatically driven to completion. Furthermore, since the burst neurons in this model encode rate-of-change-in-eye-position (the derivative of position with respect to time), there is no problem in inputting this signal directly into neural integrators. However, this still leaves the problem of implementing the position-dependent torsional axis tilts required by rotational kinematics to keep eye position in Listing's plane. To reflect our uncertainty about the role of the plant (Demer *et al.*, 1995), I have modelled this in two ways. With a plant model in which eye muscle actions are fixed with respect to the head, these were implemented by dividing the burst neuron output by the neural integrator output (possibly representing some pre-synaptic interaction at the motoneurons) to convert it into an angular velocity signal). This step is unnecessary with the second linear plant model (Tweed *et al.*, 1995) which simulates eye muscles that somehow produce torsional torques as a function of eye position during the movement, but produces zero torque independent of eye position at the end of movement. In either case (as long as these kinematics are handled properly) it makes little or no difference for the upstream visuomotor transformation.

These transformation allow this model to simulate many of the 3-D aspects of saccades that have been described above (e.g. Fig. 5.6). However, the importance of the position-dependent transformations in the visual-motor interface of this model is most clear when comparing it against a model which effects a trivial visuomotor transformation, mapping initial retinal error directly onto the initial change-in-eye-position command (a 3-D displacement model). The latter model is able to generate saccades in Listing's plane as long as it suffers no perturbations. However, due to its lack of a proper reference frame transformation and 2-D to 3-D transformation, the 3-D displacement model fails to correct torsional violations of Listing's law and to generate accurate saccades in the presence of initial torsion. Moreover, it fails to generate accurate saccades even within the range of Listing's plane (Fig. 5.7). The failing are mainly position-dependent errors in direction, resulting in simulated errors of final gaze direction of up to 15-25°, depending on the location of primary position, the size of the oculomotor range, and peripheral vision. In contrast, the new 3-D spatial model is able

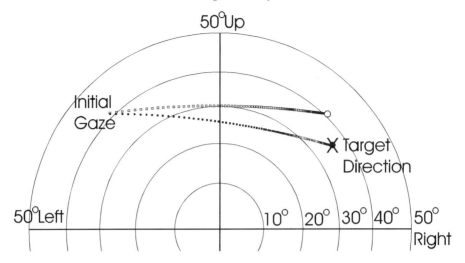

Fig. 5.6. Simulation of Listing's law with the use of the 3-D spatial model. **A** Eye position vectors following pseudo-random trajectories are shown from a "behind view". **B** Viewed from the side, these same vectors form a perfect Listing's plane. CW: Clockwise, CCW: Counterclockwise. **C** The corollary of B is that the simulated angular velocity vectors for these saccades must tilt systematically out of Listing's plane.

to simulate realistic (i.e. accurate and kinematically correct) saccades in all of these situations.

5.3.5 Implications for visuomotor coding

One of the things that has emerged in our attempts to model the saccade generator in 3-D is that true spatial representations (target direction in space relative to the eye and head, desired 3-D eye position) and comparisons with current eye position are necessary for all saccades to be simultaneously accurate and kinematically correct. Moreover, this conclusion is independent of the precise neural or mathematical implementation: it is inherent in the geometry of the oculomotor system. Since visual signals are defined relative to the eye and do not specify the third dimension for orienting, whereas eye movement is three-dimensional and defined relative to the head, a reference frame problem and degrees of freedom problem result. Moreover, since these problems grow worse as the range of motion increases, they become only more severe for control of the hand-arm system, head, and eye-in-space with the head free. The solution to these problems, in turn, necessarily includes spatial representations and transformations (as defined above).

This is disastrous for the theory that the spatial coding of visuomotor behaviours could be accomplished with the use of displacement codes alone (Jürgens *et al.*, 1981; Goldberg & Bruce, 1990; Waitzman *et al.*, 1991; Moschovakis & Highstein, 1994). The original displacement hypothesis was that retinal error signals mapped directly (presumably by a fixed point-to-point mapping from sensory to motor neural maps) onto motor error (Jürgens *et al.*, 1981), but more recent displacement models have addressed more general problems in the spatial coding of saccades. For example, the ability of subjects to saccade towards remembered targets after an intervening saccade (Hallett & Lightstone, 1976) was explained by positing that a vector representing the first saccade could be subtracted from the original retinal displacement vector in order to generate the vectorial command for the second movement. Such schemes / models work perfectly well in a 2-D vector space, where the reference frame problem and degrees-of-freedom problem do not appear. Indeed, computations of desired eye position and comparisons with current eye position in the original 1-D spatial model (Robinson, 1975) seemed somewhat redundant. However, the emergence of these problems in 3-D would cause even the simplest displacement scheme, let alone the more complicated versions, to fail in the real world (e.g. Fig. 5.7).

How then are the spatial transformations required to solve these problems implemented? This seemed problematic in the past because spatial models (Robinson, 1975) seemed to predict that the visuomotor centres of the brain would encode eye position explicitly, whereas in actuality these centres appeared to overwhelmingly code displacements explicitly. However, Zipser and Anderson (1988) showed that spatial transformations such as the eye-to-head reference frame transformation could be accomplished by more subtle eye position dependencies on these neurons, in a highly distributed fashion. Furthermore, our model (Crawford & Guitton, 1994) shows that not all displacement codes are the same: some are sensory and some are motor, and the two should be distinguishable experimentally through their fundamental geometric differences, i.e. eye position dependencies (e.g. Figs. 5.5, 5.7). Finally, it is not as clear that the retinotopic maps of the brain encode displacements as one might have thought. In our models, we have equivalently simulated retinal error as either specifying a displacement, or specifying target direction in oculocentric coordinates. This is possible because the arrangement of visual neurons, e.g. in V1 and the superficial layers of the superior colliculus, into retinotopic maps provides an unprocessed "look up table" of stimulation sites on the retina. The computational meaning of activity on each site for spatial coding is thus plenipotentiary: it depends on the downstream transformations. Thus, there is no real inconsistency

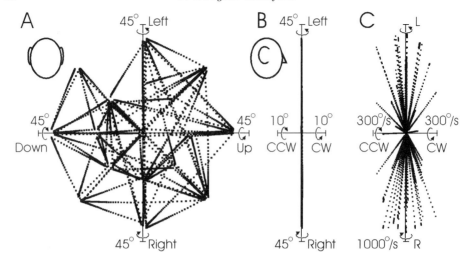

Fig. 5.7. Simulations of saccade accuracy and the reference frame problem. Concentric rings show intervals of $10°$ eccentricity from primary position, up to the maximal mechanical limit in the upper half of the oculomotor range. Gaze direction trajectories are shown for both the 3-D spatial model (■) and the 3-D displacement model (□). relative to primary position. In both cases, gaze direction was initialized at $30°$ up and $30°$ left. From this initial eye position (in Listing's plane), the target direction (X) that would stimulate $60°$ rightward retinal error was computed. Because of the oculomotor reference frame problem (Fig. 5.3), this target is obliquely displaced in the head-fixed coordinate system used in this figure. In response to an input of $60°$ rightward retinal error, the spatial model generates a saccade that lands on target (•). In contrast the displacement model misses the target (○). In the conservative case illustrated case, the error in final gaze direction is about $10°$.

between the currently known visuomotor physiology of the brain and the 3-D spatial model. To say more with certainty requires further invasive investigation.

The current experimental data do, however, leave several possibilities open for the actual neural implementation of these transformations. To illustrate these, I will discuss two possibilities that have particular pertinence to the main body of oculomotor research and spatial coding in general. The first general possibility is that coding of visual space is done in parallel for each motor system. This possibility would fit with the idea that true retinal error is encoded right down to the level of output from the deep superior colliculus. The reference frame transformations and 2-D to 3-D transformations for the eye (and head) would then have to be performed somehow in the brainstem, in between the few scant synapses upstream from the short-lead burst neurons discussed above. This scheme has all the inherent robustness inherent in parallel processing, and seems to be consistent with the idea that the superior colliculus controls, not just eye movement, but gaze in space (Munoz *et al.*, 1991). However, by the same token this scheme is highly redundant: not only in its multiple parallel spatial computations for each motor system, but also because physiological evidence indicates that the spatial transformations necessary to implement the reference frame transformation are already performed upstream from the motor map of the superior colliculus (Sparks & Mays, 1983; Schlag *et al.*, 1989). Furthermore, it fails to account for the complexity of visuomotor connections between the visual and motor maps related to saccade generation.

The second general possibility is that the cortex forms a global construct of space that is shared by all motor systems. This could include the eye-to-head reference frame transformation, which would be the first reference frame transformation stage in the visuomotor processing for all visuomotor behaviours (Andersen *et al.*, 1985; Flanders *et al.*, 1992) . This possibility is consistent with the idea that the deep motor map of the colliculus encodes a true craniotopic measure of motor error such as change-in-eye-position. Since change in eye position, is a 3-D variable, then this would suggest that must be a parallel structure (Van Opstal *et al.*, 1991; Hepp *et al.*, 1993) to generate torsional changes in eye position. Thus, the selection of signals to maintain, correct, or anticipate torsion would have already been made by this point, meaning that the 2-D to 3-D Listing's law operator was upstream from these codes. This second possibility is also intriguing because it would require a position-dependent re-mapping between the superficial superior colliculus (which along with other strictly sensory areas would still presumably encode a raw retinal signal) and the deep motor map of the colliculus, e.g. to compensate for the reference frame difference illustrated in Fig. 5.3.

If this option were correct, these position-dependent transformations would account for the complexity of the mainly indirect connections between the superficial and deep colliculus via cortical visuomotor structures (Wurtz & Albano 1980, 1980; Sparks 1988; Moschovakis & Highstein 1994). It is of interest that one of these intermediate structures, the posterior parietal cortex, has already been implicated in an eye-to-head reference frame transformation (Andersen *et al.*, 1985), because it possesses the eye-position-dependent activity necessary for such a transformation (Zipser & Andersen, 1988). This scheme is also consistent with studies of interactions between natural and stimulus-evoked saccades (Schlag *et al.*, 1989; Sparks & Mays, 1983), which suggested a comparison of visual information with eye position in the structures intermediate between the superficial and deep layers of the colliculus, but the current scheme would posit that these comparisons are necessary for all saccades. The one drawback of this hypothesis, is that if the superior colliculus does encode a kinematic variable like change-in-eye-position, and if it does control both the eye and head during gaze shifts (Munoz *et al.*, 1991), then it would follow that the superior colliculus really encodes change-in-eye-position relative to the body or space, an intuitively awkward notion.

5.4 General implications for coding of visual space

To end this chapter, I would like to take a moment to relate the computational problems we encountered in 3-D orienting movements to more general aspects of navigating through 3-D space. If we could locate and unravel the "Listing's law operator" that chooses the range of 3-D eye positions, hopefully it will shed some light on more general choices of range and trajectory in more complex movements. I suspect that this operator does not have a precise anatomical definition, but rather is part of a distributed process involving both visual and vestibular drives. However, it may transpire that the implications of Listing's law, rather than its mechanism, will have more important consequences for understanding spatial coding: in particular, the reference frame problem imposed by Listing's law and the consequent requirement for comparisons between internal spatial codes of target direction or desired eye position, and internal representations of current eye position.

As detailed above, these factors contradict any model that posits a visuomotor transformation using only displacement codes. Taken to its extreme, a displacement-only model of spatial coding would imply that our intuitive notions of an map of spatial locations (e.g. in a city) is an illusion, built up from visuomotor displacement signals (e.g. turn left at the lights, go three blocks). However, the failure of such displacement schemes in 3-D (at the cost of either accuracy or violating kinematic rules such as Listing's law), show clearly that the brain cannot do this in the real world, without producing navigational errors at a very basic level (that of individual movements). Nevertheless, it seems unlikely that the head-fixed brain would possess a complete spatial map that is fixed with respect to the earth (another reference-frame problem), and moreover we do sometimes navigate with the use of displacement instructions like those in example above. How can we explain these apparent paradoxes?

The solution to this problem lies in the basic concepts of position vs. displacement. In three-dimensions, both are 3-D vectors, but the location of the "tail" of the displacement vector is unspecified. In other words, the displacement could start anywhere. In contrast, the tail of a position vector always starts at the origin of whatever coordinate system is used to define position. Thus, positions are displacements relative to a reference position. Thus, the brain can use displacement commands to define position, as long as it keeps track of the overall relation of these displacements to some reference point. In the case of the oculomotor system, the most natural candidate for the physiological reference position of would appear to be the primary gaze direction orthogonal to Listing's plane. If, so then this head-fixed direction would take on a much larger perceptual significance that its apparently esoteric role in defining Listing's law.

The choice of reference positions become much more arbitrary when we navigating through space on a spatially mobile platform (i.e. when we walk or drive a car). Although it seemed intuitively clear earlier in the chapter that the brain might choose certain reference positions for the various body segments at a point central in their range, how would it choose reference positions in external space? Fortunately, the same basic arguments hold. The brain must choose external references, defined with the body specifically oriented within a recognizable pattern of spatially-distributed objects (e.g. a room). This is exactly the type of code seen experimentally in the so-called "place cells" of the hippocampus (O'Keefe & Dostrovsky, 1971). At a simpler level, even the some cortical visuomotor codes for saccades appear to encode displacements that are "object centred" e.g. (Olson & Gettner, 1995).

Given such external references, we are then faced with the problem of tracking them when the eyes, head, or entire body moves. Apparently we are successful at this, and there is physiological evidence that posterior parietal cortex participates at least in the shifting of visual receptive fields with eye movement (Duhamel *et al.*, 1992). Navigation then becomes a task of keeping track of subsequent displacements (using whatever visual, proprioceptive, vestibular, or internal efference information is available) relative to that initial reference position (note that following instructions like turn left, go three blocks, is fine until one looses track of the starting point - then you are lost!). Moreover, we can mentally track multiple external reference positions as long as we maintain memory of their displacements relative to each other (usually in descending hierarchies familiarity e.g. from home down to less familiar sites), and furthermore feel that we posses a complete external map by keeping track of body displacement relative to at least one of these references. Clearly, this view incorporates aspects of both the spatial and multiple-displacement models of saccade generation.

What then of the problem representing earth-fixed maps in a head-fixed brain? This is solved by a simple shift in perspective. Contrary to our intuitions, we do not really measure our movements relative to the earth, but rather that of the earth relative to us.. For example, the functional polarity of vestibular hair cells is fixed with respect to the head, so that the neural signals that result from their bending due signals movement of the inertial or gravitational reference frame relative to the head, rather than the reverse. Similarly, parietal cortex appears to represent space from an egocentric perspective (e.g. Bisiach & Luzzatti, 1978). Thus, although we may utilize certain external references to move through space, the true physiological reference frames are fixed in the body (e.g. eyes, head, or thorax, depending on the neural system): we are measuring the former relative to the latter. Therefore, in neural terms, we are always at the centre of our universe.

Finally, if this above is true, why is it that we do not perceive the inertial/visual world to move in the opposite direction to our own self-initiated motion, and perceive our position to be stable? Note that in a relativistic system like this, it is easy to switch between the egocentric and objective interpretations of space. We probably develop internal models for the way small objects act relative to the inertial reference frame very early in life. Upon becoming conscious of ourselves as such objects, we apparently incorporate ourselves into this representation, thus overcoming the inherent egocentricity of our physiology.

6

Modelling binocular neurons in the primary visual cortex

David J. Fleet

Department of Computing and Information Science,
and Department of Psychology
Queen's University

David J. Heeger

Department of Psychology, Stanford University

Herman Wagner

Department of Zoology, Aachen University

6.1 Introduction

Neurons sensitive to binocular disparity have been found in the visual cortex of many mammals and in the visual wulst of the owl, and are thought to play a significant role in stereopsis (Barlow *et al.*, 1967; Nikara *et al.*, 1968; Hubel & Wiesel, 1970; Clarke *et al.*, 1976; Pettigrew & Konishi, 1976; Poggio & Fischer, 1977; Fischer & Kruger, 1979; Ferster, 1981; Poggio & Talbot, 1981; Ohzawa & Freeman, 1986b; Ohzawa & Freeman, 1986a; LeVay & Voigt, 1988; Ohzawa *et al.*, 1990; DeAngelis *et al.*, 1991; Wagner & Frost, 1993). A number of physiologists have suggested that disparity might be encoded by a shift of receptive-field position (Hubel & Wiesel, 1962; Pettigrew *et al.*, 1968; Pettigrew, 1972; Maske *et al.*, 1984; Poggio *et al.*, 1985; Wagner & Frost, 1993). According to this *position-shift model*, disparity selective cells combine the outputs of similarly shaped, monocular receptive fields from different retinal positions in the left and right eyes. More recently, Ohzawa *et al.* (1990) and DeAngelis *et al.* (1991, 1995) have suggested that disparity sensitivity might instead be a result of interocular phase shifts. In this *phase-shift model*, the centres of the left- and right-eye receptive fields coincide, but the arrangement of receptive field subregions is different.

This chapter presents a formal description and analysis of a binocular energy model of disparity selectivity. According to this model, disparity selectivity results from a combination of position-shifts and/or phase-shifts. Our theoretical analysis suggests how one might perform an experiment

103

to estimate the relative contributions of phase and position shifts to the disparity selectivity of binocular neurons, based on their responses to drifting sinusoidal grating stimuli of different spatial frequencies and disparities.

We also show that for drifting grating stimuli, the binocular energy response (with phase and/or position shifts) is a sinusoidal function of disparity, consistent with the physiology of neurons in primary visual cortex (area 17) of the cat (Freeman & Ohzawa, 1990). However, Freeman and Ohzawa (1990) also found that the depth of modulation in the sinusoidal disparity tuning curves was remarkably invariant to interocular contrast differences. This is inconsistent with the binocular energy model.

As a consequence we propose a modified binocular energy model that incorporates two stages of divisive normalization. The first normalization stage is monocular, preceding the combination of signals from the two eyes. The second normalization stage is binocular. Our simulation results demonstrate that the normalized binocular energy model provides the required stability of the depth of response modulation. Simulations also demonstrate that the model's monocular and binocular contrast response curves are consistent with those of neurons in primary visual cortex.

6.2 Binocular interaction and disparity selectivity

There are two major classes of neurons in primary visual cortex (V1 of the monkey or A17 of the cat), namely, simple cells and complex cells (Hubel & Wiesel, 1962). Both types are selective for stimulus position and orientation. They respond vigorously to stimuli of a preferred orientation, but less well or not at all to stimuli of other orientations. Many neurons are also disparity selective.

Disparity-sensitive cells are often divided into four types: tuned-excitatory, tuned-inhibitory, near and far (Poggio & Fischer, 1977). Disparity selectivity in these different types might arise from different mechanisms (Poggio & Fischer, 1977; Ferster, 1981) (but see (Nomura *et al.*, 1990) for the opposite point of view). Tuned-inhibitory, near and far cells usually receive a strong excitatory input from one eye and an inhibitory input from the other eye (i.e., the monocular inputs are unbalanced), and most of them do not show binocular facilitation. Tuned-excitatory cells show a sharp response peak due to binocular facilitation, the responses at disparities flanking the peak are often inhibited, and they have balanced monocular inputs. This chapter is primarily concerned with tuned-excitatory complex cells, although all of the analysis and conclusions could be applied to tuned-excitatory simple cells as well.

6.2.1 *Linear neurons and energy neurons*

There is a long tradition of modelling simple cells as *linear neurons* (Hubel & Wiesel, 1962; Campbell *et al.*, 1968; Campbell *et al.*, 1969; Movshon *et al.*, 1978; Ohzawa & Freeman, 1986b; Hamilton *et al.*, 1989). This model is attractive because a linear neuron can be characterized with a relatively small number of measurements.

Figure 6.1(A) shows a schematic diagram of a monocular linear neuron. A linear neuron's response is a weighted sum of stimulus intensities within a small region of the entire visual field, called the neuron's *receptive field*. In the illustration, the three ellipses depict subregions of the receptive field, one with positive weights (the unshaded ellipse), and two with negative weights (the shaded ellipses). The neuron is excited when a bright light is flashed in the positive subregion, and inhibited when a bright light is flashed in a negative subregion. Bright lights flashed simultaneously in both positive and negative subregions tend to cancel. The positive and negative weights are balanced so the neuron does not respond to blank stimuli. Rather, its response is proportional to stimulus contrast, for patterned stimuli that vary in intensity over space and time.

Figure 6.1(B) depicts a binocular linear neuron. This neuron's response depends on a weighted sum of the stimulus intensities presented to both eyes. The left- and right-eye receptive fields are identical for the neuron depicted in the figure, but this need not be the case in general. Also, the left- and right-eye receptive fields of this particular linear neuron are in exact binocular correspondence as indicated by the small reference points below the weighting functions.

One problem with the linear model of simple cells is that linear neurons can have negative responses because they sum input intensities using both positive and negative weights. However, extracellular responses (firing rates) of real neurons are, by definition, positive. Neurons with a high maintained firing rate could encode positive and negative values by responding either more or less than the maintained rate. But simple cells have very little maintained discharge. Instead, positive and negative values may be encoded by two neurons, one responsible for the positive part and one for the negative part. The two neurons are complements of one another; an excitatory subregion of one neuron's receptive field is aligned with an inhibitory subregion of the other neuron's receptive field. The response of each neuron is halfwave-rectified so that only one of the two neurons has a non-zero response at any given time. Simple cells are often characterized as halfwave-rectified linear neurons (e.g., Movshon *et al.*, 1978; Heeger, 1992a).

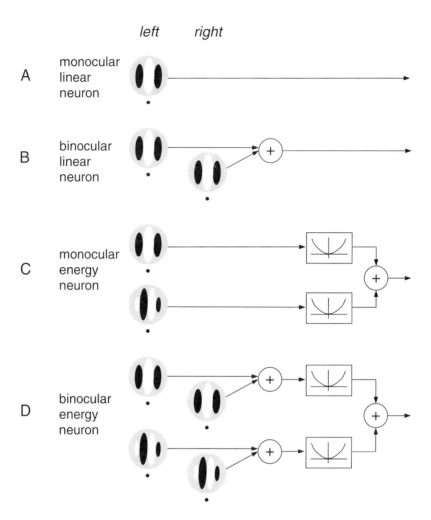

Fig. 6.1. Receptive fields of model neurons. (A) A monocular, orientation selective, linear neuron. Its response depends on a weighted sum of the stimulus intensities within its receptive field. Shaded ellipses depict inhibitory subregions of the weighting function, and the unshaded ellipse depicts an excitatory subregion. (B) A binocular linear neuron's response depends on a weighted sum of the stimulus intensities presented to both eyes. The reference points (black dots) below the weighting functions indicate that the two weighting functions are in exact binocular correspondence. (C) A monocular energy neuron sums the squared responses of two monocular, linear neurons. The weighting functions of the two linear neurons are identical except for a 90° phase shift. (D) A binocular energy neuron sums the squared responses of two binocular linear neurons. All four linear weighting functions are centred in exact (monocular and binocular) retinal correspondence.

Complex cells do not have discrete ON and OFF receptive field subregions, and have been modelled as *energy neurons* (Adelson & Bergen, 1985; Emerson *et al.*, 1992; Heeger, 1992a; Pollen & Ronner, 1983). An energy neuron sums the squared responses of a quadrature pair of linear neurons that are 90° out of phase, but with otherwise identical tuning properties (Fig. 6.1C). Equivalently, an energy neuron could sum the squared responses of four halfwave-rectified, linear neurons.

The monocular energy neuron depicted in Fig. 6.1C has one linear subunit that is even-symmetric (even phase) and another that is odd-symmetric (odd phase), but this is not necessary. The critical property is that the two subunits must be in quadrature phase (90° phase shift). Although simple cell weighting functions are not necessarily even- or odd-symmetric (Field & Tolhurst, 1986; Heggelund, 1986; Jones & Palmer, 1987), the receptive fields of adjacent simple cells tend to exhibit 90° or 180° phase relationships (Foster *et al.*, 1983; Liu *et al.*, 1992; Palmer & Davis, 1981; Pollen & Ronner, 1981). A local pool of simple cells thus provides the right combination of signals for an ideal energy neuron. Approximately the same behaviour may be obtained by summing the squared responses of many linear neurons (or halfwave-rectified, linear neurons), regardless of their phase, but with receptive fields distributed over a local spatial region.

A binocular energy neuron (Ohzawa *et al.*, 1990) is depicted in Fig. 6.1D. This neuron sums the squared responses of a quadrature pair of binocular linear neurons. This chapter is primarily concerned with the behaviour of binocular energy neurons.

6.2.2 *Disparity selectivity: position shifts and phase shifts*

Figure 6.2 depicts two ways that non-zero disparity preferences have been introduced in models of disparity selectivity. The neuron depicted in Fig. 6.2A is tuned for zero disparity because the locations of the monocular receptive fields are in exact binocular correspondence (indicated relative to the reference points) and the two pairs of weighting functions are identical. A non-zero disparity preference is introduced either by shifting the receptive field positions (Fig. 6.2B) or the receptive field phases (Fig. 6.2C). Both of the neurons in Fig. 6.2B, C are constructed to prefer uncrossed disparities; to evoke a maximal response, a visual feature (line, edge, grating) should be presented to the right eye in a position that is slightly shifted to the right.

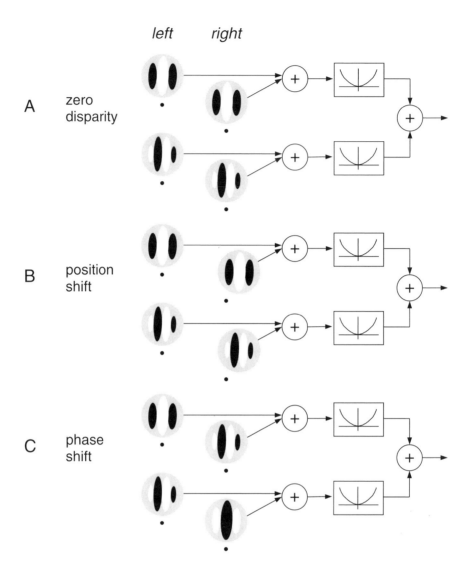

Fig. 6.2. Disparity preferences of binocular energy neurons. (A) Zero disparity preference. (B) Non-zero disparity preference is introduced by shifting the positions of both right-eye receptive fields by the same amount (relative to the reference points). (C) Non-zero disparity preference is introduced by shifting the phases of both right-eye weighting functions, in this case by 90°.

Terms	Definitions
c_l, c_r	left- and right-eye contrasts of a sinusoidal grating stimulus
$\vec{\omega} = (\omega_x, \omega_y, \omega_t)$	spatiotemporal frequency of a sinusoidal grating stimulus
L_0, L_{90}	responses of quadrature, monocular (left-eye) linear neurons
R_0, R_{90}	responses of monocular (right-eye) linear neurons
$A \equiv A(\vec{\omega})$	amplitude of linear neuron's transfer function
$\rho_l = c_l A$	response amplitude of a monocular (left-eye) linear neuron
θ	response phase of a linear neuron
B_0, B_{90}	responses of binocular linear neurons
s	receptive field position-shift
ψ	receptive field phase-shift
d	stimulus disparity
$E(d)$	binocular energy response at retinal position x
$E(d; s)$	response of binocular energy neuron with RF position-shift s
$E(d; \psi)$	response of binocular energy neuron with RF phase-shift $\Delta\psi$
$E(d; s, \psi)$	response of binocular hybrid energy neuron with position-shift s and phase-shift ψ

Table 6.1. *Symbol Table.*

6.3 Formalizing the model

In order to examine the behaviour of the model in detail, we derive formulas for the responses of these model neurons. A table of symbols (table 6.1) is provided to help the reader keep track of mathematical notation. In this chapter, we concentrate on the special case of drifting sinusoidal grating stimuli. The general case is discussed in detail in (Fleet *et al.*, 1996). We begin with linear neurons and with binocular energy neurons tuned for zero disparity. Then we introduce position-shifts and phase-shifts.

6.3.1 Monocular linear neurons

A visual neuron is linear (obeying the superposition property) if and only if its response is a weighted sum of the stimulus intensities. Mathematically, the response of a monocular linear neuron is the inner product in space and the convolution in time of a stimulus with the neuron's spatiotemporal weighting function. For a left-eye neuron with a weighting function $f_l(x, y, t)$, with stimulus $I_l(x, y, t)$, the response is given by

$$L(t) = \int \int \int_{-\infty}^{\infty} f_l(x, y, \tau)\, I_l(x, y, t - \tau) \, \mathrm{d}x \, \mathrm{d}y \, \mathrm{d}\tau . \qquad (6.1)$$

This triple integral is simply a weighted sum of the stimulus intensities over a small spatial neighbourhood and recently past time. The output response waveform, $L(t)$, is the model equivalent of a post-stimulus time histogram (PSTH), a measure of a cell's average response per unit time.

A linear neuron can be characterized by its transfer function (i.e., the Fourier transform of its weighting function). The transfer function has two components, amplitude $A(\vec{\omega})$ and phase $\theta(\vec{\omega})$, for each stimulus frequency. Here, $\vec{\omega} = (\omega_x, \omega_y, \omega_t)$ denotes the spatiotemporal frequency variables, with spatial frequency in cycles/degree and temporal frequency in Hz.

Consider a drifting sinusoidal grating stimulus,

$$I_l(x,\, y,\, t) \;=\; c_l \sin(2\pi\omega_x x \,+\, 2\pi\omega_y y \,+\, 2\pi\omega_t t)\,, \tag{6.2}$$

where c_l is the contrast of the grating. A linear neuron's response to a sinusoidal grating modulates sinusoidally over time with the same temporal frequency as the stimulus. This can be written as

$$L(t) = \rho_l(\vec{\omega})\, \sin[2\pi\omega_t t + \theta(\vec{\omega})], \tag{6.3}$$

where $\rho_l(\vec{\omega})$ is the response amplitude (peak height), and $\theta(\vec{\omega})$ is the response phase (relative peak latency).

Response amplitude depends on the amplitude component of the transfer function, $\rho_l(\vec{\omega}) = c_l A(\vec{\omega})$. Response phase depends on the phase component of the transfer function, $\theta(\vec{\omega})$, and on the receptive field position relative to the starting position of the drifting grating. A pair of monocular linear neurons with identical weighting functions, but at different receptive field positions, will respond with different phases. For example, let θ be the response phase of a neuron for a sine-grating stimulus with spatial frequency $\omega = \sqrt{\omega_x^2 + \omega_y^2}$. The response phase of a similar neuron that is a distance of s away (in the direction orthogonal to the stimulus orientation), would then be $\theta - 2\pi\omega s$. This phase behaviour is important below where position-shifts are used to introduce non-zero disparity tuning in binocular neurons.

To simplify notation we use ρ, A and θ in the equations below, dropping the explicit dependence on $\vec{\omega}$. It is important to remember that response amplitude and phase depend on the stimulus spatiotemporal frequency.

6.3.2 Monocular energy neurons

The monocular energy model depicted in Figure 6.1C consists of quadrature pairs of monocular linear neurons. These pairs of linear neurons have identical response amplitudes, but their response phases differ by 90 degrees. For example, the responses of a quadrature pair of monocular (left-eye) linear neurons can be expressed as:

$$L_0 = \rho_l \sin(2\pi\omega_t t + \theta)$$
$$L_{90} = \rho_l \cos(2\pi\omega_t t + \theta).$$

The response amplitude, $\rho_l = c_l A$, is the same for both neurons, but the response phases differ by 90 degrees. Note that we have ignored the dependence of the response on time for notational simplicity.

6.3.3 Binocular linear neurons

A binocular linear neuron computes a weighted sum of the stimulus intensities presented to both eyes. It has two weighting functions, one for each eye, as depicted in Figure 6.1B. For now, we will assume that the two monocular weighting functions are identical and in exact binocular correspondence. We can express the responses of a pair of binocular linear neurons as follows:

$$B_0 = L_0 + R_0$$
$$B_{90} = L_{90} + R_{90}$$

where L_0, R_0, L_{90}, and R_{90} are responses of the monocular linear subunits.

6.3.4 Binocular energy neurons

A binocular energy neuron (Figure 6.1D) sums the squared responses of a quadrature pair of binocular linear neurons:

$$\begin{aligned} E &= B_0^2 + B_{90}^2 \\ &= (L_0 + R_0)^2 + (L_{90} + R_{90})^2 \\ &= L_0^2 + L_{90}^2 + R_0^2 + R_{90}^2 + 2R_0 L_0 + 2R_{90} L_{90} \ . \end{aligned} \tag{6.4}$$

For now, let us assume that the drifting sinusoidal grating has a disparity of zero, so that it drifts over the same retinal positions in both eyes simultaneously. Let us further assume that the left and right monocular weighting functions are identical and in exact binocular correspondence (as depicted in Figures 6.1D and 6.2A). Then the left and right monocular responses are equal to one another, and equation (6.4) reduces to

$$E = \rho_l^2 + \rho_r^2 + 2\rho_l \rho_r \ , \tag{6.5}$$

where $\rho_l^2 = L_0^2 + L_{90}^2 = c_l^2 A^2$ is the monocular left-eye energy, and $\rho_r^2 = R_0^2 + R_{90}^2 = c_r^2 A^2$ is the right-eye energy. The binocular energy response clearly depends on stimulus contrast because ρ_r and ρ_l depend on contrast.

The binocular energy response also depends on stimulus disparity. Imagine that we introduce a small stimulus disparity d by shifting the spatial position of the sinusoidal grating in the right eye, in a direction perpendicular to the stimulus orientation. This will change the response phases of the right-eye monocular responses, R_0 and R_{90}, by an amount equal to $2\pi\omega d$, where $\omega = \sqrt{\omega_x^2 + \omega_y^2}$ is the stimulus spatial frequency. With this additional phase-offset, the the right-eye monocular responses become

$$
\begin{aligned}
R_0 &= \rho_r \sin(2\pi\omega_t t + \theta + 2\pi\omega d) \\
R_{90} &= \rho_r \cos(2\pi\omega_t t + \theta + 2\pi\omega d) \ .
\end{aligned}
$$

One can then show that the binocular energy neuron response becomes

$$
E(d) = \rho_l^2 + \rho_r^2 + 2\rho_l\rho_r \cos(2\pi\omega d) \ . \tag{6.6}
$$

To derive this equation from equation (6.4), use the trigonometry identity,

$$
\cos(\alpha - \beta) = \cos(\alpha)\cos(\beta) + \sin(\alpha)\sin(\beta) \ ,
$$

with $\alpha = 2\pi\omega_t t + \theta + 2\pi\omega d$ and $\beta = 2\pi\omega_t t + \theta$.

The binocular energy response in equation (6.6) is a sum of three terms, namely, the two monocular energies, ρ_l^2 and ρ_r^2, and a term that is a cosinusoidal function of the interocular phase difference. The response therefore has a cosinusoidal dependence on binocular disparity. When $d = 0$, the cosine term is maximal, $\cos(0) = 1$, so the response is greatest when the disparity is zero. When $d = 1/(2\omega)$, the cosine term is minimized, $\cos(\pi) = -1$, so the response is smallest when the disparity is one-half the grating period. For disparities in between these two extremes, the binocular energy response varies as the cosine of the disparity times the grating frequency. We say that this model energy neuron has a preferred disparity of zero.

Equation (6.6) simplifies further when the drifting sinusoidal gratings presented to the two eyes have the same contrast:

$$
E(d) = 2 c^2 A^2 [1 + \cos(2\pi\omega d)]. \tag{6.7}
$$

From equations (6.6) and (6.7) one can see that the binocular energy response depends on the monocular energies and the binocular phase difference. The energy response does not depend directly on the individual monocular phases θ_l and θ_r. Also note that when the stimulus is turned off in one eye (e.g., if $c_l = 0$) then the binocular energy response reduces to the monocular energy in the other eye (e.g., ρ_r^2).

The cosinusoidal dependence on disparity is consistent with physiological data. Several studies have demonstrated that binocular simple and complex cell responses exhibit a sinusoidal dependence on stimulus disparity for drifting sinusoidal grating stimuli (Ohzawa & Freeman, 1986b; Ohzawa & Freeman, 1986a; Hammond, 1991; Wagner & Frost, 1994).

However, as discussed below in Section 6.5, the contrast dependence of real binocular neurons is not consistent with predictions of the binocular energy model. Therefore we will have to modify the binocular energy model. But first, we introduce position- and phase-shifts to construct binocular energy neurons tuned for non-zero disparities.

6.3.5 Position-shift model

A non-zero disparity preference can be introduced by shifting the receptive field position in one eye (Fig. 6.2B). As noted above in Section 6.3.1, the response phase of a monocular linear neuron depends on receptive field position. If θ is the response phase for a sine-grating stimulus with spatial frequency $\omega = \sqrt{\omega_x^2 + \omega_y^2}$, then after introducing a position shift (s) of the receptive field in the direction orthogonal to the stimulus orientation, the new response phase will be $\theta - 2\pi\omega s$. If the right-eye stimulus is also shifted by the disparity d, then the right-eye monocular responses become

$$
\begin{aligned}
R_0 &= \rho_r \sin(2\pi\omega_t t + \theta + 2\pi\omega(d - s)) \\
R_{90} &= \rho_r \cos(2\pi\omega_t t + \theta + 2\pi\omega(d - s)) \,,
\end{aligned}
$$

where s is the position shift of the right-eye monocular weighting functions. Then, following the derivation above, the binocular energy response becomes

$$
E(d; s) = \rho_l^2 + \rho_r^2 + 2\rho_l\rho_r \cos(2\pi\omega(d - s)) \,.
$$

For equal contrast in both eyes, this simplifies to

$$
E(d; s) = 2\,c^2 A^2 \left[1 + \cos(2\pi\omega(d - s))\right] \,. \tag{6.8}
$$

Peaks in the energy response occur whenever the cosine term is equal to one. This happens when the disparity satisfies $2\pi\omega(s - d) = 0$, i.e., when $s = d$. The cosine term is also one when the disparity is increased or decreased by multiples of the stimulus wavelength, that is, when

$$
d = s + \frac{n}{\omega} \,, \tag{6.9}
$$

for integer values of n. Because n can be any integer, response peaks occur periodically as a function of stimulus disparity, spaced by the stimulus wavelength.

Now consider what happens when you fix the stimulus disparity, but vary the stimulus spatial frequency. One of the energy response peaks ($n = 0$)

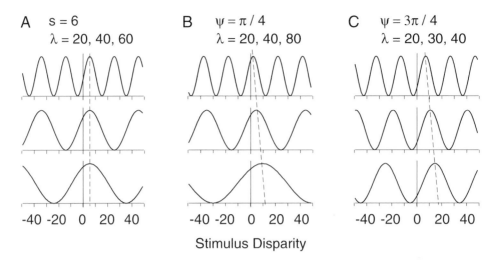

Fig. 6.3. Simulated disparity tuning curves of binocular energy neurons for drifting sine-grating stimuli. (A) A position-shift neuron with a preferred disparity of 6, and stimulus wavelengths spanning 1.5 octaves. The dashed line shows the alignment of primary response peaks. (B and C) Energy neurons with different phase-shifts, and different stimulus frequency ranges. A systematic shift in peak responses is evident for wide frequency ranges (in B) and for large phase-shifts (in C).

always occurs when the disparity equals the position-shift $d = s$, independent of the frequency of the input (Fig. 6.3A). In fact, this is a key property of the position-shift model; the location of the primary response peak does not depend on stimulus spatial frequency (Wagner & Frost, 1993; Wagner & Frost, 1994). The disparities of the other response peaks ($n \neq 0$), however, depend on stimulus frequency (see Fig. 6.3A).

6.3.6 Phase-shift model

Non-zero disparity preference can also be introduced by shifting the phase of the monocular subfields (Fig. 6.2C). Formally, let ψ denote a phase shift of the right-eye weighting functions. The right monocular responses are then

$$
\begin{aligned}
R_0 &= \rho_r \sin(\omega_t t + \theta - \psi + 2\pi\omega d) \\
R_{90} &= \rho_l \cos(\omega_t t + \theta - \psi + 2\pi\omega d) .
\end{aligned}
$$

Following the derivation used above, the binocular energy response becomes

$$
E(d; \psi) = \rho_l^2 + \rho_r^2 + 2\rho_l\rho_r \cos(2\pi\omega d - \psi) .
$$

For equal contrast in both eyes, this simplifies to

$$E(d; \psi) = 2 c^2 A^2 \left[1 + \cos(2\pi\omega d - \psi)\right]. \tag{6.10}$$

Peaks in the energy response now occur when $2\pi\omega d - \psi = n2\pi$, i.e., when

$$d = \frac{\psi}{2\pi\omega} + \frac{n}{\omega}. \tag{6.11}$$

As illustrated in Figure 6.3B, C, this means that the neuron's "disparity preference" depends in a systematic way on the stimulus frequency. Even the primary response peak ($n = 0$) depends on the stimulus spatial frequency, since $d = \psi/(2\pi\omega)$ in this case. The range of possible "disparity preferences" depends on the range of spatial frequencies to which the neuron responds (i.e., the spatial frequency bandwidth), and on the neuron's interocular phase shift. It would be inaccurate to say that a phase-shifted binocular energy neuron has a unique preferred disparity.

Position-shifts and phase-shifts (s and ψ) have different effects on disparity tuning. One way to discriminate phase-shift neurons from position-shift neurons is to measure disparity tuning curves for sine-grating stimuli with different spatial frequencies. For a position-shift neuron, the primary response peak occurs at a single preferred disparity (i.e., the position shift) for all frequencies. For a phase-shift neuron, peaks in the tuning curves will occur at different disparities for different frequencies. Data of this sort have been obtained for the owl (Wagner & Frost, 1993, 1994), and are more consistent with the position-shift model.

6.3.7 Hybrid model

As discussed below, the disparity selectivity of binocular neurons in cat and monkey primary visual cortices is probably due to a combination of position shifts *and* phase shifts. It is therefore natural to consider a hybrid model that incorporates both. Using the same analysis as above, with equal contrasts in the two eyes, one can show that the response of a hybrid binocular energy model, with a position shift s and a phase shift ψ, is given by

$$E(d; s, \psi) = 2 c^2 A^2 \left[1 + \cos(2\pi\omega(d - s) - \psi)\right]. \tag{6.12}$$

The response, $E(d; s, \psi)$, now depends cosinusoidally on both the position shift s and the phase shift ψ.

6.4 Experimental support for position-shifts and phase-shifts

The position-shift model involves binocular combinations of monocular receptive fields of similar shape at different retinal positions, while the phase-shift model combines monocular receptive fields with different shapes from the corresponding retinal locations. Only when both are tuned to a disparity of zero are they strictly equivalent. The next sections review neurophysiological evidence for position shifts and phase shifts. Then we propose an experiment for estimating both the position-shifts and phase-shifts of both simple and complex cells, based on their responses to drifting sinusoidal grating stimuli of different spatial frequencies and disparities.

6.4.1 Distribution of preferred disparities

One restriction on phase-shifted energy neurons stems from the fact that phase shifts are unique only between $-\pi$ and π. When combined with a restricted spatial frequency bandwidth, this means that for any one spatial frequency band, there is a limited range of disparities that one could hope to detect. The upper limits are reached as the phase-shift approaches $\pm\pi$ (i.e., half a wavelength) and the stimulus frequency approaches the lowest spatial frequencies to which the neurons are responsive. This limitation of the phase-shift model is particularly restrictive for neurons tuned to high spatial frequencies. Thus if a broad distribution of preferred disparities is found in a sample of neurons, relative to their preferred spatial frequencies, then one can infer that position shifts occur.

In attempting to measure the range of preferred disparities caution must be taken because eyes tend to drift and rotate under anaesthesia. To control for this, Hubel & Wiesel (1970) introduced the reference-cell method, in which a binocular cell is recorded for an extended period to find the disparity that elicits a maximal response. A second electrode is used to record from other neurons. By adjusting disparity settings to maintain the maximal response from the reference cell, one can track eye movements. Interestingly, it is not necessary to track eye drift in the owl, as their eye movements are negligible (Steinbach & Money, 1973).

In the cat, early reports gave a range of $\pm 3°$ for the distribution of preferred disparities (Barlow *et al.*, 1967). Later studies using a reference-cell method found that the range of preferred disparities of tuned-excitatory cells in area 17 is less than $1°$ for eccentricities up to $8°$ (Ferster, 1981; LeVay & Voigt, 1988). In the owl, the range of preferred disparities was found to be $\pm 2.5°$ (Pettigrew, 1979). In anaesthetized monkeys, cells with preferred disparities up to $30'$ were documented in V2 (Hubel & Wiesel, 1970).

Studies on awake, behaving monkeys seldomly found preferred disparities greater than 12′ (crossed or uncrossed) for eccentricities within 2 degrees of the fovea (Poggio & Fischer, 1977). One would expect that cells in the parafoveal region might have larger preferred disparities, but we are aware of no quantitative data regarding this issue. In the monkey, near and far cells often respond maximally at the largest disparities that have been tested (up to 1°) (Poggio & Fischer, 1977). Near and far cells of cats cover a range of at least ±5° of disparity (Ferster, 1981; LeVay & Voigt, 1988).

Unfortunately, spatial frequency tuning has usually not been measured along with disparity tuning. However, data from Ohzawa and Freeman (1986b, 1986a) suggest that the range of preferred spatial frequencies in disparity-sensitive cells is similar to the overall range of preferred frequencies in cat area 17. Assuming the same in the monkey, with foveal simple and complex cells having preferred spatial frequencies between 1 and 10 cpd (DeValois *et al.*, 1982), one can indirectly conclude that in monkeys, cats, and owls the preferred disparities cover a range that is larger than one period of the typical spatial frequency preference. This suggests that position-shifts occur, but it does not rule out the existence of additional phase-shifts.

6.4.2 Monocular receptive-field shape

To determine whether there are phase-shifts, a more elaborate method is required. One method is to directly examine the shapes of the monocular receptive fields using white noise stimuli and reverse-correlation procedures. Ohzawa *et al.* (1990) and DeAngelis *et al.* (1991, 1995) applied this method to simple cells in cat area 17. They then fitted Gabor functions to the monocular receptive fields and used the phase of the fitted Gabor functions as a measure of receptive field shape. They found that the monocular receptive field shapes of binocular cells are often different. Moreover, the differences depend on orientation; cells tuned to horizontal orientations have similar receptive field shapes, while cells tuned to near vertical orientations exhibit a wide range of phase shifts (from 0° to 180°). While these data show that phase shifts exist, the existence of additional positional-shifts cannot be excluded because eye movements were not strictly controlled.

This reverse-correlation procedure works well for simple cells as their monocular responses depend strongly on the stimulus position within the receptive field. More sophisticated procedures, analyzing higher-order kernels of the white noise responses, would be needed to determine the monocular receptive field properties underlying disparity selectivity of complex cells.

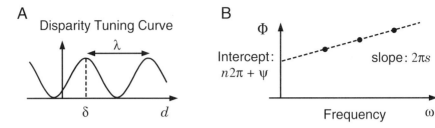

Fig. 6.4. (A) Cosinusoidal disparity tuning curve of a hybrid energy neuron. With the peak closest to the origin (zero disparity) at δ and an input spatial frequency of $\omega = 1/\lambda$, the phase of the cosinusoidal tuning curve is $\Phi = 2\pi\delta\omega$. (B) This phase Φ is a linear function of stimulus spatial frequency, the slope and intercept of which give the position-shift and the phase-shift of the monocular receptive fields.

6.4.3 Position- and phase-shifts of simple cells

Anzai *et al.* (1995b) used white noise stimuli to estimate the best fitting Gabor functions to the monocular subfields of cat simple cells . From the phases of the Gabor functions they estimate receptive field phase shifts. From the locations of the centres of the fitted Gabor functions, with respect to a reference cell, they estimate the receptive field position shift.

Their results suggest that both position- and phase-shifts contribute to the disparity selectivity of binocular simple cells. Phase-shifts appear more significant at lower spatial frequencies, while position shifts contribute more to the disparity selectivity in cells tuned to higher spatial frequencies.

6.4.4 Proposed experiment for estimating position- and phase-shifts of simple and complex cells

The method used by Anzai *et al.* (1995a) applies only to simple cells. In addition, their analysis depends on the validity of the Gabor function receptive field model. Here, we propose an experiment for estimating the phase-shift and the position-shift of all binocular (both simple and complex) neurons. Our method relies only on the cosinusoidal nature of the disparity tuning curves (see Figure 6.4).

The procedure is as follows: *1)* Measure disparity tuning curves with drifting sinusoidal gratings of various spatial frequencies ω_j. As expressed in equation (6.12) the response of a binocular energy neuron depends cosinusoidally on stimulus disparity, where the frequency of the cosinusoid is ω_j. *2)* Fit a cosinusoidal function with frequency ω_j to each tuning curve, from which a phase, denoted by $\Phi(\omega_j)$, is obtained (see Figure 6.4A). *3)* Plot these fitted phase values $\Phi(\omega_j)$ as a function of spatial frequency. From equation (6.12), these fitted phase values should depend linearly on stimulus spatial frequency, $\Phi(\omega_j) = 2\pi\omega_j s + \psi$, as depicted in Figure 6.4(B). *4)* The slope of the line gives the receptive field position shift s, and the y-intercept of the line gives the receptive field phase-shift ψ. In particular, the slope equals $2\pi s$ and the y-intercept equals $\psi + n2\pi$. Because ψ is unique only within $-\pi$ and π, one can find the phase-shift from the intercept by adding whatever multiple of 2π is required to bring the result into the range $(-\pi, \pi]$.

Similar methods have been used to explore the encoding of interaural time differences in the auditory system of cats (Yin & Kuwada, 1983). In the visual system this method can be used to measure position- and phase-shifts in simple and complex cells, without requiring that the monocular receptive fields shapes be accurately localized or described. It is necessary however to stabilize the eyes for the duration of the matrix of spatial frequency and disparity conditions. If stabilization can not be guaranteed, then one could define disparity with respect to a reference cell.

6.5 Response normalization

Many aspects of simple and complex cell responses are consistent with the linear and energy models. However, the linear/energy model falls short of a complete explanation of cell responses in primary visual cortex. One major fault with the model is the fact that cell responses saturate (level off) at high contrasts. A second fault with the linear model is revealed by testing superposition. A typical simple cell responds vigorously to its preferred orientation but not at all to the perpendicular orientation. According to the linear model, the response to the superimposed pair of stimuli (preferred plus perpendicular) should equal the response to the preferred stimulus alone. In fact, the response to the superimposed pair is about half that predicted (e.g., Bonds, 1989), a phenomenon known as cross-orientation suppression.

To explain response saturation, cross-orientation suppression, and other violations of the linear/energy models, we and others have recently proposed a new model of V1 cell responses called the *normalization* model (Robson *et al.*, 1991; Albrecht & Geisler, 1991; Heeger, 1991; Heeger, 1992b; Heeger, 1993; Carandini & Heeger, 1994; Fleet *et al.*, 1995). The normalization model is based on an underlying linear stage. The linear stage is followed by a normalization stage, where each neuron's linear response to the stimulus is divided by a quantity proportional to the pooled activity of a large number of other neurons. Thus, the activity of a large pool of neurons partially suppresses the response of each individual neuron. Normalization is a nonlinear operation: one input (a neuron's underlying linear response) is divided by another input (the pooled activity of a large number of neurons). The effect of this divisive suppression is that the response of each neuron is normalized (rescaled) with respect to stimulus contrast.

The normalization model explains a large body of otherwise unexplained physiological phenomena (Heeger, 1992b). According to the model, a cell's selectivity is attributed to summation (the linear stage) and its nonlinear behaviour is attributed to division (the normalization stage). The model explains response saturation because the divisive suppression increases with stimulus contrast. The model explains cross-orientation suppression because a given cell is suppressed by many other cells including those with perpendicular orientation tunings.

Response normalization and gain control appear to be significant in binocular neurons as well. With respect to the site of the normalization, there is evidence for response normalization both before and after the combination of signals from the two eyes.

In support of binocular normalization, Anzai *et al.* (1995a) found that binocular neurons exhibit sub-linear binocular interactions. Binocular contrast response saturates at a higher firing rate than the monocular curves, but only by a factor of about $\sqrt{2}$. In other words, the response to a binocular stimulus is less than the sum of the two responses to the component monocular stimuli. In addition, Sclar *et al.* (1985) reported that there is a significant interocular transfer of contrast adaptation.

In support of monocular normalization, the preponderance of evidence implies that cross-orientation suppression is monocular. There is little or no suppression when the preferred and perpendicular gratings are presented dichoptically (one in one eye and one in the other) (DeAngelis *et al.*, 1992; Ohzawa & Freeman, 1994). However, Bonds (1989) found no evidence for cross-orientation suppression in the LGN, suggesting that it occurs in the cortex.

A second source of evidence for monocular normalization stems from a surprising result reported by Freeman and Ohzawa (1990) and by Ohzawa and Freeman (1994). As mentioned above, simple and complex cells respond with periodic disparity-tuning curves when stimulated with drifting sinusoidal gratings. Freeman and Ohzawa measured the depth of modulation of the periodic disparity-tuning curves while varying grating contrast in one eye. As shown in Figure 6.5 they found that the depth of modulation depends surprisingly little on interocular contrast differences.

The energy model predicts a strong dependence on interocular contrast differences. As shown in Figure 6.6, when the left and right contrasts are

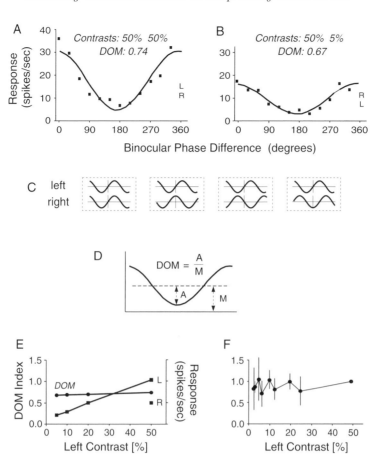

Fig. 6.5. (A) Response as a function of disparity for drifting grating stimuli with
equal (50%) contrasts in both eyes. The disparity tuning curve is nearly sinusoidal.
(B) Response as a function of disparity when the left eye contrast is reduced to 5%.
The mean response drops somewhat but the depth of modulation is virtually unaffected. (C) Left and right stimulus intensity profiles for binocular phase differences
of 0, 90, 180, and 270 degrees. (D) Depth of modulation is defined as the amplitude
of the first harmonic divided by the mean response. (E) Depth of modulation of the
binocular response as a function of left eye contrast (with right eye contrast fixed at
50%), and response as a function of contrast for monocular (left eye) stimulation.
The monocular (left eye) contrast-response curve increases monotonically with contrast, but the depth of modulation of the binocular response is virtually unaffected
by left eye contrast. (F) Mean and standard deviation of depth of modulation for
21 cells as left eye contrast was varied. (Redrawn from Freeman & Ohzawa, 1990
and Ohzawa & Freeman, 1994).

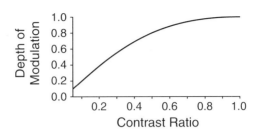

Fig. 6.6. Depth of modulation prediction of unnormalized energy model, as a function of the ratio of contrasts in the right and left stimuli.

equal, then the depth of modulation is expected to be one. But when there is a 10-fold difference in the left and right contrasts, the depth of modulation predicted by the un-normalized energy model is below 0.2. This does not agree with the data shown in Figure 6.5. The predictions in Figure 6.6 were computed from equation (6.6); a cosinusoid modulating about a mean value given by the sum of the monocular energies, and with an amplitude given by twice the product of the monocular energies.

6.5.1 Binocular normalization model

There are two simple ways that the depth of modulation can be kept nearly constant as the contrast of one eye's input is changed. Both involve monocular normalization preceding the binocular summation in the energy model. The first way, which we call the *monocular gain model*, involves independent monocular normalization of the left- and right-eye responses. This is shown schematically in Figure 6.7. The second way is an *interocular model*, where the amplitude of the right eye's response (plus an additive constant) acts as a multiplicative gain for the left signal, and vice versa. In what follows we will concentrate on the monocular gain model as this is more consistent with the lack of interocular cross-orientation suppression.

After binocular summation of the (normalized) monocular signals, we propose that there is a second stage of binocular normalization, as depicted in Figure 6.8. The binocular normalization stage is a straightforward extension of the monocular normalization model proposed by Heeger (1992a).

Monocular normalization

The monocular normalization signal is the sum of a pool of rectified linear responses plus a small constant σ_m, as shown in Figure 6.7. Since we use

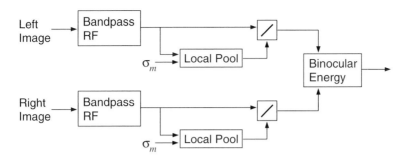

Fig. 6.7. Monocular component of response normalization. The left and right monocular neurons are normalized separately. The normalization pool includes a range of spatial positions, a range of spatial frequency preferences, and all orientation preferences.

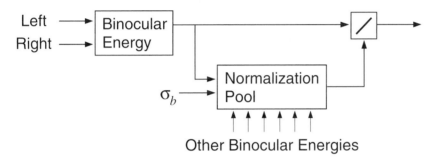

Fig. 6.8. Binocular component of response normalization. The binocular normalization pool includes a range of spatial positions, and all disparity preferences.

half-squaring for the rectifier, the monocular gain can be computed either as an average of the monocular half-squared (model simple cell) responses or as an average of the monocular energy (complex cell) responses (Heeger, 1992a). In either case the normalizing signal is proportional to the local Fourier energy of the stimulus plus a small constant.

Formally, let $\lfloor L_{90}(t) \rfloor^2$ denote the half-squared response of a monocular, left-eye, linear neuron, where $\lfloor L_{90} \rfloor^2 = L_{90} \lfloor L_{90} \rfloor$. Let $E_l(t)$ be the local monocular energy, i.e., a local average of half-squared neurons with different orientation and spatial frequency preferences, and different receptive field phases. Then, the normalized, monocular, left-eye, response is:

$$\bar{L}_{90}(t) = \frac{\lfloor L_{90}(t) \rfloor^2}{E_l(t) + \sigma_m} . \tag{6.13}$$

Since the energy in the denominator includes the half-squared response in the numerator, the normalized response will saturate at high contrasts. The

σ_m parameter is called the monocular semi-saturation constant because it determines the contrast that evokes half the maximum attainable response.

The right-eye responses are also normalized:

$$\bar{R}_{90}(t) = \frac{\lfloor R_{90}(t) \rfloor^2}{E_r(t) + \sigma_m} , \tag{6.14}$$

The inputs $L_{90}(t)$ and $R_{90}(t)$ to the energy model described by equation (6.4) are then replaced by $\bar{L}_{90}(t)$ and $\bar{R}_{90}(t)$, as depicted in Figure 6.7.

Note that there are now two stages of squaring in this model; half-squaring before the monocular normalization, and then full-squaring in the binocular energy computation. Even with this "extra" squaring step, the disparity tuning of the binocular energy responses are still (very nearly) sinusoidal.

For the simulations results reported here, we used even and odd-symmetric Gabor functions with a bandwidth of 1.5 octaves for the underlying linear weighting functions. The monocular normalization signal was pooled over a small, Gaussian weighted, spatial neighbourhood; the spatial extent of the Gaussian window was equal to that of the Gabor weighting functions.

Binocular normalization

The binocular normalization signal is the sum of a pool of binocular energy responses. The binocular pool includes the complete range of preferred binocular disparities (arising from position- and/or phase-shifts), from within a small local spatial neighbourhood. But unlike the monocular normalization, only neurons with the same spatial frequency and orientation preference are included. Formally, we write the normalized binocular energy as follows

$$\bar{E}(t) = \frac{E(t; s, \psi)}{S(t) + \sigma_b} , \tag{6.15}$$

where

$$S(t) = \sum_{x, s, \psi} E(t; s, \psi) , \tag{6.16}$$

where $E(t; s, \psi)$ is the binocular energy response computed from the position- and phase-shifted, monocularly normalized responses.

For the simulations reported here, we used position-shift energy neurons with preferred disparities that span three wavelengths. The binocular normalization signal was pooled over a Gaussian weighted spatial neighbourhood with standard deviation equal to that of the monocular spatial pooling.

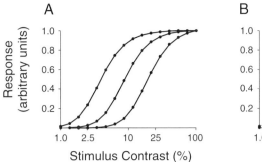 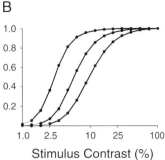

Fig. 6.9. Monocular contrast response curves for a model binocular energy neuron. (A) The three curves correspond to three different values of σ_m, with σ_b held constant. (B) The three curves correspond to three different values of σ_b, with σ_m held constant.

6.5.2 Contrast response of normalized energy neurons

The full model includes some monocular neurons and some binocular neurons. The monocular neurons in the model are identical to those in Heeger's (1992b) normalization model. The contrast response function of these monocular model neurons is given by

$$R(c) = K \frac{c^2}{c^2 + \sigma_m^2} \,, \tag{6.17}$$

that is, a hyperbolic ratio function with an exponent of 2.

The contrast response curves of the model's binocular neurons are similar: Figure 6.9(A) shows monocular contrast response curves from a model binocular energy neuron. The curves look like hyperbolic ratio functions with an exponent slightly greater than 2. Although the binocular energy neurons have gone through two squaring nonlinearities, the cumulative effect is an exponent between 2 and 3 (see *Appendix* at the end of this chapter).

The contrast-response curves also depend on the semi-saturation constants, σ_m and σ_b. In particular, changing σ_m shifts the contrast response curve laterally (Figure 6.9A). As σ_b is increased, its effect eventually diminishes and the contrast response curve depends primarily on σ_m. If σ_b is very small, however, then the contrast response curve shifts to the left and becomes somewhat steeper (Figure 6.9B). The slope on the log-contrast axis corresponds to roughly to the exponent of the hyperbolic ratio function. Therefore, Figure 6.9(B) shows that the effective exponent depends implicitly on σ_b (see *Appendix* at the end of this chapter).

Figure 6.10(A) shows the monocular and the binocular contrast response

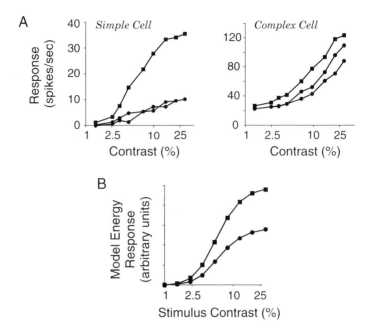

Fig. 6.10. (A) Monocular (left and right, circles) and binocular (squares) contrast response curves for a simple cell and a complex cell in A17 of the cat (redrawn from Anzai *et al.*, 1995a). (B) Monocular and binocular contrast responses curves for a normalized, binocular, energy neuron.

curves recorded extracellularly from a simple cell and a complex cell in the cat A17 (Anzai *et al.*, 1995a). The binocular contrast response curves have a lower threshold and rise somewhat more steeply than the monocular curves. Moreover they saturate at a high firing rate. Figure 6.10(B) shows that a normalized, energy neuron behaves similarly.

6.5.3 Stability of depth of modulation and mean

As discussed above, a remarkable property of binocular neurons in A17 of the cat is that the depth of modulation in their sinusoidal disparity tuning curves is invariant to interocular contrast differences. In many cells, the depth of modulation was largely unaffected even with 10-fold differences in contrast between the right-eye and left-eye (Figure 6.5). The unnormalized energy model predicts a 5-fold decrease in the depth of modulation for a 10-fold contrast difference (Figure 6.6). When normalization is included in the model, however, the depth of modulation is significantly less sensitive to interocular contrast differences, as shown in Figure 6.11. The simulations

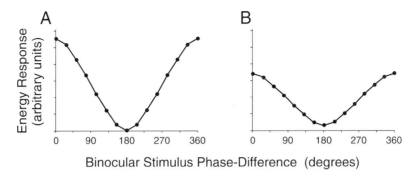

Fig. 6.11. Disparity tuning curves, using drifting sinusoidal grating stimuli, of a normalized, energy neuron. The contrast of the right-eye stimulus was fixed at 50%. (A) When left-eye contrast is 50% the depth of modulation is 1. (B) When the left-eye contrast is 5% the depth of modulation decreases only slight to 0.95. But the mean response drops by a factor of 0.75.

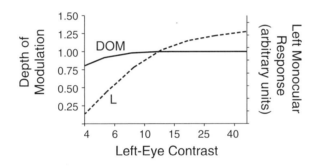

Fig. 6.12. Depth of modulation (solid curve) as a function of left-eye contrast (with right-eye contrast fixed at 50%), and monocular (left-eye) contrast-response curve (dashed curve), for a normalized, binocular energy neuron. The monocular (left eye) contrast-response curve increases monotonically with contrast, but the depth of modulation of the binocular response is largely unaffected by left-eye contrast.

of the binocular energy neuron in Figures 6.11A, B can be compared with Freeman and Ohzawa's data which is replotted here in Figures 6.5A, B. Finally, Figure 6.12 shows both the depth of modulation as a function of left eye contrast, and the contrast-response curve for monocular (left eye) stimulation. These simulation results can be compared with Freeman and Ohzawa's data, replotted here in Figure 6.5E.

As explained in the appendix, the depth of modulation is controlled mainly by the monocular semi-saturation constant σ_m. In these simulations we have therefore set σ_m in order to keep the depth of modulation above 0.95.

6.6 Discussion

To understand the neural basis for stereoscopic vision one must address several issues including the form of binocular interaction in simple and complex cells, the basis for their disparity selectivity, and the way in which they encode disparity. This article examines an energy model of binocular interaction with monocular and binocular response normalization. Disparity selectivity of the model neurons arises from a combination of position-shifts and phase-shifts between the monocular subfields of binocular receptive fields. Position- and phase-shifts have different quantitative properties, and it is argued that both likely contribute to the disparity selectivity of cells in V1. The relative contribution of position- and phase-shift can be inferred by measuring disparity-tuning curves using drifting sinusoidal grating stimuli with several different spatial frequencies.

The model also involves two stages of response normalization. There is a monocular form of normalization that occurs before binocular interaction, followed by normalization of binocular responses. These stages of normalization help to account for observed properties of the monocular and binocular contrast response curves. Normalization also accounts for the invariance of disparity tuning with response to interocular contrast differences.

Acknowledgements: This work was supported by grants from NSERC Canada and Queen's University to DJF, by a DFG grant to HW and DJF, and by an NIMH grant (MH50228) and an Alfred P. Sloan Research Fellowship to DJH.

Appendix: Mathematical notes on binocular normalization

According to equation 6.6 in Section 6.3.4, the response of an unnormalized binocular energy neuron has the form

$$E(d) = \rho_l^2 + \rho_r^2 + 2\rho_l\rho_r \cos(2\pi\omega d) .$$

The response mean is $\rho_l^2 + \rho_r^2$, and the amplitude of modulation is $2\rho_l\rho_r$. The depth of modulation, shown in Figure 6.6, is equal to the amplitude divided by the mean. In the normalized model, ρ_l^2 and ρ_r^2 are replaced by the normalized monocular energies

$$\bar{\rho}_l^2 = \bar{L}_0^2 + \bar{L}_{90}^2$$
$$\bar{\rho}_r^2 = \bar{R}_0^2 + \bar{R}_{90}^2$$

where $\bar{L}_0$ and the other normalized responses are defined by equation 6.13.

The normalized binocular response is then approximately equal to:

$$\bar{E}(d) \approx \frac{\bar{\rho}_l^2 + \bar{\rho}_r^2 + 2\bar{\rho}_l\bar{\rho}_r \cos(2\pi\omega d)}{\bar{\rho}_l^2 + \bar{\rho}_r^2 + \sigma_b}$$

Both the mean response and the modulation amplitude of the response have the same denominator. Thus the ratio of the modulation amplitude and the mean response is given by

$$\frac{2\bar{\rho}_l\bar{\rho}_r}{\bar{\rho}_l^2 + \bar{\rho}_r^2} .$$

Note that the depth of modulation does not depend on the binocular gain parameter σ_b. Rather, it depends only on the monocular energies, which depend on the input contrasts and the monocular gain parameter σ_m. Given the contrasts of the left and right stimuli, and a desired depth of modulation, one can solve for σ_m in closed form. In the simulations reported here, unless otherwise stated, we set σ_m to 0.0005.

The normalized binocular energy model has two squaring nonlinearities. The first, in equation (6.13), is monocular. The second occurs after binocular interaction, in equation (6.4). The monocular contrast response curves shown in Figure 6.9 are well approximated by equation (6.17) with an exponent between 2 and 3, rather than an exponent of 4 as one might expect.

To explain this, consider the binocular energy response when the right stimulus contrast is zero, that is

$$\bar{E} = \frac{\bar{L}_0^2 + \bar{L}_{90}^2}{\bar{L}_0^2 + \bar{L}_{90}^2 + \sigma_b} \tag{6.18}$$

One can derive this from equation 6.15 by setting $\bar{R}_0 = \bar{R}_{90} = 0$. If we substitute the normalized monocular responses defined by equation (6.13) into equation (6.18), then we obtain

$$\bar{E} \approx \frac{L_0^4 + L_{90}^4}{L_0^4 + L_{90}^4 + \sigma_b(E_l + \sigma_m)^2}$$

Here, E_l is the average broad-band monocular energy in the left stimulus. For sine-grating stimuli this is constant and equal to c_l^2.

To simplify this expression further one can approximate $L_0^4 + L_{90}^4$ by $\rho_l^4 = c_l^4 A^4$. If we ignore the attenuation of the response due to the sensitivity of the neuron's transfer function to the stimulus frequency (which introduces a multiplicative constant), then one can approximate $L_0{}^4 + L_{90}{}^4$ by c_l^4. This allows us to write the energy response as

$$\bar{E} = \frac{c_l^4}{c_l^4 + \sigma_b(c_l^2 + \sigma_m)^2}$$

$$= \frac{c_l^4}{c_l^4 + \sigma_b(c_l^4 + \sigma_m^2 + 2c_l^2\sigma_m)}$$

$$= \frac{c_l^4}{c_l^4(1 + \sigma_b) + 2c_l^2\sigma_b\sigma_m + \sigma_b\sigma_m^2} \tag{6.19}$$

The third term in the denominator will usually be extremely small, because σ_m is small in order to keep the depth of modulation stable. Thus, when c_l is relatively large, this third term can be ignored and the monocular contrast response then simplifies to

$$\bar{E} = \frac{c_l^2}{c_l^2(1 + \sigma_b) + 2\sigma_b\sigma_m} . \tag{6.20}$$

Thus for larger contrasts, the contrast response resembles a hyperbolic ratio function with an exponent of about 2. For smaller values of c_l the third term in the denominator of equation (6.19) remains significant and the exponent of the effective hyperbolic ratio function is between 2 and 4. When σ_b is small this effect is more evident.

7

Symmetries, structure and schemata in perceptual coding

Christopher W. Tyler

Smith-Kettlewell Eye Research Institute
San Francisco, CA,
USA

A comprehensive view of perceptual coding suggests that there are five basic aspects of human perceptual encoding that form the structure within which any perceptual task, such as symmetry perception, should be viewed.

(i) The *basic encoding metric* implied by the properties of the stimulus.

(ii) The *structure of the neural representation* in the coding metric: how many and what kinds of channels encode the space, and what interactions occur between them.

(iii) The *coding of image symmetries* by self-matching (neural autocorrelation) processes in the early encoding stages.

(iv) *3D object encoding* by the attentional shroud.

(v) *Dynamic manipulation* of the object representation in the coding space: allows subtle symmetries of the object structure to be evaluated by template matching of one view of the representation to a stored memory trace of another view.

7.1 The nature of neural representation

In the understanding of visual coding, a key issue is how the structure of objects in the visual world is encoded into a neural representation. How does the brain encode physical relations between parts of objects, in particular their inherent symmetries? In particular, to what degree is the neural code abstracted from an isomorphic representation of the physical properties of the object?

The Gestalt school gave the simplistic answer that representation is isomorphic with the stimulus, so that a symmetric object would have a symmetric representation in the brain. Although now generally dismissed as begging the question of the representation code, this view has been resusci-

131

tated by Shepard (1981), who argues that an isomorphic representation is necessary at some stage to allow internal transformations of the representation as a model of potential manipulations of the object in the world. Thus, the encoding of a complex object in its full complement of three-dimensional spatial relations would allow the neural representation to be manipulated to ferret out symmetry relations that are hard to detect at first glance. This manipulative view gives the isomorphic representation a significant role to play in neural coding, in contrast to the default view that assumes that the representation is given as isomorphic merely because the theoretician has failed to conceptualize deeper encoding principles.

This stress on a veridical representation principle may be derived from Young's (1962) paradoxical insight that higher organisms need to mirror the properties of the environment in the brain in order to maintain their control of the environment. This perspective emphasizes the structural symmetry between subject and object in the act of perception. The experiments of Shepard and colleagues on such transformations as mental rotation of random objects seem to provide good evidence for a 3D neural representation of the 3D world. Indeed, the classic experiments by Penfield (1959) of the sequential readout of memory sequences, and our mental ability to replay songs and speeches in temporal order, would extend the isomorphic representation to the fourth dimension of time.

However, the problem of the representation code remains. The presence of an isomorphic copy of a relevant object in the brain may have value, but it is still subject to the criticism that the object has not been encoded into some form that captures the connotations of its features to the organism. Minsky (1975) and Pylyshyn & Storm (1986), for example, argue for an entirely propositional code for object features with no coherent spatial representation. Such a code would resemble lists of attributes associated with each object, where each item would be cross-referenced to other related properties that would constitute its meaning to the organism. This view of encoding arises from the position that much of our sense of meaning must be carried by such a propositional or cognitive code because it refers to dimensional aspects of the world that are too complex to allow a representational code. It is consequently parsimonious to assume that perception is similarly coded. To encode symmetry, for example, such a code would consist of a list of attributes for the base pattern motif and a specification of the transformations required to generate the complete pattern from operations on its base motif. Without such a list of transformations, the propositional code could not be said to have encoded the symmetry of the pattern.

Shepard has argued cogently that a propositional code alone is insufficient to account for many of the properties of object recognition under spatial transformations. In particular, the speed of matching objects that are rotated copies of each other is proportional to the angle of rotation but independent of the complexity of the objects (e.g., Cooper & Shepard, 1973b, 1978). Neither result would be predicted from the inherent properties of a propositional code, but both are consistent with the idea of a neural representation of the objects in which elements that are close in physical space are represented as close in the neural connectivity space. The comparison of objects at different angles of rotation would then correspond to a matching process after the appropriate transformation has been applied to the neural representation. This transformation would correspond not to a physical rotation in the brain but to an adjustment of the local neural codes for each part of the object equivalent to such a rotation (as opposed to merely updating the propositional code for the transformation itself). One advantage of an isomorphic code is that it allows operations such as filtering, segmentation and spatial relations to be performed in a natural way by local neural operations. What is known of the neurophysiology supports the idea of the isomorphic mapping of 2D space to retinal space, depth via binocular disparity and time via velocity coding (DeYoe & van Essen, 1988).

However, the issue of how symmetry is encoded neatly underlines the limitations of an isomorphic code, which would require that the object be translated, rotated, dilated or otherwise transformed in all possible combinations for the symmetry properties to be discovered. Given the time established for mental rotation to take place (e.g., Cooper & Shepard, 1973b, 1978), the isomorphic hypothesis would require observers to take many minutes to become aware of the possible structural symmetries of even 2D images, whereas these relations seem to be immediately evident for brief presentations of less than 100 msec (Corballis & Roldan, 1974; Hogben *et al.*, 1976; Tyler *et al.*, 1995). The implication is that there must be some means of encoding the similarity relations implicit in the symmetry structure of objects in a more direct manner than is available by an isomorphic representation. Is this the point of transition to a propositional code, or is there some more geometric code for these fundamentally geometric relationships?

7.2 Properties of a perceptual encoding hierarchy

The preceding considerations lead to the view that there are five basic aspects of perceptual encoding that form the structure within which any perceptual task, such as symmetry perception, should be viewed. Beyond these processes of perceptual coding is a hierarchy of cognitive and affective en-

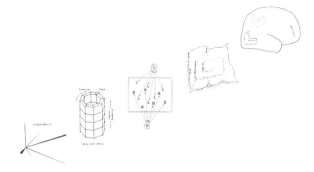

Fig. 7.1. Overview of the encoding process. From left to right: 1. Encoding metric for the stimulus space. 2. Structure of the representation in the coding metric (analyzer space; from Palmer, 1982). 3. Coding of image symmetries by a self-matching or autocorrelation process. 4. Object encoding by the attentional shroud. 5. Dynamic manipulation of the object in the coding space.

coding levels, but it is the specifically perceptual levels of coding that form the focus of the present analysis (a precursor of which is presented in Tyler, 1995). To explain the properties of perceptual coding of three-dimensional objects in a three-dimensional world, a more elaborate scheme is required than is available in most models of the process (Fig. 7.1). Beginning with an elaboration of the full dimensionality of the stimulus properties, the information is passed to sets of neural analyzers that impose a variety of coding symmetries on the encoding signals. This stage seems to be followed by a parallel self-matching process that can segregate image features according to their similarities across a variety of encoding symmetries. The final processes of perceptual coding is an active, manipulative recognition process that operates to identify object properties that are too complex to be evoked at previous stages.

7.2.1 The encoding metric for the stimulus space

The first property of perceptual encoding is the metric within which the referent space is represented in the brain. In some cases, such as retinal space, the metric is a relatively faithful match to the stimulus space. In others, such as colour, its dimensionality may be drastically reduced in comparison to the available stimulus metric. Some examples of the metrics of perceptually relevant spaces are:

- a 1D metric for time,
- a 2D metric for colour (hue),

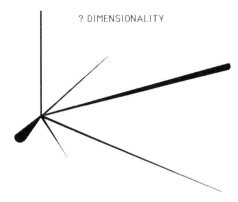

Fig. 7.2. Dimensionality of the stimulus encoding metric.

- a 3D metric for space,
- a 6D metric for rigid objects in space (three dimensions of position and three of rotation around each position).

Actually, the first three examples are each subspaces of the full sensory space for the light available for vision, which Adelson & Bergen (1991) have pointed out to be a 7D manifold that they designate the "plenoptic function". (The seven dimensions are the two dimensions of visual angle, time, wavelength, the three dimensions of object position and relative position of the two eyes from the object.) The final case of the 6D metric in Fig. 7.2 is an example of a higher-order relation between the dimensions: the configuration space of an object that exists as relationships between point across two or more dimensions will have a dimensionality corresponding to the number of combinations of those dimensions. Thus, the maximum dimensionality of the configuration space for visually specified objects is 28, the number of combinations of 7 dimensions.

Like colour vision, the dimensionality of the encoding metric in spatial vision may fall far short of the stimulus metric in dimensionality; for example, a random dot field has an N-dimensional metric, where N is the number of dots. We may encode these as mostly indiscriminable random textures, an example of failing to distinguish the metric dimensions themselves rather than just the positions along the dimension. Only idiosyncratic examples may evoke sufficient encoding response to form distinguishable dimensions. A less extreme example of encoding insufficiency is the dimensionality of perceived rotations. Intuitively, it is obvious that there are three dimensions of positional variation, but most people need to try it out to convince themselves that rotation around a point also has a dimensionality of three.

In recognition of their imperfect reflexivity, Shepard (1981) refers to the match between the encoding metric and the stimulus metric as one of complementarity, the relationship between a lock and key or a photographic negative and its print. Piaget (1969) originated a similar concept in referring to schemata, by which the organism accommodates itself to the nature of the object (in order to assimilate the object into the arrangement desired by the organism). The schema is a broader concept than Shepard's complementarity, including action components as well as the representative aspects, but it carries the full sense of the reciprocity between the mental representation and the world that is to be brought under its hegemony. The properties of a neural mechanism that instantiates the logic of Piaget's schemata in the quotidian process of every perceptual act is one of considerable interest that lies at the core of the issue of visual coding.

7.2.2 *The structure of the representation in the coding metric*

After establishment of the neural space of the coding metric, the next question is the structure of the representation in each dimension of the metric. Is the metric a continuous one, like an intensity code along the metric dimension, or are there discrete channels with local preferences? The discrete/continuous distinction has been emphasized by Foster (1982) and relates to the question of whether each dimension is intensive (coded by the intensity of a single channel) or extensive (coded by an array of similar channels differing in one respect). In this regard, a continuous code is provide by the univariate output of the single channel of an intensive dimension. For an extensive dimension, continuity implies sufficient number of overlapping channels to show no discontinuities across the dimensions on any empirical measure. The code then corresponds to identification of the most sensitive channel for any given stimulus.

Note that the logic of channel structure is opposite to the logic of the output of the code for particular images, as pointed out in a trenchant analysis by Field (1994). In a discrete channel system, it is to be expected that each channel will have some level of output signal, forming what Field calls a 'compact' or continuous code for the images. Such a code is akin to a principal components analysis that it it defines an N-dimensional component space in which to encode the images. It has the disadvantage that the component space is unconstrained with respect to the particular component projections from that space (or equivalently, unconstrained with respect to phase of the Fourier representation of the components), so there is no guarantee that the components of the code will represent the *local* receptive

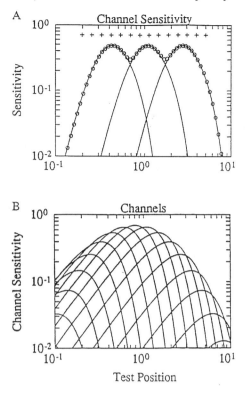

Fig. 7.3. Depiction of A. a discrete (three-channel) code and B. a continuous code (enough channels to show no discontinuities on any empirical measure).

fields with which we are familiar from neurophysiology. As an alternative, Field (1994) proposes that the neural code may be a 'sparse distributed' code, in which each image is represented by the sparse activation of elements in a continuous set of underlying channels. This matches what is know of the cortical receptive field behaviour, which is that each cell has a local tuning that is active only for a limited subset of input images. For such continuous channel codes, the main question is the form of the underlying channel and its variation over the dimension.

Note that the presence of discrete channels at one level of encoding may provide a continuous representation by a push-pull, or opponent, linkage between channels, as in the classic example of the opponent mechanisms of colour vision. This conversion highlights the properties of the encoding mechanism in determining the encoding metric. The presence of more than one channel whose outputs make essentially independent contributions to the response results in a discrete channel code; linkage between channels to determine the output generates a continuous code for each pair of linked channels (assuming a graded response for each channel alone). Another way to obtain an essentially continuous code is to have a large number of independent channels across the dimension, forming a continuous extensive coding through the channel space as opposed to the continuous intensive coding of the push-pull arrangement.

If there is a discrete channel coding, a key question to answer is how many channels lie along the coding dimension (in each local retinal region). Many techniques have been developed to address this question but few of them have been worked out in sufficient detail to have full confidence in the answers (Tyler *et al.*, 1994). Historically, channel modelling in vision began with discrete channel models, as exemplified by the threshold elevation paradigm developed in colour vision by Stiles (1939, 1959). Discrete channel analysis in spatial vision goes back to Wilson and Bergen (1979), followed by Wilson, McFarlane and Phillips (1983), Swanson and Wilson (1985) and Foley and Yang (1991), among many others. It has also been used for a variety of other stimulus domains, such as temporal frequency (Mandler & Makous, 1984; Anderson & Burr, 1985; Hess & Snowden, 1992), orientation (Regan & Beverley, 1985) and stereomotion (Beverley & Regan, 1973). See also Harris, this volume.

Most studies of the effects of adaptation or masking on visual sensitivity assume that the threshold elevation profile corresponds fairly well with the shape of the underlying channel sensitivity profile. In fact, as analyzed by Tyler, Barghout-Stein & Kontsevich (1994), there is a wide range of distorting factors that intrude to distort the measured profile. The adapted sensitivity data of Blakemore & Campbell (1969), for example, are broadened by roughly a factor of two by the compressive behaviour of the contrast adaptation function. There also is a pronounced problem with off-peak intrusion from neighbouring channels. In fact, the measured function is well-approximated by the intersection of the adapted channel profiles, in contrast to the common misconception that it is described by the envelope (or union) of the masked channel profiles (Fig. 7.4). This effect tends to narrow the measured function relative to the underlying sensitivity function, to an extent that depends on the acceleration in steepness of the flanks. A final example is that the shape and position of the measured masking profile is strongly dependent on the slope of the unmasked sensitivity function. Thus, it is a difficult task to measure unambiguously the underlying channel structure in any domain, and one that has not been successfully achieved in spatial vision despite decades of effort.

A subsequent question, when the channel distribution on each dimension

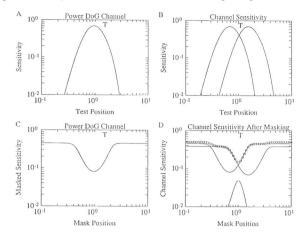

Fig. 7.4. Depiction of off-peak intrusion between neighbouring channels into the empirical masking function, a common technique for estimating channel structure. A. Typical log-log sensitivity function for a channel. B. Overlapping pair of channel profiles of the form of Fig. 7.3A. Test position is indicated by the + sign. C. Masked sensitivity of the channel as a function of the position of the mask, for a particular test position denoted by the + sign, whose unmasked sensitivity would be at the level of the dashed line. Note how masking effect is a reflection of channel shape. D. Upper full curves - masked sensitivities for the pair of channels in B. Chain curve - combined sensitivity with a probability summation exponent of 4. Lower curve - the threshold elevation function, which peaks at the test position (+), does not reflect the peak positions or bandwidths of either channel.

has been established, is the nature of the interactions between channels. Strictly speaking, a channel is an entity that is independent of its companion channels, so that sets of interacting channels constitute an overall channel. However, the situation is analogous to that of neural receptive fields, where the excitatory region of the receptive field is considered to be the primary or 'classical' receptive field. Surrounding regions that modulate the response of the excitatory region without generating a response when stimulated by themselves form the integration field that presumably represents interactions (excitatory or inhibitory) with adjacent neurons (McIlwain, 1964; Fischer & Kruger, 1974; DeAngelis *et al.*, 1992). In the same way, paradigms may be designed to distinguish between primary and interactive aspects of channel behaviour. Colour provides a canonical example of such a distinction, where the cone sensitivity functions for intensity increments may be determined by appropriate isolation techniques but these primary channels then interact in opponent fashion to provide chromatic information. As long as there is empirical access to both levels of organization, there is no categorical problem in distinguishing between the primary and interactive aspects of the channel structure.

The more concrete aspect of encoding structure, its physiological instantiation in the hardware of the brain, is tangential to the present discussion of its logical structure. For example, realizing an intensity code as a neural firing rate adds little to our appreciation of the properties of the code; the realization could equally well be a cellular voltage or a concentration of transmitter molecules, which indeed both seem to be monotonically related to the firing rate code in the operation of neurons. Rather, it is the functional organization of the encoding process that determines its effectiveness to the organism.

7.2.3 *The coding of image symmetries by a self-matching or autocorrelation process.*

Beyond the low-level structure of the representation, there arises the issue of the encoding of regularities or symmetries in the image by capitalizing on their redundancy to simplify the representation. These are issues that have been raised variously by Gibson (1950), Garner (1962) and Attneave (1954), among many venerable figures. The mechanisms for implementing this simplification remain unresolved, however.

A variety of schemes has been proposed to address the issue of how symmetries may be encoded. One of the most sophisticated is that of Palmer (1982), a transformational code based on the fact that the global structure of the coding space is determined by the symmetry relations in the local operators (cortical filters) that are generating the coding space. Thus, a symmetry relation that exists in the image will evoke multiple matching patterns in the response space (see Fig. 7.5). This operation reduces the complexity of the problem because all types of symmetry in the image space are converted simply to one type of symmetry in the coding space: translational symmetry. However, as Palmer points out, a second-order comparison mechanism is required to compare the outputs in the coding space and determine whether such matches exist.

The need for second- (and higher-) order comparison stages reveals that it is the connectivity relations in the comparison stage that determine which aspects of symmetry in the image are processed. In fact, Palmer postulates that the higher-order stages are local within the coding space, which means that global symmetries would be detected only by their local symmetry relations. If we had only local connectivity, for example, we could not detect

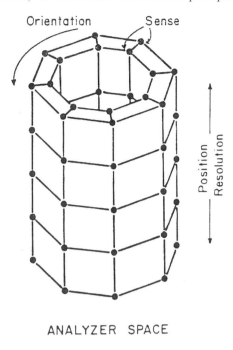

ANALYZER SPACE

Fig. 7.5. The coding metric implied by the symmetry properties of cortical receptive fields (reproduced from Palmer, 1982). Retinal position is represented on the vertical axis, orientation around the clock and ON/OFF polarity in the radial direction.

that the ears are symmetrically located in a face unless we had detectors large enough to encompass both ears in a facial image.

Rather than postulating second-, third- and higher-order matching mechanisms for detecting symmetry relations (as does Palmer, 1982), one may postulate a general-purpose autocorrelation mechanism operating in the coding space to detect symmetries of any type at any range. Tyler and Miller (1994) have shown how the core element of repeated or translationally-symmetric patterns may emerge through an autocorrelation process of mutual reinforcement. One way that such a mechanism might be implemented in the nervous system is for the local pattern vector at the focus of attention (usually the fovea) to form a template that is correlated automatically with the local pattern vector at all other locations. By 'local pattern vector' is meant the profile of response strength through the array of local detectors of all sizes, orientations and types. A high correlation of this vector between two locations means that the same pattern of inputs was present at the two locations at some orientation and scale. Any mechanism that could make such

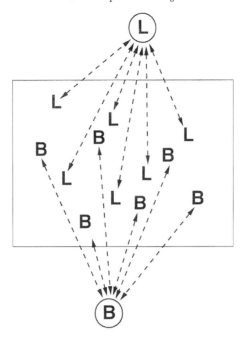

Fig. 7.6. Depiction of the operation of a self-matching process that identifies the repetition of similar patterns when spatially distributed in an arbitrary fashion.

comparisons therefore would act as a detector of all the types of symmetry present in the local pattern vector.

Interesting insights into the properties of the attention may be obtained from introspection of its operation with suitable probe stimuli, an example of which is depicted in Fig. 7.7. Steady fixation on this texture will reveal a succession of overlapping perceptual organizations in the classic pattern of Gestalt reorganization. For the purposes of inter-observer validation, a sample of the percepts observed by the author are facilitated by enhancing their local contrast in Fig. 7.8. A number of questions may be addressed from these perceptual properties. In these interpretations, it is assumed that summation of afterimages with the direct image following refixations do not play a role in these organizations since such summation is incompatible with the non-instantaneous and selective nature of the percepts to be described.

(i) In the classic literature, the reorganizations are treated as occurring globally across the whole pattern, the implication of which is that the organizing principle is controlled either in parallel or by purely local effects. Here, however, introspection suggests that the proliferation of a particular organization, though rapid, is not instantaneous.

(ii) The global organization is selective rather than complete as depicted in Fig. 7.8. One almost never observes a complete array of any particular organization. However, the selectivity seems relatively random, with no apparent correlation between independent samples. This randomness implies that the selectivity is based on noise reaching the site of attentional selection rather than structured organizational properties.

(iii) One can also ask whether the process is foveally centred or multifocal. Does the current organization originate at the fovea an then proliferate outward or is it seeded evenly across the retina? Introspection suggests an even seeding, without a foveal dominance; some organizations may even appear without a foveal representative.

(iv) A related question is whether the perceived organizations is scale-specific to retinal grain. If it were, the organizations would tend to exhibit a radial arrangement around the point of fixation. In fact, as depicted in Fig. 7.8, the organizations seem to be arbitrary in spatial position. A possible exception is the concentric pattern of Fig. 7.8B, but this structure may be more related to the inherent concentric symmetry of its ring structure than to the polar representation of the retina/cortex transform.

7.2.4 3D Object encoding by the attentional shroud

The surfaces of the natural world typically do not form flat planes; even when they do, the planes are unlikely to fall conveniently in the singular position of the observer's frontoparallel plane. An attentional process therefore would be much more valuable if it could be wrapped around the form of any spatial object, rather than being restricted to the frontoparallel plane. The wrapping process could take one of two forms - it could be an exogenous attentive process driven by the local stereoscopic information immediately preceding the test stimulus at each point in the visual field, or it could be a cooperative endogenous process in the form of a flexible planar coupling within the Keplerian array. This latter process corresponds to what Bela Julesz called "the search for dense surfaces" in stereoscopic reconstruction.

A more vivid representation of this process is to think of it as an attentional shroud, wrapping the dense locus of activated disparity detectors as a cloth wraps a structured object. A depiction of such a wrapping has been provided by René Magritte (Fig. 7.9). This depiction shows how the cloth may envelop an object (in this case, a face) to capture the broad features of

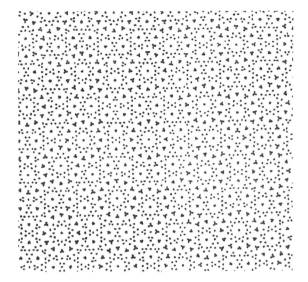

Fig. 7.7. An ambiguous texture from Marroquin (1976). Gazing at this texture elicits a variety of perceptual organizations. Of interest is the rapid proliferation of a particular organization to random locations across the field by some attentional facilitation process. If the organizations were due to afterimage overlay with refixations, the proliferation would be immediate and uniform.

its shape, although some detail may be lost. Such a loss of detail is characteristic of the stereoscopic process. The graph in Fig. 7.10, reproduced from (Tyler, 1983), shows how stereoscopic depth reconstruction of corrugated surfaces is limited to a spatial bandwidth of only about 4 cy/deg, as much as one log unit less than the bandwidth for resolution of luminance information. Thus, stereoscopic reproduction is capable of rendering depth variations only to a coarse scale of representation, as though the connectivity of depth reconstruction were by a flexible material that was too stiff to match local discontinuities in the depth information.

To validate the nature of the attentional mechanism, Tyler & Kontsevich (1995) obtained evidence for the existence of attentional enhancement in a situation where the test and priming stimuli had different slants around the vertical axis. The results (Fig. 11) show both strong attentional facilitation by the priming stimulus and selectivity for the primed depth orientation compared to other nearby slants. These results support the idea that stereoattention is not simply limited to frontoparallel planes, as would be expected if it were a hard-wired connectivity of lateral facilitation (Julesz & Johnson, 1968; Tyler, 1975; Marr & Poggio, 1979) but has the flexibility

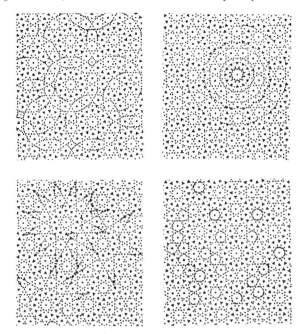

Fig. 7.8. Four examples of fluctuating attentional percepts that may be seen in the in Marroquin texture of Fig. 7.7.

to allow facilitation of first-order depth slants as opposed to frontoparallel (zero-order) depth planes

7.2.4.1 Object-oriented constraints on surface reconstruction

The concept of the attentional shroud is intended to capture the idea of a mechanism that acts like a soap film in minimizing the curvature of the perceived depth surface consistent with the available disparity information. There is evidence from Julesz (1971) that the perceived surface projects across the space between discrete disparity signs to form the minimal smooth surface. He treated this process as an extension of the "search for dense surfaces" within the disparity array and attributed it to a specialized aspect of the stereoscopic system. The present analysis proposes that this process is better viewed as a property of the attentional mechanism, and that this mechanism is not just a local spotlight but a flexible surface that can wrap subsets of the Keplerian disparity field to provide a sense of the object array in the field of view.

One corollary of this surface reconstruction approach is a postulate that the object array is represented strictly in terms of its surfaces, as proposed

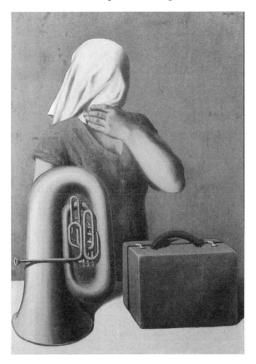

Fig. 7.9. Depiction by René Magritte of the wrapping of objects by shrouds. L'Histoire inventée, copyright (C) Renë Magritte, KINÉMAGE, Montréal, 1996. Used with permission.

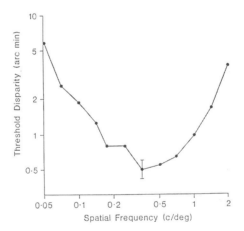

Fig. 7.10. Bandwidth limitations in the processing of disparity modulation are encapsulated by the threshold function for detection of depth corrugations, which shows an optimum at only 0.4 cy/deg and a resolution limit of less than 3 cy/deg (from Tyler, 1983).

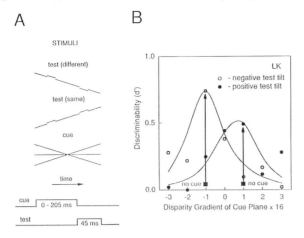

Fig. 7.11. Paradigm for demonstrating that stereoattention can wrap onto the first-order tilt of a plane in depth. Top icon shows tilted test plane with squares protruding in opposite directions on either side of fixation. Next icon shows a test plane with a different tilt from which the squares protrude in the same direction. On each trial the observer had to estimate whether square disparities were the same or opposite, to ensure that both were attended simultaneously. Third icon shows three alternative tilts for the cue plane. Lower diagram shows cue/test sequence over time. B: Tuning of stereoattention to depth tilt (circles), expressed in units of disparity gradient ratio (disparity gradient of the cue plane x 16) for the 105 ms cue. Clear enhancement was obtained for cue tilts near those of the test targets, in contrast to the lack of discriminability without a cue plane (filled squares). Enhancement data are fitted with Gaussian curves.

by Nakayama & Shimojo (1990b). As with the majority of objects in the physical world, the reconstructed surface is assumed to be inherently opaque, as seen from the point of view of the observer. However, just as Nakayama & Shimojo have postulated that the borders of ambiguous figure/ground objects "belong" to the shape perceived as "figure" at any instant, so the reconstructed surface is proposed to belong to the outside of the object that it is wrapping. The observer is constrained, on this hypothesis, always to be outside convex objects in the scene. Concave objects, on the other hand, are viewed as though from the inside (especially, perhaps, a concave "cave" filling the whole visual scene) but never as a solid object, since we could not then see through it to its surface. However, the observer can never adopt the perceptual point of view of looking back through the scene at the face, presumable because of lack of familiarity with this perspective. Even when looking at one's own image in the mirror, it seems to be impossible to adopt the perspective of the image looking at oneself.

One effect of the observer-centred viewpoint that was noted by Julesz (1971) applies to the regions of the scene that are visible to only one eye. For steeper surfaces, the nearer edge of the surface occludes the remainder from that eye, so that it is only visible to the other eye. These monocular "no man's lands" in the depth array carry no stereoscopic depth information, so they could, in principle, be perceived as anywhere behind the boundary of visibility in which the image is visible only monocularly. In practice, these regions usually are perceived as continuous with the far surface running into the monocular region rather than any other more exotic examples from the infinite set of possible percepts. This behaviour raises the question of the generality of this reconstruction process. Will it just extend the local disparity horizontally across the region being reconstructed in a simple zero-order extrapolation, or will the brain employ top-down processes to optimize the reconstructed segment according to a variety of real-world constraints?

Tyler & Kontsevich (1995) showed that some constraints are observed while others are not. Figure 7.12 shows a step between a flat and a corrugated plane. The upper and lower pairs show opposite directions of the step in depth. The pair of lines in the upper right and lower left panels are provided to define the "no man's land" of monocular dots with no corresponding mates in the opposite panel. All other dots occur in matched pairs between the two images. The question is, what depth do these uncorrelated dots appear to take when the fields are viewed stereoscopically?

Observation of Fig. 7.12 reveals that, with fixation on the rear surface close to the step, the monocular zone appears to show a vertical modulation that is continuous with that in the rear surface. This extension of the stereoscopic form into the monocular zone implies that object-oriented constraints are brought to bear on the stereoreconstruction process in selecting surface continuity over other possible interpretations.

The dependence of the interpretation of the monocular zone on the form of the surrounding surfaces is contrary to the predictions of the occlusion hypothesis of Nakayama & Shimojo (1990a). Occlusion would predict the monocular zone to appear behind the edge when the front edge was fixated, just as is observed, but that it also should be behind the fixated plane in the case of rear fixation. The observation that the front plane may be perceived as continuing across the monocular zone implies that higher-order reconstruction processes are at work beyond the simple precepts of da Vinci stereopsis (Nakayama & Shimojo, 1990a).

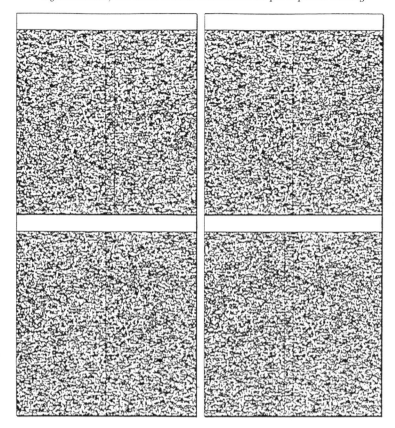

Fig. 7.12. Stereoreconstruction of indeterminate monocular regions. The left and right panels should be free-fused to obtain a stereoscopic percept. The upper and lower panels have the same image but with left-right reversal between them.

7.2.5 The dynamic manipulation of the object representation in the coding space.

Objects are represented by clusters of features with specifiable symmetry relations, but there is a kind of perceptual "surface tension" that holds the features of a specific object together in the representation space. There must be a vocabulary of object forms or schemata of the type proposed by Piaget (1969) to which are attached the features specific to the object in the current focus of attention. The concept of a schema is understood as an action structure; e.g., a 'box' is a cuboid structure with an inside in which other objects may be placed. Part of this action structure is its three-dimensional symmetry relations, i.e., the aspects or regions of the object that may be made congruent by a symmetry transformation. Unlike the

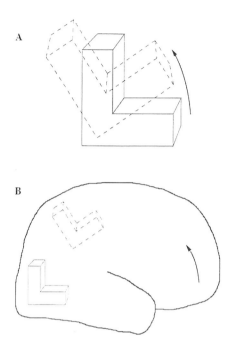

Fig. 7.13. Depiction of brain representation of visual manipulative process. A. Rotation of the object representation in some neural space. B. The component processes of the rotational manipulation are distributed through the brain.

2D symmetry structure (which, as argued in the previous section, is likely to be coded by inherent symmetries in the coding space), the complexity of generalized 3D symmetries probably require internal manipulation of the type proposed by Shepard (1981) to ascertain its symmetry structure.

The total process of object characterization thus may involve both structural and manipulative aspects in the symmetry encoding. The manipulative aspect constitutes the fifth of the perceptual processing stages identified (Fig. 7.13). For example, if a cube is viewed in perspective projection with one side facing the observer, the quartic symmetry of the front face might be perceived by inherent coding symmetries, implying that it does not need to be mentally rotated around the line of sight for the quartic symmetry to be appreciated. Conversely, the symmetrical identity of the six faces (or lack of identity if the cube is a rectangular cuboid), can perhaps be appreciated only by mental rotation of the front face into the other positions. In this way, the structural aspect of the symmetry coding process may be brought to bear in those regions of the image where manipulation is not required; the results of the structural analysis may then be carried into the manipulative phase so that features that are found to be congruent be a manipulative analysis are consequently perceived to have the same inherent symmetry structure.

There also may be a level of cognitive assumptions in the manipulative aspect of the encoding that, for symmetry operations, takes the form of avoiding the need for some mental rotations on the basis of an assumed symmetry relation. For example, when looking at a set of banisters in perspective projection, one may need only to perform the mental operation of matching one banister to the next to establish the similarity and then make the cognitive assumption that all the others are similarly matched. This assumption would economize on the number of mental manipulations that need to be made at the cost of missing deviations from the assumed symmetry in regions where manipulative testing is avoided.

Much of what we see may be only part of the total object schema, e.g., when sitting on a couch, we may have only an arm and part of the seat cushions projecting on to the retina, but perceive them as part of the complete couch. This process of amodal (or non-sensory) completion has been most fully explored by Kanizsa (1976), although he emphasized regions hidden by other objects rather than regions outside the visual field. The concept of an abstract schema representing the whole object gives a direct instantiation to the process of amodal completion; if part of an object is sufficient to evoke unambiguously the full schema, the whole object is perceived in the implied position. This evocation is similar to the process known as "lexical access" in language perception (Marslen-Wilson & Tyler, 1980), in which the full meaning of a spoken word is evoked as soon as it is unambiguously distinguishable from all other words. In the same way, the whole object may be perceived when the information from the visible parts is sufficient to identify it from the vocabulary of known objects or plausible object classes. There is the obvious proviso that the manner in which the non-visible parts are obscured must be consistent with their occlusion by an intervening object of some kind, so that the attended region of the scene is itself a plausible arrangement. That there are counterexamples in which the attended region makes an "impossible" object (Hochberg, 1981) does not reduce the general applicability of this proviso.

7.2.5.1 *Operation of schemata: The phantom limb instantiation*

The phenomenon of perceived (phantom) limbs after amputation provides a perceptual lesion that provides profound insight into the strata of perceptual representation in the somatosensory system (Ramachandran, 1993; Ramachandran *et al.*, 1995). Applying such insights to the visual system provides a radical view of its self-organizing capabilities. It is well known that amputees experience a clear and detailed sense of the presence of the limb in the space that it would have occupied before amputation. This implies that there is a neural representation of the limb that is distinct from its sensory representation in the cortex. The logic of this implication is that the sensory representation is no longer being supplied with consistent information, in the absence of the peripheral input. Any residual input will be disorganized noise, and therefore would not support a coherent representation of the pre-existing limb structure.

Less well known, but well established, is that the amputee is capable of maneuvering the perceived phantom at will (but only if it was maneuverable before amputation; a paralyzed limb remains perceptually paralyzed after amputation; Ramachandran *et al.*, 1995). This manipulable representation corresponds to the body schema of Head (1920), a complete representation of the positions of the limbs and the body that is accessible to consciousness and manipulable at will. The idea of a consciously manipulable body schema provides a challenging view of the self-organizing capabilities of the neural substrate, but one that is hard to dismiss. The properties of the body schema suggests that there are four levels of representation of the sensory world in the somatosensory system of the brain.

(i) the sensory representation in somatosensory cortex

(ii) the body image of the parietal representation, which corresponds to the phantom limb and is manipulable in position on a rapid time scale,

(iii) the will representation or corollary discharge from the frontal cortex, which represents the intended position of the limb.

(iv) the output representation in the cerebellum, which represents the body image organized in a musculature-based coordinate frame ready to implement the manipulated limb representation into an actual change of limb position.

7.2.5.2 Application to the visual representation

The same structure is presumed to apply for the visual representation of space. Here the components may be related to the coordinate frame of their representation (Pouget *et al.*, 1993) would be:

(i) the visual representation in striate cortex, which includes the neural Keplerian array of disparity detectors for encoding the 3D aspects of the image. In retinal coordinates (joint retinal coordinates of the two eyes for stereoscopic encoding).

(ii) the spatial representation in parietal cortex (in object-centred coordinates). The site of Shepard's manipulable image. It also corresponds to Gregory's hypotheses of the spatial configuration tested during perceptual alternations. The spatial representation may be conceptualized as inherently self-organizing, with the following properties:

(a) local surface tension to contract it into a data-reducing form (analogous to the physical surface minimization of soap-bubble systems). This minimization property will give the spatial representation the tendency to contract toward the densest surface of activation of the disparity detectors, corresponding to the dense planes of Julesz (1963) or the attentional shroud of Tyler & Kontsevich (1995).

(b) a tendency to self-destruct (autoinhibition) unless continually reinforced by sensory input. This self-limiting property will give the spatial representation a limited lifetime, allowing competing representations the opportunity to be expressed as suggested by Gregory (1980) when the initially dominant representation has faded. Empirical evidence for rapid fading of the spatial representation within several seconds was reported by Ramachandran *et al.* (1994).

(c) conformity to amodal instruction from distant spatial regions according to the object-based and surface-based principles elaborated by Nakayama & Shimojo (1990b) from the demonstrations of Kanizsa (1976).

(d) the intended configuration of the manipulandum in frontal cortex (in egocentric coordinates for convenient control of the manipulation process in relation to the body). This attentional manipulation is endogenous, in the sense that it can be manipulated at will according to higher cognitive instruction.

(iii) Since there is no specific output for a perceptual space representation, there seems to be no particular need for a direct cerebellar representation. However, there is a need to plan the direction of eye movements from point to point in space. Perhaps this is the reason that a positron-emission tomography study by Parsons & Fox (1995) found high activation of the cerebellum during a visual mental rotation task, suggesting that the coordinate frame transformation required in mental rotation actually takes place in the cerebellum rather than directly in the parietal representation.

One vivid demonstration of the manipulative aspect of the schema is the attentional tracking paradigm described by Culham & Cavanagh (1994). They showed that perception of a ring of rotating spokes is dominated by a pair of diametrically opposite spokes that are selected by the attentional mechanism. The observer is then able to attentionally track the rotation of the two selected spokes while fixating the centre of the display. The objective of Culham & Cavanagh's experiment is to show that attention can select between a sinusoidal luminance modulation moving in one direction and a sinusoidal chromatic modulation moving in the other. But the interest in the present context is that the attentional selection process allows not only the highlighting of two different points in the visual field, but the ability to track them in opposite directions simultaneously. This is a manipulative capability that goes well beyond the concept of attention as a 'searchlight' process drawn to one particular point in the field with a local maximum of contrast energy.

An even more dramatic example of attentional manipulation is the multi-focal experiment of Pylyshyn (1988), who showed that observers were able to maintain attentional tracking of up to five points moving independently among a masking set of other randomly moving points. Again this result attests the degree to which attentional salience is manipulable to fit the demands of a complex processing task. Although the task is framed in terms of local processing regions, it is noteworthy that the perceptual experience when tracking the independent objects is that the points are projected into 3D space to form continuously transforming figure with five vertices. To at least some observers, the figure appears as two connected triangular surfaces undergoing a non-rigid transformation. This percept is more consonant with the idea of an attentional shroud defining the structural organization than of a set of independent attentional foci tracking the individual points.

7.3 Conclusion

The processing stages described constitute a framework in which most studies of perception may be viewed. This five-stage scheme may be related to the neural network architecture proposed by Grossberg and colleagues (reviewed, for example, in Grossberg, Mingolla & Todorovic, 1989). They have a three-stage conception of preattentive processing consisting of 1) monocular preprocessing, 2) a cortical contour-processing stage and 3) an attention-driven object-recognition system that can modify and complete the boundary structures developed by the second stage according to stored representations. Without elaborating on this scheme, the relevant properties will be contrasted with those of the present conceptualization to delineate the dramatic contrasts between them.

The metric of my scheme is the two spatial dimensions of the retinal image and the implicit (constructed) third dimension of binocular disparity. This is one major difference between the two approaches for, despite several forays into the domain of 3D interpretation (Grossberg, 1987, 1994), the Grossberg approach to cortical dynamics is a fundamentally two-dimensional analysis of the image array. To a great extent, the 3D information is subsumed into a 2D representation by appealing to the size-disparity correlation whereby larger disparities are encoded by larger receptive fields. This assumption is taken to imply the corollary that image components that stimulate larger (2D) receptive fields are seen as closer, thus allowing construction of a depth representation from a 2D image. Although disparity is represented in this scheme, it has the role of a feature attached to the boundaries in the 2D contour representation rather than a fundamental dimension of the representation metric. In this respect, the Grossberg approach to 3D representation is reminiscent of the computational theory of Marr (1982), in which the 2D contour map with depth tokens for the third dimension was termed a "2 1/2 D sketch" rather than a 3D map as an indication of the subsidiary role of the disparity signal.

My scheme, on the other hand, has a fundamentally three-dimensional conception of the process of object reconstruction. Here, and in Tyler & Kontsevich (1995), the neural representation is conceived as a network structure that is manipulable in three-dimensional neural space by the attentional control mechanism.

With respect to the second stage of my scheme, Grossberg appears to assume a continuous representation of the visual input in his 2D spatial metric. When multiple channels are introduced for the representation of size, disparity, orientation, etc. the issue of their discreteness or continuity is not addressed.

In terms of coding attributes, Grossberg introduces innumerable network structures and interactions to explain a variety of illusory contour and depth effects. The basic flavour of these network interactions is bottom-up, in the sense that the interactions are assumed to reside within the network rather than being driven by an interpretive framework such as the perceptual hypotheses of Gregory (1980). This bottom-up flavour is in contrast to my scheme, which views subjective contours, amodal completion, monocular depth effects and so on as manifestations of an active, top-down process of 3D reconstruction (expressed as the manipulation of an "attentional shroud" in Tyler & Kontsevich, 1995). On this view, it is not until the image is parsed in terms of potential 3D objects that the subjective contours are formed.

This top-down view is supported by a remarkable demonstration of Ramachandran (1986) in which the 'pacmen' of the Kanizsa figure were given a binocular disparity in front of the phantom square that they usually evoke when perceived behind it. Because the near disparity was incompatible with the required occlusion interpretation, a new percept emerged of the pacmen as 'portholes' through which the corners of a square could be seen. This percept required the generation of curved subjective contours to complete the absent quadrant of the pacmen, and elimination of the normally perceived subjective contours completing the sides of the square. The fact that both changes were clearly achieved in the resulting percept implies that subjective contours are generated after the image is parsed into its 3D organization.

Thus, the key aspect of this perceptual coding scheme is in the manipulative fifth stage, which is an active reconstruction process rather than the passive memory-access stage that resides at the top of the Grossberg scheme. The essence of this active reconstruction process is surface perception through a self-organizing net with constraints akin to surface tension in liquids, some of which were explored in Tyler & Kontsevich (1995). This active apprehensive process is combined with an ability to manipulate the object representation in three dimensions (and through time) to arrange it in a optimal configuration for the apprehensive process, to characterize its properties. It is this literal manipulative aspect of the neural representation that appears to constitute the full expression of human perceptual coding. Although its properties have mainly been compared with those of known physical processes, there is no reason to suppose that the analogy will extend to all details (any more than quantum properties can be understood in terms of the macroscopic properties of materials). The challenge for the future is to develop experimental paradigms to elucidate the properties of a manipulative perceptual process. It is not until the likelihood that perceptual is a self-organizing apprehensive process is taken seriously that this conceptualization can be empirically evaluated to determine its validity.

Acknowledgements:
Supported by NEI grant 7890 and NIMH grant MH 49044.

8

The coding of self motion

Laurence Harris

Department of Psychology
York University
North York
Canada

In this chapter I outline some of the factors that must be taken into account in coding self motion. I suggest that in fact self motion is not coded as motion of a person relative to the world at all: instead only the movement of the world relative to the self is represented. Drawing on the difference between trivial, first order, transduction codes and profound, second order, goal-directed codes, I show that the coding of sub-modalities of self motion is best revealed by looking at how this information is decoded. Some possible reference frames, coordinate systems and coding methods are discussed. The ambiguous concept of 'channels' is clarified by dividing channels into the two fundamentally different types: sub-modality processing (SuMP) channels and within-sub-modality processing (WiSuMP) channels. These are compared and contrasted. Experiments are described that suggest that the sub-modality of head rotation velocity is coded by its consequences in the reference frame of the eye with the coordinate system of the canals using a coding system of WiSuMP channels. The coordinate system, units and coding system for head translation are still unclear.

8.1 Introduction

The term 'self motion' is rather imprecise since it embraces motion of any part of the self with respect to either any other part of the body or with respect to the outside world or both. Here I discuss only movement of the head with respect to the outside world. The chapter has the more general title of the coding of self motion because movements of the rest of the body are largely deduced from a knowledge of the position and movements of the head. Furthermore, people locate their selves as being within their heads (eg. Mitson *et al.*, 1976). Two important self motion detectors, the eyes and the vestibular system, are situated in the head and so the head's motion is

known most precisely. The motions and positions of other parts of the body
that might be directed towards external world targets, for example limbs
or fingers, are likely to be referred to space through a head-based coding
system.

8.2 Reference frames and coordinate systems for movement

At any instant the head has a position and an orientation and two sets of
derivatives across time: an angular set and a translational set. Each of these
sets comprises velocity and acceleration and an infinity of higher attributes
such as translational and rotational jerk (rate of change of acceleration).
Each of these terms is three dimensional: that is they require at least three
parameters to specify them. The two sets of attributes each form a sequence
of increasingly higher derivatives from position across time but the instantaneous value of any one of these, or any combination, is inadequate to deduce
the values of any other term. Given samples over time, the value of higher
derivatives can be calculated from lower ones by differentiation (acceleration from velocity for example). And lower ones can be partially, but not
completely, calculated from higher ones by integration (position from velocity for example). To calculate lower terms from higher ones, a cumulative
measure of the lower terms (eg. position, if integrating velocity) needs to be
maintained and updated by the integrated information.

To represent any of these terms (position, orientation, etc.), either as in
a mathematical notation or within the central nervous system as part of a
command to move or as a sensory report, requires a reference frame and
a coordinate system. These are not the same thing. The reference frame
refers to the anchor points of the system whereas the coordinate system
is the way in which an attribute is described with respect to those anchor
points. A coordinate might be, for example, the representation of velocity
(an external variable) in action potentials per second (an internal variable;
see below). The same component of the movement can be simultaneously
described in terms of many combinations of different reference points and
coordinate systems. It is often convenient for velocities, accelerations and
positions to share a reference frame but it does not make sense for different
attributes to share coordinates, however, because the representation rules
would be different (see below, section 8.2.5).

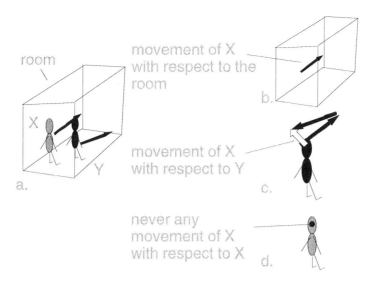

Fig. 8.1. Two people, X and Y, walk in different directions across a room. A shows the movement of X with respect to the room, B shows the movement of X with respect to Y. C shows the motion of person X with respect to themselves. No movement of the person can ever be observed in this latter case. Changing the reference frame alters all aspects of the movement observed.

8.2.1 *The consequences of choice of reference frame*

Imagine two people, X and Y, walking across a room. Obvious possible reference frames are provided by person X, person Y or the room itself. The translational movement of person X can perhaps most intuitively, from the point of view of an observer, be expressed as a vector with respect to the reference frame of the room. A vector has a magnitude and a direction. Here the magnitude represents the change in position. More specifically, the movement can be described with respect to any three non-collinear points: three such points are needed to define a three-dimensional reference frame unambiguously. This is illustrated in Fig 8.1a. The motion of person X could also be described with respect to person Y. If person Y is moving with respect to the room then movement in each of these two frames is different. This is shown by comparing Fig 8.1b and 8.1a. As an extreme case, if both people were moving in the same direction and at the same speed, then there would be no movement of person X in the reference frame defined by person Y at all, even though there *would* be movement in the reference frame defined by the room. Expressing the movement of person X in the reference frame defined by person X indicates no movement of person X at any time (Fig 8.1c). Indeed, attempting to express the motion of person X with respect to the reference frame defined by that person seems a foolish and futile thing to do. But the vestibular organs that are monitoring the movement of person X are part of person X's head and it would therefore seem likely that person X's head should form the reference frame. The vestibular system is faced with that very problem of expressing the movement of person X in the reference frame of person X! Since movement is relative, however, movement of the room, rather that the person, could be adequately described in person X's reference frame (see Crawford's chapter, this volume).

Keeping with our example, now imagine person X stops walking and, for reasons best known to themselves, executes a perfect pirouette. Examples of reference frames to describe the rotation include person X themselves, the room and person Y (who might also be caught by the same fancy). The distance between the axis of rotation of the pirouette and the reference points chosen to define the reference frame is immaterial in describing the rotation. As before, different motions of person X would be observed in each of the three reference frames. And also as before, if the reference frame is person X themselves, no rotation of the person could ever be registered! However as before, rotation of the world could be described relative to this self-based reference frame.

For a freely moving organism (or robot), it makes no sense to use external points as the anchors of a frame of reference to which every movement is related. First there is the problem of deciding which points to choose. Then the reference positions would have to be reselected every time the organism wandered out of range of the first set! Keeping track of all external points, any one of which could move with respect to all the others, is a horrendous problem and, worse, unnecessary. By instead choosing the head rather than an external frame for coding self motion the which-points-to-choose problem and the wandering-out-of-range problem disappear. And the same reference frame can be easily used for position, velocity, acceleration, etc. And it can be used for both translation and rotational information. But the disadvantage of using the head as the reference frame for coding self motion it that it allows only movement of the outside world to be registered, not of the head itself. This is not actually a problem because of the relativity of motion. As my father was fond of quoting "What would it look like if the sun did go around the earth?"

8.2.2 *The consequences of choice of coordinate system*

A coordinate system for coding position, velocity or acceleration implies a set of scales that represent that attribute with the appropriate number of dimensions. Three-dimensional spatial position could be represented, for instance, as the distance along each of three orthogonal axes that represent the distance in space from the reference point. This is a conventional Cartesian coordinate system. Choice of reference frame does not define the coordinate system to be used within that frame. For example the movement of person X with respect to the room in Fig 8.1a can be described in terms of a coordinate system parallel to the walls and floor (corresponding to x, y, z in a Cartesian grid). But an equally valid coordinate system within this same room-based reference system might use some other axes which do not line up with the walls and might not even be orthogonal. Other possible coordinate systems include a polar coordinate system of angles and directions from the chosen reference points or the use of non-linear scales along any or all axes.

8.2.3 *Confusions between coordinate systems and reference frames*

The choice of coordinate systems for describing rotations has historically introduced all sorts of complications because of confusion between the concepts of reference frame and coordinate system. This confusion can be illustrated by considering the Fick or Helmholtz systems for describing eye rotations (Helmholtz's is the same as Fick's but on its side). An example of such a system is shown in Fig 8.2. Here rotation is described in terms of three numbers, often called horizontal, vertical and torsion corresponding to x, y and z in the figure. Such a system comprises multiple reference frames which move with respect to each other during the very rotation that is being described.

If each dimension is measured in its own reference frame, then there is no problem. For example, if x, y and z were the axes of three nested motors, then signals controlling the three motors would be treated separately. But if we are using the dimensions X, Y and Z to describe the motion of a single item, for example an eyeball, then we need a *single* reference frame. And we therefore need to convert from this complex, nested system of different reference frames to just one. This conversion is complex because the contribution of each value (X, Y, Z) will depend on the values of the outer frames. Mathematical coordinate systems have been devised that avoid these complications. Quaternions, for example, describe rotation in terms

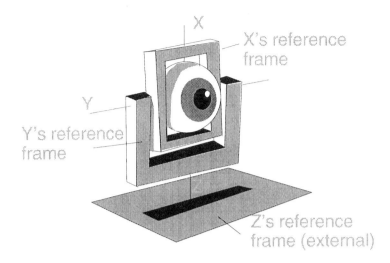

Fig. 8.2. A set of three reference frames that can all move with respect to each other is bound to be confusing! In a Fick coordinate system, the reference frame for rotation about axis Z is determined by points fixed outside the system (ie. external space). The reference frame for rotation about Y is the frame shown which moves with respect to the Z reference frame as a result of rotation about the Z axis. Because the axes Z and Y are constrained to be orthogonal, there is no significant interaction between them. But problems arise when we come to determine the third dimension: rotation about the X axis. Although X is always orthogonal to Y and therefore does not interact with Y, X does not remain orthogonal to Z and therefore its contribution in the Z coordinate system will depend on the value of Y.

of a single, non-moving frame of reference (Tweed *et al.*, 1990; Haslwanter, 1995). Quaternions use three numbers to define the orientation of the axis and then a fourth to describe the rotation. A system that uses four numbers to code a three-dimensional attribute is redundant since only three numbers are required to code a three-dimensional parameter.

8.2.4 *What sorts of coordinate systems might be used?*

Coding the static and dynamic attributes of a point in space requires a minimum of three coordinates for each of position and rotational velocity and rotational acceleration and translational velocity and translational acceleration and any higher derivatives. And any of these attributes could be multiply represented with any number of combinations of reference frames and coordinate systems. Each attribute can be described as a three-dimensional

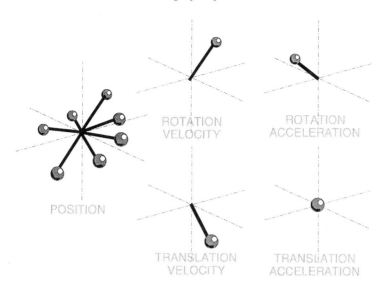

Fig. 8.3. Representation of the static and dynamic attributes of all points in the world with respect to a person at a single instant in time. The axes represent directions fixed in a reference frame (eg. the head) and the lengths and orientations of the vectors code the attributes of all points in the world. Notice that all these values are independent of each other at any one instant. However, higher attributes can be calculated from the history of lower attributes. And higher attributes (eg. acceleration) can be used to predict the values of lower derivatives (eg. velocity) in the future - given the present values. In this example, the linear acceleration of zero predicts that the linear velocity will be maintained unaltered. The rotational acceleration is around a very different axis to the prevailing rotational velocity and predicts a dramatic change in direction and amplitude of the velocity.

vector as shown in Fig 8.3: each with an magnitude and a direction. For translation, the direction of the vector is the direction of the translation, for rotation the orientation of the vector represents the orientation of the axis of the rotation. In representing the position of some point in the world, the length of the vector corresponds to the distance from the person.

Using a head-fixed reference frame and describing the movement of the world relative to this frame has the very attractive consequence that if self movement is the only source of world-relative-to-self movement, then, for everything except position, the values for all points in the world are the same: all points are affected in the same way by a given movement. That is each attribute except position can be described as a single vector. Position, however, does requires a separate vector for each point of the world. An example of an instantaneous state is illustrated in Fig 8.3. Notice that

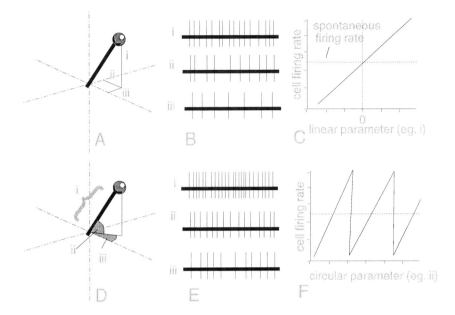

Fig. 8.4. Diagram showing how a single vector, corresponding perhaps to a rotational or translational attribute, can be coded on three equal scales (A, B, C) or as two parameters for direction and one for amplitude (D, E, F). The three dimensions shown in A could also be used to specify *just* direction and then a fourth (redundant) parameter (not shown) could be used to encode amplitude. B and E shows the activity of three sets of hypothetical cells encoding the value of these coordinates in their firing rates. On the right are graphs of the firing characteristics that would be required of these cells. The temporal properties might be carried by populations to create greater flexibility and range.

static position is affected by both rotation and translation although the rotational and translational dynamic attributes are completely independent of each other.

In Fig 8.3, the vectors have been shown in conventional 3D Cartesian coordinates. Some possible coordinate systems that might be used to represent any of these vectors are shown in Fig 8.4. One possibility is having three equivalent Cartesian-type dimensions (Fig 8.4a) although it is not necessary for these coordinates to be orthogonal in space. An alternative is to describe the vector as a direction, which needs only two coordinates, and an amplitude (Fig 8.4d). To represent all possible vectors, all the coordinate values have to be able vary symmetrically about the value that corresponds to 'no vector present' (see Figs 8.4c & 8.4f).

8.2.5 *What is the relationship between a coordinate system and a coding system?*

It is necessary to have both a coordinate system and a reference frame to represent a stimulus in neural terms. But establishing them is not the same as establishing a coding system. Representation is not enough: a method of encoding information along the chosen coordinates is also needed. A code implies a key or a decoding system by which the coded information can be extracted. The essence of all neural keys or decoding systems is the notion that the activity of a particular cell always means the same thing and that the decoder knows what that thing is: the cell is labelled in some way. The notion of labelled cells is a spatial coding system. Historically the concept originated with Müller in his Doctrine of Specific Nerve Energies (Müller, 1840). In the original, rather rigid formulation, a particular sensory experience always resulted when a particular cell was activated, no matter in what context. Interpreting the activity of a labelled cell can be much more flexible than this. In the modern, pervasive incarnation of Müller's doctrine, the notion of labelled cells is maintained as a central feature of ideas about how the brain works. The complete interpretation of a cell's message, by perception or unconscious processes, requires knowledge of the context. Nonetheless the idea of labelled cells is fundamental to the concept of hoping to elucidate the functioning of the brain by looking at individual cell's activities.

A complete coding system requires a combination of spatial and temporal aspects. The magnitude of a stimulus is generally coded in the temporal activity of a cell or group of cells. A simplistic version of how a vector might be coded is as follows. The values of each coordinate, for example the set illustrated in Fig 8.4a, could be coded as proportional to the frequency of action potentials of cells that have been labelled as representing these particular coordinates in their activity (Fig 8.4b, 8.4c). Thus, the schemas in Fig 8.4a or d could be realized by the activity of just three labelled neurons. A high spontaneous firing rate would be necessary to allow negative values of the coordinate to be encoded by reduction in firing rate. In encoding the scheme shown in Fig 8.4d, the activity of cells 2 & 3 represents the 'direction of the vector' in which the linear parameter of firing rate represents the circular parameter of angular direction. For these cells there are certain directions where the responses of the cells involved is very unstable, oscillating from minimal to maximal firing rates in response to tiny changes in the stimulus direction (Fig 8.3f).

8.3 Coding methods defined in terms of decoding methods

Paradoxically, it is in the method of decoding rather than the encoding process, in which a profound coding system is established. The difference between trivial and profound codes was introduced in chapter 1 of this book. Trivial coding is merely a re-representation of the original stimulus. Profound coding is an active, goal-oriented process in which a particular feature of the stimulus is extracted and represented. Profound coding does not have to be a high-level process: the goal is defined not by conscious intention but by a behavioural requirement. But profound coding is defined in terms of the decoding required.

Transduction of rotational acceleration into neural activity in the VIII nerve is an example of trivial coding because no goal-directed information processing occurs. The spatial and temporal filtering imposed by the transducers results in the firing rate being proportional to head angular velocity (Fernandez & Goldberg, 1971) but this does not mean that head angular velocity is coded in the activity of this nerve, any more than that this information was 'coded' in the original stimulus that excited the end organ.

Profound coding of head velocity requires that the information is extracted or decoded from the raw sensory information (the 'trivial code') and re-coded with a reference frame and coordinate system that specifies head velocity unambiguously. Deriving this information requires a systematic extraction or decoding process and a comparison between the signals from the various transducers. Such a system is useless without a matched decoding system. A profound coding system is defined in terms of the decoding system that it must be paired with. Notice that both direction and amplitude of head velocity are embedded in the trivial codes of the VIII nerve. Different profound coding systems are needed to extract and process each of them from this same set of inputs.

Possible encoding systems include population codes, channels and spatial maps (see chapter 1). All of these imply decoding systems that can understand the code and utilize appropriate coordinate systems and reference frames. Here I develop the idea of channels in the coding of self motion.

8.3.1 Channels as a decoding system

The concept of channels originated from information theory (Shannon & Weaver, 1949) and became applied to biological systems as an explanatory mechanism for psychophysical observations concerning visual perceptions (see Regan, 1982; Regan, 1989 ; Campbell & Tedeger, 1991). The basis of channel coding is that different sub-modalities are processed separately and independently: the information is divided into channels. For example, in the visual system there is are orientation-processing channels which are distinct from the colour processing channel, which are distinct from spatial-frequency-processing channels, etc. If the systems are truly independent, then things that affect one channel will have no effect on another channel: they are said to be orthogonal. A serious confusions often arises when thinking about channels because the word channel is used with two quite separate meanings. Firstly, the word channel refers to the separate processing of sub-modalities as described above. I will refer to these as SuMP channels (sub-modality processing channels). But then, within such a channel, a common mechanism for processing information is also confusingly referred to as a 'channel system' although here the word is used quite differently. The 'channels' of this second type do not function independently as SuMP channels are required to do by definition, but can only work as a cooperative team (see 8.3.3 below)! I will refer to these channels as WiSuMP channels (within sub-modality processing channels). Comparison between a set of WiSuMP channels allows the extraction of the relevant sub-modality information. WiSuMP channels represent a mechanism that enables one sub-modality processing system to be independent of other processing systems.

8.3.2 Biological realisation of sub-modality processing (SuMP) channels

The sub-modalities of self motion are defined functionally. It is of no consequence which sensory systems contribute to that functional information †. Any moving body can be described in terms of its rotation and translation which are mathematically completely independent. At the level of the end organ physical motion is parsed into its rotational and translational components by the physical structure of the vestibular system (Harris, 1994; Miles & Wallman, 1993). The semicircular canals transduce only rotational acceleration (Fernandez & Goldberg, 1971) and the otoliths of the saccule and utricle transduce only translational acceleration (Fernandez & Goldberg, 1976), including gravity. Taking rotation and translation as the main sub-modalities, they can then be further subdivided theoretically into individual, independent sub-modalities. This is illustrated in Fig 8.5. Some

---

† This is yet another source of potential confusion since the term 'modality' can refer specifically to the sense of origin, for example vision or hearing. Hence cells in the superior colliculus that receive information from both the visual and auditory systems are called 'bimodal' (e.g. Harris *et al.*, 1980). They are only bimodal in the sense that they get information from two senses: functionally they are unimodal, coding a single sub-modality, that is spatial position.

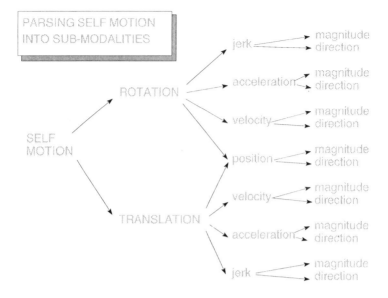

Fig. 8.5. The division of self motion into potential SuMP channels not all of which are realized biologically.

of these SuMP channels might get input from other sub-modalities, for example, position from velocity, but the information in each SuMP channel is still independent. Each sub-modality must be encoded with a separate coordinate system. Information is only extracted from the trivial codes of the early stages and profoundly coded in terms of its decoding system if it is to be used for something. It is therefore probable that most of these sub-modalities are not realized biologically unless that attribute is needed to perform some function. It is not logically required that the basic sub-modalities to which the end organs respond: linear and angular acceleration, are represented as SuMP systems. However, the direction and velocity of head rotation are likely to be biologically useful and I am hypothesizing here that the direction and amplitude of head rotational velocity are coded separately, forming two biologically-realized SuMP channels.

Lisberger et al. have suggested that certain frequency ranges of head rotation might also be processed by separate SuMP channels and that they might be processed separately and independently in parallel (Lisberger *et al.*, 1983). Such an parallel arrangement is appropriate since a complex head movement might well contain many frequencies each of which would need to appear simultaneously in an effective eye movement response. The suggestion is based on frequency-specific gain changes in the vestibulo-ocular reflex. The vestibulo-ocular reflex is very plastic and can alter its properties in response to environmental conditions (see Berthoz & Melvill-Jones, 1985). For example, if visual information indicates that the gain of the vestibulo-ocular reflex is too small, then the reflex will learn to use a larger gain. If the visual corrective experience is restricted to certain frequencies, then the change in gain of the reflex is also restricted in frequency (Lisberger *et al.*, 1983; Godaux *et al.*, 1983; Powell *et al.*, 1991). This suggests possible parallel, independent SuMP channel processing for different frequencies. It is important to distinguish this multiple SuMP channel model from a WiSuMP channel model. Lisberger *et al.* (1983) do not claim that frequency information might be coded across a set of WiSuMP channels in the same way that spatial frequency appears to be coded in the visual system (see 8.3.3 below for a description of how WiSuMP channels work). Their proposed SuMP channels are independent and do not code frequency at all. Instead they ensure independent processing for different frequency ranges that need slightly different treatments for biomechanical reasons (Donaghy, 1980).

Having identified possible SuMP channels for information we next need to consider how the information might be coded within such a channel. I will consider evidence first for a WiSuMP channel-based system for magnitude of head angular velocity and then for the direction of head angular velocity. Alternative coding mechanisms include frequency coding or population coding and are reviewed in the introductory chapter.

8.3.3 *How a within sub-modality processing (WiSuMP) channel system works*

The function of a within sub-modality processing system is to encode a particular sub-modality, for example rotation velocity, in a robust way such that the information is not affected by changes in the values of other parameters (eg. rotation direction). In a WiSuMP channel system it is the relative activity between the channels that holds the information being coded. This is illustrated in Fig 8.6b which shows that the ratio of channels a and b has an essentially monotonic relationship with the parameter being coded over a restricted range. Anything that affects all the channels equally has no effect on this relationship. This robustness is a great advantage of a WiSuMP channel system whose output, integrating the activity of its component WiSuMP channels, remains invariant in the face of potentially confusing factors. A disadvantage of a WiSuMP channel system is that it can only encode a sin-

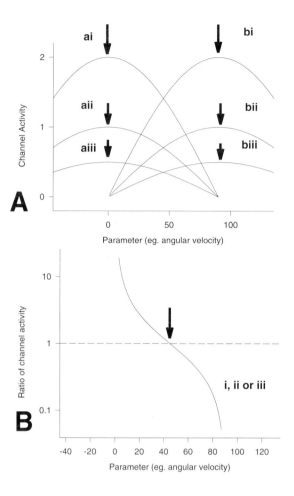

Fig. 8.6. This diagram illustrates how a within-sub-modality (WiSuMP) channel system works. Panel A shows the activities of two channels (a & b) during variations in two parameters. Variation in one parameter affects both channels equally. The responses with three values of this parameter are shown, generating curves ai, aii and aiii and bi, bii and biii. The other parameter affects the WiSuMP channels differently. Variations in this parameter are represented by the horizontal axis. The channels are tuned to the values shown by the arrows. Panel B shows the ratio of channels a and b as a function of the second parameter to which they are tuned. Variations in the first parameter has no effect on this curve.

gle value to the sub-modality in question. This is an acceptable restriction for many sub-modalities but, paradoxically, is not acceptable in the domain of spatial frequency analysis where the full frequency spectrum is required.

In the example of Fig 8.4a, the ratio of the activities of cells i, ii and iii encodes the orientation of the vector: but not its magnitude. Variations in the magnitude of the vector would affect all WiSuMP channels equally and is therefore information that is lost in the comparison. The process of coding the amplitude of the vector requires a whole additional set of WiSuMP channel, each tuned to particular values of that sub-modality. Such channels should be affected equally by changes in other sub-modalities such as direction.

8.3.4 Comparison between SuMP and WiSuMP channels

SuMP channels	*WiSuMP channels*
Each SuMP channel processes or channels information only about a specific sub-modality.	Each WiSuMP channel is affected by variation in many sub-modalities.
Its response it unambiguous	Each WiSuMP channel's response is ambiguous when taken alone.
Output is self-contained.	Output requires comparison with other WiSuMP channels.
Habituation or clinical loss of a SuMP channel affects or abolishes sensitivity to whole sub-modality but does not distort perception within sub-modality.	Habituation of a WiSuMP channel affects the BALANCE of all the WiSuMP channels involved in processing a particular sub-modality and results in perceptual distortions, for example, the tilt after effect (Carpenter & Blakemore, 1973; Howard, 1982).

The SuMP channel characteristics reflect the whole organism's response to this sub-modality.

Each WiSuMP channel has an optimal value and a bandwidth of the sub-modality to which it is tuned.   The tuned values are spread over the range of the sub-modality to which the organism responds.   The envelope of all the WiSuMP channels reflects the organism's performance.

Examples   of sub-modalities that are processed independently abound. The SuMP channel describes the whole system. A list of potential examples relevant to self motion is given in Fig 8.5. Low, medium and high frequencies of head rotation (Lisberger *et al.*, 1983) might also represent sub-modalities that can each function entirely independently.

An example of a WiSuMP channel would be a system that was tuned to a particular wavelength of light. It would also vary with other parameters.   Examples of sub-modalities that are coded by sets of overlapping WiSuMP channels like these include colour, spatial frequency and, proposed here, axis of head rotation.

SuMP channels are probably entirely theoretical constructs. They are descriptions of information processing.

WiSuMP channels represent a biologically feasible mechanism for carrying out independent sub-modality processing.

Each channel can represent the sub-modality with any degree of complexity or multiple values depending on the coding system it uses.

A WiSuMP channel system, since it works by comparison, can only provide a single value of the sub-modality in question.

8.3.5 *Revealing WiSuMP channels*

There are several methods for determining if a certain sub-modality is being coded by WiSuMP channels (see Regan, 1982; 1989). They include the following:

8.3.5.1 Revealing WiSuMP channels by variations in detection and discrimination thresholds

Detection thresholds for a particular sub-modality (eg. rotational velocity) might be lowest, the system might be most sensitive, at values corresponding to the peaks of the WiSuMP channels, indicated by the arrows in Fig 8.6a. This technique has been used successfully to hint at functional WiSuMP channels in the organization of self-movement coding (Harris & Lott, 1995; and see below section 8.4.1) and for colour (Cole *et al.*, 1993). Variations in discrimination thresholds should be best at the values midway between the peaks, where changes in the value are associated with the steepest change in relative activity (Fig 8.6b). Experiments are underway to detect such variations in self-motion discrimination thresholds.

8.3.5.2 Revealing channels by metamerism or matching

Metamers are things that are different but appear the same. Combinations of stimuli that cause a certain pattern of activity in the WiSuMP channels evoke the metamerical perception of a single stimulus that would, on its own, evoke that pattern. Historically matching colour mixes was the basis of postulating a three channel system in colour vision (see Boynton, 1979). In studying self motion however, it is difficult to mix, for example rotation around two axes or accelerations in two directions at once, since the stimuli combine externally to produce a single rotation or linear movement. But if physical rotation around one axis is combined with visual rotation around another axis, then this should stimulate patterns of hypothetical rotation channels normally associated with rotation about another axis. The eye movements evoked by such combinations suggest just such metamerism (Harris & Mente, 1995; and see below section 8.4.2).

8.3.5.3 Revealing channels by the effects of adaptation

Adaptation represents a classic tool for investigating a possible channel coding mechanism. This technique has been widely used in visual psychophysics to reveal WiSuMP channels for many sub-modalities (see Campbell & Tedeger, 1991). Channels that are most active during any particular stimulation will be most adapted or knocked out by the experience. Exposure to this stimulation thus alters the relative activity between affected and relatively unaffected channels that were not so active during the adaptation regime. The alteration in activity affects thresholds and supra-threshold processing of that sub-modality specifically in ways that can be predicted. Preliminary experiments have started in my laboratory using this technique to look at self-motion WiSuMP channels (unpublished observations). They are unique studies.

Unfortunately, the word 'adaptation' has been used even more ambiguously than the word 'channels'! In the above context adaptation refers to a simple, tiring out process due to one channel working harder than the others for some period of time. This is how the term adaptation is usually used in visual psychophysics. Adaptation can however refer to a goal-directed change in a system which can learn to adjust appropriately to changed circumstances. This is how the term is usually used in studying self-motion where the systems have been shown to be very flexible to learning demands (see Berthoz & Melvill-Jones, 1985). Adaptation of the goal-directed kind has suggested some independent sub-modality channels in the self motion system (Lisberger *et al.*, 1983) but has only once been used to explore WiSuMP channels (Harris & Mente, 1995).

8.4 Biological realization of within sub-modality processing (WiSuMP) channels for the direction-of-head-rotational-velocity SuMP channel

8.4.1 Data from Psychophysics

Thresholds for the detection of full-field visual motion of the pattern normally associated with self rotation, vary depending on the axis of rotation. This variation among axes is compatible with a within sub-modality (WiSuMP) channel system for encoding the orientation of the axis of visual full-field rotation (Harris & Lott, 1995).

To measure detection thresholds for full-field motion we used a pattern of random dots projected by a planetarium projector onto a 57 cm radius hemispherical screen (range: 0.04 deg/s to 74 deg/s; resolution: 0.02 deg/s). Velocity detection thresholds were measured under binocular viewing conditions for 29 axes of planetarium rotation. Subjects kept their chin in a chin rest and maintained fixation on an LED. During pattern presentation the LED was off but subjects were instructed to continue to stare where it had been. A two-alternative forced choice method was used (Wetherill & Levitt, 1965; Levitt, 1971). Each trial consisted of two 1 sec periods separated by 1 sec. The dot pattern moved during only one of the periods. Subjects indicated in which period they thought the movement occurred. The velocity of the movement was varied by a staircase procedure depending on whether the subjects were correct (Wetherill & Levitt, 1965). Detection threshold rotation velocities for full field movement around some of the tested axes are shown in Fig. 8.7.

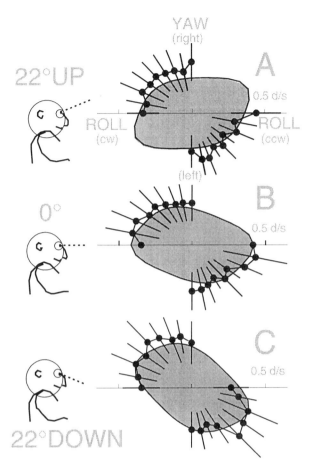

Fig. 8.7. Velocity thresholds for detection of full-field visual rotation as a function of eye position. Each data point represents the mean of three repetitions for each of the four subjects along with the standard deviations. In each graph the distance of each symbol (filled circle) from the centre represents the threshold rotation velocity. The direction of the data point from the centre represents the orientation of the axis of rotation. The directions of rotation have been separated using a left hand rule where the fingers of the left hand curl in the direction of rotation of the stimulus when the left thumb is aligned with the axis. All axes are defined with respect to the head. The data for panel B was obtained with the subjects looking straight ahead. The data shown in panels A and C were obtained with the subjects looking 22° up and down respectively. Also plotted in each of the panels is the output expected from a model having three channels for the detection of full-field rotation (shaded zones: see Harris & Lott, 1995). The model's outputs shown in panels A and C are simply that of B tilted up or down by 22°. (After Harris & Lott, 1995).

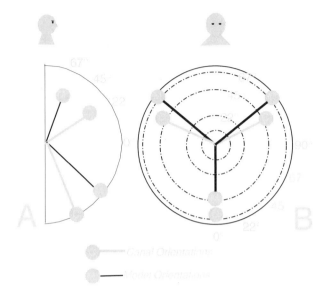

Fig. 8.8. The orientations of the best-fit model WiSuMP channels compared to the orientation of the semi-circular canals. The orientations are shown from the side (panel a) and from the front (panel b). The downward-directed canal vector corresponds to the orientation of the axis of rotation which maximally stimulates the horizontal canals. The others represent anterior/posterior canal pairs (Curthoys *et al.*, 1977). From Harris & Lott, 1995.

An important point is that these data cannot be explained in terms of the detection of local motion of features relative to each other (eg. McKee & Nakayama, 1984) or to the subject (Wright & Johnston, 1985). However the data could be well described using a model in which full-field rotation is detected by three WiSuMP channels (Quick, 1974; Cole *et al.*, 1993). Each hypothetical channel in this model is represented by a rotation vector which lies along the axis of rotation to which it is most sensitive. The channel's activity falls off as the cosine between this vector and the axis of rotation. Typical of WiSuMP channels, then, rotation about almost any axis would stimulate all these hypothetical channels. The best locations for the channel orientations are shown in Fig 8.8. The orientation of the semicircular canals is given for comparison. The model required that the visual full-field rotation channel that closely aligned with the horizontal canals orientation had a significantly higher threshold (lower sensitivity) than the other two (0.29 deg/s as opposed to 0.17 deg/s). The thresholds predicted by the three channel model are shown as shaded zones along with the actual data in Fig. 8.7 (shaded zones). The key features of the data are reproduced convincingly.

To narrow down the coordinates of these hypothetical channels, detection thresholds were determined with the eyes held either 22 up or 22 down (Fig. 8.7a and c) and the results compared with when the eyes were looking straight ahead (Fig 8.7b). If the channels were in head (or space) coordinates, they would not be affected by eccentric eye position and the distribution of thresholds in space would be unaffected. A comparison of Fig 8.7a, b and c shows that the pattern of thresholds in fact moves with the eyes, that is, it stays constant in retinal coordinates. The model prediction obtained when the eyes were looking straight ahead (shaded zone), continues to fit the data well, provided it too is rotated by the amount of the eye deviation. This suggests that the WiSuMP channels for encoding the sub-modality of head angular velocity use a retinal frame of reference.

The standard WiSuMP comparison system for extracting information (see 8.3.3 above) in which the ratio of activity between the channels is important, makes this sub-modality coding system for determining the axis of rotation independent from the consequences of translation. Comparing the output of three WiSuMP channels might form a convenient way to extract full-field rotation information in a visual stimulus that contains both rotational and translational components.

These data are by no means conclusive of a WiSuMP channel system, or even for it to be reasonable to consider the axis of head rotation as a separate sub-modality. However, this variation in detection thresholds is very suggestive of self-rotation being detected by such channels. It now remains to be demonstrated that knowledge of the orientation of the rotation axis is deduced from such channels.

If the axis of head rotation is a genuine, independently-processed sub-modality encoded by WiSuMP channels, what are the consequences for systems that refer to this code: that are driven by the output of the system? Eye movements that are reflexively generated in response to head rotation should show characteristics that reveal the signature of a WiSuMP system.

8.4.2 Data from Eye movements

In order to reveal some of the consequences of a channel representation of head rotation, the eye movements of cats were measured as the animals were exposed to rotation about two different axes of rotation at the same time: one rotation was entirely visual and the other entirely vestibular (Harris & Mente, 1995; Harris & Mente, 1996). Cats were chosen because of the insignificant contribution of smooth pursuit in this species (Evinger & Fuchs, 1978). WiSuMP channel processing for the axis of head rotation predicts that each channel is partially activated by each stimulus depending on the angle between the rotation axis and the orientation of the channel (see section 8.4.1 above).

The eye movements elicited in response to combinations of vestibular yaw and visual pitch stimuli were in an oblique direction (Fig. 8.9). This shows that stimulation of the two axes combined to evoke an eye movement: rotation around two axes separately evoked a response identical to the response that would be elicited by rotation (either visual or vestibular) about an oblique axis.

An oblique eye movement when the visual stimulus is entirely up and down (pitch) creates a retinal slip with pitch components due to the visual stimulus itself but also yaw components due the vestibularly-evoked eye movements around the yaw axis (Figs 8.9 and 8.10). The responses to different velocity combinations show that the pitch (vertical) component of the eye movement response for any one visual stimulus speed remains fairly constant despite a huge range in the concurrent yaw (horizontal) vestibular stimulation from 0 to 32 deg/sec and a concomitant huge change in the retinal slip (Fig. 8.11).

Conventional descriptions of visual-vestibular interactions take the reduction of retinal slip as their goal (eg. Robinson, 1977; Raphan & Cohen, 1985). But this is not the 'aim' of a channel-based system. For such a system the goal is to generate an internal representation of the ongoing head movement (using all information available) and produce eye movements that are compensatory for that movement. Normally of course the eye movements required for 'retinal slip reduction' are identical to those required to 'compensate for a head movement'. But with the two-axis stimuli used in this study, these goals do not necessarily correspond because the visual stimulus and the vestibular stimulus are not around the same axis. For example, in the graphs of Fig 8.10, the point of maximal retinal slip reduction is the point on the horizontal axis corresponding to the velocity of the visual stimulus (see key). But the data do not lie on routes between the vestibular alone conditions and this point of zero retinal slip.

8.4.3 Conclusions about the coding mechanism for head rotation

The idea of a small number of roughly orthogonal, spatially-tuned channels coding head rotation is naturally suggested by the anatomy of the semicircular canals (Graf, 1988). This is a misleading suggestion however because the division of head rotation information into three dimensions by the canals

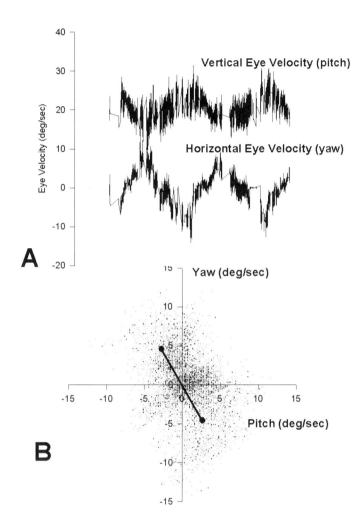

Fig. 8.9. The eye movements evoked by a combination of 32 deg/sec vestibular yaw stimulation and 16 deg/sec visual pitch. Panel A shows horizontal and vertical eye velocity, with the fast phases removed, as a function of time. The vertical eye velocity has been displayed for clarity. Panel B shows them as a function of each other. For panel B, the abscissa is the pitch axis, corresponding to the orientation of the axis of pitch rotation and the ordinate is the yaw axis. Each dot represents eye velocity at a given moment: the velocity is the distance from the origin and the orientation of a line from the dot to the origin represents the axis of eye rotation. Also shown in Panel B is the in-phase, best-fit sinusoid through the horizontal and vertical components. The peak velocities of this fit are shown as filled circles. In later plots (fig 8.10 and 8.11), these best-fit peak velocities are used to describe the whole eye movement response.

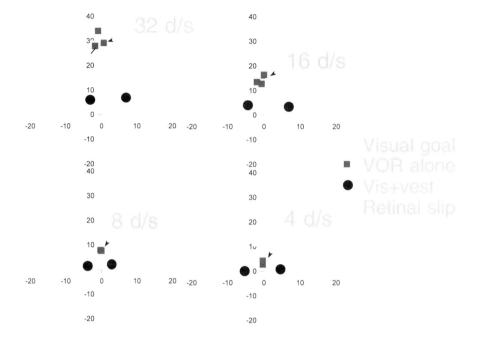

Fig. 8.10. Each panel shows the effect of combining one speed of vestibular yaw stimulation (32, 16, 8 or 4 deg/sec) with visual pitch stimulation at 32 deg/sec. The axes are as in Fig 9. The peak amplitude (distance from the origin) and direction (orientation of a line from the origin) of evoked eye movements for vestibular only (filled squares) and visual-vestibular combinations (filled circles) are shown. The open circles show the peak velocity of the sinusoidal visual stimulus. The dashed line joins the vestibular-only responses with the visual stimulus. The line represents the retinal slip to be nulled during the visual-vestibular stimulation. Clearly the data do not fall on this line.

represents a trivial code (see section 3 above and the Introductory Chapter). A profound code for representing head rotation might use the canals' information as one of its inputs but is in no way restricted to using that coordinate system or reference frame or only one sensory modality. Similarly, the profound code would take input from a visual representation of head rotation but would not be restricted by this input.

   Coding mechanisms suggested for visual motion are usually population based (Georgopolous *et al.*, 1986) with no particular directions being picked out (Heeger, 1987). But physiological evidence is accumulating which identifies visually-responsive cells that are broadly tuned in their spatial properties and that pass information compatible with rotation around certain restricted axes to converge with the vestibular system (Graf, 1988; Grasse

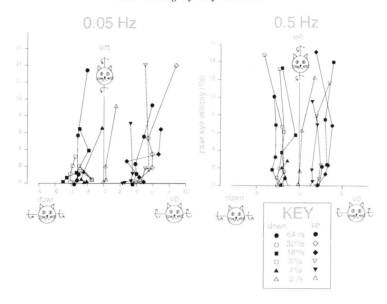

Fig. 8.11. The direction and peak velocity of eye movements evoked by in-phase sinusoidal combinations of visual pitch and vestibular yaw stimuli with various combinations of peak velocities. The axes are head space in degs/sec. The orientation of a line (not shown) joining each symbol to the origin of the graph is the axis of the eye rotation. The distance from the origin represents the peak velocity. The left side of diagram shows data obtained at 0.05 Hz, and the right side was obtained at 0.5 Hz. The key shows the peak velocities of the visual pitch stimuli. Stimuli in which the same visual pitch peak velocity was combined with a range of vestibular peak velocities are joined with solid lines. Starting from the top of each line, the vestibular yaw peak velocities are 32, 16, 8, 4 and 0 deg/sec respectively. The bottom point of each line corresponds to what is usually misleadingly described as 'vision alone' or 'optokinesis'. Notice that the data lines are predominantly straight and parallel to the ordinate axis of the graphs. This indicated that the pitch component of the eye movement response remains fairly constant despite a huge range in the concurrent vestibular stimulation around the yaw axis. These data are all from one animal. A second animal showed qualitatively similar effects.

& Cynader, 1991; Leonard *et al.*, 1988; Simpson *et al.*, 1988a; Simpson *et al.*, 1988b; Wylie & Frost, 1993; Wylie *et al.*, 1993). Such cells might represent the visual input to a neural basis for these proposed head rotation WiSuMP channels.

WiSuMP head rotation channels are illustrated in Fig 8.12. Each channel has a response depending on the sine of the angle between the stimulated axis and the channel. But neither the frame of reference nor the coordinate system are necessarily determined by either the visual or the vestibular input. Rotation about any axis activates all three channels with visual,

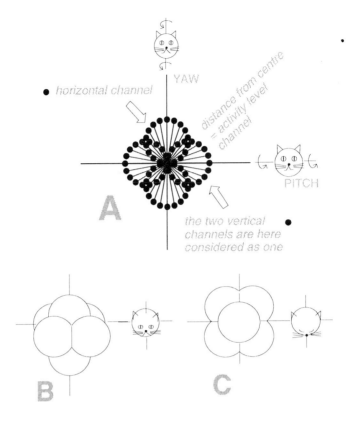

Fig. 8.12. A description of WiSuMP head movement coding channels. The distance from the centre is the response of each channel as the orientation of a fixed-magnitude head rotation varies. The fall-off has been represented as perfectly sinusoidal which results in a pair of circles for each channel. Opposite ends of the same axis represent motions in opposite directions of rotation and require neural representation of negative values. The channels do not have to be in the frame of reference of the head.

vestibular and possibly other information to create a pattern of activity that uniquely encodes the orientation and the magnitude of the rotation.

The suggestion that the reference frame for head rotation might be retinal rather than the head is intriguing in its implications and despite the practical issues of shifting the canal-coded vestibular afferent information, surprisingly intuitive. Once it is realized that the only movements of the outside world can be coded (section 2.1) and that a profound code of some kind has to be derived from the trivial codes of the vestibular afferent nerve (section 3) then an eye, rather than a head, based system becomes more appealing. There are precedents for shifting an apparently rock-solid, head-based coding system into the ephemeral and arbitrary world of retinal coordinates: the codes for localizing auditory targets can sometimes be in retinal coordinates (Jay & Sparks, 1984; Jay & Sparks, 1987).

8.4.4 Coding Mechanisms for other sub-modalities of the self motion system

Coding systems must be in place for all of the sub-modalities that are used biologically to describe self motion for whatever purposes (see Fig 8.5). This chapter has presented some evidence and some speculation about the coding of head rotation and has perhaps presumed more than it should that rotation velocity is of central importance. Linear motion represents a parallel set of problems, complicated slightly by the linear force of gravity. As for rotation, both visual and vestibular information are significantly involved functionally (Harris, 1994; Howard, 1982; Harris & Jenkin, 1996; Lathan *et al.*, 1995; Wall *et al.*, 1992) and biologically (Daunton & Thomsen, 1979; Fukushima & Fukushima, 1991; Xerri *et al.*, 1988). But, also as for rotation, we have almost no idea how linear-motion sub-modalities are coded in the brain.

Acknowledgements

LRH is supported by grants OGP 46271 and CPG 0181883 from the National Science and Research Council (NSERC) of Canada and the Institute of Space and Terrestrial and Science (ISTS) of Ontario. I would like to thank J. Douglas Crawford for comments on an earlier draft of this chapter.

9

A neurophysiological and computational approach to the functions of the temporal lobe cortical visual areas in invariant object recognition.

Edmund T. Rolls

Oxford University,
Department of Experimental Psychology,
South Parks Road, Oxford, OX1 3UD, England.

Mechanisms by which the brain could perform invariant recognition of objects including faces are addressed neurophysiologically, and then a computational model of how this could occur is described. Some neurons that respond primarily to faces are found in the macaque cortex in the anterior part of the superior temporal sulcus (in which region neurons are especially likely to be tuned to facial expression, and to face movement involved in gesture). They are also found more ventrally in the TE areas which form the inferior temporal gyrus. Here the neurons are more likely to have responses related to the identity of faces. These areas project on to the amygdala and orbitofrontal cortex, in which face-selective neurons are also found.

Quantitative studies of the responses of the neurons that respond differently to the faces of different individuals show that information about the identity of the individual is represented by the responses of a population of neurons, that is, ensemble encoding is used. The rather distributed encoding (within the class faces) about identity in these sensory cortical regions has the advantages of maximizing the information in the representation useful for discrimination between stimuli, generalization, and graceful degradation. In contrast, the more sparse representations in structures such as the hippocampus may be useful to maximize the number of different memories stored. There is evidence that the responses of some of these neurons are altered by experience so that new stimuli become incorporated in the network, in only a few seconds of experience with a new stimulus. It is shown that the representation that is built in temporal cortical areas shows considerable invariance for size, contrast, spatial frequency and translation. Thus the representation is in a form which is particularly useful for storage and as an output from the visual system. It is also shown that one of the representations which is built is view-invariant, which is suitable for recognition and as an input to associative memory. Another is viewer-centred, which is appropriate for conveying information about gesture. It is shown that these computational processes operate rapidly, in that in a backward masking paradigm, 20-40 ms of neuronal activity in a cortical area is sufficient to support face recognition.

In a clinical application of these findings, it is shown that humans with ventral frontal lobe damage have in some cases impairments in face and voice expression identification. These impairments are correlated with and may contribute to the problems some of these patients have in emotional and social behaviour.

To help provide an understanding of how the invariant recognition described could be performed by the brain, a neuronal network model of processing in the ventral visual system is described. The model uses a multistage feed-forward architecture, and is able to learn invariant representations of objects including faces by use of a Hebbian synaptic modification rule which incorporates a short memory trace (0.5 s) of preceding activity to enable the network to learn the properties of objects which are spatiotemporally invariant over this time scale.

9.1 Introduction

This paper draws together evidence on how information about visual stimuli is represented in the temporal cortical visual areas and the brain areas to which these are connected; on how these representations are formed; and on how learning about these representations occurs. The evidence comes from neurophysiological studies of single neuron activity in primates. It also comes from closely related theoretical studies which consider how the representations may be set up by learning, about the utility of the different representations found, and about how learning occurs in the brain regions which receive information from the temporal cortical visual areas. The recordings described are made mainly in non-human primates, firstly because the temporal lobe, in which this processing occurs, is much more developed than in non-primates, and secondly because the findings are relevant to understanding the effects of brain damage in patients, as will be shown. In this paper, particular attention will be paid to neural systems involved in processing information about faces, because with the large number of neurons devoted to this class of stimuli, this system has proved amenable to experimental analysis; because of the importance of face recognition and expression identification in the primate social behaviour; and because of the application of understanding this neural system to understanding the effects of damage to this system in humans on behaviour.

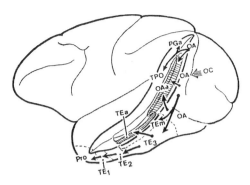

Fig. 9.1. Lateral view of the macaque brain (left) and coronal section (right) showing the different architectonic areas (e.g. TEm, TPO) in and bordering the anterior
part of the superior temporal sulcus (STS) of the macaque (see text). The coronal
section is through the temporal lobe 133 mm P (posterior) to the sphenoid reference
(shown on the lateral view). HIP - hippocampus; RS - rhinal sulcus.

9.2 Neuronal responses found in different temporal lobe cortex visual areas

Visual pathways project by a number of cortico-cortical stages from the
primary visual cortex until they reach the temporal lobe visual cortical areas
(Seltzer & Pandya, 1978; Maunsell & Newsome, 1987; Baizer et al., 1991) in
which some neurons which respond selectively to faces are found (Desimone
& Gross, 1979; Bruce et al., 1981; Desimone et al., 1984; Gross et al.,
1985; Rolls, 1981, 1984, 1991, 1992a, 1992c; Perrett, Rolls & Caan, 1982;
Desimone, 1991). The   inferior temporal visual cortex, area TE, is divided
on the basis of cytoarchitecture, myeloarchitecture, and afferent input into
areas TEa, TEm, TE3, TE2 and TE1. In addition there is a set of different
areas in the cortex in the superior temporal sulcus (Seltzer & Pandya, 1978;
Baylis et al., 1987) (see Fig. 9.1). Of these latter areas, TPO receives inputs
from temporal, parietal and occipital cortex; PGa and IPa from parietal and
temporal cortex; and TS and TAa primarily from auditory areas (Seltzer &
Pandya, 1978).

In order to investigate the information processing being performed by
these parts of the temporal lobe cortex, the activity of single neurons was
analyzed in each of these areas in a sample of more than 2600 neurons in
the rhesus macaque monkey during the presentation of simple and complex
visual stimuli such as sine wave gratings, three-dimensional objects, and
faces; and auditory and somatosensory stimuli (Baylis et al., 1987). Considerable specialization of function was found. For example, areas TPO,
PGa and IPa are multimodal, with neurons which respond to visual, audi-

tory and/or somatosensory inputs; the inferior temporal gyrus and adjacent areas (TE3,TE2,TE1,TEa and TEm) are primarily unimodal visual areas; areas in the cortex in the anterior and dorsal part of the superior temporal sulcus (e.g. TPO, IPa and IPg) have neurons specialized for the analysis of moving visual stimuli; and neurons responsive primarily to faces are found more frequently in areas TPO, TEa and TEm (Baylis *et al.*, 1987), where they comprise approximately 20% of the visual neurons responsive to stationary stimuli, in contrast to the other temporal cortical areas in which they comprise 4-10%. The stimuli which activate other cells in these TE regions include simple visual patterns such as gratings, and combinations of simple stimulus features (Gross *et al.*, 1985; Tanaka *et al.*, 1990)). Although face-selective neurons are thus found in the highest proportion in areas TPO within the superior temporal sulcus and TEa and TEm on the ventral lip of the sulcus, their extent is great in the anteroposterior direction (they are found in corresponding regions within the anterior half of the sulcus), and they are present in smaller proportions in many other temporal cortical areas (e.g. TE3, TE2 and TE1) (Baylis *et al.*, 1987). Due to the fact that face-selective neurons have a wide distribution, it might be expected that only large lesions, or lesions that interrupt outputs of these visual areas, would produce readily apparent face-processing deficits. Further, as described below, neurons with responses related to facial expression, movement, and gesture are more likely to be found in the cortex in the superior temporal sulcus, whereas neurons with activity related to facial identity are more likely to be found in the TE areas (see also Hasselmo, *et al.*, 1989a. These neurophysiological findings suggest that the appropriate tests for the effects of STS lesions will include tests of facial expression, movement, and gesture; whereas facial identity is more likely to be affected by TE lesions.

9.3 The selectivity of one population of neurons for faces

The neurons described in our studies as having responses selective for faces are selective in that they respond 2-20 times more (and statistically significantly more) to faces than to a wide range of gratings, simple geometrical stimuli, or complex 3-D objects (see Rolls, 1984; Baylis *et al.*, 1985, 1987; 1992a)†. The responses to faces are excitatory, sustained and are time-locked

† In fact, the majority of the neurons in the cortex in the superior temporal sulcus classified as showing responses selective for faces responded much more specifically than this. For half of these neurons, their response to the most effective face was more than five times as large as to the most effective non-face stimulus, and for 25% of these neurons, the ratio was greater than 10:1. The degree of selectivity shown by different neurons studied is illustrated in Fig. 6 of Rolls, 1992c and by Baylis, *et al.*, 1985, and the criteria for classification as face-selective are elaborated further by Rolls, 1992c.

to the stimulus presentation with a latency of between 80 and 160 ms. The cells are typically unresponsive to auditory or tactile stimuli and to the sight of arousing or aversive stimuli. The magnitude of the responses of the cells is relatively constant despite transformations such as rotation so that the face is inverted or horizontal, and alterations of colour, size, distance and contrast (see below). These findings indicate that explanations in terms of arousal, emotional or motor reactions, and simple visual feature sensitivity or receptive fields, are insufficient to account for the selective responses to faces and face features observed in this population of neurons (Perrett *et al.*, 1982; Baylis *et al.*, 1985; Rolls & Baylis, 1986). Observations consistent with these findings have been published by Desimone *et al.* (1984), who described a similar population of neurons located primarily in the cortex in the superior temporal sulcus which responded to faces but not to simpler stimuli such as edges and bars or to complex non-face stimuli (see also Gross *et al.*, 1985).

In a recent study, further evidence has been obtained that these neurons are tuned to provide information about which face has been seen, but not about which non-face has been seen (Rolls & Tovee, 1995b). In this study a wide range of different faces (23) and non-face images (45) of real-world scenes was used. This enabled the function of this brain region to be analyzed when it was processing natural scenes. The information available about which stimulus had been shown was measured quantitatively using information theory. This analysis showed that the responses of these neurons contained much more information about which (of 20) face stimuli had been seen (on average 0.4 bits) than about which (of 20) non-face stimuli had been seen (on average 0.07 bits). Multidimensional scaling to produce a stimulus space represented by this population of neurons showed that the different faces were well separated in the space created, whereas the different non-face stimuli were grouped together. The information analyses and multidimensional scaling thus provided evidence that what was made explicit in the responses of these neurons was information about which face had been seen. Information about which non-face stimulus had been seen was not made explicit in these neuronal responses. These procedures provide an objective and quantitative way to show what is "represented" by a particular population of neurons.

9.4 The selectivity of these neurons for whole faces or for parts of faces

Masking out or presenting parts of the face (e.g. eyes, mouth, or hair) in isolation reveal that different cells respond to different features or subsets of features. For some cells, responses to the normal organization of cut-out or line-drawn facial features are significantly larger than to images in which the same facial features are jumbled (Perrett *et al.*, 1982). These findings are consistent with the hypotheses developed below that by competitive self-organization some neurons in these regions respond to parts of faces by responding to combinations of simpler visual properties received from earlier stages of visual processing, and that other neurons respond to combinations of parts of faces and thus respond only to whole faces. Moreover, the finding that for some of these latter neurons the parts must be in the correct spatial configuration show that the combinations formed can reflect not just the features present, but also their spatial arrangement.

9.5 Ensemble encoding of face identity

An important question for understanding brain function is whether a particular object (or face) is represented in the brain by the firing of one or a few gnostic (or 'grandmother') cells (Barlow, 1972), or whether instead the firing of a group or ensemble of cells each with somewhat different responsiveness provides the representation. We have investigated whether the face-selective neurons encode information which could be used to distinguish between faces and, if so, whether gnostic or ensemble encoding is used. First, it has been shown that the representation of which particular object (face) is present is rather distributed. Baylis *et al.* (1985) showed this with the responses of temporal cortical neurons that typically responded to several members of a set of 5 faces, with each neuron having a different profile of responses to each face. At the same time, the neurons discriminated between the faces reliably, as shown by the values of d', taken in the case of the neurons to be the number of standard deviations of the neuronal responses which separated the response to the best face in the set from that to the least effective face in the set. The values of d' were typically in the range 1-3. A measure of the breadth of tuning (Smith & Travers, 1979) which takes the value 0 for a local representation and 1 if all the neurons are equally active for every stimulus, had values that were for the majority of neurons in the range 0.7-0.95.

In the most recent study, the responses of another set of temporal cortical neurons to 23 faces and 45 non-face natural images was measured, and again a distributed representation was found (Rolls & Tovee, 1995b). The tuning was typically graded. The measure used of the tuning of the neurons was one useful in analyzing the quantitative implications of sparse representation in neuronal networks, namely

$$a = (\sum_{s=1,S} r_s/S)^2 / \sum_{s=1,S} (r_s^2/S)$$

where r_s is the mean firing rate to stimulus s in the set of S stimuli. If the neurons were binary (either firing or not to a given stimulus), then a would be 0.5 if the neuron responded to 50% of the stimuli, and 0.1 if a neuron responded to 10% of the stimuli. It was found that the sparseness of the representation of the 68 stimuli by each neuron had an average across all neurons of 0.65. This indicates a rather distributed representation. It is of interest to note that if neurons had a continuum of responses equally distributed between zero and maximum rate, a would be 0.75; while if the probability of each response decreased linearly, to reach zero at the maximum rate, a would be 0.67; and if the probability distribution had an exponentially decreasing probability of high rates, a would be 0.5. If the spontaneous firing rate was subtracted from the firing rate of the neuron to each stimulus, so that the changes of firing rate, i.e. the *active responses* of the neurons, were used in the sparseness calculation, then the 'response sparseness' had a lower value, with a mean of 0.33 for the population of neurons, or 0.60 if calculated over the set of faces rather than over all the face and non-face stimuli. Thus the representation was rather distributed. It is, of course, important to remember the relative nature of sparseness measures, which (like the information measures to be discussed below) depend strongly on the stimulus set used. Nevertheless, the results obtained are clearly not those expected for a local (i.e. grandmother cell) representation, in which each neuron codes for one object.

Complementary evidence comes from applying information theory to analyze how information is represented by a population of these neurons. The information required to identify which of S equiprobable events occurred (or stimuli were shown) is $\log_2 S$ bits. (Thus 1 bit is required to specify which of two stimuli was shown, 2 bits to specify which of 4 stimuli was shown, 3 bits to specify which of 8 stimuli was shown, etc. The important point for the present purposes is that if the encoding was local, the number of stimuli encoded by a population of neurons would be expected to rise approximately linearly with the number of neurons in the population. In contrast, with distributed encoding, provided that the neuronal responses are sufficiently independent, and are sufficiently reliable (not too noisy), the number of stimuli encodable by the population of neurons might be expected to rise exponentially as the number of neurons in the sample of the population was increased. The information available about which of 20 equiprobable faces had been shown that was available from the responses of different numbers of these neurons is shown in Fig. 9.2. First, it is clear that some information is available from the responses of just one neuron - on average approximately 0.34 bits. Thus knowing the activity of just one neuron in the population does provide some evidence about which stimulus was present. This evidence that information is available in the responses of individual neurons in this way, without having to know the state of all the other neurons in the population, indicates that information is made explicit in the firing of individual neurons in a way that will allow neurally plausible decoding, involving computing a sum of input activities each weighted by synaptic strength, to work (see below). Second, it is clear (Fig. 9.2) that the information rises approximately linearly, and the number of stimuli encoded thus rises approximately exponentially, as the number of cells in the sample increases (Rolls *et al.*, 1996; Abbott *et al.*, 1996).

This direct neurophysiological evidence thus demonstrates that the encoding is distributed, and the responses are sufficiently independent and reliable, that the representational capacity increases exponentially. The consequence of this is that large numbers of stimuli, and fine discriminations between them, can be represented without having to measure the activity of an enormous number of neurons. Although the information rises approximately linearly with the number of neurons when this number is small, gradually each additional neuron does not contribute as much as the first (see Fig. 9.2). In the sample analyzed by Rolls *et al.*, 1996, the first neuron contributed 0.34 bits, on average, with 3.23 bits available from the 14 neurons analyzed. This reduction is however exactly what could be expected to derive from a simple ceiling effect, in which the ceiling is just the information in the stimulus set, or $\log_2 20 = 4.32$ bits, as shown in Fig. 9.2. This indicates that, on the one hand, each neuron does not contribute independently to the sum, and there is some overlap or redundancy in what is contributed by each neuron; and that, on the other hand, the degree of redundancy is not a property of the neuronal representation, but just a contingent feature dependent on the particular set of stimuli used in probing that representation. The data available is consistent with the hypothesis, explored by Abbott *et al.* (1996) through simulations, that if the ceiling provided by the limited number of stimuli that could be presented were at much higher levels, each neuron would continue to contribute as much as the first few, up to much larger neuronal populations, so that the number of stimuli that can be en-

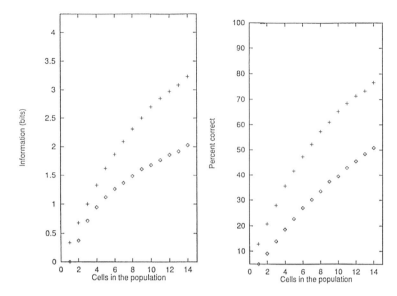

Fig. 9.2. (a) The values for the average information available in the responses of different numbers of these neurons on each trial, about which of a set of 20 face stimuli has been shown. The decoding method was Dot Product (DP, diamonds) or Probability Estimation (PE, crosses), and the effects obtained with cross validation procedures utilizing 50% of the trials as test trials are shown. The remainder of the trials in the cross-validation procedure were used as training trials. The full line indicates the amount of information expected from populations of increasing size, when assuming random correlations within the constraint given by the ceiling (the information in the stimulus set, I=4.32 bits). (b) The percent correct for the corresponding data to those shown in Fig. 9.4a. (From Rolls, Treves and Tovee, 1996).

coded still continues to increase exponentially even with larger numbers of neurons (Fig. 9.3; Abbott *et al.*, 1996). The redundancy observed could be characterized as flexible, in that it is the task that determines the degree to which large neuronal populations need to be sampled. If the task requires discriminations with very fine resolution between many different stimuli (i.e. in a high-dimensional space), then the responses of many neurons must be taken into account. If very simple discriminations are required (requiring little information), small subsets of neurons or even single neurons may be sufficient. The importance of this type of flexible redundancy in the representation is discussed below. The important point is that the information increases linearly with the number of cells used in the encoding, subject to a ceiling due to the fact that cells cannot add much more information as the ceiling imposed by the amount of information needed for the task is approached.

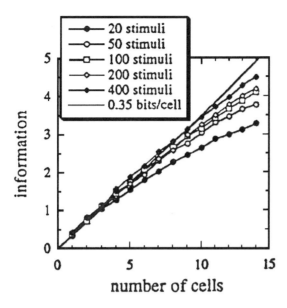

Fig. 9.3. The information available about which stimulus was seen when the responses of many neurons to many stimuli are simulated (from Abbott *et al.*, 1996). Reprinted with permission of Oxford University Press.

It may be noted that it is unlikely that there are further processing areas beyond those described where ensemble coding changes into grandmother cell (local) encoding. Anatomically, there does not appear to be a whole further set of visual processing areas present in the brain; and outputs from the temporal lobe visual areas such as those described, are taken to limbic and related regions such as the amygdala and via the entorhinal cortex the hippocampus. Indeed, tracing this pathway onwards, we have found a population of neurons with face-selective responses in the amygdala, and in the majority of these neurons, different responses occur to different faces, with ensemble (not local) coding still being present (Leonard *et al.*, 1985; Rolls, 1992b). The amygdala in turn projects to another structure which may be important in other behavioural responses to faces, the ventral striatum, and comparable neurons have also been found in the ventral striatum (Williams *et al.*, 1993).

9.6 Advantages of the distributed representation found of objects for brain processing

Three key types of evidence that the visual representation provided by neurons in the temporal cortical areas, and the olfactory and taste representations in the orbitofrontal cortex, are distributed have been provided, and reviewed above. One is that the coding is not sparse (Baylis *et al.*, 1985; Rolls & Tovee, 1995b). The second is that different neurons have different response profiles to a set of stimuli, and thus have at least partly independent responses (Baylis *et al.*, 1985; Rolls & Tovee, 1995b). The third is that the capacity of the representations rises exponentially with the number of neurons (Rolls *et al.*, 1996; Abbott *et al.*, 1996). The advantages of such distributed encoding are now considered, and apply to both fully distributed and to more sparse (but not to local) encoding schemes.

9.6.1 Exponentially High Coding Capacity

This property arises from a combination of the encoding being sufficiently close to independent by the different neurons (i.e. factorial), and sufficiently distributed. Part of the biological significance of such exponential encoding capacity is that a receiving neuron or neurons can obtain information about which one of a very large number of stimuli is present by receiving the activity of relatively small numbers of inputs from each of the neuronal populations from which it receives. For example, if neurons received in the order of 100 inputs from the population described here, they would have a great deal of information about which stimulus was in the environment. In particular, the characteristics of the actual visual cells described here indicate that the activity of 15 would be able to encode 192 face stimuli (at 50% accuracy), of 20 neurons 768 stimuli, of 25 neurons 3,072 stimuli, of 30 neurons 12,288 stimuli, and of 35 neurons 49,152 stimuli (Abbott *et al.*, 1996; the values are for the optimal decoding case). Given that most neurons receive a limited number of synaptic contacts, in the order of several thousand, this type of encoding is ideal. It would enable for example neurons in the amygdala and orbitofrontal cortex to form pattern associations of visual stimuli with reinforcers such as the taste of food when each neuron received a reasonable number, perhaps in the order of hundreds, of inputs from the visually responsive neurons in the temporal cortical visual areas which specify which visual stimulus or object is being seen (see Rolls, 1990, 1992a, 1992b, 1995). Such a representation would also be appropriate for interfacing to the hippocampus, to allow an episodic memory to be formed, that for example a particular visual object was seen in a particular place in the environment (Rolls, 1989b, 1989c, 1989a; Treves and Rolls, 1994). Here we should emphasize that although the sensory representation may have exponential encoding capacity, this does not mean that the associative networks that receive the information can store such large numbers of different patterns. Indeed, there are strict limitations on the number of memories that associative networks can store (Rolls & Treves, 1990; Treves & Rolls, 1991). The particular value of the exponential encoding capacity of sensory representations is that very fine discriminations can be made as there is much information in the representation, and that the representation can be decoded if the activity of even a limited number of neurons in the representation is known.

One of the underlying themes here is the neural representation of objects. How would one know that one has found a neuronal representation of objects in the brain? The criterion we suggest that arises from this research (Rolls, 1994) is that when one can identify the object or stimulus that is present (from a large set of stimuli, that might be thousands or more) with a realistic number of neurons, say in the order of 100, then one has a representation of the object. This criterion appears to imply exponential encoding, for only then could such a large number of stimuli be represented with a relatively small number of units, at least for units with the response characteristics of actual neurons. Equivalently, we can say that there is a representation of the object when the information required to specify which of many stimuli or objects is present can be decoded from the responses of a limited number of neurons.

The properties of the representation of faces, and of olfactory and taste stimuli, have been evident when the readout of the information was by measuring the firing rate of the neurons, typically over a 500 ms period. Thus, at least where objects are represented in the visual, olfactory, and taste systems (e.g. individual faces, odours, and tastes), information can be read out without taking into account any aspects of the possible temporal synchronization between neurons (Engel *et al.*, 1992), or temporal encoding within a spike train (Tovee *et al.*, 1993; Rolls *et al.*, 1996). Further, as shown in section 11, the information is available so rapidly in the responses of these neurons that temporal encoding is unlikely to be a fundamental aspect of neuronal spike trains in this part of the brain.

9.6.2 Ease With Which The Code Can Be Read By Receiving Neurons

For brain plausibility, it would also be a requirement that the decoding process should itself not demand more than neurons are likely to be able to perform. This is why when we have estimated the information from populations of neurons, we have used in addition to a probability estimating measure (PE, optimal, in the Bayesian sense), also a dot product measure, which is a way of specifying that all that is required of decoding neurons would be the property of adding up postsynaptic potentials produced through each synapse as a result of the activity of each incoming axon (Rolls *et al.*, 1996; Abbott *et al.*, 1996). It was found that with such a neurally plausible algorithm (the Dot Product, DP, algorithm), which calculates which average response vector the neuronal response vector on a single test trial was closest to by performing a normalized dot product (equivalent to measuring the angle between the test and the average vector), the same generic results were obtained, with only a 40% reduction of information compared to the more efficient (PE) algorithm. This is an indication that the brain could utilize the exponentially increasing capacity for encoding stimuli as the number of neurons in the population increases. For example, by using the representation provided by the neurons described here as the input to an associative or autoassociative memory, which computes effectively the dot product on each neuron between the input vector and the synaptic weight vector, most of the information available would in fact be extracted (see Rolls & Treves, 1990; Treves & Rolls, 1991).

9.6.3 Higher Resistance to Noise

This, like the next few properties, is in general an advantage of distributed over local representations, which applies to artificial systems as well, but is presumably of particular value in biological systems in which some of the elements have an intrinsic variability in their operation. Because the decoding of a distributed representation involves assessing the activity of a whole population of neurons, and computing a dot product or correlation, a distributed representation provides more resistance to variation in individual components than does a local encoding scheme.

9.6.4 Generalization

Generalization to similar stimuli is again a property that arises in neuronal networks if distributed but not if local encoding is used. The generalization arises as a result of the fact that a neuron can be thought of as computing the inner or dot product of the stimulus representation with its weight vector. If the weight vector leads to the neuron having a response to one visual stimulus, then the neuron will have a similar response to a similar visual stimulus. This computation of correlations between stimuli operates only with distributed representations. If an output is based on a single X,Y (input firing, synaptic weight) pair, then if the X or the Y is lost, the correlation drops to zero.

9.6.5 Completion

Completion occurs in associative memory networks by a similar process. Completion is the property of recall of the whole of a pattern in response to any part of the pattern. Completion arises because any part of the stimulus representation, or pattern, is effectively correlated with the whole pattern during memory storage. Completion is thus a property of distributed representations, and not of local representations. It arises for example in autoassociation (attractor) neuronal networks, which are characterized by recurrent connectivity. It is thought that such networks are important in the hippocampus in enabling incomplete recent episodic memories to be completed, and in the cerebral cortex, where the association fibres between nearby pyramidal cells may help the cells to retrieve a representation which depends on many neurons in the network (Treves & Rolls, 1994).

9.6.6 Graceful Degradation or Fault Tolerance

This also arises only if the input patterns have distributed representations, and not if they are local. Local encoding suffers sudden deterioration once the few neurons or synapses carrying the information about a particular stimulus are destroyed.

9.6.7 Speed of Readout of the Information

The information available in a distributed representation can be decoded by an analyzer more quickly than can the information from a local representation, given comparable firing rates. Within a fraction of an inter-spike interval, with a distributed representation, much information can be extracted (Treves, 1993; Treves *et al.*, 1996; Rolls *et al.*, 1996; Simmen *et al.*, 1995). In effect, spikes from many different neurons can contribute to calculating the angle between a neuronal population and a synaptic weight vector within an inter-spike interval. With local encoding, the speed of information readout depends on the exact model considered, but if the rate of firing needs to be taken into account, this will necessarily take time, because of the time needed for several spikes to accumulate in order to estimate the firing rate. It is likely with local encoding that the firing rate of a neuron would need to be measured to some degree of accuracy, for it seems implausible to suppose that a single spike from a single neuron would be sufficient to provide a noise-free representation for the next stage of processing.

9.7 Invariance in the neuronal representation of stimuli

One of the major problems which must be solved by a visual system is the building of a representation of visual information which allows recognition to occur relatively independently of size, contrast, spatial frequency, position on the retina, angle of view, etc. To investigate whether these neurons in the temporal lobe visual cortex are at a stage of processing where such invariance is being represented in the responses of neurons, the effect of such transforms of the visual image on the responses of the neurons was investigated.

To investigate whether the responses of these neurons show some of the perceptual properties of recognition including tolerance to isomorphic transforms (i.e. in which the shape is constant), the effects of alteration of the size and contrast of an effective face stimulus on the responses of these neurons were analyzed quantitatively in macaque monkeys (Rolls & Baylis, 1986). It was shown that the majority of these neurons had responses which were relatively invariant with respect to the size of the stimulus. The median size change tolerated with a response of greater than half the maximal response was 12 times. Also, the neurons typically responded to a face when the information in it had been reduced from 3D to a 2D representation in grey on a monitor, with a response which was on average 0.5 of that to a real face.†
Another transform over which recognition is relatively invariant is spatial frequency. For example, a face can be identified when it is blurred (when it contains only low spatial frequencies), and when it is high-pass spatial frequency filtered (when it looks like a line drawing). It has been shown that if the face images to which these neurons respond are low-pass filtered in the spatial frequency domain (so that they are blurred), then many of the neurons still respond when the images contain frequencies only up to

---

† This reduction in amplitude does not by itself mean that the point in multidimensional space represented by the ensemble of neurons has moved. The point represented by a facial identity ensemble will move only to the extent that the responses of neurons in the facial identity ensemble are affected differently by this transform. The original data are shown in Rolls & Baylis, 1986.

8 cycles per face. Similarly, the neurons still respond to high-pass filtered images (with only high spatial frequency edge information) when frequencies down to only 8 cycles per face are included (Rolls *et al.*, 1985). Face recognition shows similar invariance with respect to spatial frequency (see Rolls *et al.*, 1985). Further analysis of these neurons with narrow (octave) bandpass spatial frequency filtered face stimuli shows that the responses of these neurons to an unfiltered face can not be predicted from a linear combination of their responses to the narrow band stimuli (Rolls *et al.*, 1987). This lack of linearity of these neurons, and their responsiveness to a wide range of spatial frequencies, indicate that in at least this part of the primate visual system recognition does not occur using Fourier analysis of the spatial frequency components of images.

To investigate whether neurons in the inferior temporal visual cortex and cortex in the anterior part of the superior temporal sulcus operate with translation invariance in the awake behaving primate, their responses were measured during a visual fixation (blink) task in which stimuli could be placed in different parts of the receptive field (Tovee *et al.*, 1994). It was found that in most cases the responses of the neurons were little affected by which part of the face was fixated, and that the neurons responded (with a greater than half-maximal response) even when the monkey fixated 2-5 degrees beyond the edge of a face which subtended 8 - 17 degrees at the retina. Moreover, the stimulus selectivity between faces was maintained this far eccentric within the receptive field. These results held even across the visual midline. It was also shown that these neurons code for identity and not fixation position, in that there was approximately six times more information in the responses of these neurons about which face had been seen than about where the monkey fixated on the face. It is concluded that at least some of these neurons in the temporal lobe visual areas do have considerable translation invariance so that this is a computation which must be performed in the visual system. Ways in which the translation and size invariant representations shown to be present in the brain by these studies could be built are considered below in section 9.12. It is clearly important that translation invariance in the visual system is made explicit in the neuronal responses, for this simplifies greatly the output of the visual system to memory systems such as the hippocampus and amygdala, which can then remember, or form associations about, objects. The function of these memory systems would be almost impossible if there were no consistent output from the visual system about objects (including faces), for then the memory systems would need to learn about all possible sizes, positions etc of each object, and there would be no easy generalization from one size or position of an object to that object when seen with another retinal size or position.

Until now, research on translation invariance has considered the case in which there is only one object in the visual field. The question then arises of how the visual system operates in a cluttered environment. Do all objects that can activate an inferior temporal neuron do so whenever they are anywhere within the large receptive fields of inferior temporal neurons? If so, the output of the visual system might be confusing for structures which receive inputs from the temporal cortical visual areas. To investigate this we measured the responses of inferior temporal cortical neurons with face-selective responses of rhesus macaques performing a visual fixation task. We found that the response of neurons to an effective face centred 8.5 degrees from the fovea was decreased to 71% if an ineffective face stimulus for that cell was present at the fovea. If an ineffective stimulus for a cell is introduced parafoveally when an effective stimulus is being fixated, then there was a similar reduction in the responses of neurons. More concretely, the mean firing rate across all cells to a fixated effective face with a non-effective face in the periphery was 34 spikes/s. On the other hand, the average response to a fixated non-effective face with an effective face in the periphery was 22 spikes/s.† Thus these cells gave a reliable output about which stimulus is actually present at the fovea, in that their response was larger to a fixated effective face than to a fixated non-effective face, even when there are other parafoveal stimuli ineffective or effective for the cell (Rolls & Tovee, 1995a). Thus the cell provides information biased towards what is present at the fovea, and not equally about what is present anywhere in the visual field. This makes the interface to action simpler, in that what is at the fovea can be interpreted (e.g. by an associative memory) partly independently of the surroundings, and choices and actions can be directed if appropriate to what is at the fovea (cf. Ballard, 1993). These findings are a first step towards understanding how the visual system functions in a normal environment.

9.8 A view-independent representation of visual information

For recognizing and learning about objects (including faces), it is important that an output of the visual system should be not only translation and size invariant, but also relatively view invariant. In an investigation of whether there are such neurons, we found that some temporal cortical neurons re-

---

† These firing rates reflected the fact that in this population of neurons, the mean response for an effective face was 49 spikes/s with the face at the fovea, and 35 spikes/s with the face 8.5 degrees from the fovea.

liably responded differently to the faces of two different individuals independently of viewing angle (Hasselmo *et al.*, 1989b), although in most cases (16/18 neurons) the response was not perfectly view-independent. Mixed together in the same cortical regions there are neurons with view-dependent responses (e.g. Hasselmo *et al.*, 1989b). Such neurons might respond for example to a view of a profile of a monkey but not to a full-face view of the same monkey (Perrett *et al.*, 1985b). These findings, of view-dependent, partially view independent, and view independent representations in the same cortical regions are consistent with the hypothesis discussed below that view-independent representations are being built in these regions by associating together neurons that respond to different views of the same individual. These findings also provide evidence that the outputs of the visual system are likely to include representations of what is being seen, in a view independent way that would be useful for object recognition and for learning associations about objects; and in a view-based way that would be useful in social interactions to determine whether another individual is looking at one, and for selecting details of motor responses, for which the orientation of the object with respect to the viewer is required.

Further evidence that some neurons in the temporal cortical visual areas have object-based rather than view-based responses comes from a study of a population of neurons that responds to moving faces (Hasselmo *et al.*, 1989b). For example, four neurons responded vigorously to a head undergoing ventral flexion, irrespective of whether the view of the head was full face, of either profile, or even of the back of the head. These different views could only be specified as equivalent in object-based coordinates. Further, for all of the 10 neurons that were tested in this way, the movement specificity was maintained across inversion, responding for example to ventral flexion of the head irrespective of whether the head was upright or inverted. In this procedure, retinally encoded or viewer-centred movement vectors are reversed, but the object-based description remains the same. It was of interest that the neurons tested generalized across different heads performing the same movements.

Also consistent with object-based encoding is the finding of a small number of neurons which respond to images of faces of a given absolute size, irrespective of the retinal image size (Rolls & Baylis, 1986).

9.9 Different neural systems are specialized for recognition and for face expression decoding

To investigate whether there are neurons in the cortex in the anterior part of the superior temporal sulcus of the macaque monkey which could provide information about facial expression (Rolls, 1981, 1984, 1986a, 1986b, 1990), neurons were tested with facial stimuli which included examples of the same individual monkey with different facial expressions (Hasselmo *et al.*, 1989a). The responses of 45 neurons with responses selective for faces were measured to a set of 3 individual monkey faces with three expressions for each monkey, as well as to human expressions. Of these neurons, 15 showed response differences to different identities independently of expression, and 9 neurons showed responses which depended on expression but were independent of identity, as measured by a two-way ANOVA. Multidimensional scaling confirmed this result, by showing that for the first set of neurons the faces of different individuals but not expressions were well separated in the space, whereas for the second group of neurons, different expressions but not the faces of different individuals were well separated in the space. The neurons responsive to expression were found primarily in the cortex in the superior temporal sulcus, while the neurons responsive to identity were found in the inferior temporal gyrus. These results show that there are some neurons in this region the responses of which could be useful in providing information about facial expression, of potential use in social interactions (Rolls, 1981, 1984, 1986a, 1986b, 1990). Damage to this population may contribute to the deficits in social and emotional behaviour which are part of the Kluver-Bucy syndrome produced by temporal lobe damage in monkeys (see Rolls, 1981, 1984, 1986a, 1986b, 1990; Leonard *et al.*, 1985).

A further way in which some of these neurons may be involved in social interactions is that some of them respond to gestures, e.g. to a face undergoing ventral flexion, as described above and by Perrett *et al.* (1985a). The interpretation of these neurons as being useful for social interactions is that in some cases these neurons respond not only to ventral head flexion, but also to the eyes lowering and the eyelids closing (Hasselmo *et al.*, 1989b). Now these two movements (head lowering and eyelid lowering) often occur together when a monkey is breaking social contact with another, e.g. after a challenge, and the information being conveyed by such a neuron could thus reflect the presence of this social gesture. That the same neuron could respond to such different, but normally co-occurrent, visual inputs could be accounted for by the Hebbian competitive self-organization described below. It may also be noted that it is important when decoding facial expression not to move entirely into the object-based domain (in which the description would be in terms of the object itself, and would not contain information about the position and orientation of the object relative to the observer), but to retain some information about the head direction of the face stimulus being seen relative to the observer, for this is very important in determining whether a threat is being made in your direction. The presence of view-dependent representations in some of these cortical regions is consistent with this requirement. Indeed, it may be suggested that the cortex in the superior temporal sulcus, in which neurons are found with responses related to facial expression (Hasselmo *et al.*, 1989a), head and face movement involved in for example gesture (Hasselmo *et al.*, 1989b), and eye gaze (Perrett *et al.*, 1985b), may be more related to face expression decoding; whereas the TE areas (more ventral, mainly in the macaque inferior temporal gyrus), in which neurons tuned to face identity (Hasselmo *et al.*, 1989a) and with view-independent responses (Hasselmo *et al.*, 1989b) are more likely to be found, may be more related to an object-based representation of identity. Of course, for appropriate social and emotional responses, both types of subsystem would be important, for it is necessary to know both the direction of a social gesture, and the identity of the individual, in order to make the correct social or emotional response.

Outputs from the temporal cortical visual areas reach the amygdala and the orbitofrontal cortex, and evidence is accumulating that these brain areas are involved in social and emotional responses to faces (Rolls, 1990, 1992a, 1992b, 1992c, 1994). For example, lesions of the amygdala in monkeys disrupt social and emotional responses to faces, and we have identified a population of neurons with face-selective responses in the primate amygdala (Leonard *et al.*, 1985), some of which may respond to facial and body gesture (Brothers *et al.*, 1990). We (observations of E. T. Rolls and H. D. Critchley) and Wilson *et al.* 1993, have also found a small number of face-responsive neurons in the orbitofrontal cortex, and also in the ventral striatum, which receives projections from the amygdala and orbitofrontal cortex (Williams *et al.*, 1993).

We have applied this research to the study of humans with frontal lobe damage, to try to develop a better understanding of the social and emotional changes which may occur in these patients. Impairments in the identification of facial and vocal emotional expression were demonstrated in a group of patients with ventral frontal lobe damage who had behavioural problems such as disinhibited or socially inappropriate behaviour (Hornak *et al.*, 1995). A group of patients with lesions outside this brain region, without these behavioural problems, was unimpaired on the expression identification tests. The impairments shown by the frontal patients on these expression identification tests could occur independently of perceptual difficulties. Face expression identification was severely impaired in some patients whose recognition of the identity of faces was normal. Severe impairments on the vocal expression test (which consisted of non-verbal emotional sounds) were found in patients who produced excellent imitations of the sounds they could not identify, and whose identification of environmental sounds was also normal.

These findings suggest that some of the social and emotional problems associated with ventral frontal lobe or amygdala damage may be related to a difficulty in identifying correctly facial (and vocal) expression (Hornak *et al.*, 1995). The question then arises of what functions are performed by the orbitofrontal cortex and amygdala with the face-related outputs they receive from the temporal cortical visual areas. The hypothesis has been developed that these regions are important in emotional and social behaviour because of their role in reward-related learning (Rolls, 1986b, 1986a, 1990, 1995). The amygdala is especially involved in learning associations between visual stimuli and primary (unlearned) rewards and punishments such as food taste and touch, and the orbitofrontal cortex is especially involved in the rapid reversal (i.e. adjustment or relearning) of such stimulus reinforcement associations. According to this hypothesis, the importance of projecting face-related information to the amygdala and orbitofrontal cortex is so that they can learn associations between faces, using information about both face identity and facial expression, and rewards and punishments. Now it is particularly in primate social behaviour that rapid relearning about individuals, identified by their face, and depending on their facial expression, must occur very rapidly and flexibly, to keep up with the continually changing social exchanges between different individuals and groups of individuals. It is crucial to be able to remember recent reinforcement associations of different individuals, and to be able to continually adjust these. It is suggested that these factors have led to the very major development of the orbitofrontal cortex in primates, to receive appropriate inputs (about identity from faces, and about facial expression), and to provide a very rapid and flexible learning mechanism for the current reinforcement associations of these inputs. Consistent with this, the same patients that are impaired in face expression identification are also impaired on stimulus-reinforcement relearning tasks such as visual discrimination reversal and extinction (Rolls *et al.*, 1994a). Moreover, this learning impairment is highly correlated with the social and behavioural changes found in these patients (Rolls *et al.*, 1994a).

9.10 Learning of new representations in the temporal cortical visual areas

Given the fundamental importance of a computation which results in relatively finely tuned neurons which across ensembles but not individually specify objects including individual faces in the environment, we have investigated whether experience plays a role in determining the selectivity of single neurons which respond to faces. The hypothesis being tested was that visual experience might guide the formation of the responsiveness of neurons so that they provide an economical and ensemble-encoded representation of items actually present in the environment. To test this, we investigated whether the responses of temporal cortex face-selective neurons were at all altered by the presentation of new faces which the monkey had never seen before. It might be for example that the population would make small adjustments in the responsiveness of its individual neurons, so that neurons would acquire response tuning that would enable the population as a whole to discriminate between the faces actually seen. We thus investigated whether when a set of totally novel faces was introduced, the responses of these neurons were fixed and stable from the first presentation, or instead whether there was some adjustment of responsiveness over repeated presentations of the new faces. First, it was shown for each neuron tested that its responses were stable over 5-15 repetitions of a set of familiar faces. Then a set of new faces was shown in random order (with 1 s for each presentation), and the set was repeated with a new random order over many iterations. Some of the neurons studied in this way altered the relative degree to which they responded to the different members of the set of novel faces over the first few (1-2) presentations of the set (Rolls *et al.*, 1989). If in a different experiment a single novel face was introduced when the responses of a neuron to a set of familiar faces was being recorded, it was found that the responses to the set of familiar faces were not disrupted, while the responses to the novel face became stable within a few presentations. Thus there is now some evidence from these experiments that the response properties of neurons in the temporal lobe visual cortex are modified by experience, and that the modification is such that when novel faces are shown, the relative responses of individual neurons to the new faces alter. It is suggested that alteration of the tuning of individual neurons in this way results in a good discrimination over the population as a whole of the faces known to the monkey. This evidence is consistent with the categorization being performed by self-organizing competitive neuronal networks, as described below and elsewhere (Rolls, 1989a, b, c). ,).

Further evidence that these neurons can learn new representations very rapidly comes from an experiment in which binarized black and white images of faces which blended with the background were used. These did not activate face-selective neurons. Full grey-scale images of the same photographs were then shown for ten 0.5s presentations. It was found that in a number of cases, if the neuron happened to be responsive to that face, that when the binarized version of the same face was shown next, the neurons responded to it (Rolls *et al.*, 1993). This is a direct parallel to the same phenomenon which is observed psychophysically, and provides dramatic evidence that these neurons are influenced by only a very few seconds (in this case 5 s) of experience with a visual stimulus.

Such rapid learning of representations of new objects appears to be a major type of learning in which the temporal cortical areas are involved. Ways in which this learning could occur are considered below. It is also the case that there is a much shorter term form of memory in which some of these neurons are involved, for whether a particular visual stimulus (such as a face) has been seen recently, for some of these neurons respond differently to recently seen stimuli in short term visual memory tasks (Baylis & Rolls, 1987; Miller & Desimone, 1994), and neurons in a more ventral cortical area respond during the delay in a short term memory task (Miyashita, 1993).

9.11 The speed of processing in the temporal cortical visual areas

Given that there is a whole sequence of visual cortical processing stages including V1, V2, V4, and the posterior inferior temporal cortex to reach the anterior temporal cortical areas, and that the response latencies of neurons in V1 are about 40-50 ms, and in the anterior inferior temporal cortical areas approximately 80-100 ms, each stage may need to perform processing for only 15-30 ms before it has performed sufficient processing to start influencing the next stage. Consistent with this, response latencies between V1 and the inferior temporal cortex increase from stage to stage (Thorpe & Imbert, 1989). This seems to imply very fast computation by each cortical area, and therefore to place constraints on the type of processing performed in each area that is necessary for final object identification. We note that rapid identification of visual stimuli is important in social and many other situations, and that there must be strong selective pressure for rapid identification. For these reasons, we have investigated the speed of processing quantitatively, as follows.

In a first approach, we measured the information available in short temporal epochs of the responses of temporal cortical face-selective neurons about which face had been seen. We found that if a period of the firing rate of 50 ms was taken, then this contained 84.4% of the information available in a much longer period of 400 ms about which of four faces had been seen. If the epoch was as little as 20 ms, the information was 65% of that available from the firing rate in the 400 ms period (Tovee *et al.*, 1993). These high information yields were obtained with the short epochs taken near the start of the neuronal response, for example in the post-stimulus period 100-120 ms. Moreover, we were able to show that the firing rate in short periods taken near the start of the neuronal response was highly correlated with the firing rate taken over the whole response period, so that the information available was stable over the whole response period of the neurons (Tovee *et al.*, 1993). We were able to extend this finding to the case when a much larger stimulus set, of 20 faces, was used. Again, we found that the information available in short (e.g. 50 ms) epochs was a considerable proportion (e.g. 65%) of that available in a 400 ms long firing rate analysis period (Tovee & Rolls, 1995). These investigations thus showed that there was considerable information about which stimulus had been seen in short time epochs near the start of the response of temporal cortex neurons.

The next approach was to address the issue of for how long a cortical area must be active to mediate object recognition. This approach used a visual backward masking paradigm. In this paradigm there is a brief presentation of a test stimulus which is rapidly followed (within 1-100 ms) by the presentation of a second stimulus (the mask), which impairs or masks the perception of the test stimulus. This paradigm used psychophysically leaves unanswered for how long visual neurons actually fire under the masking condition at which the subject can just identify an object. Although there has been a great deal of psychophysical investigation with the visual masking paradigm (Turvey, 1973; Breitmeyer, 1980; Humphreys & Bruce, 1989), there is very little direct evidence on the effects of visual masking on neuronal activity. For example, it is possible that if a neuron is well tuned to one class of stimulus, such as faces, that a pattern mask which does not activate the neuron, will leave the cell firing for some time after the onset of the pattern mask. In order to obtain direct neurophysiological evidence on the effects of backward masking of neuronal activity, we analyzed the effects of backward masking with a pattern mask on the responses of single neurons to faces (Rolls & Tovee, 1994). This was performed to clarify both what happens with visual backward masking, and to show how long neurons may respond in a cortical area when perception and identification are just possible. When there was no mask the cell responded to a 16 ms presentation of the test stimulus for 200-300 ms, far longer than the presentation time. It is suggested that this reflects the operation of a short term memory system implemented in cortical circuitry, the importance of which in learning invariant representations is considered below in section 9.12. If the mask was a stimulus which did not stimulate the cell (either a non-face pattern mask consisting of black and white letters N and O, or a face which was a non-effective stimulus for that cell), then as the interval between the onset of the test stimulus and the onset of the mask stimulus (the stimulus onset asynchrony, SOA) was reduced, the length of time for which the cell fired in response to the test stimulus was reduced. This reflected an abrupt interruption of neuronal activity produced by the effective face stimulus. When the SOA was 20 ms, face-selective neurons in the inferior temporal cortex of macaques responded for a period of 20-30 ms before their firing was interrupted by the mask (Rolls & Tovee, 1994). We went on to show that under these conditions (a test-mask stimulus onset asynchrony of 20 ms), human observers looking at the same displays could just identify which of 6 faces was shown (Rolls *et al.*, 1994b).

These results provide evidence that a cortical area can perform the computation necessary for the recognition of a visual stimulus in 20-30 ms. This provides a fundamental constraint which must be accounted for in any theory of cortical computation. The results emphasize just how rapidly cortical circuitry can operate. This rapidity of operation has obvious adaptive value, and allows the rapid behavioural responses to the faces and face expressions of different individuals which are a feature of primate social and emotional behaviour. Moreover, although this speed of operation does seem fast for a network with recurrent connections (mediated by e.g. recurrent collateral or inhibitory interneurons), recent analyses of networks with analog membranes which integrate inputs, and with spontaneously active neurons, shows that such networks can settle very rapidly (Treves, 1993; Treves *et al.*, 1996).

9.12 Possible computational mechanisms in the visual cortex for object recognition

The neurophysiological findings described above, and wider considerations on the possible computational properties of the cerebral cortex (Rolls, 1989b, 1989c, 1992a, 1994), lead to the following outline working hypotheses on object recognition by visual cortical mechanisms. The principles underlying the processing of faces and other objects may be similar, but more neurons may become allocated to represent different aspects of faces because of the need to recognize the faces of many different individuals, that is to identify many individuals within the category faces.

Cortical visual processing for object recognition is considered to be organized as a set of hierarchically connected cortical regions consisting at least of V1, V2, V4, posterior inferior temporal cortex   (TEO), inferior temporal cortex (e.g. TE3, TEa and TEm), and anterior temporal cortical areas (e.g. TE2 and TE1)†. There is convergence from each small part of a region to the succeeding region (or layer in the hierarchy) in such a way that the receptive field sizes of neurons (e.g. 1 degree near the fovea in V1) become larger by a factor of approximately 2.5 with each succeeding stage (and the typical parafoveal receptive field sizes found would not be inconsistent with the calculated approximations of e.g. 8 degrees in V4, 20 degrees in TEO, and 50 degrees in inferior temporal cortex, Boussaoud *et al.*, 1991) (see Fig. 9.4). Such zones of convergence would overlap continuously with each other (see Fig. 9.4). This connectivity would be part of the architecture by which translation invariant representations are computed. Each layer is considered to act partly as a set of local self-organizing competitive neuronal networks with overlapping inputs‡. These competitive nets operate by a single set of forward inputs leading to (typically non-linear, e.g. sigmoid) activation of output neurons; of competition between the output neurons mediated by a set of feedback inhibitory interneurons which receive from many of the principal (in the cortex, pyramidal) cells in the net and project back (via inhibitory interneurons) to many of the principal cells which serves to decrease the firing rates of the less active neurons relative to the rates of the more active neurons; and then of synaptic modification by a modified Hebb rule, such that synapses to strongly activated output neurons from active input axons strengthen, and from inactive input axons weaken (see Rolls, 1989a).§ Such competitive networks operate to detect correlations between the activity of the input neurons, and to allocate output neurons to respond to each cluster of such correlated inputs. These networks thus act as categorizers. In relation to visual information processing, they would remove redundancy from the input representation, and would develop low entropy representations of the information (cf. Barlow, 1985; Barlow *et al.*, 1989). Such competitive nets are biologically plausible, in that

---

† This stream of processing has many connections with a set of cortical areas in the anterior part of the superior temporal sulcus, including area TPO.

‡ The region within which competition would be implemented would depend on the spatial properties of inhibitory interneurons, and might operate over distances of 1-2 mm in the cortex.

§ A biologically plausible form of this learning rule that operates well in such networks is

$$\delta w_{ij} = k.f_i.(r'_j - w_{ij})$$

where k is a learning rate constant, r'_j is the jth input to the neuron, f_i is the output of the i'th neuron, w_{ij} is the jth weight on the ith neuron and f_i is a non-linear function of the output activation which mimics the operation of the NMDA receptors in learning (see Rolls, 1989a, 1989b,1989c).

they utilize Hebb-modifiable forward excitatory connections, with competitive inhibition mediated by cortical inhibitory neurons. The competitive scheme I suggest would not result in the formation of "winner-take-all" or "grandmother" cells, but would instead result in a small ensemble of active neurons representing each input (Rolls, 1989a, 1989b, 1989c). The scheme has the advantages that the output neurons learn better to distribute themselves between the input patterns (cf. Bennett, 1990), and that the sparse representations formed (which provide "coarse coding") have utility in maximizing the number of memories that can be stored when, towards the end of the visual system, the visual representation of objects is interfaced to associative memory (Rolls, 1989b, 1989c; Rolls & Treves, 1990). In that each neuron has graded responses centred about an optimal input, the proposal has some of the advantages with respect to hypersurface reconstruction described by Poggio and Girosi (1990a). However the system I propose learns differently in that instead of using perhaps non biologically-plausible algorithms to locate the centres of the receptive fields of the neurons optimally, the neurons use graded competition to spread themselves throughout the input space, depending on the statistics of the inputs received, and perhaps with some guidance from back projections (see below). The finite width of the response region of each neuron which tapers from a maximum at the centre is important for enabling the system to generalize smoothly from the examples with which it has learned (cf. Poggio & Girosi, 1990a, 1990b), to help the system to respond for example with the correct invariances as described below.

Translation invariance would be computed in such a system by utilizing competitive learning to detect regularities in inputs when real objects are translated in the physical world. The hypothesis is that because objects have continuous properties in space and time in the world, an object at one place on the retina might activate feature analyzers at the next stage of cortical processing, and when the object was translated to a nearby position, because this would occur in a short period (e.g. 0.5 s), the membrane of the postsynaptic neuron would still be in its "Hebb-modifiable" state (caused for example by calcium entry as a result of the voltage dependent activation of NMDA receptors), and the presynaptic afferents activated with the object in its new position would thus become strengthened on the still-activated postsynaptic neuron. It is suggested that the short temporal window (e.g. 0.5s) of Hebb-modifiability helps neurons to learn the statistics of objects moving in the physical world, and at the same time to form different representations of different feature combinations or objects, as these are physically discontinuous and present less regular correlations to the visual system. Foldiak

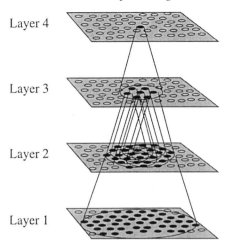

Layer 4

Layer 3

Layer 2

Layer 1

Fig. 9.4. Schematic diagram showing convergence achieved by the forward projections in the visual system, and the types of representation that may be built by competitive networks operating at each stage of the system from the primary visual cortex (V1) to the inferior temporal visual cortex (area TE) (see text). LGN - lateral geniculate nucleus. Area TEO forms the posterior inferior temporal cortex. The receptive fields in the inferior temporal visual cortex (e.g. in the TE areas) cross the vertical midline (not shown) (Boussaoud *et al.*, 1991).

(1991) has proposed computing an average activation of the postsynaptic neuron to assist with the same problem. One idea here is that the temporal properties of the biologically implemented learning mechanism are such that it is well suited to detecting the relevant continuities in the world of real objects. Another suggestion is that a memory trace for what has been seen in the last 300 ms appears to be implemented by a mechanism as simple as continued firing of inferior temporal neurons after the stimulus has disappeared, as was found in the masking experiments described above (see also Rolls & Tovee, 1994; Rolls *et al.*, 1994b). I also suggest that other invariances, for example size, spatial frequency, and rotation invariance, could be learned by a comparable process.† It is suggested that this process takes place at each stage of the multiple-layer cortical processing hierarchy, so that invariances are learned first over small regions of space, and then over successively larger regions. This limits the size of the connection space within which correlations must be sought.

Increasing complexity of representations could also be built in such a

† Early processing in V1 which enables different neurons to represent inputs at different spatial scales would allow combinations of the outputs of such neurons to be formed at later stages. Scale invariance would then result from detecting at a later stage which neurons are almost conjunctively active as the size of an object alters.

multiple layer hierarchy by similar mechanisms. At each stage or layer the self-organizing competitive nets would result in combinations of inputs becoming the effective stimuli for neurons. In order to avoid the combinatorial explosion, it is proposed, following Feldman (1985), that low-order combinations of inputs would be what is learned by each neuron†. Evidence consistent with this suggestion that neurons are responding to combinations of a few variables represented at the preceding stage of cortical processing is that some neurons in V2 and V4 respond to end-stopped lines, to tongues flanked by inhibitory subregions, or to combinations of colours (see references cited by Rolls, 1991); in posterior inferior temporal cortex to stimuli which may require two or more simple features to be present (Tanaka *et al.*, 1990); and in the temporal cortical face processing areas to images that require the presence of several features in a face (such as eyes, hair, and mouth) in order to respond (see above and Yamane *et al.*, 1988)‡. It is an important part of this suggestion that some local spatial information would be inherent in the features which were being combined. For example, cells might not respond to the combination of an edge and a small circle unless they were in the correct spatial relation to each other§. The local spatial information in the features being combined would ensure that the representation at the next level would contain some information about the (local) arrangement of features. Further low-order combinations of such neurons at the next stage would include sufficient local spatial information so that an arbitrary spatial arrangement of the same features would not activate the same neuron, and this is the proposed, and limited, solution which this mechanism would provide for the feature binding problem (cf. von der Malsburg, 1990). By this stage of processing a *view-dependent* representation of objects suitable for view-dependent processes such as behavioural responses to face expression and gesture would be available.

It is suggested that view-independent representations could be formed by the same type of computation, operating to combine a limited set of views of objects. The plausibility of providing view-independent recognition of objects by combining a set of different views of objects has been proposed by a number of investigators (Koenderink & van Doorn, 1979; Poggio & Edelman, 1990; Logothetis *et al.*, 1994). Consistent with the suggestion that the

---

† Each input would not be represented by activity in a single input axon, but instead by activity in a set of active input axons.

‡ Precursor cells to face-responsive neurons might, it is suggested, respond to combinations of the outputs of the neurons in V1 that are activated by faces, and might be found in areas such as V4.

§ This is in fact consistent with the data of Tanaka *et al.*, 1990, and with our data on face neurons, in that some faces neurons require the face features to be in the correct spatial configuration, and not jumbled, Rolls *et al.*, 1994b.

view-independent representations are formed by combining view-dependent representations in the primate visual system, is the fact that in the temporal cortical areas, neurons with view-independent representations of faces are present in the same cortical areas as neurons with view-dependent representations (from which the view-independent neurons could receive inputs) (Hasselmo *et al.*, 1989a; Perrett *et al.*, 1987). This solution to "object-based" representations is very different from that traditionally proposed for artificial vision systems, in which the coordinates in 3D-space of objects are stored in a database, and general-purpose algorithms operate on these to perform transforms such as translation, rotation, and scale change in 3D space (e.g. Marr, 1982). In the present, much more limited but more biologically plausible scheme, the representation would be suitable for recognition of an object, and for linking associative memories to objects, but would be less good for making actions in 3D-space to particular parts of, or inside, objects, as the 3D coordinates of each part of the object would not be explicitly available. It is therefore proposed that visual fixation is used to locate in foveal vision part of an object to which movements must be made, and that local disparity and other measurements of depth then provide sufficient information for the motor system to make actions relative to the small part of space in which a local, view-dependent, representation of depth would be provided (cf. Ballard, 1990).

The computational processes proposed above operate by an unsupervised learning mechanism, which utilizes regularities in the physical environment to enable representations with low entropy to be built. In some cases it may be advantageous to utilize some form of mild teaching input to the visual system, to enable it to learn for example that rather similar visual inputs have very different consequences in the world, so that different representations of them should be built. In other cases, it might be helpful to bring representations together, if they have identical consequences, in order to use storage capacity efficiently. It is proposed elsewhere (Rolls, 1989b, 1989c) that the back projections from each adjacent cortical region in the hierarchy (and from the amygdala and hippocampus to higher regions of the visual system) play such a role by providing guidance to the competitive networks suggested above to be important in each cortical area. This guidance, and also the capability for recall, are it is suggested implemented by Hebb-modifiable connections from the back-projecting neurons to the principal (pyramidal) neurons of the competitive networks in the preceding stages (Rolls, 1989b, 1989c).

The computational processes outlined above use coarse coding with relatively finely tuned neurons with a graded response region centred about an optimal response achieved when the input stimulus matches the synaptic weight vector on a neuron. The coarse coding and fine tuning would help to limit the combinatorial explosion, to keep the number of neurons within the biological range. The graded response region would be crucial in enabling the system to generalize correctly to solve for example the invariances. However, such a system would need many neurons, each with considerable learning capacity, to solve visual perception in this way. This is fully consistent with the large number of neurons in the visual system, and with the large number of, probably modifiable, synapses on each neuron (e.g. 5,000). Further, the fact that many neurons are tuned in different ways to faces is consistent with the fact that in such a computational system, many neurons would need to be sensitive (in different ways) to faces, in order to allow recognition of many individual faces when all share a number of common properties.

9.13 A computational model of invariant visual object recognition

To test and clarify the hypotheses just described about how the visual system may operate to learn invariant object recognition, we have performed a simulation which implements many of the ideas just described, and is consistent and based on much of the neurophysiology summarized above. The network simulated can perform object, including face, recognition in a biologically plausible way, and after training shows for example translation and view invariance (Wallis *et al.*, 1993).

In the four layer network, the successive layers correspond approximately to V2, V4, the posterior temporal cortex, and the anterior temporal cortex. The forward connections to a cell in one layer are derived from a topologically corresponding region of the preceding layer, using a Gaussian distribution of connection probabilities to determine the exact neurons in the preceding layer to which connections are made. This schema is constrained to preclude the repeated connection of any cells. Each cell receives 100 connections from the 32 x 32 cells of the preceding layer, with a 67% probability that a connection comes from within 4 cells of the distribution centre. Fig. 9.5 shows the general convergent network architecture used, and may be compared with Fig. 9.4. Within each layer, lateral inhibition between neurons has a radius of effect just greater than the radius of feedforward convergence just defined. The lateral inhibition is simulated via a linear local contrast enhancing filter active on each neuron. Note that this differs from the global 'winner-take-all' paradigm implemented by Foldiak

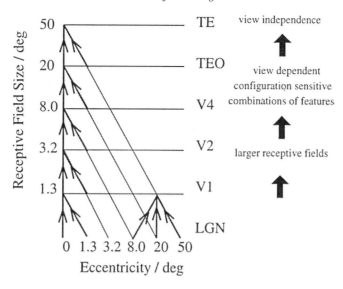

Fig. 9.5. Hierarchical network structure of VisNet

1991. The cell activation is then passed through a non-linear cell output activation function, which also produces contrast enhancement of the firing rates.

In order that the results of the simulation might be made particularly relevant to understanding processing in higher cortical visual areas, the inputs to layer 1 come from a separate input layer which provides an approximation to the encoding found in visual area 1 (V1) of the primate visual system. These response characteristics of neurons in the input layer are provided by a series of spatially tuned filters with image contrast sensitivities chosen to accord with the general tuning profiles observed in the simple cells of V1. Currently, only even-symmetric (bar detecting) filter shapes are used. The precise filter shapes were computed by weighting the difference of two Gaussians by a third orthogonal Gaussian (see Wallis *et al.*, 1993). Four filter spatial frequencies (in the range 0.0625 to 0.25 pixels^{-1} over four octaves), each with one of four orientations (0° to 135°) were implemented. Cells of layer 1 receive a topologically consistent, localized, random selection of the filter responses in the input layer, under the constraint that each cell samples every filter spatial frequency and receives a constant number of inputs.

The synaptic learning rule used can be summarized as follows:

$$\delta w_{ij} = k.m_i.r'_j$$

and

$$m_i' = (1 - \eta)f_i^{(t)} + \eta m_i^{(t-1)}$$

where r_j' is the jth input to the neuron, f_i is the output of the ith neuron, w_{ij} is the jth weight on the ith neuron, governs the relative influence of the trace and the new input (typically 0.4 - 0.6), and $m_i^{(t)}$ represents the value of the ith cell's memory trace at time t. In the simulation the neuronal learning was bounded by normalization of each cell's dendritic weight vector, as in standard competitive learning. An alternative, more biologically relevant implementation, using a local weight bounding operation, has in part been explored using a version of the Oja update rule (Oja, 1982; Kohonen, 1988). To train the network to produce a translation invariant representation, one stimulus was placed successively in a sequence of 7 positions across the input, then the next stimulus was placed successively in the same sequence of 7 positions across the input, and so on through the set of stimuli. The idea was to enable the network to learn whatever was common at each stage of the network about a stimulus shown in different positions. To train on view invariance, different views of the same object were shown in succession, then different views of the next object were shown in succession, and so on.

One test of the network used a set of three non-orthogonal stimuli, based upon probable 3-D edge cues (such as 'T, L and +' shapes). During training these stimuli were chosen in random sequence to be swept across the 'retina' of the network, a total of 1000 times. In order to assess the characteristics of the cells within the net, a two-way analysis of variance was performed on the set of responses of each cell, with one factor being the stimulus type and the other the position of the stimulus on the 'retina'. A high F ratio for stimulus type (F_s), and low F ratio for stimulus position (F_p) would imply that a cell had learned a position invariant representation of the stimuli. The discrimination factor of a particular cell was then simply the ratio F_s/F_p (a factor useful for ranking at least the most invariant cells). To assess the utility of the trace learning rule, nets trained with the trace rule were compared with nets trained with standard Hebbian learning without a trace, and with untrained nets (with the initial random weights). The results of the simulations, illustrated in Fig. 9.6, show that networks trained with the trace learning rule do have neurons with much higher values of the discrimination factor. An example of the responses of one such cell are illustrated in Fig. 9.7. Similar position invariant encoding has been demonstrated for a stimulus set consisting of 8 faces. View invariant coding has also been demonstrated for a set of 5 faces each shown in 4 views (Wallis *et al.*, 1993).

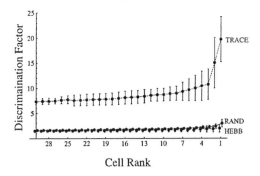

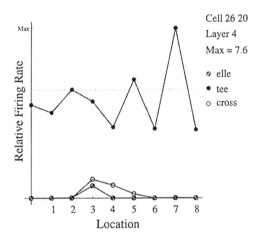

Fig. 9.6. Comparison of network discrimination when trained with the trace learning rule (TRACE), with a Hebb rule (HEBB), and when not trained (RAND) on three stimuli, +, T and L, at nine different locations.

Fig. 9.7. The responses of a layer 4 cell in the simulation shown in Fig. 9.6. The cell had a translation invariant response to stimulus 1.

In recent simulations, we have extended the analysis of VisNet to investigate whether it can still form invariant responses when there are many more locations over which it must show translation invariant representations of objects such as faces. In one such investigation, Rolls and Milward trained VisNet on 7 faces shown at each of 49 training locations. Each face is a 32 x 32 pixel image with 256 grey scale values. The image is presented in each of 49 locations in a 64 x 64 part of the retina during training. With a value of of 0.6 the trace effect remaining from a previous presentation of a stimulus decays to a small value after the stimulus image has been presented in 7 different retinal locations. Therefore we did not present the 49 locations for any one image during training in a standard serial sequence, but instead

Visnet (7 faces, 49 locations)

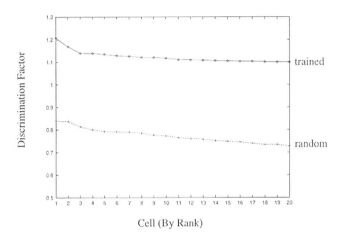

Fig. 9.8. The results of training VisNet on 7 faces at 49 locations. The discrimination factor for the 20 most translation invariant cells in layer 4 when VisNet was trained with the trace rule, or was untrained (random weights) as a control, are shown.

used a set of short-range movements across the retina, followed by a longer jump. The idea here is that during inspection of an object during learning, there is a set of small eye movements, followed by a longer saccade to another part of the object, which occurs several times. In detail, the sequence of presentations of any image consisted of 7 small movements to adjacent testing locations (which were arranged in a pattern which consisted of 7 rows of seven points in the 64 x 64 grid), followed by a random long jump to another training location to start on another set of small movements. Each of the 49 locations was visited once per training epoch for each image. 8000 such training trials were run. During testing, each face was presented at the 49 training locations, and the responses of the cells in layer 4 were measured to determine whether they showed responses which display selectivity for one of the faces but invariance with respect to where that face was shown.

The results of training VisNet on 7 faces at 49 locations are shown in Fig. 9.8. The discrimination factor for the 20 most translation invariant cells in layer 4 when VisNet was trained with the trace rule, or was untrained (random weights) as a control, are shown. Fig. 9.9 shows the results from the same simulation expressed as the amount of information in bits about which of the 7 faces had been shown (calculated across all 49 training

Visnet (7 faces, 49 locations)

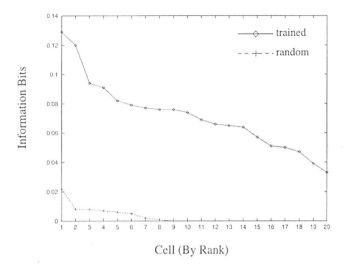

Cell (By Rank)

Fig. 9.9. The results from the same simulation as that shown in Fig. 9.8 expressed as the amount of information in bits about which of the 7 faces had been shown (calculated across all 49 training locations) represented by the 20 most selective cells. The results for VisNet trained with the trace rule, and left untrained as a control with random weights are shown separately.

locations) represented by the 20 most selective cells. The results are shown separately for VisNet trained with the trace rule, and left untrained as a control with random weights. These results show that this architecture can still perform reasonably at the very difficult task of learning translation invariant representations over 49 training locations of seven different complex images, faces. To enable it to learn, the eyes had effectively to jump to different parts of the object several times, so that the trace rule could make associations not just over short distances across the retina, but also (using its higher layers) across longer distances across the retina.

These results show that the proposed learning mechanism and neural architecture can produce cells with responses selective for stimulus type with considerable position or view invariance. The ability of the network to be trained with natural scenes may also help to advance our understanding of encoding in the visual system.

Acknowledgements

The author has worked on some of the investigations described here with

P. Azzopardi, G. C. Baylis, P. Foldiak, M. Hasselmo, C. M. Leonard, G. Littlewort, T. J. Milward, D. I. Perrett, M. J. Tovee, A. Treves and G. Wallis, and their collaboration is sincerely acknowledged. Different parts of the research described were supported by the Medical Research Council, PG8513790; by a Human Frontier Science Program grant; by an EC Human Capital and Mobility grant; by the MRC Oxford Interdisciplinary Research Centre in Brain and Behaviour; and by the Oxford McDonnell-Pew Centre in Cognitive Neuroscience.

10

Integrating qualitative and quantitative object representations in the recovery and tracking of 3-D shape

Sven J. Dickinson

Department of Computer Science and Rutgers Center for Cognitive Science (RuCCS)
Rutgers University, New Brunswick, NJ

Dimitri Metaxas

Department of Computer and Information Science
University of Pennsylvania
Philadelphia, PA

Data-driven models such as active contours in 2-D and deformable surfaces in 3-D have become prevalent in the computer vision community, particularly in the areas of shape tracking and shape recovery. They provide an important alternative to typical model-based recognition and tracking approaches that assume knowledge of the exact geometry of the object. Despite the power of these approaches, data-driven models often encode too little model information. As a consequence, active 3-D model recovery schemes often require manual segmentation or good model initialization, and active contour trackers have been able to track only an object's translation in the image. To overcome these problems requires bridging the representational gap between over-constrained geometric models and under-constrained active models. In previous work, we introduced a qualitative object representation integrating object-centred and viewer-centred models. In this paper, we first show how this representation provides the missing constraints on the recovery of quantitative 3-D deformable models from 2-D images. We then show how this same representation provides the missing constraints needed to qualitatively track an object's rotation in depth or to quantitatively track an object's pose.

10.1 Introduction

In the computer vision community, there exists a continuum of approaches to recovering two- and three-dimensional shape from two- and three-dimensional images. This continuum is bounded by two extremes. At one end lie the purely data-driven approaches to shape recovery, while at the other end lie

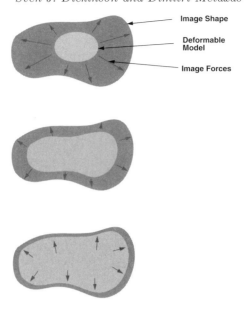

Fig. 10.1. Data-driven shape recovery

the purely model-driven approaches. Moreover, this continuum also applies to object tracking where, at one end, model-driven trackers assume knowledge of exact object geometry, while at the other end, data-driven trackers simply track the translation of an object's outline in the image. Although these purely data-driven and model-driven paradigms are extremely powerful, each of these two schools suffers from serious limitations. The solution, we believe, is a class of techniques for shape recovery and tracking whose underlying representations are intermediate between the two extremes.

The purely data-driven approaches to shape recovery are exemplified by the class of deformable or active model recovery techniques, in which a model contour (in 2-D) or surface (in 3-D) adapts itself to the image data under the influence of "forces" exerted by the image data (Kass *et al.*, 1988; Terzopoulos *et al.*, 1987; Terzopoulos *et al.*, 1988; Terzopoulos & Metaxas, 1991). As shown in Figure 10.1, points on the model are "pulled" towards corresponding (e.g., closest) data points in the image, with the integrity of the model often maintained by giving the model physical properties such as mass, stiffness, and damping. Having such flexible models is critical in an object recognition system, particularly when object models are more generic and do not specify exact geometry.

As powerful as these data-driven, deformable model recovery techniques are, they are not without their limitations. Their success relies on both the accuracy of initial image segmentation and initial placement of the model given the segmented data. For example, such techniques often assume that the bounding contour of a region belongs to the object, a problem when the object is occluded. Furthermore, focusing only on an object's silhouette assumes 3-D models with rotational symmetry, i.e., no surface discontinuities, e.g., (Terzopoulos & Metaxas, 1991). In addition, such techniques often require a manual segmentation of an object into parts to which models are fitted, e.g., (Terzopoulos *et al.*, 1987). If the models are not properly initialized, a canonical fit may not be possible, e.g., (Pentland & Sclaroff, 1991). These limitations are a consequence of using such unconstrained models.

At the other extreme lie the purely model-driven approaches to shape recovery, in which the exact geometry of the object is captured in a model, e.g., (Lowe, 1985; Huttenlocher & Ullman, 1990; Lamdan *et al.*, 1988; Thompson & Mundy, 1987). As shown in Figure 10.2, simple image features such as corners or changes in curvature are paired with similar features on a 3-D model to yield a set of hypothesized correspondences. In order to verify a given hypothesis, the model is transformed to bring the chosen model features into alignment with their corresponding image features. Because the correspondence is weak, other features belonging to the aligned model must be projected into the image and compared to other image features. If there is sufficient agreement between the two, the object is "recognized." In this case, shape recovery is essentially provided by the model in the form of a 2-D template extracted from a 3-D model.

For machine vision applications, where the number of object models is small and exact object geometry is known, this approach is highly effective, requiring the extraction of simple, robustly-recoverable image features and offering insensitivity to occlusion. However, for large databases, combinatorial complexity renders the search intractable. Furthermore, since the approach is dominated by the verification of local features, such as lines or corners, the approach is very sensitive to minor changes in the shapes of the objects. For example, if the dimensions or curvature of an object part changes, a new object model must be added.

In the tracking domain, a similar continuum exists. Purely data-driven approaches, as shown in Figure 10.3, track the silhouette of a blob in 2-D or surface of a blob in 3-D (e.g., Kass *et al.*, 1988; Curven *et al.*, 1991; Terzopolous & Szeliski, 1992). Although 2-D translation can be recovered and, in some cases, translation in depth (e.g., Cipolla & Blake, 1992), lack of any model information prevents the recovery of rotation in depth. At the other extreme, as shown in Figure 10.4, purely model-driven approaches can track an object's six degrees of freedom accurately, but require an exact

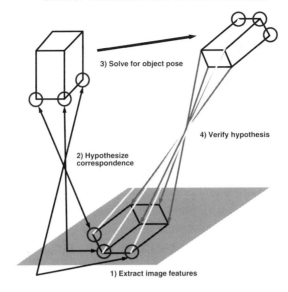

Fig. 10.2. Model-driven object recognition

specification of the object's geometry, and cannot support non-rigid object tracking, e.g., (Lowe, 1991; Gennery, 1990; Verghese *et al.*, 1990; Wu *et al.*, 1989).

In this paper, we describe both shape recovery and shape tracking paradigms that attempt to close the gap between under-constrained data-driven approaches and over-constrained model-driven approaches. The critical component of our approach is a parts-based object representation that combines both object-centred and viewer-centred models. In the following sections, we review the object representation, and show how its application to both shape recovery and tracking can overcome the limitations of the data-driven and model-driven techniques described above.

10.2 Bridging the representational gap

In this section, we first describe a representation which models an object's 3-D shape in terms of a set of qualitatively-defined volumetric parts. This representation, combining both object-centred and viewer-centred models, will not only form the backbone of our qualitative shape recovery and tracking paradigms, but will be used to govern our quantitative shape recovery and tracking paradigms. We therefore include in this section a description of our quantitative shape model.

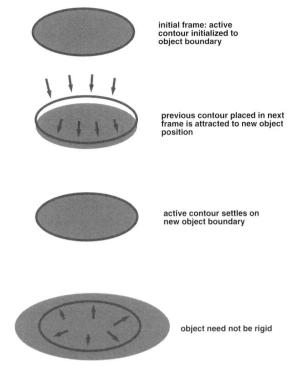

Fig. 10.3. Data-driven object tracking

10.2.1 Qualitative shape modelling

The hybrid representation we use to describe objects draws on two prevalent representation schools in the computer vision community. The first school is called object-centred modelling, whereby three-dimensional object descriptions are invariant to changes in their position and orientation with respect to the viewer. The second school is called viewer-centred modelling, whereby an object description consists of the set of all possible views of an object, often linked together to form an aspect graph. Object-centred models are compact, but their recognition from 2-D images requires making 3-D inferences from 2-D features. Viewer-centred models, on the other hand, reduce the recognition problem from three dimensions down to two, but incur the cost of having to store many different views for each object.

In order to meet the goals of qualitative object modelling and matching, we first model objects as object-centred constructions of qualitatively-defined volumetric parts chosen from some arbitrary, finite set (Dickinson *et al.*, 1990). The part classes are qualitative in the sense that they are invariant to degree of curvature, relative dimensions, degree of tapering, etc.

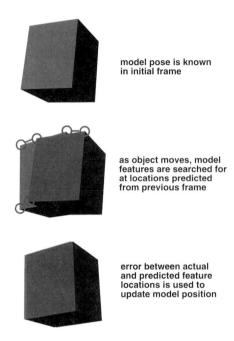

model pose is known
in initial frame

as object moves, model
features are searched for
at locations predicted
from previous frame

error between actual
and predicted feature
locations is used to
update model position

Fig. 10.4. Model-driven object tracking

Their choice was inspired by a set of volumetric shapes (called geons) proposed by the psychologist Biederman as a set of shapes which the human visual system could quickly recover from a 2-D image and which were rich enough to describe a large number of everyday objects (Biederman, 1985). Unlike Biederman however, we do not restrict our representation to geons; we borrow only the notion of a finite set of qualitatively-defined volumetric parts used to build objects.

It is at the volumetric part modelling level, that we invoke the concept of viewer-centred modelling. Traditional aspect graph representations of 3-D objects model an entire object with a set of aspects (or views), each defining a topologically distinct view of an object in terms of its visible surfaces (Koenderink & van Doorn, 1979). Our approach differs in that we use aspects to represent a (typically small) set of volumetric parts from which objects appearing in our image database are constructed, rather than representing the entire object directly. Consequently, our goal is to use aspects to recover the 3-D volumetric parts that make up the object in order to carry out a recognition-by-parts procedure, rather than attempting to use aspects to recognize entire objects. The advantage of this approach is that since the number of qualitatively different volumes is generally small, the number of possible aspects is limited and, more important, *independent* of the number of objects in the database. By having a sufficiently large set of volumetric part building blocks, and by assuming that objects appearing in the image database can be composed from this set, our training phase which computes the part views is independent of the contents of the image database.

The disadvantage of our hybrid representation is that if a volumetric part is occluded from a given 3-D viewpoint, its projected aspect in the image will also be occluded. We must therefore accommodate the matching of occluded aspects, which we accomplish by use of a hierarchical representation we call the *aspect hierarchy*. The aspect hierarchy consists of three levels, consisting of the set of *aspects* that model the chosen volumes, the set of component *faces* of the aspects, and the set of *boundary groups* representing all subsets of contours bounding the faces. The ambiguous mappings between the levels of the aspect hierarchy are captured in a set of upward and downward conditional probabilities, mapping boundary groups to faces, faces to aspects, and aspects to volumes (Dickinson, 1991). The probabilities are estimated from a frequency analysis of features viewed over a sampled viewing sphere centred on each of the volumetric classes.

To demonstrate our techniques for shape recovery, object recognition, and tracking, we have selected an object representation similar to that used by Biederman (1985), in which the Cartesian product of contrastive shape properties gives rise to a set of volumetric primitives called geons. For our investigation, we have chosen three properties including cross-section shape, axis shape, and cross-section size variation (Dickinson *et al.*, 1990). The values of these properties give rise to a set of ten primitives (a subset of Biederman's geons), modelled using Pentland's SuperSketch 3-D modelling tool (Pentland, 1986) and illustrated in Figure 10.5. Figure 10.6 illustrates a portion of the corresponding aspect hierarchy. To construct objects, the primitives are attached to one another with the restriction that any junction of two primitives involves exactly one distinct surface from each primitive.

10.2.2 *Quantitative shape modelling*

The qualitative object models described in the previous section will play a critical role in both the recovery of quantitative 3-D shape models from an image and the quantitative tracking of 3-D shape models in an image sequence. Geometrically, these quantitative shape models are closed surfaces in space whose intrinsic (material) coordinates are $u = (u, v)$, defined on a domain Ω (Terzopoulos & Metaxas, 1991; Dickinson & Metaxas, 1994). The

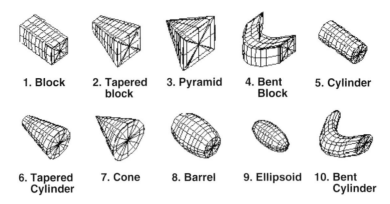

Fig. 10.5. The ten modelling primitives

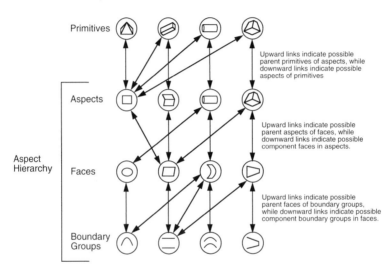

Fig. 10.6. The aspect hierarchy

positions of points on the model relative to an inertial frame of reference Φ in space are given by a vector-valued, time-varying function of u:

$$\mathbf{x}(\mathrm{u}, t) = (x_1(\mathrm{u}, t), x_2(\mathrm{u}, t), x_3(\mathrm{u}, t))^\top \qquad (10.1)$$

where $^\top$ is the transpose operator. We set up a noninertial, model-centred reference frame ϕ (Metaxas, 1992), and express these positions as:

$$\mathbf{x} = \mathbf{c} + \mathbf{R}\mathbf{p}, \qquad (10.2)$$

where $\mathbf{c}(t)$ is the origin of ϕ at the center of the model, and the orientation of ϕ is given by the rotation matrix $\mathbf{R}(t)$. Thus, $\mathbf{p}(\mathrm{u}, t)$ denotes the canonical

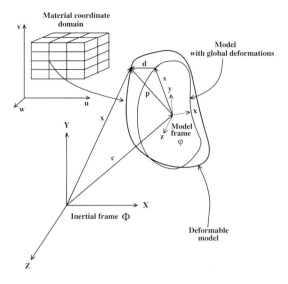

Fig. 10.7. Geometry of deformable models

positions of points on the model relative to the model frame. We further express $\mathbf{p}$ as the sum of a reference shape $\mathbf{s}(\mathrm{u}, t)$ (global deformation) and a displacement function $\mathbf{d}(\mathrm{u}, t)$ (local deformation):

$$\mathbf{p} = \mathbf{s} + \mathbf{d}. \tag{10.3}$$

We define the global reference shape as:

$$\mathbf{s} = \mathbf{T}(\mathbf{e}(\mathrm{u}; a_0, a_1, \ldots); b_0, b_1, \ldots). \tag{10.4}$$

Here, a geometric primitive $\mathbf{e}$, defined parametrically in u and parameterized by the variables a_i, is subjected to the *global deformation* $\mathbf{T}$ which depends on the parameters b_i. Although generally nonlinear, $\mathbf{e}$ and $\mathbf{T}$ are assumed to be differentiable (so that we may compute the Jacobian of $\mathbf{s}$) and $\mathbf{T}$ may be a composite sequence of primitive deformation functions $\mathbf{T}(\mathbf{e}) = \mathbf{T}_1(\mathbf{T}_2(\ldots \mathbf{T}_n(\mathbf{e})))$. We concatenate the global deformation parameters into the vector:

$$\mathbf{q}_s = (a_0, a_1, \ldots, b_0, b_1, \ldots)^\top. \tag{10.5}$$

Even though our technique for defining $\mathbf{T}$ is independent of the primitive $\mathbf{e} = (e_1, e_2, e_3)^\top$ to which it is applied, we will use superquadric ellipsoid primitives due to their suitability in vision applications.

We first consider the case of superquadric ellipsoids (Barr, 1981b), which are given by the following formula:

$$\mathbf{e} = a \begin{pmatrix} a_1 C_u^{\epsilon_1} C_v^{\epsilon_2} \\ a_2 C_u^{\epsilon_1} S_v^{\epsilon_2} \\ a_3 S_u^{\epsilon_1} \end{pmatrix}, \tag{10.6}$$

where $-\pi/2 \leq u \leq \pi/2$ and $-\pi \leq v < \pi$, and where $S_w^\epsilon = \mathrm{sgn}(\sin w)|\sin w|^\epsilon$ and $C_w^\epsilon = \mathrm{sgn}(\cos w)|\cos w|^\epsilon$, respectively. Here, $a \geq 0$ is a scale parameter, $0 \leq a_1, a_2, a_3 \leq 1$ are aspect ratio parameters, and $\epsilon_1, \epsilon_2 \geq 0$ are "squareness" parameters.

We then combine linear tapering along principal axes 1 and 2, and bending along principal axis 3 of the superquadric $\mathbf{e}$† into a single parameterized deformation $\mathbf{T}$, and express the reference shape as:

$$\mathbf{s} = \mathbf{T}(\mathbf{e}, t_1, t_2, b_1, b_2, b_3) = \begin{pmatrix} \left(\frac{t_1 e_3}{a a_3 w} + 1\right) e_1 + b_1 \, \cos\left(\frac{e_3 + b_2}{a a_3 w} \pi b_3\right) \\ \left(\frac{t_2 e_3}{a a_3 w} + 1\right) e_2 \\ e_3 \end{pmatrix}, \tag{10.7}$$

where $-1 \leq t_1, t_2 \leq 1$ are the tapering parameters in principal axes 1 and 2, respectively; b_1 defines the magnitude of the bending and can be positive or negative; $-1 \leq b_2 \leq 1$ defines the location on axis 3 where bending is applied; and $0 < b_3 \leq 1$ defines the region of influence of bending. Our method for incorporating global deformations is not restricted to only tapering and bending deformations. Any other deformation that can be expressed as a continuous parameterized function can be incorporated in our global deformation in a similar way.

We collect the parameters in $\mathbf{s}$ into the parameter vector:

$$\mathbf{q}_s = (a, a_1, a_2, a_3, \epsilon_1, \epsilon_2, t_1, t_2, b_1, b_2, b_3)^\top. \tag{10.8}$$

The above global deformation parameters are adequate for quantitatively describing the ten modelling primitives shown in Figure 10.5. In the following section, we describe how these global deformation parameters, describing a volume's quantitative shape, are recovered from an image. In cases where local deformations $\mathbf{d}$ are necessary to capture object shape details, we use the finite element theory and express the local deformations as:

$$\mathbf{d} = \mathbf{S}\mathbf{q}_d, \tag{10.9}$$

where $\mathbf{S}$ is the shape matrix whose entries are the finite element shape functions, and $\mathbf{q}_d$ are the model's nodal local displacements (Metaxas, 1992).

---

† These coincide with the model frame axes x, y and z respectively.

10.3 Recovering 3-D shape

Identifying or recognizing the object's class may require only that we recover the coarse shape of the object. However, if we need to recover a more accurate, quantitative shape description for subclass recognition or for grasping, then a qualitative description is insufficient. In the following two subsections, we first outline an approach to qualitative shape recovery using the aspect hierarchy (Dickinson *et al.*, 1992b; Dickinson *et al.*, 1992a; Dickinson *et al.*, 1994a). Next, we show how the recovered aspects, along with the recovered qualitative shape, can be used to constrain a physics-based deformable model recovery process that will yield the quantitative shapes of the object's parts (Dickinson & Metaxas, 1994; Dickinson *et al.*, 1994c).

10.3.1 Qualitative shape recovery

An analysis of the conditional probabilities in the aspect hierarchy (Dickinson *et al.*, 1992b; Dickinson *et al.*, 1994a) suggests that for 3-D modelling primitives which resemble the commonly used generalized cylinders, superquadrics, or geons, the most appropriate image features for recognition appear to be image regions, or faces. Moreover, the utility of a face description can be improved by grouping the faces into the more complex aspects, thus obtaining a less ambiguous mapping to the primitives and further constraining their orientation. Only when a face's shape is altered due to primitive occlusion or intersection should we descend to analysis at the contour or boundary group level. Our approach, therefore, first segments the input image into regions and then determines the possible face labels for each region. Next, we assign aspect labels to the faces, effectively grouping the faces into aspects. Finally, we map the aspects to primitives and extract primitive connectivity.

The first step in recovering a set of faces is a region segmentation of the input image. We begin by applying Saint-Marc, Chen, and Medioni's edge-preserving adaptive smoothing filter to the image (Saint-Marc *et al.*, 1991). Next, we apply a fast region segmentation algorithm due to Kristensen and Nielsen (Kristensen & Nielsen, 1992), resulting in a region label image. In this method, a queue-based technique is used to merge pixels which differ by less than a similarity threshold. The comparison is based on simple pooled statistics for the regions. Given scale information about the objects in the field of view, an additional threshold is used to reject small regions.

From the resulting 2-D region label image, we build a *region topology graph*, in which nodes represent regions and arcs specify region adjacencies. Each node (region) encodes the 2-D bounding contour of a region as well as a mask which specifies pixel membership in the region. From the region topology graph, each region is characterized according to the qualitative shapes of its bounding contours. The steps of partitioning the bounding contour and classifying the resulting contours are performed simultaneously using a minimal description length algorithm (Li, 1992). From a set of initial candidate contour breakpoints (derived from a polygonal approximation), the algorithm considers all possible groupings of the inter-breakpoint contours. The best partitioning is chosen as the grouping with the minimum description length based on how well lines and elliptical arcs can be fit to the segment groups in terms of the cost of coding the various segments. The result is a *region boundary graph* representation for a region, in which nodes represent bounding contours, and arcs represent relations between the contours, including cotermination, parallelism, and symmetry.†

Once we have established a description for each image region, the next step is to match that description against the faces in the aspect hierarchy using an interpretation tree search (Grimson & Lozano-Pérez, 1984). Descriptions that exactly match a face in the aspect hierarchy will be given a single label with probability 1.0. For region boundary graphs that do not match due to occlusion or segmentation errors, we descend to an analysis at the boundary group level and match subgraphs of the region boundary graph to the boundary groups in the aspect hierarchy. Each subgraph that matches a boundary group generates a set of possible face interpretations (labels), each with a corresponding probability defined by the non-zero conditional probabilities mapping boundary groups to faces in the aspect hierarchy. The result is a *face topology graph* in which each node contains a set of face labels (sorted by decreasing order of probability) associated with a given region.

10.3.1.1 *Unexpected object recognition*

In an unexpected object recognition domain, in which there is no a priori knowledge of scene content, each face in the face topology graph (recall that there may be many faces at each node) is used to infer a set of aspect hypotheses, using the non-zero conditional probabilities mapping faces to aspects in the aspect hierarchy. A search through the space of aspect hypotheses for a covering of the regions of the image is guided by a heuristic based on the conditional probabilities in the aspect hierarchy (Dickinson *et al.*, 1992a; Dickinson *et al.*, 1992b). During the search process, aspect verification, like face matching, is accomplished through the use of an interpretation tree search (Grimson & Lozano-Pérez, 1984). Once a set of aspects has been recovered, each aspect is used to infer one or more volume

---

† See Dickinson *et al.* (1992b) for a discussion on how parallelism and symmetry are computed.

hypotheses based on the non-zero conditional probabilities mapping aspects to volumes in the aspect hierarchy. This time, we search through the space of volume hypotheses until we find a set of volumes that is consistent with the objects in the database (Dickinson *et al.*, 1992a; Dickinson *et al.*, 1992b).

10.3.1.2 Expected object recognition

In an expected or top-down object recognition domain, in which we are searching for a particular object or part, we use the aspect hierarchy as an attention mechanism to focus the search for an aspect at appropriate regions in the image. This technique was applied to the top-down recognition of multipart objects in (Dickinson *et al.*, 1994c). Moving down the aspect hierarchy and guided by a Bayesian utility measure, target objects map to target volumes which, in turn, map to target aspect predictions which, in turn, map to target face predictions. Those faces in the face topology graph whose labels match the target face prediction provide an ordered (by decreasing probability) set of ranked search positions at which the target aspect prediction can be verified. If the mapping from a verified aspect to a target volume is ambiguous, this attention mechanism can be used to drive an active recognition system which moves the camera to obtain a less ambiguous view of the volume (Dickinson *et al.*, 1994c). Finally, it should be noted that for either top-down (expected) or bottom-up (unexpected) volume recovery, each recovered volume encodes the aspect in which it it viewed; the aspect, in turn, encodes the faces that were used in instantiating the aspect, while each face specifies those contours in the image used to instantiate the face.

10.3.1.3 Example

To illustrate our approach to qualitative shape recovery and recognition, consider the image of a table lamp, as shown in Figure 10.8; the results of the bottom-up (unexpected) qualitative shape recovery algorithm are shown in Figure 10.9. At the top, the image window contains the regions extracted from the image, along with the region (face) numbers. To the left is a window describing the recovered primitives (primitive covering). The mnemonics, PN, PL, and PP, refer to primitive number (simply an enumeration of the primitives in the covering), primitive label (see Figure 10.5), and primitive probability, respectively. The mnemonics AN, AL, AP, and AS refer to the aspect number (an enumeration), aspect label (see Dickinson *et al.*, 1992b), aspect probability, and aspect score (how well aspect was verified), respectively. The mnemonics FN, FL, FP, and PS refer to face number (in image window), face label (see Dickinson *et al.*, 1992b), face probability, and

Fig. 10.8. Image of a table lamp (256 x 256)

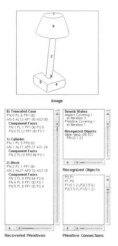

Fig. 10.9. Recovered qualitative primitives. Reprinted from *International Journal of Computer Vision*, Vol. 13, No. 3, Copyright (1994) with kind permission of Kluwer Academic Publishers.

corresponding primitive attachment surface (see Dickinson *et al.*, 1992b), respectively, for each component face of the aspect. The search window indicates the status of the aspect and primitive covering searches, along with the recognized object (table lamp) and a goodness of fit. There were seven objects in the database.

10.3.2 Quantitative shape recovery

In the previous section, we outlined a technique for recognizing a 3-D object from a single 2-D image. Although the technique segments the scene into a set of qualitatively-defined parts, no metric information is recovered for the parts nor is the 3-D position and orientation of the parts recovered. For problems such as subclass recognition, where finer shape distinctions are necessary, and grasping, where accurate localization is critical for grip-

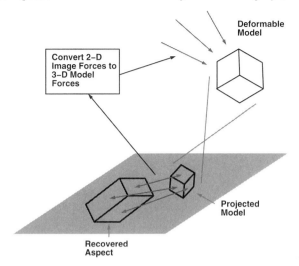

Fig. 10.10. Using qualitative shape to constrain physics-based deformable shape recovery

per placement, the above qualitative recognition strategy does not recover sufficient metric shape information.

In this section, we describe a technique whereby the recovered qualitative shape is used to constrain the physics-based recovery of a deformable quantitative model (described in Section 10.2.2) from the recovered image contours. As shown in Figure 10.10, distances between a recovered aspect and a projected model aspect are converted to 2-D image forces. These forces, in turn, are mapped to a set of generalized forces which deform the model and bring its projection into alignment with the recovered aspect. The technique: 1) ensures that only data used to infer object shape will exert forces on the model; 2) is not sensitive to model initialization; 3) is able to recover shapes with surface discontinuities; and 3) uses qualitative shape knowledge to constrain shape recovery. Details of the algorithm can be found in (Metaxas & Dickinson, 1993; Dickinson & Metaxas, 1994), while an extension of the technique to shape recovery from range data can be found in (Dickinson *et al.*, 1994c).

10.3.2.1 Simplified numerical simulation

When fitting the quantitative model to visual data, our goal is to recover $\mathbf{q} = (\mathbf{q}_c^\top, \mathbf{q}_\theta^\top, \mathbf{q}_s^\top, \mathbf{q}_d^\top)^\top$, the vector of degrees of freedom of the model. The components $\mathbf{q}_c$, $\mathbf{q}_\theta$, $\mathbf{q}_s$, and $\mathbf{q}_d$, are the translational, rotational, global deformation, and local deformation degrees of freedom, respectively.   Our approach carries out the coordinate fitting procedure in a physics-based way. We make our model dynamic in $\mathbf{q}$ by introducing mass, damping, and a deformation strain energy. This allows us, through the apparatus of Lagrangian dynamics, to arrive at a set of equations of motion governing the behaviour of our model under the action of externally applied forces.

The Lagrange equations of motion take the form (Terzopoulos & Metaxas, 1991):

$$\mathbf{M}\ddot{\mathbf{q}} + \mathbf{D}\dot{\mathbf{q}} + \mathbf{K}\mathbf{q} = \mathbf{g}_q + \mathbf{f}_q, \qquad (10.10)$$

where $\mathbf{M}$, $\mathbf{D}$, and $\mathbf{K}$ are the mass, damping, and stiffness matrices, respectively, where $\mathbf{g}_q$ are inertial (centrifugal and Coriolis) forces arising from the dynamic coupling between the local and global degrees of freedom, and where $\mathbf{f}_q(\mathbf{u}, t)$ are the generalized external forces associated with the degrees of freedom of the model. If it is necessary to estimate local deformations in (10.10), we tessellate the surface of the model into linear triangular elements.

For fast interactive response, we employ a first-order Euler method to integrate (10.10).† However, in fitting a model to static data, we simplify these equations by setting both $\mathbf{M}$ and $\mathbf{K}$ to zero, yielding a model which has no inertia and comes to rest as soon as all the applied forces vanish or equilibrate.

10.3.2.2 Applied forces

In the dynamic model fitting process, the data are transformed into an externally applied force distribution $\mathbf{f}(\mathbf{u}, t)$. We convert the external forces to generalized forces $\mathbf{f}_q$ which act on the generalized coordinates of the model (Terzopoulos & Metaxas, 1991). We apply forces to the model based on differences between the model's projected points and points on the recovered aspect's contours. Each of these forces is then converted to a generalized force $\mathbf{f}_q$ that, based on (10.10), modifies the appropriate generalized coordinate in the direction that brings the projected model closer to the data. The application of forces to the model proceeds in a face by face manner. Each recovered face in the aspect, in sequence, affects particular degrees of freedom of the model. In the case of occluded volumes, resulting in both occluded aspects and occluded faces, only those portions (boundary groups) of the regions used to infer the faces exert external global deformation forces on the model.

---

† In Section 10.4, we will see how Equation (10.10) is also used in object tracking.

10.3.2.3 Model initialization

One of the major limitations of previous deformable model fitting approaches is their dependence on model initialization and prior segmentation (Terzopoulos *et al.*, 1988; Terzopoulos & Metaxas, 1991; Pentland & Sclaroff, 1991). Using the qualitative shape recovery process as a front end, we first segment the data into parts, and for each part, we identify the relevant non-occluded data belonging to the part. In addition, the extracted qualitative volumes explicitly define a mapping between the image faces in their projected aspects and the 3-D surfaces on the quantitative models. Moreover, the extracted volumes can be used to immediately constrain many of the global deformation parameters. For example, from the qualitative shape classes, we know if a volume is bent, tapered, or has an elliptical cross-section.

Although the initial model can be specified at any position and orientation, the aspect that a volume encodes defines a qualitative orientation that can be exploited to speed up the model fitting process. Sensitivity of the fitting process to model initialization is also overcome by independently solving for the degrees of freedom of the model. By allowing each face in an aspect to exert forces on only one model degree of freedom at a time, we remove local minima from the fitting process and ensure correct convergence of the model.

10.3.2.4 Example

To illustrate the fitting stage, consider the contours belonging to the recovered lamp shade shown in Figure 10.9. Having determined during the qualitative shape recovery stage that we are trying to fit a deformable superquadric to a truncated cone, we can immediately fix some of the parameters in the model. In addition, the qualitative shape recovery stage provides us with a mapping between faces in the image and physical surfaces on the model. For example, we know that the elliptical face (FN 1, in Figure 10.9) maps to the top of the truncated cone, while the body face (FN 0) maps to the side of the truncated cone. For the case of the truncated cone, we will begin with a cylinder model (superquad) and will compute the forces that will deform the cylinder into the truncated cone appearing in the image. Assuming that the x and y dimensions are equal, we compute the following forces:

(i) The cylinder is initially oriented with its z axis orthogonal to the image plane. The first step involves computing the centroid of the elliptical image face (known to correspond to the top of the cylinder). The distance between the centroid and the projected center of the cylinder top is converted to a force which translates the model cylinder. Figure 10.11(a) shows the image contours corresponding to the lamp shade and the cylinder following application of this force. Figure 10.11(b) shows a different view of the image plane, providing a better view of the model cylinder.

(ii) The distance between the two image points corresponding to the extrema of the principal axis of the elliptical image face and two points that lie on a diameter of the top of the cylinder is converted to a force affecting the x and y dimensions with respect to the model cylinder. Figures 10.11(c) and 10.11(d) show the image and the cylinder following application of this force.

(iii) The distance between the projected model contour corresponding to the top of the cylinder and the elliptical image face corresponds to a force affecting the orientation of the cylinder. Figures 10.11(e) and 10.11(f) show the image and the cylinder following application of this force. This concludes the application of forces arising from the elliptical image face, i.e., top of the truncated cone.

(iv) Next, we focus on the image face corresponding to the body of the truncated cone to complete the fitting process. The distance between the points along the bottom rim of the body face and the projected bottom rim of the cylinder corresponds to a force affecting the length of the cylinder in the z direction. Figures 10.11(g) and 10.11(h) show the image and the cylinder following application of this force.

(v) Finally, the distance between points on the sides of the body face and the sides of the cylinder corresponds to a force which tapers the cylinder to complete the fit. Figures 10.11(i) and 10.11(j) show the image and the tapered cylinder following application of this force.

As shown in the above example, the recovered aspect plays a critical role in constraining the fitting process. In the next section we will examine two object trackers and show how the aspect also plays a critical role in object tracking.

10.4 Tracking 3-D shape

There are two ways in which an object can be tracked. If we have identified the object in the image from the qualitative shapes of its parts, we would like to be able to qualitatively track the object as it moves, for example, from "front" to "side" to "back" without knowing the exact geometry of

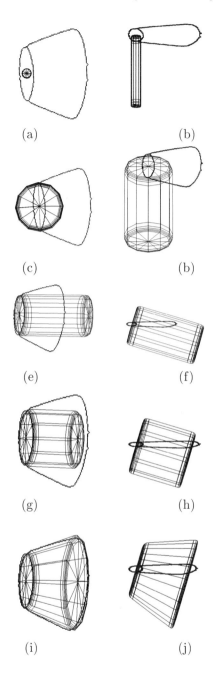

(a) (b)

(c) (b)

(e) (f)

(g) (h)

(i) (j)

Fig. 10.11. Quantitative shape recovery for lamp shade

the object. Alternatively, if we have used the recovered qualitative shape to recover the exact geometry of the object, then we would also like to be able to track the object's exact position and orientation, and possibly its shape if it is non-rigid. In the following subsections, we outline our approach to each of these problems.

10.4.1 A qualitative tracker

Our approach to qualitative object tracking, as shown in Figure 10.12, combines a symbolic tracker and an image tracker (Dickinson *et al.*, 1994b). Just as we used a qualitative shape model to govern a data-driven shape recovery process, we will use the same qualitative shape model to govern a data-driven shape tracking process.

10.4.1.1 Image tracker

The image tracker employs a representation called an adaptive adjacency graph, or AAG. The AAG is initially created from a recovered aspect, and consists of a network of active contours (snakes) (Kass *et al.*, 1988). In addition, the AAG encodes the topology of the network's regions, as defined by minimal cycles of contours. Contours in the AAG can deform subject to both internal and external (image) forces while retaining their connectivity at nodes. Connectivity of contours is achieved by imposing constraints (springs) between the contour endpoints. If an AAG detected in one image is placed on another image that is slightly out of registration, the AAG will will be "pulled" into alignment using local image gradient forces.

The basic behaviour of the AAG is to track image features while maintaining connectivity of the contours and preserving the topology of the graph. This behaviour is maintained as long as the positions of active contours in consecutive images do not fall outside the zones of influence of tracked image features. This, in turn, depends on the number of active contours, the density of features in the image, and the disparity between successive images. If either the tracked object or the camera moves between successive frames, the observed scene may change due to disappearance of one of the object faces. The shape of the region corresponding to the disappearing face will change and eventually the size of the region will be reduced to zero. The image tracker monitors the sizes and shapes of all regions in the AAG and detects such events. When such an event is detected, a signal describing the event is sent to the symbolic tracker.

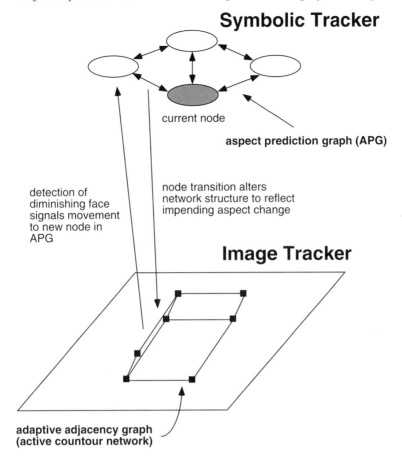

Fig. 10.12. Qualitative object tracking

10.4.1.2 Symbolic tracker

The symbolic tracker tracks movement from one node to another in a representation called the aspect prediction graph (Dickinson *et al.*, 1994a). Each of the nodes in this representation, derived from an aspect graph (Koenderink & van Doorn, 1979) and the aspect hierarchy, represents a topologically different viewpoint of the object, while arcs between nodes specify the visual events or changes in image topology between nodes. The role of the symbolic tracker is to:

(i) Determine which view or aspect of the object is currently visible (current node).

(ii) Respond to visual events detected by the image tracker by predicting which node (aspect) will appear next (target node).

(iii) From the visual event specification defined by the current and target nodes, add or delete structure from the active contour network (predictions).

(iv) If predicted aspects cannot be verified by the image tracker or visual event predictions cannot be recognized by the symbolic tracker, the symbolic tracker must be able to bootstrap the system to relocate itself in the aspect prediction graph.

10.4.1.3 Visual event recognition

The symbolic tracker specifies the criteria for which a visual event will be detected by the image tracker. Currently, we use region area as the single event criteria. If at any time during the image tracking of an aspect, one or more of its faces' areas falls below some threshold, we interpret that to mean that the face is undergoing heavy foreshortening and will soon disappear. When a region's area drops below the threshold, the image tracker sends a signal to the symbolic tracker. Given its current position (node) in the aspect prediction graph, the symbolic tracker compares the outgoing arcs, or visual events, with the events detected by the image tracker. The arc in the aspect prediction graph matching the observed visual event defines a transition to a new aspect.

The transition between the current aspect and the predicted aspect defines a set of visual events in terms of the faces in the aspect defined by the current APG node. If one or more faces disappear from the current aspect to the predicted aspect, the symbolic tracker directs the image tracker to delete those contours from the adaptive adjacency graph which both belong to the disappearing faces and are not shared by any remaining faces. Alternatively, if one or more new faces are expected to appear, the symbolic tracker directs the image tracker to add structure to the adaptive adjacency graph. Since the symbolic tracker knows along which existing contours new faces should appear, it can specify between which nodes in the adaptive adjacency graph new contours should be added.

10.4.1.4 Example

In Figure 10.13, we demonstrate our tracking technique on a sequence of images taken of a rotating block. Note that for the first frame, the AAG was created from the recovered aspect. For subsequent frames, a blurred, thresholded, gradient image is used to exert external forces on the AAG. Moving left to right, top to bottom, we can follow the AAG as it tracks the image faces. When the foreshortened face's area falls below a threshold, the visual event is signaled to the symbolic tracker. Consequently, the nodes and

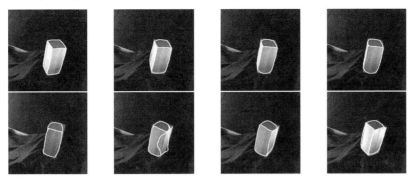

Fig. 10.13. Tracking a rotating block. There were 11 images in the sequence with 10 iterations of the AAG per image, for a total of 110 snapshots of the AAG. Working left to right and top to bottom, we show snapshots 1, 23, 32, 41, 70, 82, 90, and 110. Note that when the disappearing face is detected (70), the new face is predicted and contours are added (82). The added contours are automatically "pulled apart" to ensure that they do not converge to the same image edge; final position of the new edge is shown in frame 90.

contours belonging to the disappearing faces are removed while nodes and contours belonging to the face predicted to appear are added. Note that in order to ensure that new contours and old contours do not "lock on" to the same image gradient ridge, the contours are automatically "pulled apart", so that they will converge to the correct edges in the image. We are currently investigating the use of repulsion forces that would more effectively prevent network contours from converging.

10.4.2 Quantitative object tracking

Our approach to quantitative tracking (Chan *et al.*, 1994a; Chan *et al.*, 1994b) makes use of our frameworks for qualitative and quantitative shape recovery described in previous sections, as well as a physics-based framework for quantitative motion estimation (Metaxas & Terzopoulos, 1993). To be able to track multiple objects, initialization of the models is performed in the first frame of the sequence based on our quantitative shape recovery process. For successive frames, the qualitative shape recovery process can be avoided in favour of a physics-based model updating process requiring only a gradient computation in each frame, as shown in Figure 10.14. Assuming small deformations between frames, local forces derived from stereo images are sufficient to update the positions, orientations, and shapes of the models in 3-D; no costly feature extraction or correspondence is necessary.

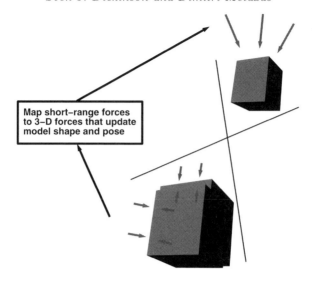

Fig. 10.14. Quantitative object tracking

10.4.2.1 Tracking and prediction

Kalman filtering techniques have been applied in the vision literature for the estimation of dynamic features (Deriche & Faugeras, 1990) and rigid motion parameters (Dickmanns & Graefe, 1988; Broida *et al.*, 1990) of objects from image sequences. We use a Kalman filter to estimate the object's shape and motion in a sequence of images. This allows us to predict where the object will appear in the image at some future time, thereby increasing the likelihood of the projected model falling within the local gradient field.

We incorporate a Kalman filter into our dynamic deformable model formulation by treating the model's Lagrangian equations of motion (10.10) as system models. Based on the use of the corresponding extended Kalman filter, we perform tracking by updating the model's generalized coordinates **q** according to the following equation:

$$\dot{\hat{\mathbf{u}}} = \mathbf{F}\hat{\mathbf{u}} + \mathbf{g} + \mathbf{P}\mathbf{H}^\top \mathbf{V}^{-1}(\mathbf{z} - \mathbf{h}(\hat{\mathbf{u}})), \qquad (10.11)$$

where $\mathbf{u} = (\dot{\mathbf{q}}^\top, \mathbf{q}^\top)^\top$ and matrices $\mathbf{F}, \mathbf{H}, \mathbf{g}, \mathbf{P}, \mathbf{V}$ are associated with the model dynamics, the error in the given data, and the measurement noise statistics (Metaxas & Terzopoulos, 1993). Since we are measuring local short range forces directly from the image potential, the term $\mathbf{z} - \mathbf{h}(\hat{\mathbf{u}})$ represents the 2-D image forces. Using the above Kalman filter, we can predict at every step the expected location of the data in the next image frame, based on the magnitude of the estimated parameter derivatives $\dot{\mathbf{q}}$.

10.4.2.2 Computing Forces on the Model

Only those nodes on the model surface that are visible should respond to image forces. A modal node is made active if: 1) it lies on the occluding contour of the model from that viewpoint (Terzopoulos *et al.*, 1988), or 2) the local surface curvature at the node is sufficiently large and the node is visible. Visibility of the nodes can be determined in two ways. Since we have a 3-D model, we can easily test the visibility of each node on the model, turning off those nodes that are self-occluded. A more elegant approach involves the symbolic tracker used in the qualitative tracker. By maintaining which aspect prediction graph node is visible, the symbolic tracker can activate only those nodes corresponding to visible faces. Determining which aspect is visible can be computed directly from knowledge of the model's exact pose. Alternatively, we can also pursue a data-driven approach to determining which aspect is visible. Analogous to our qualitative tracker, local image events can be used to detect a change in aspect with the aspect governing which nodes on the model are active (visible). In this case, a sudden vanishing of forces along a contiguous set of projected model nodes belonging to a face would signify an aspect change.

We must also deal with occlusion due to both known and unknown objects passing in front of the object being tracked. If the occluding object geometry and pose is known, then node visibility of the tracked object can be easily computed. Forces at occluded nodes can be simply turned off until they become visible again. For occlusion by an unknown (untracked) object, we can monitor changes in the image forces exerted on the tracked model's nodes. If the local forces at a particular node suddenly vanish or greatly increase, this erratic behaviour can be used to suggest local occlusion, resulting in deactivation of those nodes. The Kalman filter can still maintain the track based on prior motion as well as other active nodes until the object becomes disoccluded.

10.4.2.3 Examples

We demonstrate our approach in a series of tracking experiments involving real stereo image sequences. Figure 10.15(a) shows the first pair of stereo images. The initial pose and shape of both objects are recovered using a stereo extension of our quantitative shape recovery algorithm. The objects are subsequently tracked using only image gradient forces, shown as a set of blurred edges in the image. Figures 10.15(b-f) show snapshots of the two objects being tracked with the wire-frame models overlaid on the image potential. This example illustrates our ability to track an object when a known object partially occludes it. The nodes on either model which are

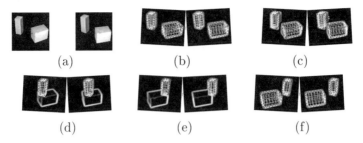

Fig. 10.15. Tracking two independently moving blocks in a sequence of stereo images: (a) stereo pair, (b) initialized models, (c) start of occlusion, (d) taller block partially occluded (occluding model not shown), (e) taller block becoming disoccluded (occluding model not shown), (f) end of occlusion. Note that only the active model nodes are marked, with occluded nodes at the bottom of the taller block unmarked. Reprinted from *International Journal of Computer Vision*, Vol. 13, No. 3, Copyright (1994) with kind permission of Kluwer Academic Publishers.

determined to be occluded (through either self-occlusion or occlusion by another known model) are deactivated until they become visible.

In the second experiment, we consider a sequence of stereo images (24 frames) of a scene containing multiple objects, including a two-part object. Figure 10.16 shows the initial stereo images of the multi-object scene. Figure 10.17(a) shows the initialized models using the same technique as before. Figure 10.17(b) shows the image potentials at an intermediate time frame where the aspects of some parts have changed and some parts have become partially occluded. Figures 10.17(c-f) show that each object is still successfully tracked under these circumstances with the individual part models overlaid on the image potentials.

10.5 Conclusions

We have shown how the representational gap between under-constrained data-driven shape recovery and over-constrained model-driven object recognition can be bridged using an intermediate representation. Our part-based probabilistic aspect hierarchy combines the advantages of object-centred and viewer-centred modelling, offering a unifying representation that: 1) encodes sufficient shape information to support part segmentation and generic object recognition based on coarse shape, 2) provides the missing constraints on physics-based deformable model recovery, allowing more accurate shape recovery *if needed*, 3) provides a control mechanism for an active contour network that can qualitatively track an object's translation *and* rotation in

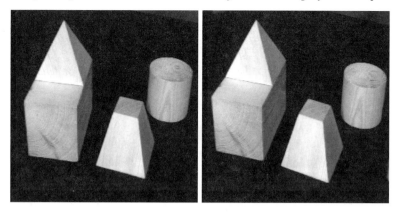

Fig. 10.16. Initial stereo images of the multi-object scene. Reprinted from *International Journal of Computer Vision*, Vol. 13, No. 3, Copyright (1994) with kind permission of Kluwer Academic Publishers.

depth, and 4) provides a control mechanism that can control node activation when quantitatively tracking an object's motion and shape.

The results reported here are still preliminary, with much work remaining. The techniques are still sensitive to region segmentation performance, and the objects used in the experiments are simplified. Our goal has been to explore a number of closely-related object recognition behaviours that must be addressed by an active agent in a dynamic environment. Our object representation has so far provided a common framework for novel algorithms for these and other behaviours (e.g., active object recognition Dickinson *et al.*, 1994a). We continue to refine these algorithms while at the same time attempting to work with more complex scenes containing more realistic objects.

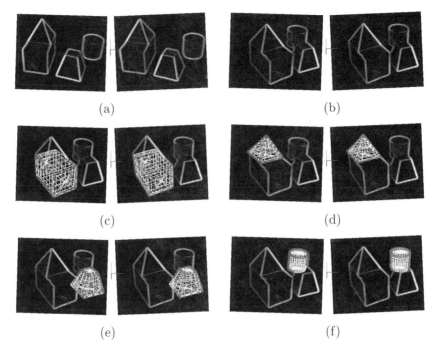

Fig. 10.17. Tracking multiple objects in a sequence of stereo images: (a) initialized models, (b) image potentials of an intermediate frame (both occlusions and visual events have occurred), (c-f) each object part correctly tracked with part models overlaid on the image potentials. Note that only the active model nodes are marked.

11

Coding of position and orientation

Dennis M. Levi

University of Houston
College of Optometry,
Texas 77204-6052

Human observers demonstrate an exquisite ability to judge whether a pair of target features is aligned. This ability, known as Vernier acuity has sometimes been referred to as a hyperacuity, because the thresholds, under ideal conditions, may be just a few seconds of arc, considerably smaller than the eyes blur function, or the size or spacing of foveal cones (Westheimer, 1975).

Although a good deal has been made about the high precision of position acuities (such as Vernier acuity), the elegant work of Geisler (1984; 1989) shows that an "ideal discriminator" limited only by the optics and photoreceptors of human observers can achieve hyperacuity thresholds. Furthermore both retinal ganglion cells (Shapley & Victor, 1986) and cortical neurons (Parker & Hawken, 1985) have the requisite sensitivity to signal changes in position of a few arc seconds. Recently, Morgan (1991) has argued based on radar theory, that some blur (either optical or neural) may actually be helpful rather than detrimental to hyperacuity, and indeed may be a necessary condition for precise position judgements. Thus, the question is not "why is Vernier acuity so good?", but what processes or structures limit performance, and how is precise position information coded in the human visual system?

11.1 Limits to position acuity

Geisler & Davila (1985) compared their photon based ideal discriminator with data of real humans on contrast discrimination, two dot resolution and two dot separation discrimination. For all three tasks the human observers had an efficiency of between 5 and 20% of the ideal. That is, humans needed to absorb about 5 to 20 times the number of photons than did the ideal observer. Since the ideal observer's predictions are about 3 times too small

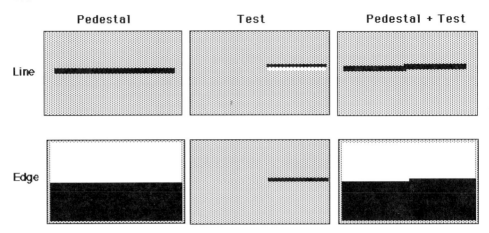

Fig. 11.1. Schematic illustration of stimuli for multipole Vernier acuity and detection. The pedestal and test stimuli are shown in the left and middle columns respectively. The right column shows the effect of adding the pedestal and test stimuli. The top row illustrates the classical line Vernier stimulus. The bottom row shows an edge Vernier target (two abutting horizontal contrast edges). The offset cue is shown in the middle column. For line Vernier, the offset cue is a dipole, i.e. a pair of opposite polarity lines, while the offset cue for edge Vernier acuity is a line (from Levi, *et al.*, 1994a). Copyright (1994), reprinted with kind permission of Elsevier Science Ltd., The Boulevard, Langford Lane, Kidlington, OX5 1GB, UK.

(square root of efficiency), this implies that the noise limiting performance comes mainly from sources other than photon statistics.

A long standing notion about the limits of hyperacuity, is that performance is limited by the ability of adjacent retinal cones to signal local contrast differences (Hartridge, 1923; Morgan & Aiba, 1985a; Morgan & Aiba, 1985b; Morgan, 1986). Morgan & Aiba calculated that the approximately 3 arc sec Vernier limit corresponds closely to the approximately 1/can be discriminated by human observers. More recently, Klein *et al.*, (1990) have shown that the Vernier acuity for abutting targets can be predicted using a simple test-pedestal approach. For example in edge Vernier the edge is the "pedestal", and the Vernier offset is equivalent to adding a "test" line to this pedestal (Fig. 11.1 lower panel). Similarly, for line Vernier, the line is the pedestal, and the Vernier offset is formally equivalent to a line with a dipole (a pair of adjacent opposite contrast lines) added (Fig. 11.1 upper panel). Klein *et al.* were able to show that for abutting Vernier targets, the Vernier threshold could be directly predicted on the basis of the detection threshold for the "test". Thus for abutting Vernier acuity in the normal fovea, the ultimate limit on performance seems to be the observer's "sensitivity" to the local contrast information. Interestingly in peripheral vision and in the

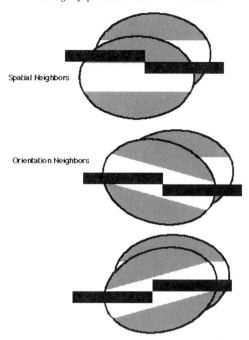

Fig. 11.2. Schematically illustrates two ways in which contrast sensitive filters might signal a Vernier offset. In the top panel, spatially neighbouring filters, oriented parallel to the target lines would be differentially sensitive to a vertical shift in the target position. In the lower panels, obliquely oriented filters (i.e., filters at neighbouring orientations to the target lines) would be differentially sensitive to a vertical shift in the target position.

central field of strabismic amblyopes, Vernier acuity appears to be limited by other factors (Levi *et al.*, 1994a), but that's another story!

11.2 Computational models for Vernier acuity

There are now a number of computational models which can account for the high precision of position acuity (e.g. Geisler, 1984, 1989; Klein & Levi, 1985; Watt & Morgan, 1985; Wilson, 1986), and a common feature of these models is their strong dependence on stimulus contrast. The most fully developed and tested of these models is that of Wilson (1986), which is based upon the responses of contrast sensitive spatial filters. Fig. 11.2 illustrates two different ways in which contrast sensitive filters might signal a Vernier offset. In the top panel, spatially neighbouring filters, oriented parallel to the target lines would be differentially sensitive to a vertical shift in the target position. In the lower panels, obliquely oriented filters (i.e., filters at neighbouring orientations to the target lines) would be differentially sensitive to a vertical shift in the target position. As might be expected based on a model of contrast sensitive spatial filters, abutting Vernier acuity depends strongly on the visibility of stimuli (Watt & Morgan, 1984; Morgan & Aiba, 1985b; Morgan & Regan, 1987; Morgan, 1991; Bradley & Skottun, 1987; Klein, Casson, & Carney, 1990; Wehrhahn & Westheimer, 1990; Banton & Levi, 1991; Waugh & Levi, 1993c and 1993b). For example, Fig. 11.3 shows that abutting Vernier acuity depends on (and indeed is almost inversely proportional to) the visibility of the target features, with little dependence on stimulus duration (the different symbol sizes represent different durations, Waugh & Levi, 1993c) or luminance (not shown, but see Waugh & Levi, 1993b).

11.3 Unmasking the mechanisms of Vernier acuity

One psychophysical method which has been useful in uncovering the mechanisms of spatial vision of human observers has been the paradigm of simultaneous masking (e.g., Gilinsky, 1967; Braddick *et al.*, 1978; Wilson *et al.*, 1983; Regan & Beverley, 1985). The basic concept is simple: if stimulus A and B interact in their psychophysical effects (e.g. stimulus B makes stimulus A more difficult to discern), while stimulus B and C do not interact in this way, then A and B must be some share some common process or structure, which is not shared by stimulus C. As described below, masking experiments have been quite helpful in uncovering the mechanisms of Vernier acuity.

Fig. 11.4 shows the orientation tuning revealed by masking an abutting line Vernier target with band-limited one-dimensional noise masks (solid symbols). The tuning curve is bimodal, showing distinct peaks at about 10 deg on either side of the line orientation. In contrast, the orientation tuning curve for line detection (open symbols) is unimodal, with peak masking corresponding to the line orientation. After accounting for effects of the masks on line visibility (Fig. 11.5 - for details see Waugh *et al.*, 1993), the resultant tuning function is very similar to the post-adaptation orientation thresholds reported by Regan & Beverley (1985). One clear implication of these results is that the mechanisms most sensitive to a Vernier offset are filters at neighbouring orientations to the mechanisms which detect the targets (Fig. 11.2 lower panels) rather than parallel filters at neighbouring spatial locations (Fig. 11.2 upper panel).

The bimodal orientation tuning of Vernier acuity is not a new result. Findlay (1973) reported similar tuning curves. In Findlay's study, observers

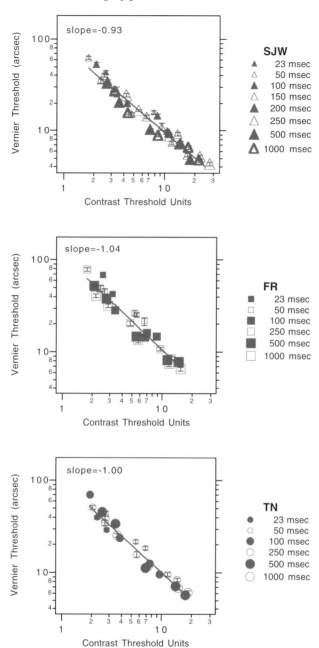

Fig. 11.3. Abutting Vernier acuity is plotted as a function of the visibility of the target features (in contrast detection threshold units). The different symbol sizes represent different durations. (from Waugh & Levi, 1993c). Note that thresholds depend on (and indeed are almost inversely proportional to) visibility. Copyright (1993), reprinted with kind permission of Elsevier Science Ltd., The Boulevard, Langford Lane, Kidlington, OX5 1GB, UK.

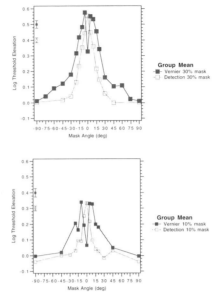

Fig. 11.4. Orientation tuning of Vernier acuity (solid symbols) and line detection (open symbols) revealed by masking with band-limited (2-octaves) one-dimensional noise masks. The tuning curve for Vernier is bimodal, showing distinct peaks at about 10 deg on either side of the line orientation. The tuning curve for line detection (open symbols) is unimodal, with peak masking corresponding to the line orientation (from Waugh *et al.*, 1993). Copyright (1993), reprinted with kind permission of Elsevier Science Ltd., The Boulevard, Langford Lane, Kidlington, OX5 1GB, UK.

adjusted the offset between the Vernier lines, and it is reasonable to assume that the offset was sometimes in one direction (e.g. up) and sometimes in the other (e.g. down). Given this paradigm, Findlay's results can be quite simply explained, with reference to Fig. 11.2 (bottom two panels). In Findlay's experiment, a mask which affects the sensitivity of the "tilted" filter in the middle panel, would reduce sensitivity to an upward shift of the left line - a mask which reduced the sensitivity of the "tilted" filter in the lower panel would reduce sensitivity to a downward shift of the left line. Surprisingly, Waugh *et al.* (1993) also found bimodal masking - but used a unidirectional shift (only up). They argued that their bimodal masking results cannot be easily explained by masking a single oriented filter; rather, the bimodal tuning requires a model in which the responses of filters at 2 or more orientations are combined.

As is evident in Fig. 11.6, similar bimodal masking occurs with plaid masks as it does with grating masks. Thus, the masking effect is not simply

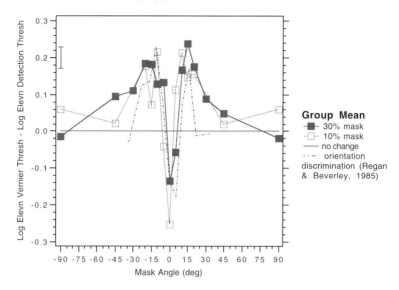

Fig. 11.5. Orientation tuning of Vernier acuity, after accounting for effects of the masks on line visibility (for details see Waugh *et al.*, 1993). The resultant tuning function is very similar to the post-adaptation orientation thresholds reported by Regan & Beverley (1985) and shown by the dot-dashed lines. Copyright (1993), reprinted with kind permission of Elsevier Science Ltd., The Boulevard, Langford Lane, Kidlington, OX5 1GB, UK.

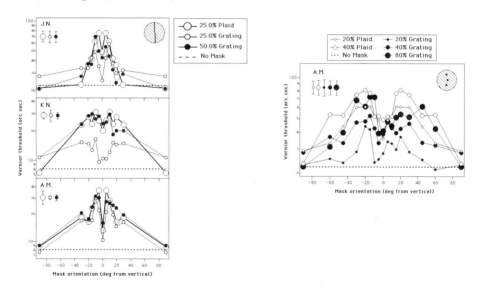

Fig. 11.6. Bimodal masking occurs with plaid masks and is similar to that found with grating masks. Thus, the masking effect is not simply a consequence of a perceived shift in orientation, or due to off-axis looking (from Mussap & Levi, 1996). Reprinted from Vision Research with kind permission from Elsevier Science Ltd., The Boulevard, Langford Lane, Kidlington, OX5 1GB, UK.

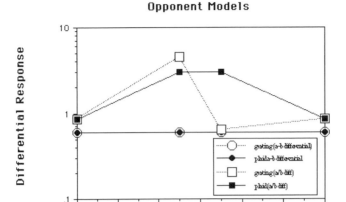

Fig. 11.7. The differential activity predicted by two different opponent models, for grating and plaid masks. One model is based on the ratio of activity in a pair of orthogonally oriented filters. The other is based on the difference in activity in a pair of orthogonally oriented filters. While the differential response (response of opponent mechanism with an offset - response of opponent mechanism with no offset) predicted by the difference model is identical for plaid and grating masks, it is quite different for the ratio model.

a consequence of a perceived shift in orientation, or due to off-axis looking (Mussap & Levi, 1996). The results are consistent with Wilson's (1986) line element model, where offsets are detected on the basis of pooled differential filter activity. According to the line element model, masking with plaids would be expected to produce the same bimodal pattern of masking as a single grating. It is interesting to note that masking with a 25% contrast plaid produces similar effects to that obtained with a 50% contrast grating, implying that pooling of differential filter activity is quasi- linear (Mussap & Levi, 1996). It is difficult to distinguish between a line element model, and an opponent model if both are linear; however, the plaid results may place some constraints on the type of model needed. Fig. 11.7 shows the differential activity predicted by two different opponent models, for grating and plaid masks. One model is based on the ratio of activity in a pair of orthogonally oriented filters. The other is based on the difference in activity in a pair of orthogonally oriented filters. While the differential response (response of opponent mechanism with an offset - response of opponent mechanism with no offset) predicted by the difference model is identical for plaid and grating masks, it is quite different for the ratio model.

Bimodal masking occurs under dichoptic conditions (Vernier target to one eye, mask to the other (Mussap & Levi, 1995a)), and taken together with the strong orientation dependence, it seems likely that the mechanisms revealed by masking are cortical (possibly in V1).

11.4 Gaps in the mask

The mechanisms most sensitive to offset are tuned to fairly high spatial frequencies (the peak spatial frequency is at 10 - 12 c/deg - Waugh et al., 1993) - thus, making the target lines longer than about 5' has little effect on Vernier thresholds (Westheimer & McKee, 1977). Masks falling outside the classical receptive field would not be expected to have an influence on Vernier thresholds, but they do (Mussap & Levi, 1995b). Fig. 11.8 shows that placing a 22' gap in the mask produces essentially the same effect on Vernier thresholds as having no gap in the mask, after the effect of the mask on target visibility has been taken into account. The mask in this experiment had a spatial frequency of 12 c/deg, so the length of the mechanism sensitive to the mask would be expected to be considerably smaller than the 22' gap (Wilson, 1986). Similar effects are seen with gaps as large as 1 deg (Mussap & Levi, 1995b). The gap-mask experiment poses a difficulty for a simple first-stage filter model. As described below, separated targets pose some further difficulties.

11.5 Gaps in the target

Perhaps more important to the coding of information in natural scenes than the hyperacuity thresholds obtained with abutting lines, is the precision with which observers can judge a misalignment between two separated features (e.g., 2 dots) about 1-2% of the separation between the dots (Fig. 11.9). This is an example of Weber's Law for position. Two general classes of models have been proposed to account for Weber's law in alignment judgements:

(i) A simple filter model (Fig. 11.10 - top). The most sensitive mechanism for detecting the offset would be an oriented filter, tilted at a slight angle to the imaginary horizontal. This filter fires differentially when there is an offset. As the gap increases, so does the filter size, so Weber's law or a constant orientation threshold is obtained.

(ii) A "local sign" model (Fig. 11.10 - bottom). In this model, the position of each dot is coded by a single filter whose position is labelled or tagged, and which has some associated positional uncertainty. As the

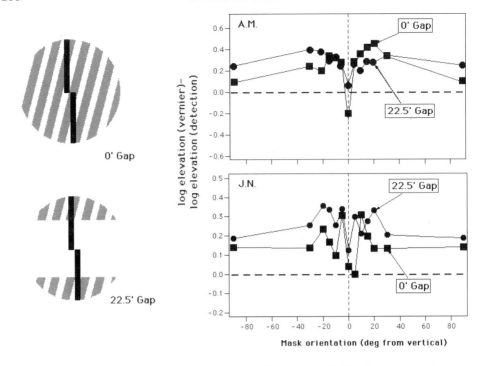

Fig. 11.8. Placing a 22' gap in the mask produces essentially the same effect on Vernier thresholds as having no gap in the mask, after the effect of the mask on target visibility has been taken into account. Results are shown for two observers (from Mussap & Levi, 1995b). Reprinted from Vision Research with kind permission from Elsevier Science Ltd., The Boulevard, Langford Lane, Kidlington, OX5 1GB, UK.

gap increases, so does the eccentricity of the outer dot. In this model, the positional uncertainty of the filter increases with the eccentricity of the outer dot, and hence threshold increases.

While the filter model is strongly contrast dependent, a local sign mechanism should be relatively immune to stimulus contrast. Fig. 11.11 shows that unlike abutting Vernier (Fig. 11.4), with widely separated targets thresholds show little contrast dependence once the stimulus is more than 2-3 times above the detection threshold (Waugh & Levi, 1993a). Similarly, while a local sign model would be indifferent to the relative contrast polarity of the target, opposite polarity targets cause some difficulties for linear spatial filters. Fig. 11.12 shows 2-dot alignment thresholds vs gap for same and opposite polarity dots. While offset thresholds for same polarity dots increase with gap size, thresholds for opposite polarity dots are more or less a constant offset ($\approx$ .35' or 20") up to a gap of 20' or so, and then increase

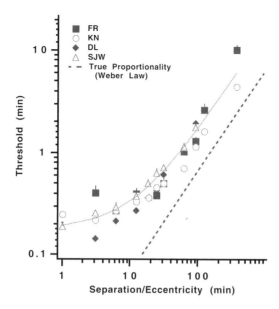

Fig. 11.9. Two 2-dot alignment thresholds of 4 observers are plotted as a function of the separation between the dots. Since one of the dots served as a fixation point, the eccentricity of the nonfixated dot covaries with the dot separation (as indicated by the legend - from Waugh & Levi, 1995). Used with permission.

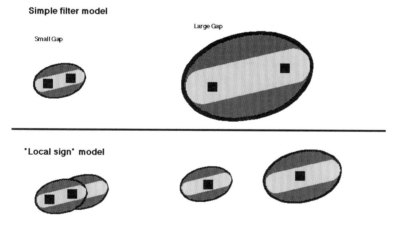

Fig. 11.10. Two models for 2-dot alignment. 1. A simple filter model (top). The most sensitive mechanism for detecting the offset would be an oriented filter, tilted at a slight angle to the imaginary horizontal. This filter fires differentially when there is an offset. As the gap increases, so does the filter size, so Weber's law or a constant orientation threshold is obtained. 2. A "local sign" model (bottom). The position of each dot is coded by a single filter whose position is labelled or tagged, and which has some associated positional uncertainty. As the gap increases, so does the eccentricity of the outer dot. In this model, the positional uncertainty of the filter increases with the eccentricity of the outer dot, and hence threshold increases.

for larger gaps. Note that for gaps greater than about 20' thresholds for same & opposite polarity stimuli are identical, and both follow Weber's law. Thus, it seems clear that different processes are at work at small vs. large separations. A simple proposition is that the filter model (the prediction is shown by the solid line in Fig. 11.12) operates over small gaps, and the local sign model (the prediction is shown by the dotted line in Fig. 11.12) holds across large gaps; however, as will be seen below, things are a bit more complicated.

11.6 Unmasking mechanisms underlying 2-dot alignment

Reprinted from Vision Research with kind permission from Elsevier Science Ltd., The Boulevard, Langford Lane, Kidlington, OX5 1GB, UK. Fig. 11.13 plots the orientation tuning of 2-dot alignment. Each curve represent a different gap (from 3-30') for same polarity dots. Noise masking produced a bimodal orientation tuning function, with peak masking at about ± 20 - 30 deg on either side of the virtual line connecting the dots when aligned. The peak of the tuning function doesn't seem to change much with the gap, at least over this range, and it is quite similar to that described by Findlay (1973) for abutting line Vernier acuity, and to the post-adaptation orientation discrimination data of Regan & Beverley (1985). This is not an effect of the masks on the visibility of the dots; since the dots are broadband in both spatial frequency and orientation, noise masking has only a small (≈ 10%) uniform effect on dot detection thresholds.

Fig. 11.14 shows spatial frequency tuning for gaps of 3-30' for same polarity dots. The data are clearly tuned to the mask spatial frequency, with a peak near 10c/deg, and it is interesting to note that for gaps between 3-30' the peak spatial frequency shows little dependence on the gap size. Recall, that the simple single filter model predicts that the peak spatial frequency increases in proportion to the gap size. At bigger gaps, where the eccentricity of the test dot is significant, the peak spatial frequency does shift gradually toward lower spatial frequencies. Fig. 11.15 summarizes the data of four observers by plotting the spatial period at which peak masking occurred as a function of the gap. At gaps less than about 30' the peak spatial period is ≈ 6', increasing gradually with separation, so that it doubles at between 2 & 3 degrees. The 1:1 line shows the simple filter prediction, that filter size increases in proportion to the gap. Clearly the data do not support this model. Rather, the very modest increase in peak spatial period is consistent with the slow rate of increase of contrast sensitive filters in peripheral vision

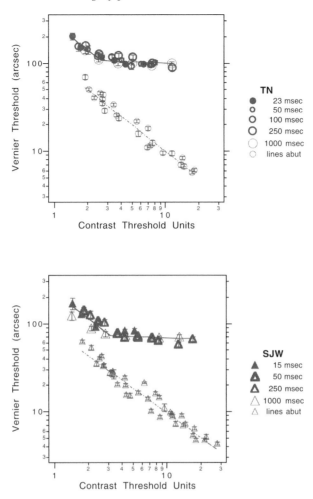

Fig. 11.11. Vernier acuity for well-separated targets (gap of 90 min - circles or triangles) is plotted as a function of the visibility of the target features (in contrast-detection threshold units). The different symbol sizes represent different durations. (from Waugh & Levi, 1993c). Note that unlike abutting Vernier (bows and propellers), these widely separated targets thresholds show little contrast dependence once the stimulus is more than 2-3 times above the detection threshold (from Waugh & Levi, 1993a). Copyright (1993), reprinted with kind permission of Elsevier Science Ltd., The Boulevard, Langford Lane, Kidlington, OX5 1GB, UK.

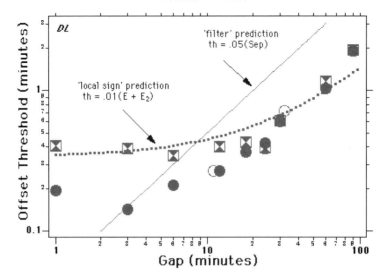

Fig. 11.12. 2-dot alignment thresholds (in arc min) vs. gap for same- and opposite-contrast polarity dots. Note that for gaps > 20' thresholds for same & opposite polarity stimuli are quite similar. The prediction of a simple filter model in which the threshold is equal to .05*gap is shown by the solid line in Fig. 11.12. The prediction of a local sign model in which the threshold is equal to $.01(E_{cc} + E_2)$ is shown by the dotted line (E_{cc} is the target eccentricity, and E_2 is the eccentricity at which the foveal threshold doubles).

(Levi & Waugh, 1994), and cannot account for the increase in alignment thresholds.

The masking results are consistent with the notion that orientation and spatial frequency tuned filters play a role in the processing of relative position information for both abutting Vernier acuity and 2-dot alignment tasks. However, even if simple filter models do predict a degradation of acuity for closely separated opposite polarity stimuli, other aspects of the present study are not easily accounted for. In particular, the simple filter model predicts that filter size should increase in proportion to the separation between targets. Clearly the data do not support this model. Over the 10 fold range of separations from 3 to 30', the peak spatial period of the most effective mask is almost constant. While we cannot rule out an explanation in which there are multiple filters of a fixed preferred spatial frequency with a range of lengths, a 10 fold range of filter aspect ratios seems rather implausible†. We do not believe that our results can be simply explained by longer (first

† In Wilson's model, oriented spatial filters have an aspect ratio of 3.2:1 so that the length standard deviation of an 8c/deg filter is ≈ 7.3'

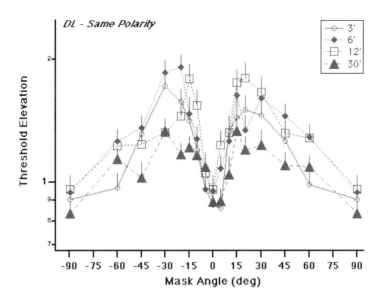

Fig. 11.13. Orientation tuning functions for same-polarity dots obtained with broadband masks. The ordinate axis shows the threshold elevation (masked/unmasked threshold); the abscissa is the mask angle relative to the horizontal (the aligned condition). Data are shown for gaps of 3, 6, 12, and 30 min) (from Levi & Waugh, 1996). Reprinted from Vision Research with kind permission from Elsevier Science Ltd., The Boulevard, Langford Lane, Kidlington, OX5 1GB, UK.

stage) filters, because we find masking extends over gaps of at least 6 degrees (Waugh & Levi, 1995), much larger than any plausible early filter.

An alternative model proposed by Hering (1899) involves a comparison of local signs. A local sign mechanism should be insensitive for example, to the contrast polarity of the stimuli, and it has been suggested as a plausible mechanism for position acuity with widely separated stimuli (Klein & Levi, 1987; Levi & Klein, 1990; Wang & Levi, 1994). Each local sign mechanism would be expected to operate on target features which fall in separate filters.

However, there are problems with the simple local sign model:

(i) A simple local sign mechanism would not be expected to be susceptible to pattern masking which is suggestive of an orientation tuned process.

(ii) In addition, masks placed between but not overlapping the targets, also degrade relative position thresholds (Fig. 11.15).

In order to model all of the results, we suggest that signals from early linear

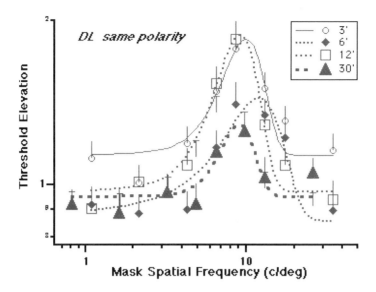

Fig. 11.14. Spatial frequency tuning functions for 2-dot alignment for gaps of 3-30'
for same- polarity dots. Spatial frequency tuning functions were measured with a
1-octave band of spatial frequencies oriented at an angle of 10 deg (3, 6 & 12') or
20 deg (30'). The data are clearly tuned to the mask spatial frequency, with a peak
at ≈ 10c/deg, with little dependence on the gap (from Levi & Waugh, 1996).

filters are collected in a nonlinear 2nd stage filter, which collates information
along an orientation trajectory (Levi & Waugh, 1996).

11.7 A 2-stage model for Vernier alignment

Fig. 11.16 illustrates schematically such a 2-stage model. The 1st stage consists of linear contrast sensitive filters. While there is a range of filter sizes
available for the task, there is a trade off between filter size and sensitivity. Based on the masking results, it appears that the visual system uses
relatively small, but very sensitive filters, i.e., the optimum filters for foveal
vision appear to be those with a peak spatial frequency of about 10c/deg.
For gaps less than the filter length, differential contrast signals in oriented
linear filters are highly sensitive to misalignments of same polarity targets,
but are degraded by opposite polarity targets. Thus at small gaps, a process
whereby absolute position labels, i.e. local signs, are compared, is more sensitive for opposite polarity stimuli. When the gap exceeds the filter length,
a second stage mechanism which appears to collect information along an
orientation trajectory is more sensitive for both same and opposite polarity
stimuli than is the differential response of larger filters.

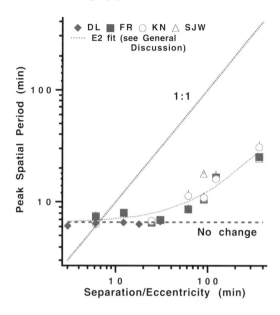

Fig. 11.15. The peak spatial periods (min) calculated from masking functions (1/peak spatial frequency of mask*60) are plotted against each dot separation condition (min) measured for 4 observers. The thick dashed line represents constancy in size of the measured spatial period. A proportional increase in size with increasing separation is represented by the thick dotted line (1:1) (from Waugh & Levi, 1995). Used with permission.

The 2nd stage can be thought of as a nonlinear rectifying filter which collates the (squared) response of the 1st stage filters along an orientation trajectory. In Figure 11.16 the "subunits" are represented with identical orientations; however, in reality, there may be increased scatter in the preferred orientations of the subunits as the 2nd stage filter becomes more elongated (this would lead to the slightly broader orientation tuning evident at large separations). These, long, but relatively high spatial frequency nonlinear second stage filters may underlie the "local sign" mechanism, providing a broad orientation specificity over long distances.

Nonlinear filters of this sort have been suggested previously. Morgan & Hotopf (1989) proposed a model in which like-oriented first-stage filters are collected over space into a second- stage "collector" filter, in order to explain why diagonal lines are seen running between the intersections in repetitive grid patterns, and to explain several other illusions involving diagonal lines (not readily explained by a simple Fourier model). More recently, Moulden (1994) has provided psychophysical evidence consistent with the existence

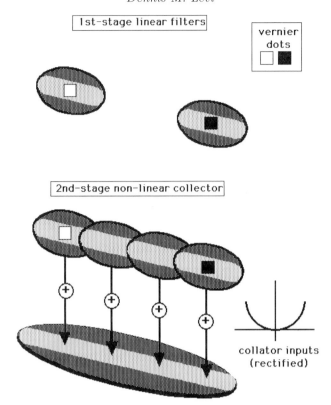

Fig. 11.16. Illustrates schematically the 2-stage nonlinear collator model. The 1st stage consists of linear contrast sensitive filters. The 2nd stage is an elongated nonlinear filter which collects the squared outputs of the 1st stage filters. The nonlinear filters collects signals from 1st stage filters along an orientation trajectory.

of collector filters of this sort, which linearly collate the responses of up to 7 subunits.

Collector filters of this sort may also be useful in trying to explain some old results and some more recent ones too. For example, Meer & Zeevi (1986) found that perturbing the ends of long, abutting Vernier lines interfered with Vernier acuity - a result which is not consistent with highly localized high spatial frequency filters. This result can be readily explained by a collator mechanism. Similarly, the collator model can account for the bimodal orientation tuning obtained with stimuli comprised of long abutting Vernier bars, and superimposed masks with gaps (Fig. 11.8). Interestingly similar masking is obtained when the 12c/deg masks have gaps up to 1 deg wide. This result seems surprising because Vernier acuity is generally thought to improve little for lines longer than 10 or so (e.g. Westheimer & McKee, 1977).

However, recent studies with low contrast, sampled lines suggest that all samples are used over line lengths far longer than 10 (Wang & Levi, 1994; Wang *et al.*, 1996). Nor are the results easily attributed to large low spatial frequency filters, because the masks are high spatial frequency. Moreover, the collator model also predicts that masks placed between the bars will produce orientation specific threshold elevation, while masks placed beyond the bars have little or no effect.

Alignment thresholds may be limited at either stage, by the properties of the linear filters, or by noise at the second stage (Levi & Waugh, 1994; Levi *et al.*, 1994b; Levi *et al.*, 1994a).

A nonlinear collator mechanism like the one we are proposing here would be very useful in global pattern perception, and may be similar to the standard complex cells in V1 layer 6 described by Gilbert, 1977. These cells have long receptive fields (up to several degrees) and have inputs from smaller layer 5 cells. They demonstrate length summation, prefer stimulus bars which are much thinner than the overall receptive field width and show sharpened orientation tuning due to their increased length. For the 2-dot alignment task, it seems that the optimal orientation trajectory is about 20 deg to the virtual horizontal line connecting aligned targets. The signals collected along this path result in very fine orientation thresholds.

Acknowledgements

I gratefully acknowledge the contributions of Sarah Waugh and Alex Mussap to both the data and the ideas presented here. This research was supported by grant RO1EY01728 from the National Eye Institute, NIH, Bethesda, MD.

12

A historical review of the imagery debate

Heather L. Jenkin

Department of Psychology
York University
North York
Canada

Fundamental to all human cognition is the representation of knowledge: how information, derived from sensory experiences, is symbolized and combined with information already stored in the brain. One of the problems we have in communicating with each other, or solving tasks, is that the world is never identically represented. What you see, hear, smell, taste or feel is not the same as I experience and represent in memory. And what I experience and store in memory is not identical to your experience. In spite of these inherent dissimilarities between representations of knowledge, most humans do experience and depict experiences in similar enough ways to get along well in the world.

The lively interest in representational knowledge has evoked the same fundamental questions: How is knowledge acquired, stored, transformed, and used? What is the nature of perception and memory? What is thought? and How do these abilities develop? These questions reflect the essential issue of representational knowledge - how ideas, events, and things are stored and schematized in the mind.

Throughout history, from the earliest of writings of the Egyptians and Greeks, the question of representation has been discussed. What has changed with the passage of time is the perspective from which representation is examined. The Greek philosophers dealt with the issue of mental representation within the context of structure and process. Aristotle believed that knowledge was represented in the heart, while Plato wrote that the brain was the locus of the mind.

Discussion of structure and process has continued for centuries, with the focus of interest passing from one to the other over the years. Clearly, the modern view encompasses both working together. The dichotomy and interaction between structure and process have been described by Solso as the structure of a bee's honeycomb and the processes that operate within the comb (Solso, 1991). The structure of the honeycomb is formed by the bee and is generally fixed (for example, its size, shape, position, and capacity are relatively stable), while the activity or processes - such as the gathering, transformation, and storage of honey - are constantly in flux although acting in conjunction with the structure (Solso, 1991).

This chapter will examine different models of representation in modern psychology, moving from a description of external representation to one of internal representation. The shift of symbolic representation to subsymbolic forms will be traced by a historic examination of the imagery debate, and the movement toward neural network solutions of representation issues. The imagery debate focused on the empirical evidence for analogical versus propositional internal representations. Neural network solutions look at distributed versus local representations. The changing technology available has allowed for different empirical research to be explored by neurologists, computer scientists as well as cognitive psychologists interested in the problem of representation. Each new perspective influences the direction of empirical investigation and adds to the knowledge base. Issues that determined the imagery debate in the seventies and eighties have not necessarily been resolved, for perhaps flux in ongoing research has changes the perspective and perhaps even the question. What were clear issues are revealed to be pseudo-issues and at a tangent to the new line of research.

There are many distinctions that can be made about the form of representations. There is a broad distinction between external and internal (or mental) representations in the literature. External representations are representations that are available for examination in either pictorial or notational form and as such can be used by different individuals and at different times. Written text is a good example of a well-understood external representation. The symbols that make up the representation are available and are communally understood. Internal representations, on the other hand, are the way in which we each represent the information within ourselves. Internal representations are private, and not available for direct examination. Even if two persons read the same standard external representation of information (e.g., this text), their internal representations may be quite different. Each person relates information with knowledge previously internalized. Connections are made between ideas and concepts, based upon previous experience of the individual.

A representation must be constructed so that it is useful for some collection of salient tasks. As information that is not encoded is lost from short term memory, great care must be taken that information that is essential for the task or collection of tasks is incorporated within the representation.

It is quite possible to have a poor representation that does not allow for successful task completion. A critical feature or event may be unnoticed the first time around, only a lack of success highlights missing information from the internal representation. A simple example is of parking your car in a large parking area and noticing that you parked beside a white van. A more appropriate cues for recall might be the signs which indicate parking sub-area (e.g., Red-6), or which store door is located closest to your car.

An external representation is any notation, sign or set of symbols that can 're-present' something to us (Beakley & Ludlow, 1992). External representations can occur in many different forms, although they fall into two distinct categories; notational, and pictorial. For example a musical score represents music, while a mathematical equation represents some mathematical system. Both take notational form. On the other hand, a picture represents a scene, and similarly a map represents geographical information. There are occasions when the same object or event can support both kinds of external representation. The chemical equation CH_3OH and it's molecular diagram both represent some aspect of a concept in the real world. Neither representation indicates the taste, the colour or even the effect of consumption. The pictorial representation may be more informative (i.e., give a chemist more information about the three-dimensional structure of the molecule) than the textual description, but both represent the molecular makeup of alcohol. In the previous parked car example – when describing your car's location to someone else you might draw a map where 'X' marks the spot or write a description of the car's location '3 cars to the left just to the south of the mall's west-end door'.

The statement "The glass is on the table" represents the spatial relationship between two objects in the world. This information could be quite easily represented by a drawing of a glass on a table. Both representations only represent some aspects of the world. With the linguistic statement we do not know what kind of glass it is. However, the picture can provide more information about the glass, such as "martini glass versus beer stein." Often a pictorial representation is cited as being *more natural* than linguistic descriptions. After all 'A picture is worth a thousand words.' A pictorial representation seems to capture more about the world. Other relationships can be inferred, by a further examination of the picture, such as that it is in the centre of the table and dangerously close to the edge.

Kosslyn (1980, 1983) found several differences between linguistic and pictorial forms of representation. First, any linguistic system is made up of discrete symbols. Sentences can be broken down into words (e.g., glass, table), and words can be further broken down into letters (e.g., 'g', 'l'), but letters are the smallest units and cannot be meaningfully broken down any further. A part of a letter does not really represent anything in any linguistic sense. Kosslyn asserts that because there is no smallest unit of a picture, there are no pictorially discrete symbols. For example, the glass, the olive, and the table are basic elements in the picture. These can be further broken down, for example, the bowl of the glass and the stem.

Second, the linguistic representation 'stands' for something. The words "the glass is on the table" explicitly stands for the two items (*glass, table*) and the relationship between them (*on*). Pictures do not have explicit symbols to state relationships between objects. Rather, relationships (such as *on*) are implicit within the pictorial representation. The fact that the glass is depicted upon the table allows the viewer to understand the relative relationship between the two objects (i.e. the glass is not shown under the table, but rather *on* the table).

Third, in normal usage there are grammatical rules for the combination of symbols in any linguistic representation. The two sentences: "the glass is on the table" and "the table is on the glass" represent two different things although they are both grammatically correct. But not all combinations of words give rise to meaningful sentences. In English there are rules about which words go first, and linguistics representations that disobey these rules represent nothing. For example the sentence "glass the table on is the" holds no relevant information concerning the two items involved. Special forms of language may impose their own rules of combination, for example Haiku poetry does not necessarily follow the formal grammatical rules of English, but there are still complex rules to follow. Abstract poetry allows for personal interpretations to be made by the reader, that may or may not follow from the poets' intentions.

There are no clear cut 'grammatical' rules about combination for pictorial representation. There is no steadfast pictorial 'verb' or 'noun'. If there are rules they do not seem to hold a tight control concerning meaningfulness. A painting that does not follow a set of 'grammatical' rules may still be understood. For example in a Picasso painting, eyes do not have to be on either side of the nose. Picasso was able to portray faces while appearing to break standard 'grammatical' rules. Viewers can recognize the face even though the face 'breaks' the normal syntax.

Any linguistic representation is arbitrary and abstract in nature (Fodor, 1981). With any language, even musical notation, the symbols used are arbitrary although they have been agreed upon by the user community. The representation can take information from any of the senses and interpret it in some arbitrary abstract way. For example, the colour, nose, texture and taste of single malt scotch can be linguistically described:

"Lagavulin: Its attack is reminiscent of Lapsang Souchong tea, but supported by a big, malty, sweetish (Darjeeling this time?), background. The third generous element is sherry. A big, immensely sophisticated whisky. Some devotees feel the dryness is better expressed in the 12-year-old, which was the principal version until it was largely replaced by the 16-year-old. Others feel that the greater sherry character of the 16-year-old makes for a more complete symphony." (Jackson, 1989 p.165)

A picture of a glass of single malt is a more concrete or absolute representation of the colour, because a pictorial representation usually acquires information from the visual sense, rather than others senses. Through close association with the visual modality pictorial representations fail to fully represent information from all the senses (i.e. the taste of the single malt).

Traditionally external models of representation have been used to provide a model for understanding the nature of internal representations. One, perhaps, should be cautious as the constraints are somewhat different. In the past, internal representations have been described by relating them to external representations. The distinction between notational and pictorial external representations has been paralleled in the descriptions of internal representations. Pyslshyn (1981) described two types of symbolic internal representation; analogical, corresponding to pictorial external representation; and propositional, corresponding to notational internal representation The basic view of this approach is that human cognition is dependent upon the manipulation of symbolic representations in some organized way.

More recently researchers have examined cognition as a computational model. Changes in technology, the growth of computer science and artificial intelligence, and a new understanding of neural processes in the brain has lead to an alternative approach to understanding internal representations at a sub-symbolic level. This connectionist approach to cognition, allows for representing information without dealing with symbols. Information is held within distributed representations that do not require specific rules for combination, and because of the influence of neuron-like processing units, there is the possibility of mapping onto actual neurophysiological areas (Clark, 1989; Rumelhart *et al.*, 1986b; Smolensky, 1988).

The following sections examine analogical and propositional forms of symbolic internal representation. Further sections will outline the theoretical debate that developed primarily between Anderson, Pylyshyn and Kosslyn in the late 1970's and early 1980's (Anderson, 1978; Anderson, 1979; Kosslyn, 1973; Kosslyn, 1975; Kosslyn, 1976; Kosslyn, 1980; Pylyshyn, 1973;

Pylyshyn, 1979; Pylyshyn, 1981). Some aspects of the empirical research involved will be examined, highlighting the point at which the debate started and then later stalled. The rise of neural network-connectionist thinking steered intellectual interest from a debate between propositional and analogical representation to a search for an implementable paradigm. That is, technology made previously impossible systems possible. Further, these advances in computer representation and acquisition blurred the distinction between representational types (Boden, 1981; Boden, 1988; Hayes, 1985).

12.1 Analogical representations

Analogical representations are non-discrete images that have loose rules of combination and are concrete in the sense that they are linked in some way to the original presentation modality. Analogical representations need not be limited to the visual sense (unlike pictures) but can represent information gleaned from all the senses. We represent the taste, texture, smell, etc., internally. Memories of what a good wine tastes like, what the summer sun feels like, the sound of waves lapping on the shore, etc.. Despite this, research on analogical representations has primarily dealt with visual imagery rather than other sense imagery (Glass *et al.*, 1979).

Visual imagery has occupied centre stage in the debate concerning the nature of thinking. The debate arose because of experimental findings on imagery, and their interpretation, challenged the then dominant view of cognitive representation (McGuiness, 1989). First, it questioned the view that the mind favours a single mode of representation. Second, it raised doubts about the general-purpose digital computer as an appropriate model of thinking. Finally the relationship between traditional methods of experimental psychology (i.e., hypothesis testing) and new methods of cognitive modelling used by connectionists is not yet clear. One perspective looks at paradigm driven models for explanation, while the other simulates possible explanations. These issues are still unresolved.

Imagery is indicated as a mnemonic device and has been used for centuries. A classical memory trick for memorizing a list of items is to imagine a familiar route, perhaps from home to work. At specific points along the way visualize the items you are trying to remember (Glass *et al.*, 1979). Part of the remembering is the ability to travel along that familiar route in your mind and 'see' those items again. A closer look at memory for objects and events follows with an examination of Paivio's dual-coding theory.

12.1.1 Paivio's dual-coding theory

The reawakening of interest in imagery research was given a jump start by Paivio's formulation of a dual-coding theory (see Paivio, 1971, 1983, 1986 and 1991). Working from a verbal-learning tradition Paivio outlined a theoretical treatment of cognitive representation. He argued that imagery was a memory code or associate mediator between stimulus and response. He and his colleagues studied how characteristics of words (e.g. meaningfulness, familiarity, concreteness, imagability) affected their memorability. For example, concrete words are easier to remember than abstract words, and pictures of concrete objects are the easiest to remember (Paivio & Csapo, 1973). To account for these types of findings Paivio appealed to imagery as a mediating code and formulated his Dual Coding theory. The essence of the theory is that there are two distinct systems for the representation and processing of information. Paivio describes logogens and imagens as units in the verbal and image systems respectively. Memory consists of both verbal and imagery codes; concrete words and pictures are redundantly stored by an image code as well as a verbal code, whereas abstract words are stored by a verbal code alone. The two codes work in harmony, but they are distinct, and processing benefits accrue through the use of two codes rather than one (Paivio, 1986).

When a spoken word is processed, it is identified by a logogen for the auditory sound of the word. Paivio characterizes a logogen as a modality-specific unit that "can function as an integrated, informational structure or as a response generator" (Paivio 1986, p.66,)†. There may be logogens for the word 'cat'. Logogens are modality-specific, in the sense that there are separate logogens for identifying the spoken sound 'cat' and its visual form (i.e. the letters c-a-t). The corollary of logogen in the nonverbal systems is imagen. The verbal and nonverbal systems communicate in a functional fashion through relations by way of logogens and imagens. The simplest case of such a relation is the referential link between an object and its name. That is, if you see a visual object (e.g. a cat climbs the curtain) it would be recognized by an imagen and a link between this imagen and an auditory logogen for the word 'cat' may bring the word 'cat' to mind.

Logogens and imagens allow for a processing unit that identifies or represents a particular item (i.e. an image of a cat or a particular word) without having to specify the internal workings of this processing unit or the detailed representation of the item being processed.

Evidence for the dual-coding theory has been provided in a number of

† Copyright 1986 Oxford University Press. Used by Permission of Oxford University Press.

different task areas: memory tasks, problem solving situations, etc. (Paivio, 1986). These experiments typically try to test two main predictions: (1) that the two symbolic systems operate in an independent fashion in some circumstances; and (2) that the two symbolic systems produce additive effects in other circumstances.

Paivio (1971) and Paivio and Csapo (1973) gave subjects either a series of words or a series of pictures to remember. When the pictures were of common objects then subjects would spontaneously name the objects during the memorizing part of the experiment. Thus, both systems are brought into play, and hence there should be increased recall for pictures, while memorizing words simply involves the verbal system. This is typically what is found. Pictures are more readily remembered in both free-recall and recognition tasks than words alone. Word recall can be improved if one uses an imagery mnemonic strategy, thereby bringing both systems into play.

The importance of Paivio's dual coding theory (1971) and the subsequent revision (1986) is not so much in their precise detail, but rather as their impact on the general discussion about mental representation.

So what exactly is the image your head? Paivio made no strong claims as to the nature of the image other than it was 'quasi-perceptual'. In a common sense way an image is simply what you have in your head when you imagine something. However this is not enough for scientific investigation. Questions such as; what is the exact nature of the images? What are the special properties of images? What kinds of operations are possible with the images is your head? Others have been asked to examine whether or not images have any functional significance.

Do images (analogue representations) differ in any significant way from internal propositional representations? This last question became the central issue in the imagery debate (Kosslyn, 1983; Pylyshyn, 1981). First, images are picture-like representations that operate in the same way as external pictorial representations. Images have been defined as having one-to-one correspondence with the real world, that is distinct from propositional (linguistic) internal representations (Shepard & Cooper, 1982). Alternatively, images have been described as ultimately no different from propositional representations, rather an alternative way of revealing propositional information. Experiments in mental rotation (see Shepard & Cooper, 1982 for a review) and image scanning (Kosslyn, 1973, 1983) are the two general paradigms used in this investigation of the functional nature of analogical representation.

12.1.2 Mental rotation

In the early 1970's, Shepard and his associates (see Shepard, 1978;1982)
developed an experimental paradigm to study 'images in action' by timing
how long it took to manipulate and transform them. The most intensively
studied transformation was rotation. In this chronometric study of imaging
subjects were asked to imagine objects, numbers, and letters rotating about
various axes. In the first of these studies Shepard and Metzler (1971) asked
subjects to determine if pairs of line drawings of complex 3-D objects were
the same or different. The pairs differed in orientation from 0° and 180°.
Reaction times (RTs) of subjects' judgements were a linear increasing function of the extent of the rotation between the pairs. They proposed that
the reaction times reflected the mental rotation of one object into congru-
ence with the other and the check for a match or a mismatch. Subjects'
introspective reports supported this interpretation. The continuous nature
of the RT function was taken to indicate that mentally rotating the objects
had characteristics in common with rotation in real space. Mental rotation,
they claim, was an analogue process.

Cooper and Shepard (1973a) modified the paradigm from comparison of
two objects to a decision about one object. For example, subjects were
asked to identify whether a figure was a 'normal' letter **R** or its mirror image. Test figures of either the **R** or its mirror image were presented in a
variety of orientations. It was found that the length of time subjects needed
to decide whether the figure was 'normal' or 'mirror' increased as the orientation moved further from the upright. Again, reaction times (RTs) of
subjects' judgements were a linear increasing function of the extent of the
rotation from the upright orientation associated with the letter **R**. When
reaction time latencies are plotted against increasing differences in orientation angle an increasing straight line is obtained (or an inverted V function
centred on 180°, if both clockwise and counter-clockwise rotations are used).

Metzler and Shepard (1982) argued that for a process to be analogical it
must pass through "a certain trajectory of intermediate states each of which
has a one-to- one correspondence to an intermediate stage of external physical rotation of the object"† (p.28). Again, the impression is that images
function in the same way as objects in the real world would. The mental representation relates specifically to the physical world. Images can be mentally
moved (for example, rotated) in the same way real objects can be physically
manipulated. Shepard and associates distinguished analogue processes from
other types of processes such as feature search, symbol manipulation, verbal

---

† Copyright (1982) MIT Press. Used with permission.

analysis or other digital computation. The representations are analogue in the sense that they preserved some degree of the spatial structure inherent in the object (Cooper & Podgorny, 1976; Shepard & Cooper, 1982)).

Shepard and his colleagues explicitly articulated a form of representation that was in direct opposition to propositional formats. But Shepard's is not a computational model, it lacks the detailed specifications that would be requires to implement it as a simulation. During the same period Kosslyn and his associates began to report on a series of experiments that eventually culminated in a computer simulation of imagery.

12.1.3 Image scanning

In image scanning experiments, subjects are asked to examine an image of some object and then respond to questions about it. The classic question used by Kosslyn (1973) required subjects to first imagine an elephant and rabbit together. Questions about the elephant were answered more accurately and with greater detail than questions about the rabbit. When subjects were then asked to imagine a rabbit and a fly together, the same information previously asked about the rabbit was now available faster and in greater detail. Kosslyn concluded that the subjects were scanning an image that kept the relative metric information about the two animals consistent with the metric information appropriate for the real animals. When the rabbit is imaged with the elephant, the image is much smaller and therefore loses detail. This changes when the rabbit is imaged with the much smaller fly, i.e. the rabbit is now the larger, more detailed, part of the image and therefore information about the rabbit is more easily accessible than information concerning the fly. Analogical representations are therefore described as being like looking at a picture.

Other empirical evidence about the possible nature of images comes from scanning an imaged map. Kosslyn, Ball and Reiser (1978) had subjects study a map of an island, on which a number of different locations had been marked. When subjects could produce a complete external representation of the map, (they were able to draw it for themselves), they were asked to imagine the island in their heads. They were then asked to focus on one landmark in their image. Five seconds later a second landmark was named and subjects had to scan from the first location to the second by imagining a flying black dot. Kosslyn found that scanning time was linearly related to the actual distances between the two locations. This evidence that increases in scanning time are related to increases in actual distances supports the hypothesis that images have special properties that are analogous to the real world.

12.1.4 Problems with imagery

There is some concern with these results from image scanning and mental rotation experiments. In both methods instructions to subjects may be 'leading the witness'. Baddeley (1986, p.130) is more direct:

"I have a nagging concern that, implicitly, much of the experimental work in this field consists of instructing the subjects to behave as if they were seeing something in the outside world.......Whether this tells us how the system works, or indeed tell us much about the phenomenology, I am as yet uncertain."†

Introspective reports from subjects used in Mental Rotation tasks attest to the fact that subjects claim that they

"(a) form a mental picture of the anticipated stimulus and then (b) carry out a mental rotation of that picture into its anticipated orientation."‡ (Shepard & Cooper, 1982 p. 74).

Some researchers who have used these two image paradigms have uncovered conditions in which the linear-disparity function is not found. Pylyshyn (personal communication, 1993) has spoken on aids that influence image scanning. If the subjects focus on the imaginary island while facing a breeze-block wall then scanning time is very fast regardless of distance and subjects report making use of the grid system on the wall to anchor their image.

With regard to mental rotation tasks, it has been found that if the object to be rotated is very simple, for example if subjects are told that certain aspects of the objects are redundant, then the slope of the angular-disparity function decreases, on occasion to a flat-line (Friedman *et al.*, 1988; Hochberg & Gellman, 1977; Shepard & Metzler, 1988; Takano, 1989). On the other hand when the object becomes very complex, then subjects are less able to make correct judgements about the expected rotated appearance of objects and subsequently do not produce linear angular disparity results. Studies examining the role of frame, the influence of symmetry, colour and the objects' own internal structure on recognition have been shown to produce non-linear results (Bialystok, 1989; Jenkin, 1987; Rock, 1973; Rock *et al.*, 1989; Tarr & Pinker, 1989). The effect of manipulating the complexity of an object is a problem that would not occur in the physical rotation of a real world complex object.

---

† Copyright 1986 Oxford University Press. Used by Permission of Oxford University Press.
‡ Copyright 1982 MIT Press. Used with permission.

When aids for recognition are available to the subject then the linear angular disparity function also changes; the use of vertical-horizontal cues aid in object recognition, when the final orientation aligns with the vertical-horizontal axes (Jenkin, 1987; Shiffrar & Shepard, 1991). In these cases, then no linear effect is found and a series of high RT's and low RT's are reported. Low when some categorical cue is available, high when complexity and/or orientation makes the task difficult. Shepard and Cooper (1982) have said that subjects could be trained to non-rotational strategies, (although none of their expert subjects spontaneously did so) and therefore theoretically the linear-disparity function would change. Yuille and Steiger (1982) have suggest other non-holistic processing strategies for mental rotation tasks.

There is some evidence that subjects may use an analogical representation (Shepard & Cooper, 1982), but it is not the whole story. If the subjects are given other tools, cues, more simple shapes or more complex shapes the linear function breaks down (Jenkin, 1987; Takano, 1989). Perhaps as in Paivio's theory, more than one encoding mechanism is at work and the overall theory is more complex than a straightforward imagistic model.

12.2 Propositional representations

The arguments in favour of propositions as a representational format for imagery have been posed primarily by Pylyshyn. Internal representations and processes involved in tasks such as mental rotation or image scanning, bear no structural resemblance to their corresponding external objects and operations (Pylyshyn, 1973). Propositional representations are considered to be explicit, discrete and abstract entities that follow certain combinatorial rules. These internal representations are notational in nature and are used to represent information presented in all modalities.

The representations can be described as a form of predicate calculus (Johnson-Laird, 1980, 1983, 1990; Olson & Bialystok, 1983). Predicate calculus is a method that uses schematic descriptions to show how representations are structured. The propositions can be related in various ways. The links between the objects are known as predicates, and the object representations are called the arguments of the predicates. Predicates can show how concepts are related. For example, 'the glass is on the table' has two arguments (glass, table) linked by the predicate 'on'. The formal notation for this information is:

ON (glass, table).

This type of notation can be used to describe the structure of propositional concepts. These propositions can be logically combined to represent additional information. For example:

ON (glass, table) AND TYPE (glass, martini)

represent the information "the martini glass is on the table".

As such the representations and processes underlying mental rotation tasks can be described as follows. Visual objects are represented propositionally in the form of networks, and orientation is represented in the network in the form of a reference point and position predicates, which relate the orientation of subparts of the representation to the reference point. Rotation is accomplished by successively changing these orientation predicates.

In an empirical context, the basic properties of propositions are rarely tested directly but are simply assumed. Where they can be tested is when they are combined to represent knowledge, for example semantic networks (Collins & Quillian, 1969). In practical terms propositional representations are very useful for computer modelling. The predicate calculus can be implemented in artificial intelligence computing languages (e.g. LISP, PROLOG). This has allowed computer modelling of propositional representations to be run successfully.

12.2.1 *The debate*

Pylyshyn's position Analogue and propositional theories of representation have matured considerably with the growing interest in cognition in the scientific realm of Psychology. The notion that analogue and propositional representations existed as equal possibilities for internal symbolic representation came under fire in the 1970's when Pylyshyn began to explore the use of analogue representations. He started questioning the evidence supporting analogical representations; concluding that there is no need to postulate images at all, that cognition should only be analyzed in terms of propositions. This question was debated by Pylyshyn (1973, 1979), Anderson (1978, 1979) and Kosslyn (1980, 1983) among others. (For a well-rounded introduction to the imagery debate see Tye, 1991).

The main thrust of the debate being that despite the 'naturalness' of describing images as pictures, there is still a vagueness surrounding the concept of imagery. Pylyshyn (1973) stated that neither the experience of imagery nor the observed empirical regularities were in question but rather whether "the concept of image can be used as a primitive explanatory concept (i.e., one not requiring further reduction) in psychological theories of cognition"†

(p.2) His main complaint with the concept of imagery (Paivio's dual-coding theory mainly) was that the picture-metaphor of imagery and the common sense understandings of the word had slipped into psychological theorizing. Images are not pictures. Pylyshyn pointed out that if images are like pictures then you need a 'Mind's eye' to see them (1973). This is a circular response i.e. 'What does the Mind's eye see'? 'An image', and so on.

Pylyshyn (1973, 1981) argued that one could posit a propositional code in which all processing (verbal and nonverbal) could be carried out. Much like the dual coding theory, if verbal and nonverbal codes are in different formats then some relational code must be specified to link them together. Pylyshyn argued that the third code that relates the other two can be described as an interlingua or common code, and this abstract code would be propositional or descriptive rather than resembling the surface properties of words and images.

Even evidence from mental rotation studies can be re-interpreted within a propositional framework. For example, the same object can be represented in several different orientations. A letter in the upright position could be represented propositionally by predicates that specify the features of the letter that are at the top, bottom, left and right. In this way the letter **A** could have the proposition

$$\text{TOP}(35^o\text{- VERTEX, LETTER - A})$$

to indicate that the pointed feature is the top of the letter 'A' (Eysenck & Keane, 1990). So when the letter is to be rotated 180°, then

$$\text{BOTTOM}(35^o\text{- VERTEX, LETTER - A})$$

describes an inverted letter $\forall$. In this way there can be a process to simply switch the top to the bottom. The orientation predicates (e.g. top, bottom, 5° tilt, 60° tilt) can carry out a rotation in the same simple number of steps.

Anderson (1978, 1979) made the point that even using the propositional code as outlined above, it is often important to simulate how the object would actually move in space. In that case then the propositional operators might change the orientation predicates in a step-by-step fashion. In the rotation example the movement would be from top to 30° tilt, from 30° to 60° tilt ... 150° to bottom. This may produce the same predictions as from the imagery theory. As such it is impossible to determine unequivocally the

† Copyright (C) American Psychological Association. Used with permission.

format of a representation used in any cognitive task, because a theory can be mimicked in part by any other theory. For Pylyshyn (1981) such cognitive confusions can be dealt with when it is understood that what people report, and what imagery experiments show, are not the properties of images but rather the properties of the objects they are imaging.

Pylyshyn (1981) used the criterion of cognitive penetrability as an empirical method for assessing the representational status of imagery. If images are cognitively penetrable, subject to the influences of tacit knowledge, then they are descriptions and as such are governed by the general processes that operate on symbolic encodings of rules and representations. If images are cognitively impenetrable then they should be viewed as intrinsic properties of certain mechanisms that are not alterable, by tacit knowledge. Clearly, Pylyshyn is convinced that images are of the former class while Kosslyn believes that they are of the latter (McGuiness, 1989).

Kosslyn's position Kosslyn (1976, 1980, 1983) put forward counter-arguments to Pylyshyn's criticisms. Primarily he rejected the picture metaphor of imagery. He theorized that images partially involve propositional information, but also include non-propositional representations and are represented in a medium with special properties. Images are not pictures but quasi-spatial entities generated from some store of perceptual experience in long term memory. In this way Kosslyn acknowledged that some aspects of imaging may be more susceptible to cognitive penetration than others. The components of imaging that are shared with perception, the spatial structure of the visual buffer for example, are not likely to be cognitively penetrated. On the other hand, components that interface with general knowledge, for example image generation, may well be.

At one point the propositional/analogical debate looked as if it was about to turn into the cognitive penetrability/impenetrability debate. The penetrability criterion applies only to individual components of tasks and experimental tasks are usually made up of several components. Identifying which components are cognitively penetrable and which are not, may be as dogged as making any other decision about representation and process based on experimental data (Pinker, 1985).

The argument that all imagery phenomena can be accounted for by propositional accounts is perhaps the hardest to answer. The imagery theorists must specify how images can operate without relying on a "Mind's eye", and to specify the special properties that make images distinctive from representations that are propositionally based.

Kosslyn's theory of imagery deals with representation in a spatial medium

(Kosslyn 1975, 1980, 1983). This spatial medium has four properties: (1) there is a specified shape and capacity to depict spatial relations; (2) there is an area of high resolution in the centre; (3) there is a grain to the medium that can obscure small features; and (4) there is a timing constraint in that once an image is generated it begins to fade. In simplified terms Kosslyn's model of imagery has been likened to a cathode ray tube (CRT). The mental television screen has spatial extent, limited capacity, can fade and therefore requires re-activation. The images shown on the screen can be rotated, scanned, enlarged or reduced in scale; the images can be blurred or finely focused (Kosslyn *et al.*, 1978; Kosslyn & Schwartz, 1977; Kosslyn & Schwartz, 1978).

Kosslyn's subsequent computer simulation of imagery was deliberately designed to capture the characteristics of the prototype model (Kosslyn *et al.*, 1992). Two types of information are used in his simulation to sustain an image: propositional representation in long term memory and a spatial array in a visual buffer that sustains the surface image. As such image information is kept in image files in long term memory in analogical format, while information about the parts of objects is kept in propositional files in another part of long term memory. Computational processes use image files, propositional files and the spatial medium to generate, interpret and transform images.

Within this theory several structures and processes are involved to generate an image; for example the image of a cat. The spatial medium in which the cat is to be represented, the propositional and image files that store the knowledge about the cat, and the processes that generate the image in the medium from these files (Kosslyn, 1980, 1983).

The idea that the spatial medium is like a cathode-ray tube gives a sense of physical space, if images move too far they will move out of the medium space (like film images move out of shot). Resolution is not uniform with the centre being in clearer focus, as the image moves further out resolution begins to deteriorate. Associated with the changing resolution of the spatial medium is the grain; the size of the pixels on the cathode-ray tube. The grain limits what can and cannot be represented clearly. Details of an image may be lost when an image is reduced in size. For example some fonts are illegible when the size is reduced. The image may also have a time constraint in that if the image is to be maintained in the medium, it needs to be regenerated or refreshed.

If the image is represented in this spatial medium the next question is how is the image generated? Image files can represent a whole object or various parts of one. Details can be represented in different image files;

different colouring image files allow for different cat images (e.g. tabby cats, black and white cats, gray cats). Propositional files list the properties of cats (e.g. HAS-TAIL, HAS-WHISKERS). The propositional files might contain entries that relate parts to the whole. Propositional files also contain general information, (for example, very small, small, large, very large) and information about superordinate categories.

When one is asked to image a cat, several processes go to work using various propositional and image files. In the model proposed by Kosslyn, the main process is called IMAGE and it breaks down into three sub-processes: PICTURE, FIND, and PUT. When asked to image, the IMAGE process first checks to see whether the object (i.e. the cat) mentioned has a propositional file with links to an image file. If such a file is available then the PICTURE process takes the information about the coordinates of the image and represents it in the spatial medium the location for highest resolution (in the centre, and in focus). The PUT process directs the PICTURE process to add details from other image files, e.g. turn the cat silhouette into a black and white cat with distinctive markings. In cases when more specific instructions are given, i.e. rotate the cat 180°, look at the whiskers up close, processes ROTATE and SCAN operate on the image.

Kosslyn's crucial claim is that the spatial medium is a dedicated medium for depicting (not describing) visual-spatial information and that this medium is also used in perceptual processing. As well as the array-like structure, the model also includes procedures for generating images from long-term memory, for detecting parts of images, and for carrying out transformations (Kosslyn, 1980; Kosslyn *et al.*, 1978; Kosslyn & Schwartz, 1978). Kosslyn is here eliminating the vagueness or imprecision surrounding imagery by specifying the different processes and data structures in computational terms. His theory was one of the first that changed the focus toward computer modelling of the mind and associated processes. In the best tradition of the computational approach, he specified an imagery model at a level that is computable. This leaves an important question: Is it an adequate model?

The propositional case In 1984, Pylyshyn introduced a second wave of arguments in an attempt to define imagery out of cognitive science. Pylyshyn's work adds support to Baddeley's (1986) criticisms of experiment methodology especially Kosslyn's image scanning. For Pylyshyn, subjects are simply doing what they are told to do: i.e. simulating what it would be like to look at something and scan across it. Subject behaviour therefore does not reflect any special properties of an imagery system, rather their behaviour reflects the experimental instructions.

The criterion of cognitive penetrability is fundamental to Pylyshyn's view of computation and cognition. He uses it to distinguish between those processes that are ultimately computable (explainable by rules and representations) and those that are part of the functional architecture of the system (the biological system). As Pylyshyn's general view is that all computational processes are formal operations carried out on symbol structures, then either imagery must be within the computational domain or it must be part of the functional architecture.

To further the computer analogy, the hardware of a computer is unchanging; for example, until you buy a new system the monitor, keyboard, silicone chips and wiring remain the same. On the other hand the software of a computer can be changed in a number of different ways; new programs can be bought that create data structures, text files, graphics files etc., without changing the hardware of the computer. Pylyshyn (1984) takes the argument that the mind has a functional architecture like the hardware of the computer that cannot be modified by the software of the mind (beliefs, goals etc.).

Pylyshyn argues that if images operate as described by Kosslyn in a special medium then they are part of the functional architecture (the hardware) of the mind and as such are cognitively impenetrable. Since beliefs and goals are inherently propositional, and if one shows that images are cognitively penetrable then they must be fundamentally the same as propositions and therefore be reducible to propositional representations.

Pylyshyn has used these proposals to reinterpret those experiments that provide evidence for the imagery. In a series of experiments he found that like Kosslyn and associates that if subjects were asked to image a black spot moving from point to point, or imagine really walking from point to point, then the times taken to 'scan' corresponded to the relative distances between the points on the map. However, he also found that if subjects were asked to shift their gaze as quickly as possible, the effects disappeared, and if they were asked to imagine running between locations then the time taken was faster than in the original (walking) experiment. For Pylyshyn this shows that people do not seem to be scanning an image in a uniform fashion because instruction changes shouldn't increase or decrease scan rate, and furthermore imagery was clearly under the control of the kind of transformations one expected or believed to occur. In short imagery is cognitively penetrable. To imagine something means to represent something as if it were real. Thus imaging traversing a space entails imagining being successively at intermediate points – otherwise it would not be traversing that was being imagined. It seems as if subjects are better at following instructions than one would expect and that a special representational format is not required to explain the results. Mental rotation studies can be accounted for in the same way (see Rock, 1973). It is harder to judge rotation effects in more complex 3-D shapes (Hinton, 1979; Jenkin, 1987; Takano, 1989).

Other ideas regarding the imagery debate Imagery research has taken a number of directions, not all of which are directly relevant to the representation question, although it is never far away. Pinker (1985) suggested that there are now competing scientific theories of imagery that can be empirically disentangled. Pinker outlines the basic question as whether a specially dedicated cognitive module for image processing is required (the old question). If it is required, is it like Kosslyn's representation in a spatial medium, or like Hinton's (1979) model that is centred on structural descriptions along with special processes that manipulate information in images. Or is it something else?

Not all researchers dealing with propositional representation took Pylyshyn's formal position. Boden (1988) rejects Pylyshyn's adherence to the dichotomy of mental representations as being too simplistic. She argues that it is more correct to admit a three-fold division between propositions, analogue-as-a-special medium representations, and simply analogical representations (in a sense that lacks any special medium claim). This means that even though images may be cognitively penetrable (and therefore based on propositions), it does not follow that the imagery has to be explained in terms of propositional representations that do not operate in a special medium.

Anderson (1983) has acknowledged an alternate tri-code theory of knowledge representation. This model includes propositions, strings and images. For Anderson it is not the notation that expresses the knowledge structure that is important, rather the processes that operate on that knowledge.

Another point is that any arguments hinging on cognitive penetrability are inappropriate and a misguided treatment of the issues. Johnson-Laird (1983) has argued that Pylyshyn's penetrability argument can be used against him. He points out that one might maintain that Pylyshyn's constructs of beliefs and goals are epiphenomenal because they can be 'imagistically penetrated'; that is, the way in which they govern behaviour can be influenced in a rationally explicable way by images. Johnson-Laird (1983, p.152) concludes:

"The moral is plain: images and beliefs are both high-level constructs, and it is a mistake to argue that they are epiphenomenal just because they 'penetrate' each other."

12.3 Mental models

Johnson-Laird (1990) cites Kenneth Craik as the modern author of the concept of mental models. Craik argued in his 1943 monograph *The Nature of Explanation*, that we translate external events into internal models and reason by manipulating these symbolic representations. We can translate the resulting symbols back into actions or recognize a correspondence between them and external events. For Craik a mental model was preeminently a dynamic representation or simulation of the world.

A mental model, according to Johnson-Laird (1983), is a representation that can be wholly analogical, or partly analogical and partly propositional, which is distinct from but related to an image. He uses a philosophical approach to propositional representations. Propositions are the conscious objects of thoughts that allow the linguistic expression of such entities that we entertain, believe, think, doubt etc. In this sense a propositional representation is a representation that is verbally expressible and close to the surface form of natural language.

Johnson-Laird distinguishes among three types of representational constructs; images, mental models, and propositions. He argues that images and mental models are high-level representations that are essential to an understanding of human cognition. Even though the brain may at a base level compute images and mental models in some form of propositional code, it is nevertheless important to study the ways in which people use these high-level representations. The reasons can be appreciated by analogy to the use of high-level programming languages in computers.

Computers use a programming language called machine language at their lowest level of organization (Eysenck & Keane, 1990). Machine language carries out the basic operations of assigning bits of information to different memory registers. While one can program in machine code, it is not "user-friendly" because it is terse and difficult to read. To circumvent this problem, a variety of high-level programming languages have been developed (e.g., BASIC, C++, PASCAL etc.) which can be used by programmers. These languages can be translated by the computers into machine language when compiled, and are useful in that they allow a programmer to think about what the computer has to do in a shorter and clearer fashion. Johnson-Laird argues that mental models and images are like high-level programming languages for the brain in the sense that they free human cognition from operating at a machine-code-like propositional level. So from this perspective, the researchers concern shifts from proving the existence of a representational format to the goals of understanding how people use dif-

ferent representations to carry out different tasks. As such, Johnson-Laird
has mainly looked at how models are used in thinking and reasoning.

Propositions are representations of things that are verbally expressible,
while in contrast, mental models include varying degrees of analogical structure. In some cases, the model may be spatially analogical to the world in
that it captures two- or three- dimensional layouts. It may also represent
analogically the dynamics of a sequence of events. The essential properties
of mental models are that they are analogical, determinate, and concrete
(they represent specific entities). In contrast, propositions, like linguistic
descriptions, are usually indeterminate. That is, propositions can be taken
to describe many different possible states of affair. For example, "The glass
is on the table" is true of the glass in the centre of the table, the edge of the
table, the glass standing upright on the table, lying on its side on the table,
and so on. Propositional representations retain this indeterminacy. Mental
models are made determinate through the action of various inference and
comprehension processes. So the mental model, "the glass is on the table"
might represent a specific glass as being on the table in a particular location and position. If further sentences contradict this model then it can be
revised.

Many of these attributes make them sound like images, but there are
specific differences. Johnson-Laird states that:

"images correspond to views of models; as a result either of perception or imagina-
tion, they represent the perceptible features of corresponding real-world objects."
(Johnson-Laird, 1983, p.157)

In this way, a model of a glass on a table would represent the relative
position of the glass with respect to the table in an analogical manner that
parallels the structure of that state of affairs in the world. An image of a
glass on a table would contain the same information but also involve a view
of the glass on the table from a particular angle.

Johnson-Laird's framework for representation is useful for making predictions about the different types of representations that people are likely to
use in different task situations.

The determinacy differences between propositions and mental models have
been examined experimentally by Mani & Johnson-Laird (1982). They rea-
soned that if subjects were given descriptions that were either determinate
or indeterminate they would form a model of the determinate description
and would not form a model of the indeterminate description because it is
consistent with two models. Later, subjects were given a recognition test
and it was found that they tended to recognize false sentences that described

Descriptions   Layouts

Determinate
The spoon is to the left of the knife.
The plate is to the right of the knife.   spoon   knife   plate
The fork is in front of the spoon.   fork   cup
The cup is in front of the knife.

Indeterminate
The spoon is to the left of the knife.   spoon   knife   plate
The plate is to the right of the spoon.   fork   cup
The plate is to the right of the knife.   **OR**
The cup is in front of the knife.   spoon   plate   knife
                                               fork   cup

Table 12.1. *Examples of the Verbal Descriptions of Spatial Arrays of Objects (Mani & Johnson-Laird, 1982).*

aspects of the inferred model, even though those aspects were never stated explicitly. The determinate and indeterminate descriptions given to subjects are given in Table 12.1. Note that the indeterminate descriptions are consistent with two different states of affairs.

In the experimental procedure, subjects heard a verbal description, and then were shown a diagram of the layout of the objects and asked to decide whether the diagram was consistent or inconsistent with the description. After this decision task subjects were given an unexpected memory test in which they had to rank four descriptions in terms of their resemblance to the original description. One of these descriptions contained a sentence that should have been inferred if subjects had constructed a mental model, even though it had never been mentioned explicitly: namely, that 'The fork is to the left of the cup.' The experiments revealed two main findings. First, subjects tended to recognize falsely the inferred description of determinate items. They did not do this for indeterminate items. This was interpreted as indicating that subjects build models of determinate descriptions and hence make the inference that 'The fork is to the left of the cup'; but they abandon model construction for indeterminate descriptions because of the multiplicity of models that can be produced. Second, subjects tend to remember the verbatim detail of descriptions, because having abandoned model construction, they resort to remembering the propositional structure of the descriptions (Mani & Johnson-Laird, 1982).

While this type of symbolic-logical description of how we do things in our minds has been a driving force in the study of cognition, and primarily information processing; there has been a new perspective developing recently. Rather than trying to distinguish between various models, researchers have side-stepped the representation question and have tried to establish the degree to which imagery and perception share the same processing mechanisms (Finke, 1980, 1985, 1989), or investigate where imaging and perception engage cortical areas (Farah, 1988). Even Kosslyn (1987) has gone 'into the brain' looking at shared processing and brain mechanisms of seeing and imagining in a new computational theory of hemispheric specialization.

The turning away from the basic representational question has resulted in the demise of the propositional/analogical debate. More specifically the arrival of parallel distributed processing and connectionist models have turned the debate toward the examination of the nature of computational psychology. As previously stated, concerns are now expressed in terms of formal operations carried out on symbol structures (Pylyshyn, 1981).

12.4 Connectionist approach

In the previous sections the examination of representations has primarily taken the traditional symbolic approach. The basic view of this approach is that human cognition is centrally dependent on the manipulation of symbolic representations by various rule-like processes. Kosslyn's imagery theory is a prime example of theorizing from this perspective, in which rule-based processes – like IMAGE and PUT – manipulate various symbols. Even though the symbolic approach has been the dominant one within information-processing psychology, some researchers have wondered whether this is ultimately the best way to understand human cognition. They have pointed to a number of possible difficulties in the symbolic approach (Kosslyn, 1983).

First, within a symbolic tradition one has to state explicitly how mental content is represented (whether it be by analogical representations or propositions). Moreover, one has to specify exactly how these representations are manipulated by various rules. So even for relatively simple tasks, symbolic theories can become very complicated. When one moves away from laboratory tasks and looks at everyday tasks (like driving a car), it is sometimes difficult to envision how such a complicated scheme could be at work. People can operate quite efficiently by taking multiple sources of information into account at once. While a symbolic account might be able to deal with a task such as driving, many feel that the account would be too inelegant and cumbersome. A second concern with the symbolic approach is that it has tended to avoid the question of how cognitive processes are realized in the brain. Granted, it provides evidence for the gross localization of cognitive processes in the brain, but we are left with no idea of how these symbols are represented and manipulated at the level of a particular neuron (or set of neurons).

In response to these and other issues, there has been a growing movement in the last few years that has attempted to mount a new approach to cognition: the connectionist approach. (Anderson, 1983; Ballard, 1986; Rumelhart *et al.*, 1986a). The new debate is about the nature of computational psychology (McGuiness, 1989).

Connectionists use computational models consisting of networks of neuron-like units, allowing for several advantages over their symbolic competitors. First, connectionist schemes represent information without recourse to symbolic entities like propositions. Difficulties dealing with propositions and image representation are avoided as information is described at a sub-symbolic level, using distributed representations (Smolensky, 1988). Second, as they do not have to use large sets of explicit propositional rules they have the potential to model complex behaviours (Bechtel & Abrahamsen, 1991; Holyoak & Thagard, 1989; Rumelhart *et al.*, 1986a). Third, in their use of neuron-like processing units they hold out the possibility of theories of cognition that map directly onto detailed aspects of the neurophysiological substrate (Smolensky, 1988).

In contrast to the symbolic tradition, Boden (1988) cites several differences associated with connectionism. Connectionist models stress low-level computational, most of the research is in vision. They involve massive parallel processing, with their 'representations' distributed over networks of computational units. Also, their preferred implementation is on dedicated hardware rather than general purpose digital machines. It is already clear that connectionist ideas suggest significant answers to many questions concerning human cognition. What is not so clear is whether human cognition can in fact be characterized in this way.

The idea of a distributed representation can be illustrated by a simple network of weighted associations. Within the symbolic tradition, the sight and taste of a single malt might be represented as some set of coordinates (for the image of the glass of Lagavulin) or as a proposition (i.e. SINGLE MALT). A distributed representation does not have symbols that represent the single malt explicitly but rather stores the connection strengths between units that will allow either the sight or taste of the single malt to be recreated.

The sight and taste of a single malt can be viewed as being coded in terms of simple signals in certain input cells. These input cells are sense specific (i.e. vision units for sight, and flavour units for taste). Simply, the network is capable of associating the pattern of activation that arrives at the vision units with that arriving at the flavour units and vice versa. This generates a distributed representation of the sight and taste of a single malt as a matrix of weighted activation over the units in the network. The sight and taste of other objects (e.g. glass of iced tea) can be represented by a different pattern of activation in the same network. The units themselves may have no meaning. In a distributed representation it is the pattern as a whole that is the meaningful unit of analysis.

Distributed representations have two important properties to add to this discussion. First, the representation is content-addressable (Eysenck & Keane, 1990). This refers to the fact that in human memory any part of a past occurrence can lead to its full retrieval from memory (one sensory memory jog can bring back an entire episode from memory). In this way, a partial representation of an object is sufficient to reinstate the whole representation. The sight of the single malt will trigger the taste memory as well. Further, distributed representations allow for generalization. While the activation matrices are not exactly the same for a glass of Lagavulin and a glass of iced tea, the visual units are very close indeed. This can lead to disappointment upon tasting the iced tea.

Not all connectionist models use distributed representations. They also use representations similar to those used in the symbolic approach, even though the models still use networks of units. Connectionists call the latter local representations. The difference between distributed and local representations is sometimes subtle. A distributed representation is one in which the units represent small feature-like entities and the full pattern becomes the meaningful unit of analysis (Rumelhart *et al.*, 1986a). The essential tenet of the distributed scheme is that different items correspond to alternative patterns of activity in the same units. A local representation, on the other hand, has a one-unit-one-concept representation in which single units represent entire concepts or other large meaningful units.

Research on network representation is relatively new and the local/distributed distinction can often be equivocal. Hinton (1989, 1991) admits that semantic networks which use spreading activation are not very distinguishable from other distributed representations even though they have units which correspond to single concepts.

What is the relationship between distributed representation and symbolic representation? Do the connectionists actually have a distinctly different approach to representation? Hinton (1990, 1991) has argued that the two views of symbolic and sub-symbolic representation do not contradict one another, but may work in complement. In this way higher level propositions may themselves be represented at lower levels in a distributed fashion (see Clark, 1989; Rumelhart *et al.*, 1986b). This complementarity depends upon the properties of the lower-level distributed representation being recognized and fundamental aspects of the higher-level representations.

The symbolic framework may in fact characterize the macro-structure of cognitive representation (i.e. the broad outlines of symbols and their organization) while the distributed representations characterize the micro-structure of cognitive representation. This is an area that requires further investigation, not everyone shares Hinton's view of complementarity. In some ways reminiscent of the imagery debate, some researchers' have taken sides and attempted to argue that one view is redundant or inappropriate. A case in point is Smolensky's (1988) 'proper treatment of connectionism' argument against complementarity. Again, current interest in cognitive psychology concerns the final resolution of this debate.

12.5 Conclusions

The current consensus follows two basic premises. First, any effort to prove that one format of representation is redundant is a waste of time. In fact, the terms of the argument were misplaced, perhaps even the issue was not empirically decidable, or possibly both groups of proponents were attempting to answer radically different questions (Anderson, 1978; Baddeley, 1986; McGuiness, 1989). Second, there is general agreement that different representational constructs are needed to characterize the richness of human cognition and that imagery should be counted as one of these constructs (Anderson, 1983; Johnson-Laird, 1983).

Despite the fact that the debate may have been ill-conceived in itself, it has provoked a clarification of the concept of imagery and a resurgence in interest and creative experimentation in a field long ignored by past behaviourist theories. Block (1981), Finke (1980, 1985) and Tye (1991) are examples of new perspective regarding imagery in psychology. Although the question of analogical or propositional representation with respect to imagery is central to the issue, it is certainly not the only one. Others include: Why do some tasks engage visual imagery while others do not? Are there changes in visual imagery with increasing expertise in a domain? Is there any method to maximize the usefulness of imagery?

Instead of freeing researchers to examine these questions, the question of representation has dominated the research. Apart from the analysis of imagery as a mnemonic, and the relationship between imagery and perception, there has been little attention paid to the role of imagery in problem solving, planning, performance on spatial cognition tasks in general (McGuiness, 1989). The upsurgence of imagery research was part of the pendulum swing that was an attempt to redress the balance from a one-sided propositional research focus of the 1960s and 1970s. What has occurred is more balanced, with both forms of symbolic representation (analogical representation and propositions) drawing research interest and speculation.

If there is any lesson to be learned from the propositional-analogical debate it is that wide ranging empirical regularities must be established if experimental psychology is to make any impact on the principled accounts of cognitive modellers (Logie & Denis, 1991). Reducing the mind to the level of a CPU as proposed by connectionism and neural networks may also be simplifying the issue. In fact Gardner's statement that

"...humans may be an amalgam of several kinds of computers, computer models, or may deviate from any kind of computer yet described." (Gardner, 1985 p.387).†

may be found to have a great deal of truth to it.

To describe and understand complex systems we require a multiplicity of representations. It is not possible to state that one of them "is true," or that it is the final answer. Dalegroot (1990) suggests that we need to live with a multitude of approaches. The best we can aim for is to understand the relationship between different approaches. He argues "that this is in essence the nature of understanding: relating new representations to old familiar ones"‡ (Dalegroot, 1990, p.236). This is constructivism in action, assimilating and accommodating information as we experience it.

The representation debate stems from the inability to consider the possibility that more than one of representation can be used. Perhaps one should look at task analysis to posit a feasible underlying representation. In the issue of mental rotation and image scanning, clearly instruction's given to subjects provide a suggested method for task completion. When redundancies are explained to subjects, thereby reducing task difficulty, the subjects' responses change. If task complexity is increased then subjects' responses differ again. Human cognition may be 'opportunistic'. Based on experience one represents the salient information necessary for task completion. The co-existence of analog and propositional representations for symbolic manipulation is a possibility, especially if different tasks are examined. Often researchers who deal with neural networks preface their descriptions of the visual system, by stating that while modelling the human visual systems

† Copyright (1985) Howard Gardner, Harper Collins Publishers Inc., Used with permission.
‡ Copyright (1990) Springer-Verlag New York. Used with permission.

performance on specific tasks, their model is a best guess at what is going on inside our heads, and may not transfer to model human vision on other tasks.

Different performances across domains leads one to wonder if representation will ever be fully understood. For the future perhaps the new perspective brought forward by neural network researchers may have an impact upon the imagery debate. If the concept of cognitive redundancies can be examined in a distributed (or even local) representation, perhaps similar to dual-coding, then inferences regarding accuracy and efficiency in human performance on cognitive tasks may be made. Some combination of paradigm driven evidence and computer modelling may lead to new questions and answers. Whether this would lead to a parsimonious model of representation is yet to be discovered.

Perhaps the final word should be from Hatfield.

"One often suspects that the competing 'isms' overplay their differences in order to maintain their respective identities."† (Hatfield, 1990, p.243).

† Copyright (C) American Psychological Association. Used with permission.

13

A simple algorithm that discovers efficient perceptual codes

Brendan J. Frey, Peter Dayan and Geoffrey E. Hinton

Department of Computer Science, University of Toronto
Toronto, Ontario, M5S 1A4, Canada

We describe the "wake-sleep" algorithm that allows a multilayer, unsupervised, neural network to build a hierarchy of representations of sensory input. The network has bottom-up "recognition" connections that are used to convert sensory input into underlying representations. Unlike most artificial neural networks, it also has top-down "generative" connections that can be used to reconstruct the sensory input from the representations. In the "wake" phase of the learning algorithm, the network is driven by the bottom-up recognition connections and the top-down generative connections are trained to be better at reconstructing the sensory input from the representation chosen by the recognition process. In the "sleep" phase, the network is driven top-down by the generative connections to produce a fantasized representation and a fantasized sensory input. The recognition connections are then trained to be better at recovering the fantasized representation from the fantasized sensory input. In both phases, the synaptic learning rule is simple and local. The combined effect of the two phases is to create representations of the sensory input that are efficient in the following sense: On average, it takes more bits to describe each sensory input vector directly than to first describe the representation of the sensory input chosen by the recognition process and then describe the difference between the sensory input and its reconstruction from the chosen representation.

13.1 Introduction

Artificial neural networks are typically used as bottom-up recognition devices that transform input vectors into output vectors via one or more layers of hidden neurons. The networks are trained by repeatedly adjusting the weights on the connections to minimize the discrepancy between the actual output of the network on a given training case and the target output supplied by a teacher. During training, the hidden neurons are forced to extract informative features from the input vector in order to produce the correct outputs. Although this kind of learning works well for many practical problems, it is unrealistic as a model of real perceptual learning because it requires a teacher who specifies the target output of the network.

When there is no explicit teacher, it is much less obvious what learning should be trying to achieve. In this chapter, we show how it is possible to get target activities for training the hidden neurons of a network without requiring a teacher. This leads to a very simple, local rule for adjusting the weights on connections. We then show that this simple rule can be viewed as a way of optimizing the coding efficiency of the representations extracted by the network.

13.2 A simple stochastic neuron and how to train it

There are many different idealized models of neurons. Here we use a particular model in which the neuron has two possible activity states, 1 and 0. The inputs to the neuron only have a probabilistic influence on its state of activity. Big positive inputs tend to turn it on and big negative ones tend to turn it off, but there is always some chance that the neuron will adopt the less probable of its two states. A neuron, i, first computes its total input, x_i

$$x_i = b_i + \sum_j s_j w_{ji}$$

where b_i is the bias of the neuron, s_j is the binary state of another neuron, and w_{ji} is the weight on the connection from j to i. The probability that the neuron turns on then depends only on x_i

$$p_i = prob(s_i = 1) = \frac{1}{1 + e^{-x_i}}$$

If a teacher supplies target states for the neuron it is relatively straightforward to adjust the weights on the incoming connections so as to maximize the probability that the neuron will adopt the correct target states on all the various training cases. This overall probability is just the product over all training cases of the probability that the neuron adopts each target activity. First we note that maximizing the product of these probabilities is equivalent to maximizing the sum of their logarithms. This can be done by an online procedure that simply adjusts a weight to improve the log-probability of the target value on each training case as it is presented. Provided these improvements are small and in proportion to the derivative of the log-probability with respect to the weight, the combined effect of the weight changes over all of the different training cases will be to improve the overall log-probability. Fortunately, the derivative of the log-probability is very simple and leads to the following learning rule:

$$\Delta w_{ji} = \epsilon s_j(t_i - p_i) \qquad (13.1)$$

where ϵ is the learning rate and t_i is the target value.

The nice thing about this learning rule is that all of the information it requires is local to a synapse (assuming that the synapse can find out p_i or the actual postsynaptic activity s_i which is a stochastic estimate of p_i). The major difficulty in applying this simple rule to a multilayer network is that we do not generally have targets for the hidden neurons.

13.3 How bottom-up and top-down models can train each other

One way of solving the problem of hidden targets for a network that performs vision is to use synthetic images that are generated by a realistic graphics program. This program randomly chooses a sensible representation and then produces a synthetic image using its graphics rules. It can therefore provide pairings of images with their underlying representations and these pairings can be used to train a recognition network to recover the underlying representation from the image. If the graphics program is written as a top-down hierarchical network of binary stochastic neurons (see figure 13.1), each top-down pass will produce an image together with a set of targets for all the hidden neurons in the layers above. So, given a graphics program in this form, we can train a vision program that inverts the generation process. Of course, images will typically be ambiguous in the sense that the graphics program could have generated them using different representations. This means that, given the image, the best we can hope to do is to assign probabilities to the underlying representations. The stochastic neurons we use are therefore entirely appropriate.

The rule for learning the weight, ϕ_{ij}, on the recognition connection from neuron i to neuron j is:

$$\Delta \phi_{ij} = \epsilon s_i(t_j - q_j) \qquad (13.2)$$

where t_j is the actual binary state of neuron j produced by the generation process and q_j is the probability that neuron j would be turned on by the recognition connections and the recognition bias, ϕ_{0j}:

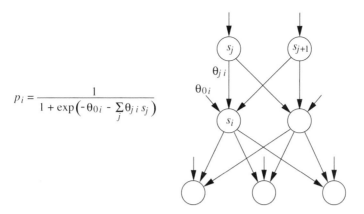

$$p_i = \frac{1}{1 + \exp\left(-\theta_{0i} - \sum_j \theta_{ji} s_j\right)}$$

Fig. 13.1. A top-down generative model composed of stochastic neurons. The model can be used to generate data in the bottom layer. Because the neurons are stochastic, many different data vectors can be generated by the same model. A neuron is turned on with probability p_i so its binary state depends on its generative bias and on the binary states already chosen for neurons in the layer above. At the top layer the neurons have uncorrelated states. The correlations between neurons become more and more complicated in lower layers.

$$q_j = \frac{1}{1 + \exp(-\phi_{0j} - \sum_i s_i \phi_{ij})}$$

So far we seem to have merely exchanged one problem for another. In order to get the hidden targets to train a network to do vision, we have appealed to a network that can already do graphics. But where does this network come from?

Suppose we already have a multilayer bottom-up vision network that can recover underlying representations from images. It would then be easy to train a top-down graphics network since the vision network can provide training examples in which images are paired with the higher level representations from which they should be generated.

The rule for learning the weight, θ_{ji}, on the generative connection from neuron j to neuron i is:

$$\Delta\theta_{ji} = \epsilon s_j(t_i - p_i) \tag{13.3}$$

where t_i is the actual binary state of neuron i produced by the recognition process and p_i is the probability that neuron i would be turned on by the generative connections and generative bias.

So, given a graphics network we can train a vision network and vice versa. Now comes the leap of faith. Given a *poor* graphics network, we use the images it generates to train a vision network. When this vision network is then applied *to real images* we can use it to improve the graphics network. Intuitively, the reason the two networks can improve each other is that the mutual training keeps decreasing the discrepancy between the distribution of the real images and the distribution of the fantasies generated by the graphics network. As we shall see later, this intuitive reasoning is only approximately correct.

13.4 A statistical perspective

There are two equivalent but very different approaches to analyzing what the wake-sleep algorithm does. In one approach we view the generative model as primary and the aim is to adjust the top-down generative connections so as to maximize the likelihood that the generative model would produce the observed data. This type of maximum likelihood model fitting is a standard statistical approach. In order to perform the maximization, we need to know how the current generative model explains each data vector. An explanation of a data vector is an assignment of 1's and 0's to all of the hidden neurons in the network. For a given set of generative weights, each possible explanation will have some posterior probability of having generated each data vector and these probabilities are needed in order to adjust the generative weights correctly. This is tricky because the number of possible explanations is exponential in the number of hidden neurons so it is completely intractable to compute all those posterior probabilities.

The recognition connections can be viewed as a way of approximating the posterior probabilities of explanations. Given a data vector, a bottom-up pass through the network will produce a particular explanation. Since the neurons are stochastic, another bottom-up pass may well produce a different explanation for the same data vector. The recognition connections therefore determine a probability distribution over explanations for each data vector. Although this is not the true posterior distribution, the learning in the sleep phase makes it approximate the posterior distribution which is good enough to allow the generative weights to be improved. A more rigorous account from this perspective is given by Dayan *et al.* (1995). In this chapter we focus on a coding perspective (Hinton & Zemel, 1994; Hinton *et al.*, 1995).

13.5 The minimum description length perspective

Consider the following communication game: A *sender* must communicate an ensemble of binary data vectors to a *receiver* using as few bits as possible. The simplest method is for the sender to treat all the components of each data vector as independent and to communicate each component separately. The cost of communicating the binary value of a component depends on how often that component is on in the whole ensemble of data vectors. It can be shown that the best possible code for an event that occurs with probability p requires at least $-\log_2 p$ bits. Moreover, by using clever coding techniques it is always possible to approach this limit, so to simplify matters we shall simply assume that an event with probability p can be communicated using $-\log_2 p$ bits. This is only possible if the sender and the receiver both know the value of p, which would require some additional communication. For large ensembles, this additional communication can be amortized across many data vectors so it is negligible and we shall ignore it here. So, taking into account the two possible states of component i of the data vector, the cost of communicating that component is:

$$C_i = -s_i \log_2 p_i - (1 - s_i) \log_2 (1 - p_i) \tag{13.4}$$

where p_i is the probability that it is on and s_i is its actual binary state.

If the components of the data vector are not independent it is wasteful to communicate them separately and independently. It is more efficient to transform the data into a different representation in which the components *are* approximately independent. Then this representation is communicated together with any errors that occur when the raw data is reconstructed from the representation. This gives rise to an interesting criterion for what constitutes a good representational scheme. We simply measure the cost of communicating the representations of all the data vectors in the ensemble plus the cost of communicating the reconstruction errors. The smaller this combined description length, the better the representational scheme. This is a simplified version of the minimum description length (MDL) approach introduced by Rissanen (1989). In MDL it is usually important to include the cost of communicating the representational scheme itself since this is needed in order to reconstruct each data vector from its representation. For our current purposes we ignore this additional cost.

A simple idea about how to communicate images may make the MDL perspective clearer. Instead of sending the individual pixel intensities, we could first extract edges from the image and then extract instances of objects from the edges as shown in figure 13.2. To communicate the image we first

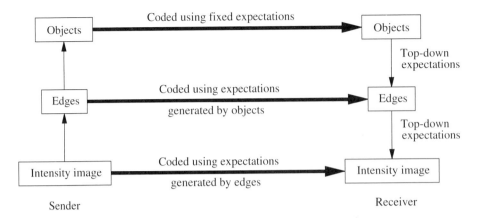

Fig. 13.2. An illustration of the relationship between good representations and economical communication. If the images are well-modelled in terms of objects and edges, then they can be communicated cheaply by using this representation. The top-down expectations produced by the generative model operating on representations at one level will assign high probabilities to the data actually observed at the next level down, so by using the top-down expectations it is possible to communicate the data cheaply.

send the top-level representation in terms of instantiated objects. If the number of possible object types is limited and if each type of object only has a few degrees of freedom in how it can be instantiated (*eg.* position, size and orientation) it will be much cheaper to send the top-level representation than to send the raw image. Once the receiver knows the instantiated objects he can use a top-down generative model to predict where the edges are. More specifically, his predictions can take the form of a probability distribution across the various possible instantiated edges. If the predictions are good, they will assign fairly high probabilities to the actual edges. Since both the sender and the receiver can construct the predicted probability distributions, these distributions can be used for communicating the edges. This should be much more efficient than communicating the edges under the assumption that all possible edges are equally likely. In effect, an edge is only expensive to communicate if it violates the expectations created from the layer above by the top-down model. Finally, the edges (plus the contrast across them) can be used to create expectations for the pixel intensities so that intensities which meet these expectations can be communicated cheaply.

For an appropriate ensemble of images, this whole scheme is an efficient way to compress the images for communication. But even if we are not interested in communication, the efficiency of the compression can be used as a criterion for whether the representational scheme is any good. The MDL criterion allows us to take an ensemble of images and decide that it really is sensible to code them in terms of edges and objects even if we have no prior bias towards this type of representation†.

13.5.1 *Quantifying the description length*

Figure 13.3 shows how a multi-layer network could be used to communicate data vectors to a receiver. To communicate an individual data vector, the sender first performs a bottom-up recognition pass which assigns a binary value s_j to each hidden neuron†. This value is chosen stochastically using the recognition probability distribution for the neuron $\{q_j, 1 - q_j\}$, where q_j is determined by the states of the neurons in the layer below and the recognition weights. The binary states of neurons are then sent to the receiver starting with the top layer and working down. Each top-layer neuron s_i has a generative bias, θ_{0i}, that adapts during learning. Applying the logistic function to this bias yields the generative probability p_i that the neuron is on. Assuming that the sender and receiver use the distribution $\{p_i, 1 - p_i\}$ as an agreed prior distribution for communicating the binary state s_i, the cost is given by equation 13.4‡. For neurons in the middle and bottom layers, the generative probability p_j depends not only on the generative bias of the neuron but also on the states of neurons in the higher layers and the generative weights from those neurons.

Summing over all neurons, the number of bits that would have to be sent across a channel to communicate a data vector is:

$$C = \sum_i C_i = -\sum_i \left(s_i \log_2 p_i + (1 - s_i) \log_2(1 - p_i) \right) \qquad (13.5)$$

C is a stochastic quantity because it depends on the states s_i that are stochastically picked during the bottom-up recognition pass. Apart from this, the only peculiar property of equation 13.5 is that it is wrong, for reasons explained in the next section.

---

† To be fair, we need to also take into account the cost of communicating the generative model itself — how object instantiations predict edges and how edges predict pixel intensities. This raises some tricky issues about what probability distribution to use for communicating the generative models, but these difficulties can be handled.

† Notice that the states of neurons within one layer are conditionally independent given the particular binary states chosen for neurons in the layer below, but this still allows the states of neurons in the top layer to be far from independent given the data.

‡ To approach this theoretical limit it is necessary to combine the states of many neurons into one message, so what would actually have to be sent across a channel would be much more complicated than just sending the binary value s_i.

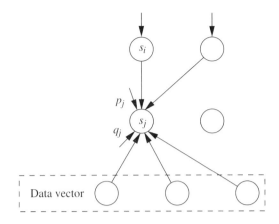

Fig. 13.3. A multi-layer network can be used to communicate data vectors. Binary values for the hidden neurons are obtained by a bottom-up sweep of the recognition network. Assuming that the sender and receiver have identical copies of the generative weights, the generative probability p_j can be used to encode each binary activity.

13.5.2 The bits-back argument

Consider the simple network shown in figure 13.4a which might be obtained by training on the data set shown in figure 13.4b. Since there is only one hidden neuron, the network has two alternative ways of representing each data vector. The generative bias of the hidden neuron, h, is 0 so its generative probability is $p_h = 0.5$. It therefore costs 1 bit to communicate the state of the hidden neuron whichever representation is used. The generative probabilities for the two input neurons are $(0.5, 0.75)$ if neuron h is on and $(0.25, 0.5)$ if it is off. Either way, if the data vector is $(1, 0)$ it costs an additional 3 bits to communicate the states of the two data neurons once s_h has been communicated. The network has two equally good ways of coding the data vector $(1, 0)$ and each way takes a total of 4 bits. Now we show a rather surprising result: Two 4 bit methods are as good as one 3 bit method.

We start with a vague intuitive argument. If we can send the data using two different messages each of which costs 4 bits, why can't we save a bit by being vague about which of the two messages we are actually sending? This intuition can be made precise using the scheme illustrated in figure 13.5. Imagine that in addition to the data vector, the sender and the receiver are also trying to communicate some totally separate information across the same channel. This other information has already been efficiently encoded into a string of binary digits that appears totally random. We show how to

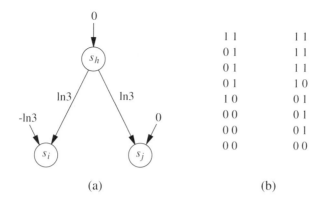

Fig. 13.4. a) A simple example of a generative model. The logistic of $-ln3$ is $1/4$, so it costs 2 bits to communicate $s_i = 1$ when $s_h = 0$ because the top-down distribution $(p_i, 1-p_i)$ under which the state of s_i must be coded is then $(1/4, 3/4)$. Similarly, when s_h is off it only takes 1 bit to communicate the state of s_j. b) A data-set which is well-modelled by the simple network. Note that the frequency of the vector $(1,0)$ in the dataset is $1/8$ so the optimal code takes 3 bits.

communicate both the data vector and the first bit of this random bit-string using only the 4 bits that are required to communicate the data vector. So the net cost of sending the data vector is really only 3 bits which is just what it should be for a vector that occurs one eighth of the time.

During the bottom-up recognition pass, the sender discovers that $q_h = 0.5$ because there are two equally good choices for s_h. Instead of using a random number generator to make the decision, the sender simply uses the first bit in the other message since these bits conveniently have a probability of 0.5 of being on. Using whatever value of s_h gets selected, the sender then communicates s_h and the data vector for a total cost of 4 bits. Assuming the receiver has access to the same recognition model as the sender, the receiver can now recreate the choice that the sender was faced with. He also knows what value was chosen for s_h so he can figure out the first bit of the other message.

In general, the various alternative representations will not give equal description lengths for the data vector, and the recognition probabilities will not be 0.5. In the general case, there are many alternative codes, α, each requiring E_α bits, where E_α includes the cost of communicating the reconstruction error. If we have a probability Q_α of picking each code, the expected number of bits that are used to send the data is $\sum_\alpha Q_\alpha E_\alpha$ and the expected number of bits from the other message used to pick a single code

Fig. 13.5. An illustration of how to make effective use of the freedom of choice available when there are several alternative ways of coding the data. Another source of information is used to decide between alternative codes. This allows the other information to be communicated as well as the data. So the true cost of communicating the data is reduced by the amount of information needed to choose between the alternative codes.

from the Q distribution is the entropy of this distribution, $-\sum_\alpha Q_\alpha log_2 Q_\alpha$. So the net cost of communicating a data vector is:

$$F = \sum_\alpha Q_\alpha E_\alpha - \left(-\sum_\alpha Q_\alpha log_2 Q_\alpha\right) \qquad (13.6)$$

Frey and Hinton (1996) describe an actual implementation of this coding method. Equation 13.6 is well known in physics. We interpret α as a particular configuration of a physical system, E_α as its energy measured in appropriate units and Q as a probability distribution over configurations. F is then the Helmholtz free energy of the system at a temperature of 1. We call a model that uses separate recognition connections to minimize the Helmholtz free energy in equation 13.6 a "Helmholtz machine".

The probability distribution that minimizes F is the Boltzmann distribution:

$$Q_\alpha = \frac{e^{-E_\alpha}}{\sum_\gamma e^{-E_\gamma}} \qquad (13.7)$$

The generative weights and biases define the "energy" of each representation and the Boltzmann distribution is then the best possible recognition distribution to use. But F is perfectly well defined for any other recognition distribution over representations and it is generally not worth the effort of computing the full Boltzmann distribution. Our simple bottom-up recognition network builds up the Q distribution as a product of lots of $\{q_i, 1 - q_i\}$ distributions within each hidden layer.

When we take into account the savings that occur when the generative model allows many alternative ways of representing the same data, the coding perspective tells us to minimize free energy. If we also decide to restrict the recognition model to using a product distribution in each hidden layer, the free energy can be rewritten as:

$$F = \sum_i \left(q_i \log_2 \frac{q_i}{p_i} + (1 - q_i) \log_2 \frac{1 - q_i}{1 - p_i} \right) \tag{13.8}$$

where i is an index over all of the neurons, and most of the p's and q's are stochastic quantities that depend on choices of s in higher or lower layers. A pleasing aspect of equation 13.8 is that each neuron makes a separate additive contribution which is just the asymmetric divergence between the recognition and generative probability distributions for the state of the neuron. A less pleasing aspect of the equation is that changes in the recognition weights in lower layers cause changes in q's and hence p's in higher layers, so the derivatives of the free energy with respect to the recognition weights are complicated. Dayan *et al.* (1995) show how the derivatives can be approximated accurately and efficiently using a back-propagation scheme if the recognition process is modified. However, this is much less biologically plausible than the simple wake-sleep algorithm.

13.5.3 Does the wake-sleep algorithm minimize free energy?

All that remains to be shown is that the simple, local wake-sleep algorithm defined by equations 13.2 and 13.3 is actually performing gradient descent in the free energy. For the wake phase, this is easy because the q's are unaffected by changes in the generative weights. When averaged over the stochastic choices of states for the hidden neurons, the right hand side of equation 13.3 is exactly $-\epsilon$ times the derivative of the free energy with respect to the generative weight θ_{ji}. So wake-phase learning does exactly the right thing.

The sleep phase is more problematic for two reasons. First, the sleep phase uses fantasy data produced by the generative model instead of real data. Early on in the learning the fantasies will be quite different from the real data. Later in the learning, however, the distribution of fantasies comes to resemble the distribution of real data. The second problem is more serious. Instead of performing gradient descent in the free energy, the sleep phase performs descent in a similar expression with the p's and q's interchanged:

$$G = \sum_i \left(p_i \log_2 \frac{p_i}{q_i} + (1 - p_i) \log_2 \frac{1 - p_i}{1 - q_i} \right)$$

Fortunately, the free energy and G have very similar gradients when the

p's and q's have soft values that are not close to 1 or 0. Extensive simulations have shown that so as long as we avoid large weights, following the gradient of G almost always reduces the free energy. Naturally, during on-line learning there are stochastic fluctuations in the frèe energy because the binary states produced by the recognition process are stochastic.

13.6 An example: Extracting structure from noisy images

An interesting problem relevant to vision is that of extracting independent horizontal and vertical bars from an image (Foldiak, 1990; Saund, 1995; Zemel, 1994; Dayan & Zemel, 1995; Hinton *et al.*, 1995). Figure 13.6 shows 48 examples of the binary images we are interested in. Each image is produced by randomly choosing between horizontal and vertical orientations with equal probability. Then, each of the 16 possible bars of the chosen orientation is independently instantiated with probability 0.25. Finally, additive noise is introduced by randomly turning on with a probability of 0.25 each pixel that was previously off. So, the graphics program used to produce the training data has three levels of hierarchy: the first and lowest level represents pixel noise, the second represents bars that consist of groups of 16 pixels each, and the third represents the overall orientation of the bars in the image.

Using the wake-sleep algorithm, we trained a Helmholtz machine that has 4 top-layer neurons, 36 middle-layer neurons, and 256 bottom-layer image neurons. Learning is performed through a series of iterations, where each iteration consists of one bottom-up wake phase sweep used to adjust the generative connections and one top-down sleep phase sweep used to adjust the recognition connections. Every 5,000 iterations, an estimate of the free energy and the variance of this estimate are computed. To do this, 1,000 recognition sweeps are performed without learning. During each recognition sweep, binary values for the hidden neurons are obtained for the given training image. The negative log-likelihood of these values under the recognition model gives an unbiased estimate of the second (entropy) term in the free energy of equation 13.6. The negative log-likelihood of the values of *all* the neurons under the generative model gives an unbiased estimate of the first (energy) term in the free energy of equation 13.6. In this way we obtain 1,000 independent, identically distributed, noisy unbiased estimates of the free energy. The average of these values gives a less noisy unbiased estimate of the free energy. Also, the variance of this estimate is estimated by dividing the sample variance by 999.

Since we are interested in solutions where the generative model can con-

Fig. 13.6. Examples of training images produced by a graphics program with three levels of hierarchy. First, an orientation (*ie.*, horizontal or vertical) is randomly chosen with fair odds. Second, each bar of the chosen orientation is randomly instantiated with probability 0.25. Third, additive noise is introduced by randomly turning on with a probability of 0.25 each pixel that was previously off.

struct the image by adding features, but cannot remove previously instantiated features, we constrain the middle-to-bottom connections to be positive by setting to zero any negative weights every 20th learning iteration. In order to encourage a solution where each image can be succinctly described by the minimum possible number of causes in the middle layer, we initialize the middle-layer generative biases to -4.0 which favours most middle-layer neurons being off on average. All other weights and biases are initialized to zero. For the first 100,000 iterations, we use a learning rate of 0.1 for the generative connections feeding into the bottom layer and for the recognition connections feeding into the middle layer; the remaining learning rates are set to 0.001. After this, learning is accelerated by setting all learning rates to 0.01.

Figure 13.7 shows the learning curve for the first 300,000 iterations of a

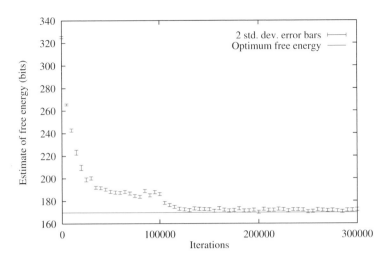

Fig. 13.7. Variation of free energy with the number of wake-sleep learning iterations.

simulation consisting of a total of 1,000,000 iterations. Aside from several minor fluctuations, the wake-sleep algorithm minimizes free energy in this case. Eventually, the free energy converges to the optimum value (170 bits) shown by the solid line. This value is computed by estimating the free energy for the graphics program that was used to produce the training images (*ie.*, in this case, how many random bits it uses when generating an image).

By examining the generative weights after learning, we see that it has extracted the correct 3-level hierarchical structure. Figure 13.8 shows the generative incoming weights, incoming biases, and outgoing weights for the middle-layer neurons. A black blob indicates a negative weight and a white blob indicates a positive weight; the area of each blob is proportional to the magnitude of the weight (the largest weight shown has a value of 7.77 and the smallest a value of -7.21). There are 36 blocks arranged in a 6x6 grid and each block corresponds to a middle-layer neuron. The 4 blobs at the upper-left of a block show the weights from each of the top-layer neurons to the corresponding middle-layer neuron. The single blob at the upper-right of a block shows the bias for the corresponding middle-layer neuron. The 16x16 matrix that forms the bulk of a particular block shows the weights from the corresponding middle-layer neuron to the bottom-layer image. The outgoing weights clearly indicate that 32 of the 36 middle-layer neurons are used by the network as "bar neurons" to represent the 32 possible bars. These bar neurons are controlled mainly by the right-most top-layer "orientation" neuron – the weights from all the other top-layer neurons are nearly zero. If

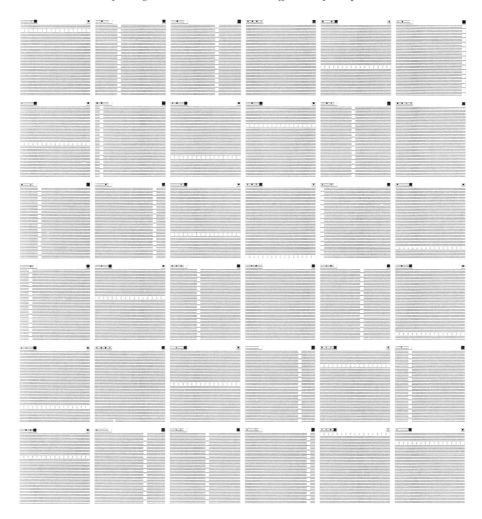

Fig. 13.8. Weights for connections that feed into and out of the middle-layer neurons. A black blob indicates a negative weight and a white blob indicates a positive weight; the area of each blob is proportional to the weight's magnitude (the largest weight shown has a value of 7.77 and the smallest a value of -7.21).

the orientation neuron is off, the probability of each bar neuron is determined mainly by its bias. Vertical bar neurons have significantly negative biases, causing them to remain off if the orientation neuron is off. Horizontal bar neurons have only slightly negative biases, causing them to fire roughly 25% of the time if the orientation neuron is off. The vertical bar neurons have significantly positive incoming weights from the orientation neuron, so that when the orientation neuron is on the net inputs to the vertical bar neurons are slightly negative, causing them to fire roughly 25% of the time. The horizontal bar neurons have significantly negative incoming weights from the orientation neuron, so that when the orientation neuron is on the net inputs to the horizontal bar neurons are significantly negative, causing them to remain off. The 4 middle-layer neurons that are not used to represent bars are usually inactive, since they have large negative biases and all incoming weights are negative. Because the bottom-layer biases (not shown) are only slightly negative, a pixel that is not turned on by a bar neuron still has a probability of 0.25 of being turned on. This accounts for the additive noise.

Once learned, the recognition model can nonlinearly filter the noise from a given image, detect the underlying bars, and determine the orientation of these bars. To clean up each of the training images shown in figure 13.6, we apply the learned recognition model to the image and obtain middle-layer activities which reveal an estimate of which bars are on. The results of this procedure are shown in figure 13.9 and clearly show that the recognition model is capable of filtering out the noise. Usually, the recognition model correctly identifies which bars were instantiated in the original image. Occasionally, a bar is not successfully detected. In two cases a bar is detected that has an orientation that is the opposite of the dominant orientation; however, usually the recognition model preserves a single orientation. Inspection of the original noisy training images for these two cases shows that aside from the single-orientation constraint, there is significant evidence that the mistakenly detected bars *should* be on. Further training reduces the chance of misdetection.

If all the weights and biases are initialized to zero, the middle-to-bottom connections are not constrained to be positive, and all the learning rates are set to 0.01, the trained network is not able to separate the horizontal bars from the vertical bars. Figure 13.10 shows the middle-to-bottom weights after 5,000,000 learning iterations. The black bars indicate that some middle-layer neurons are capable of uninstantiating bars that may be instantiated by other neurons. Although it is imaginable that such a complex scheme is still capable of modelling the training images, the free energy for this trained network is 190 bits – significantly higher than the optimum value of 170 bits.

Although this bar extraction problem may seem simple, it must be kept in mind that the network is not given *a priori* topology information – a fixed random rearrangement of the pixels in the training images would not change the learning performance of the network. So, insofar as the network is concerned, the actual training examples look like those shown in figure

Fig. 13.9. Filtered versions of the training examples from figure 13.6 extracted using the the learned recognition model.

13.11 which were produced by applying a fixed random rearrangement to the pixels in the images from figure 13.6.

13.7 Summary

We have shown that a very simple local algorithm for adjusting synapse strengths is capable of constructing sensible hierarchical representations from the sensory input alone. The algorithm performs approximate gradient descent in a measure of the coding efficiency of the representations. The top-down generative connections are required both for defining the measure that is to be optimized and for generating fantasies to train the recognition weights.

Although the wake-sleep algorithm performs moderately well, we believe that there is room for considerable further development in order to make it more useful in practice (Frey *et al.*, 1996) and more realistic as a neural model (Dayan & Hinton, 1996). The simple form of the algorithm presented

Fig. 13.10. Weights for connections that feed out of the middle-layer neurons after learning without special initialization of the weights, without different learning rates between layers, and without positive weight constraints.

here is unable to account for top-down influences *during* recognition (Palmer, 1975) because it lacks top-down recognition weights. Nor does it explain the role of lateral connections within a cortical area which seem to be important in modelling a number of psychophysical phenomena (Somers *et al.*, 1995). The whole approach would be more plausible if the learning could be driven by the discrepancy between recognition probabilities and generative expectations *during recognition*. How to achieve this without making recognition tediously slow is an open issue.

Acknowledgements

Fig. 13.11. Training examples from figure 13.6 after a fixed random rearrangement of the pixels has been applied. These are indicative of the difficulty of the bars problem in the absence of a topological prior that favours local intensity coherence.

This research was funded by the Information Technology Research Center and Natural Sciences and Engineering Research Council. Hinton is a fellow of the Canadian Institute for Advanced Research. We thank Radford Neal, Rich Zemel and Carl Rasmussen for helpful discussions.

Bibliography

Abbott, L. A., Rolls, E. T., & Tovee, M. J. (1996). Representational capacity of face coding in monkeys. *Cerebral Cortex.* in press.

Adelson, E. H. & Bergen, J. R. (1985). Spatiotemporal energy models for the perception of motion. *J. Opt. Soc. Am. A*, 2:284–299.

Adelson, E. H. & Bergen, J. R. (1991). The plenoptic function and the elements of early vision. In Landy, M. S. & Movshon, J. A., editors, *Computational Models of Visual Processing*, pp. 3–20. MIT Press, Cambridge, MA.

Albrecht, D. G. & Geisler, W. S. (1991). Motion sensitivity and the contrast-response funtion of simple cells in the visual cortex. *Vis. Neurosci.*, 7:531–546.

Albright, T. D., Desimone, R., & Gross, C. G. (1984). Columnar organization of directionally selective cells in visual area MT of macaques. *J. Neurophysiol.*, 51:16–31.

Allman, J., Miezin, F., & McGuinness, E. L. (1985). Direction- and velocity-specific responses from beyond the classical receptive field in the middle temporal visual area (MT). *Perception*, 14:105–126.

Allman, J., Miezin, F., & McGuinness, E. L. (1991). Effects of background motion on the responses of neurons in the first and second cortical visual areas. In Edelman, G. M., Gall, W. E., & Cowan, M. W., editors, *Signal and Sense: Local and Global Order in Perceptual Maps*, pp. 131–142. Wiley-Liss, New York, NY.

Andersen, R. A., Essick, G. K., & Siegel, R. M. (1985). Encoding of spatial location by posterior parietal neurons. *Science*, 230:456–458.

Anderson, J. R. (1978). Arguments concerning representations for mental imagery. *Psych. Rev.*, 85:249–277.

Anderson, J. R. (1979). Further arguments concerning representation for mental imagery: A response to Hayes-Roth and Pylyshyn. *Psych. Rev.*, 86:395–406.

Anderson, J. R. (1983). *The Architecture of Cognition.* Harvard University Press, Cambridge, MA.

Anderson, S. J. & Burr, D. C. (1985). Spatial and temporal selectivity of the human motion detection system. *Vis. Res.*, 25:1147–1154.

Anstis, S. M. (1967). Visual adaptation to gradual change of intensity. *Science*, 155:710–712.

Anstis, S. M. (1990). Motion aftereffects from motionless stimulus. *Perception*, 19:301–306.

Anstis, S. M., Giaschi, D., & Cogan, A. I. (1985). Adaptation to apparent motion. *Vis. Res.*, 25:1051–1062.

Anzai, A., Bearse, M. A., Freeman, R. D., & Cai, D. (1995a). Contrast coding in cells in the cat's striate cortex: Monocular vs binocular detection. *Vis. Neurosci.*, p. (in press).

Anzai, A., Ohzawa, I., Freeman, R. D., & Cohn, T. E. (1995b). Do simple cells in the cat's striate cortex encode binocular disparity through position and phase incongruities? *Soc. Neurosci. Abst.*, 21:1648.

Arnold, K. & Anstis, S. (1993). Properties of the visual channels that underlie adaptation to gradual change of luminance. *Vis. Res.*, 33:47–54.

Attneave, F. (1954). Some informational aspects of visual perception. *Psych. Rev.*, 61:183–193.

Baddeley, A. D. (1986). *Working Memory.* Oxford University press, Oxford.

Baizer, J. S., Ungerleider, L. G., & Desimone, R. (1991). Organization of visual inputs to the inferior temporal and posterior parietal cortex in macaques. *J. Neurosci.*, 11:168–190.

Ballard, D. H. (1986). Cortical connections and parallel processing: structure and function. *Behav. Brain Sci.*, 9:67–120.

Ballard, D. H. (1990). Animate vision uses object-centred reference frames. In Eckmiller, R., editor, *Advanced Neural Computers*, pp. 229–236. North-Holland, Amsterdam.

Ballard, D. H. (1993). Subsymbolic modelling of hand-eye co-ordination. In Broadbent, D. E., editor, *The Simulation of Human Intelligence*, pp. 71–102. Blackwell, Oxford.

Banton, T. & Levi, D. M. (1991). Binocular summation in vernier acuity. *J. Opt. Soc. Am. A*, 8:673–680.

Barlow, H. B. (1972). Single units and sensation: a neuron doctrine for perceptual psychology? *Perception*, 1:371–394.

Barlow, H. B. (1985). Cerebral cortex as model builder. In Rose, D. & Dobson, V. G., editors, *Models of the Visual Cortex*, pp. 37–46. Wiley, Chichester.

Barlow, H. B., Blakemore, C., & Pettigrew, J. D. (1967). The neural mechanism of binocular depth discrimination. *J. Physiol. (Lond.)*, 193:327–342.

Barlow, H. B. & Hill, R. M. (1963). Selective sensitivity to direction of movement in ganglion cells of the rabbit retina. *Science*, 139:412–414.

Barlow, H. B., Kaushal, T. P., & Mitchison, G. J. (1989). Finding minimum entropy codes. *Neural Computat.*, 1:412–423.

Barlow, H. B. & Levick, W. R. (1965). The mechanism of directionally selective units in rabbit retina. *J. Physiol. (Lond.)*, 178:477–504.

Barr, A. H. (1981a). Superquadrics and angle-preserving transformations. *IEEE Comp. Graphics and Appl.*, 1:1–120 1–20.

Barr, A. H. (1981b). Superquadrics and angle-preserving transformations. *IEEE Comp. Graphics and Appl.*, 1:11–23.

Baylis, G. C. & Rolls, E. T. (1987). Responses of neurons in the inferior temporal cortex in short term and serial recognition memory tasks. *Exp. Brain Res.*, 65:614–622.

Baylis, G. C., Rolls, E. T., & Leonard, C. M. (1985). Selectivity between faces in the responses of a population of neurons in the cortex in the superior temporal sulcus of the monkey. *Brain Res.*, 342:91–102.

Baylis, G. C., Rolls, E. T., & Leonard, C. M. (1987). Functional subdivisions of temporal lobe neocortex. *J. Neurosci.*, 7:330–342.

Beakley, B. & Ludlow, P., editors (1992). *The Philosophy of Mind: Classical Problems/Contemporary Issues*. MIT Press, Cambridge, MA.

Bechtel, W. & Abrahamsen, A. (1991). *Connectionism and the Mind: An Introduction to Parallel Processing in Networks*. Basil Blackwell Inc., Cambridge, MA.

Beck, J. (1967). Perceptual grouping produced by line figures. *Percept. & Psychophys.*, 2:491–495.

Beck, J. (1982). Textural segmentation. In Beck, J., editor, *Organization and Representation in Perception*, pp. 285–317. Erlbaum, Hillsdale, NJ.

Beck, J., Rosenfeld, A., & Ivry, R. (1989). Line segregation. *Spatial Vision*, 4:75–101.

Bennett, A. (1990). Large competitive networks. *Network*, 1:449–462.

Bergen, J. R. (1991). Theories of visual texture perception. In Regan, D., editor, *Spatial Vision*, pp. 114–134. MacMillan Press, Houndmills Basingstoke, UK.

Bergen, J. R. & Landy, M. S. (1991). Computational modeling of visual texture segregation. In Landy, M. S. & Movshon, J. A., editors, *Computational Models of Visual Processing*, pp. 253–271. MIT Press, Cambridge, MA.

Berkley, M. A. (1982). Neural substrates of the visual perception of movement. In Wertheim, A. H., Wagenaar, W. A., & Leibowitz, H. W., editors, *Tutorials on Motion Perception*, pp. 201–229. Plenum Press, New York, NY.

Berman, N. & Cynader, M. (1972). Comparison of receptive-field organization of the superior colliculus in siamese and normal cats. *J. Physiol. (Lond.)*, 224:363–389.

Bernstein, N. (1967). *The Coordination and Regulation of Movements*. Pergamon Press, Oxford.

Berthoz, A. & Melvill-Jones, G. (1985). *Adaptive Mechanisms in Gaze Control*. Elsevier, North Holland.

Beverley, K. I. & Regan, D. (1973). Evidence for the existence of neural mechanisms selectively sensitive to the direction of movement in space. *J. Physiol.*, 235:17–29.

Bialystok, E. (1989). Children's mental rotations of abstract displays. *J. Exp. Child Psych.*, 47:47–71.

Biederman, I. (1985). Human image understanding: Recent research and a theory. *Computer Vision, Graphics, and Image Processing*, 32:29–73.

Biederman, I. (1987). Recognition by components. *Psychological Review*, 94:115–147.

Bisiach, J. G. & Luzzatti, C. (1978). Unilateral neglect of representational space. *Cortex*, 14:129–133.

Blakemore, C. & Campbell, F. W. (1969). On the existence of neurones in the human visual system selectively sensitive to the orientation and size of retinal images. *J. Physio.*, 203:237–260.

Blakemore, C. & Tobin, E. A. (1972). Lateral inhibition between orientation detectors in the cat's visual cortex. *Exp. Brain Res.*, 15:439–440.

Block, N. (1981). *Imagery*. MIT Press, Cambridge, MA.

Boden, M. (1981). *Minds and Mechanisms: Philosophical Psychology and Computational Models*. The Harvester Press Ltd., Sussex.

Boden, M. (1988). *Computer Models of Mind: Computational Approaches in Theoretical Psychology*. Cambridge University Press, Cambridge.

Bonds, A. B. (1989). Role of inhibition in the specification of orientation selectivity of cells in the cat striate cortex. *Vis. Neurosci.*, 2:41–55.

Born, R. T., Groh, J. M., & Newsome, W. T. (1995). Functional architecture of primate area MT probed with microstimulation: effects on eye movements. *Soc. Neurosci. Abst.*, 21:281.

Boussaoud, D., Desimone, R., & Ungerleider, L. G. (1991). Visual topography of area TEO in the macaque. *J. Comp. Neurol.*, 306:554–575.

Boynton, R. M. (1979). *Human Color Vision*. Holt, Rinehart and Winston, New York, NY.

Braddick, O., Campbell, F. W., & Atkinson, J. (1978). Channels in vision: Basic aspects. In Held, R., Leibowitz, H. W., & Teuber, H. L., editors, *Handbook of Sensory Physiology, Vol. 8*, pp. 3–38. Springer-Verlag, New York, NY.

Bradley, A. & Skottun, B. (1987). Effects of contrast and spatial frequency on vernier acuity. *Vis. Res.*, 27:1817–1824.

Breitmeyer, B. G. (1980). Unmasking visual masking: a look at the "why" behind the veil of the "how". *Psych. Rev.*, 87:52–69.

Bridgeman, B. (1995). A review of the role of efference copy in sensory and oculomotor control-systems. *Ann. Biomed. Eng.*, 23:409–422.

Broida, T. J., Chandrashekhar, S., & Chellappa, R. (1990). Recursive 3-D motion estimation from a monocular image sequence. *IEEE Trans. Aerospace and Electronic Systems*, 26:639–656.

Brooks, R. A. (1981). Symbolic reasoning among 3-d models and 2-d images. *AI*, 17:285–348.

Brotchie, P. R., Anderson, R. A., Snyder, L. H., & Goodman, S. J. (1995). Head position signals used by parietal neurons to encode locations of visual-stimuli. *Nature*, 375:232–235.

Brothers, L., Ring, B., & Kling, A. S. (1990). Response of neurons in the macaque amygdala to complex social stimuli. *Behav. Brain Res.*, 41:199–213.

Bruce, C., Desimone, R., & Gross, C. G. (1981). Visual properties of neurons in a polysensory area in superior temporal sulcus of the macaque. *J. Neurophys.*, 46:369–384.

Buisseret, P. (1995). Influence of extraocular muscle proporioception on vision. *Physiol. Rev.*, 75:323–338.

Büttner, U., Büttner-Ennever, J. A., & Henn, V. (1977). Vertical eye movement related activity in the rostral mesencephalic reticular formation of the alert monkey. *Brain Res.*, 130:239–252.

Caelli, T. (1995). A brief overview of texture processing in machine vision. In Papathomas, T. V., Chubb, C., Gorea, A., & Kowler, E., editors, *Early Vision and Beyond*, pp. 79–87. MIT Press, Cambridge, MA.

Campbell, F. W., Cleland, B. G., Cooper, G. F., & Enroth-Cugell, C. (1968). The angular selectivity of visual cortical cells to moving gratings. *J. Physiol. (Lond.)*, 198:237–250.

Campbell, F. W., Cooper, G. F., & Enroth-Cugell, C. (1969). The spatial selectivity of visual cells of the cat. *J. Physiol. (Lond.)*, 203:223–235.

Campbell, F. W. & Tedeger, R. W. (1991). A survey of channels and challenges of information and meaning. In *Channels in the Visual Nervous System: Neurophysiology, Psychophysics and Models*. Freund, London.

Cannon, S. C. & Robinson, D. A. (1987). Loss of the neural integrator of the oculomotor system from brain stem lesions in monkey. *J. Neurophysiol.*, 57:1383–1409.

Canny, J. F. (1986). A computational approach to edge detection. *IEEE PAMI*, 8:679–698.

Carandini, M. & Heeger, D. J. (1994). Summation and division by neurons in primate visual cortex. *Science*, 264:1333–1336.

Carpenter, R. H. S. & Blakemore, C. B. (1973). Interactions between orientations in human vision. *Exp. Brain. Res.*, 18:287–303.

Chan, M., Metaxas, D., & Dickinson, S. (1994a). A new approach to tracking 3-D objects in 2-D image sequences. In *Proc. AAAI '94*, Seattle, WA.

Chan, M., Metaxas, D., & Dickinson, S. (1994b). Physics-based tracking of 3-D objects in 2-D image sequences. In *Proc. ICPR*, pp. 326–330, Jerusalem, Israel.

Chelazzi, L., Miller, E. K., Duncan, J., & Desimone, R. (1993). A neural basis for visual search in inferior temporal cortex. *Nature*, 363:345–347.

Cheron, G. & Godaux, E. (1987). Disabling of the oculomotor neural integrator by kainic acid injections in the prepositus-vestibular complex of the cat. *J. Physiol. (Lond.)*, 394:267–290.

Cipolla, R. & Blake, A. (1992). Motion planning using image divergence and deformation. In Blake, A. & Yuille, A., editors, *Active Vision*, pp. 189–201. MIT Press.

Clark, A. (1989). *Microcognition: Philosophy, Cognitive Science, and Parallel Distributed Processing*. The MIT Press, Cambridge, MA.

Clarke, P. G. H., Donaldson, I. M. L., & Witteridge, D. (1976). Binocular visual mechanisms in cortical areas I and II of the sheep. *J. Physiol. (Lond.)*, 256:509–526.

Cohen, B. & Bender, A. K. M. B. (1968). Electrooculographic syndrome in monkeys after pontine reticular formation lesions. *Arch. Neurol.*, 18:78–92.

Cole, G. R., Hine, T., & McIlhagga, W. (1993). Detection mechanisms in L-, M- and S-cone contrast space. *J. Opt. Soc. Am. A.*, 10:38–51.

Collewijn, H., Van der Steen, J., Ferman, L., & Jansen, T. C. (1985). Human ocular counterroll: assessment of static and dynamic properties from electromagnetic scleral search coil recordings. *Exp. Brain Res.*, 59:185–196.

Collins, A. M. & Quillian, M. R. (1969). Retrieval time from semantic memory. *J. Verbal Learn. & Verbal Behav.*, 8:240–247.

Cooper, L. A. & Podgorny, P. (1976). Mental transformations and visual comparison processes: Effects of complexity and similarity. *J. Exp. Psych.: Human Perception and Performance*, 2:503–514.

Cooper, L. A. & Shepard, R. N. (1973a). Chronometric studies of the rotation of mental images. In Chase, W. G., editor, *Visual Information Processing*. Academic Press, New York, NY.

Cooper, L. A. & Shepard, R. N. (1973b). The time required to prepare for a rotated stimulus. *Memory & Cognition*, 1:246–250.

Cooper, L. A. & Shepard, R. N. (1978). Transformations on representations of objects in space. In Carterette, E. C. & Friedman, M. P., editors, *Handbook of Perception (Vol. 8)*, pp. 105–146. Academic Press, New York, NY.

Corballis, M. C. & Roldan, C. E. (1974). On the perception of symmetrical and repeated patterns. *Perception and Psychophysics*, 16:136–142.

Cornsweet, T. N. (1970). *Visual Perception*. Academic Press, New York, NY.

Craik, K. J. W. (1966). *The Nature of Psychology. A Selection of Papers, Essays and Other Writings by the Late K. J. W. Craik*. Cambridge University Press, Cambridge, UK. Edited by S. L. Sherwood.

Crawford, J. D. (1994). The oculomotor neural integrator uses a behavior-related coordinate system. *J. Neurosci.*, 14:6911–6923.

Crawford, J. D., Cadera, W., & Vilis, T. (1991). Generation of torsional and vertical eye position signals by the interstitial nucleus of Cajal. *Science*, 252:1551–1553.

Crawford, J. D. & Guitton, D. (1994). A model for the sensorimotor transformations required for accurate 3-D saccades. *Soc. Neurosci. Abstr.*, 20:234.

Crawford, J. D. & Guitton, D. (1995). Motor adpaptation of 2-D and 3-D aspects of eye-head coordination in monkeys. *Soc. Neurosci. Abstr.*, 21:1271.

Crawford, J. D. & Vilis, T. (1991). Axes of eye rotation and Listing's law during rotations of the head. *J. Neurophysiol.*, 65:407–423.

Crawford, J. D. & Vilis, T. (1992). Symmetry of oculomotor burst neuron coordinates about Listing's plane. *J. Neurophysiol.*, 68:432–448.

Crawford, J. D. & Vilis, T. (1993). Modularity and parallel processing in the oculomotor integrator. *Exp. Brain Res.*, 96:443–456.

Crawford, J. D. & Vilis, T. (1995). How does the brain solve the problems of rotational motion? *J. Motor Behav.*, 27:89–99.

Culham, J. C. & Cavanagh, P. (1994). Motion capture of luminance stimuli by equiluminance color gratings and by attentive tracking. *Vis. Res.*, 34:2701–2706.

Curthoys, I. S., Blanks, R. H. I., & Markham, C. H. (1977). Semicircular canal functional anatomy in cat, guinea pig and man. *Acta Oto-Laryngolica*, 83:258–265.

Curven, R., Blake, A., & Cipolla, R. (1991). Parallel implementation of lagrangian dynamics for real-time snakes. In *Proc. British Machine Vision Conference (BMVC '91)*, pp. 27–35.

Dalenoort, G. J. (1990). Towards a general theory of representation. *Psych. Res.*, 52:229–237.

Daunton, N. & Thomsen, D. (1979). Visual modulation of otolith-dependent units in cat vestibular nuclei. *Exp. Brain Res.*, 37:173–176.

Dayan, P. & Hinton, G. E. (1996). Varieties of Helmholtz machine. *Neural Networks.* (in press).

Dayan, P., Hinton, G. E., Neal, R. M., & Zemel, R. S. (1995). The Helmholtz machine. *Neural Computation*, 7:889–904.

Dayan, P. & Zemel, R. S. (1995). Competition and multiple cause models. *Neural Computation*, 7:565–579.

DeAngelis, G. C., Ohzawa, I., & Freeman, R. D. (1991). Depth is encoded in the visual system by a specialized receptive field structure. *Nature*, 352:156–159.

DeAngelis, G. C., Ohzawa, I., & Freeman, R. D. (1995). Neuronal mechanisms underlying stereopsis: how do simple cells in the visual cortex encode binocular disparity? *Perception*, 24:3–32.

DeAngelis, G. C., Robson, J. G., Ohzawa, I., & Freeman, R. D. (1992). Organization of suppression in receptive fields of neurons in the cat's visual cortex. *J. Neurophysiol.*, 68:144–163.

Demer, J. L., Miller, J. M., Poukens, V., Vinters, H. V., & Glasgow, B. J. (1995). Evidence for fibromuscular pulleys of the recti extraocular muscles. *Invest. Ophthal. Vis. Sci.*, 36:1125–1136.

Deriche, R. & Faugeras, O. (1990). Tracking line segments. *Image and Vision Computing*, 8:261–270.

Desimone, R. (1991). Face-selective cells in the temporal cortex of monkeys. *J. Cog. Neurosci.*, 3:1–8.

Desimone, R., Albright, T. D., Gross, C. G., & Bruce, C. (1984). Stimulus-selective properties of inferior temporal neurons in the macaque. *J. Neurosci.*, 4:2051–2062.

Desimone, R. & Gross, C. G. (1979). Visual areas in the temporal lobe of the macaque. *Brain Res.*, 178:363–380.

DeValois, R. L., Albrecht, D. G., & Thorell, L. G. (1982). Spatial frequency selectivity of cells in macaque visual cortex. *Vis. Res.*, 22:545–559.

DeWeerd, P., Vandenbussche, E., & Orban, G. A. (1992). Texture segregation in the cat: a parametric study. *Vis. Res.*, 32:305–322.

DeYoe, E. A. & van Essen, D. C. (1988). Concurrent processing streams in monkey visual cortex. *Trends in Neurosci.*, 11:219–226.

Dickinson, S. (1991). The recovery and recognition of three-dimensional objects using part-based aspect matching. Technical Report CAR-TR-572, Center for Automation Research, University of Maryland.

Dickinson, S., Christensen, H., Tsotsos, J., & Olofsson, G. (1994a). Active object recognition integrating attention and viewpoint control. In *Proc. ECCV '94*, Stockholm, Sweden.

Dickinson, S., Jasiobedzki, P., Christensen, H., & Olofsson, G. (1994b). Qualitative tracking of 3-D objects using active contour networks. In *Proc. IEEE CVPR*, Seattle.

Dickinson, S. & Metaxas, D. (1994). Integrating qualitative and quantitative shape recovery. *IJCV*, 13:311–330.

Dickinson, S., Metaxas, D., & Pentland, A. (1994c). Constrained recovery of deformable models from range data. In *Proc. 2nd Int. Workshop Visual Form*, Capri, Italy.

Dickinson, S., Pentland, A., & Rosenfeld, A. (1990). A representation for qualitative 3-D object recognition integrating object-centered and viewer-centered models. In Leibovic, K., editor, *Vision: A Convergence of Disciplines*. Springer Verlag, New York.

Dickinson, S., Pentland, A., & Rosenfeld, A. (1992a). From volumes to views: An approach to 3-D object recognition. *CVGIP: Image Understanding*, 55:130–154.

Dickinson, S., Pentland, A., & Rosenfeld, A. (1992b). 3-D shape recovery using distributed aspect matching. *IEEE PAMI*, 14:174–198.

Dickmanns, E. D. & Graefe, V. (1988). Applications of dynamic monocular machine vision. *Machine Vision and Applications*, 1:241–261.

Donaghy, M. (1980). Cats vestibulo-ocular reflex. *J. Physiol. (Lond.)*, 300:337–351.

Donders, F. C. (1847). Bietrag zur lehr von den bewigungen des men-schlichen auges. *Hollandeshen Beitragen zu den Anatomischen und Physiologischen Wissenschaften*, 1:104–145.

Duhamel, J.-R., Colby, C. L., & Goldberg, M. E. (1992). The updating of the representation of visual space in parietal cortex by intended eye movements. *Science*, 255:90–92.

Duncker, K. (1929). Uber induzierte bewegung. *Psychol. Forschung*, 22:180–259.

Emerson, R. C., Bergen, J. R., & Adelson, E. H. (1992). Directionally selective complex cells and the computation of motion energy in cat visual cortex. *Vis. Res.*, 32:203–218.

Engel, A. K., Konig, P., Kreiter, A. K., Schillen, T. B., & Singer, W. (1992). Temporal coding in the visual cortex: new vistas on integration in the nervous system. *Trends in Neurosci.*, 15:218–226.

Evinger, C. & Fuchs, A. F. (1978). Saccadic, smooth pursuit and optokinetic eye movements in the trained cat. *J. Physiol. (Lond.)*, 285:209–229.

Eysenck, M. & Keane, M. (1990). *Cognitive Psychology: A students hand-book*. Lawrence Erlbaum Associates, Hillsdale, NJ.

Fahle, M. & Koch, C. (1995). Spatial displacement, but not temporal asyn-chrony, destroys figural binding. *Vis. Res.*, 35:491–494.

Fahle, M., Leonards, U., & Singer, W. (1993). Figure-ground discrimination from temporal phase. *Invest. Ophthal. & Vis. Sci.*, 34:785.

Farah, M. J. (1988). Is visual imagery really visual? overlooked evidence from neuropsychology. *Psych. Rev.*, 95:307–317.

Feldman, J. A. (1985). Four frames suffice: a provisional model of vision and space. *Behav. Brain Sci.*, 8:265–289.

Ferman, L., Collewijn, H., Jansen, T. C., & Ven den Berg, A. V. (1987a). Human gaze stability in the horizontal, vertical, and torsional direction during voluntary head movements, evaluated with a three-dimensional scleral induction coil technique. *Vis. Res.*, 27:811–828.

Ferman, L., Collewijn, H., & Van den Berg, A. V. (1987b). A direct test of listing's law-I. Human ocular torsion measured in static tertiary posi-tions. *Vis. Res.*, 27:929–938.

Ferman, L., Collewijn, H., & Van den Berg, A. V. (1987c). A direct test of Listing's law-II. Human ocular torsion measured under dynamic condi-tions. *Vis. Res.*, 27:939–951.

Fernandez, C. & Goldberg, J. M. (1971). Physiology of peripheral neurons innervating semicircular canals of the squirrel monkey. ii response to sinusoidal stimulation and dynamics of peripheral vestibular system. *J. Neuophysiol.*, 34:661–675.

Fernandez, C. & Goldberg, J. M. (1976). Physiology of peripheral neurons innervating otolith organs of the squirrel monkey. ii. directional selectivity and force-response relations. *J. Neurophysiol.*, 39:985–995.

Ferster, D. (1981). A comparison of binocular depth mechanisms in areas 17 and 18 of the cat visual cortex. *J. Physiol. (Lond.)*, 311:623–655.

Fetter, M., Tweed, D., Misslisch, M., Fischer, D., & Koenig, E. (1982). Multidimensional descriptions of the optokinetic and vestibuloocular reflexes. *Annals New York Acad. Sci.*, 656:841–842.

Field, D. J. (1994). What is the goal of sensory coding? *Neural Computation*, 6:559–601.

Field, D. J., Hayes, A., & Hess, R. F. (1993). Contour integration by the human visual system: evidence for a local "association field". *Vis. Res.*, 33:173–193.

Field, D. J. & Tolhurst, D. J. (1986). The structure and symmetry of simple-cell receptive field profiles in the cat's visual cortex. *Proc. Roy. Soc. Lond. B*, 228:379–400.

Findlay, J. M. (1973). Feature detectors and vernier acuity. *Nature*, 241:135–137.

Finke, R. (1980). Levels of equivalence in imagery and perception. *Psych. Rev.*, 87:113–132.

Finke, R. (1985). Theories relating mental imagery to perception. *Psychological Bulletin*, 98:236–259.

Finke, R. (1989). *Principles of Mental Imagery*. MIT Press, Cambridge, MA.

Fischer, B. & Kruger, J. (1974). The shift effect in the cat's lateral geniculate nucleus. *Exp. Brain Res.*, 21:225–227.

Fischer, B. & Kruger, J. (1979). Disparity tuning and binocularity of single neurons in cat visual cortex. *Exp. Brain Res.*, 35:1–8.

Flanders, M., Helms-Tillery, S. I., & Soechting, J. F. (1992). Early stages in a sensorimotor transformation. *Behav. Brain Sci.*, 15:309–362.

Fleet, D. J., Heeger, D. J., & Wagner, H. (1995). Computational model of binocular disparity. *Investigative Opthalmology and Visual Science Supplement*, 36:365.

Fleet, D. J., Wagner, H., & Heeger, D. J. (1996). Neural encoding of binocular disparity: Energy models, position shifts and phase shifts. *Vis. Res.*, (in press).

Fodor, J. A. (1981). *Representations: Philosophical Essays on the Foundations of Cognitive Science*. A Bradford Book, MIT Press, Cambridge, MA.

Foldiak, P. (1990). Forming sparse representations by local anti-Hebbian learning. *Biol. Cybernetics*, 64:165–170.

Foldiak, P. (1991). Learning invariance from transformation sequences. *Neural Comp.*, 3:193–199.

Foley, J. M. & Yang, Y. (1991). Forward pattern masking: effects of spatial frequency and contrast. *J. Opt. Soc. Am. A*, 8:2026–2037.

Foster, D. H. (1982). Analysis of discrete internal representations of visual pattern stimuli. In Beck, J., editor, *Organization and Representation in Perception*, pp. 319–341. Lawrence Erlbaum, Hillsdale, NJ.

Foster, K. H., Gaska, J. P., Marcelja, S., & Pollen, D. A. (1983). Phase relationships between adjacent simple cells in the feline visual cortex. *J. Physiol. (Lond.)*, 345:22P.

Freeman, R. D. & Ohzawa, I. (1990). On the neurophysiological organization of binocular vision. *Vis. Res.*, 30:1661–1676.

Frey, B. J. & Hinton, G. E. (1996). Free energy coding. In *Proc. Data Compression Conf. 1996*. IEEE Computer Society Press. (to appear).

Frey, B. J., Hinton, G. E., & Dayan, P. (1996). Does the wake-sleep algorithm produce good density estimators? In Touretzky, D. S., Mozer, M. C., & Hasselmo, M. E., editors, *Advances in Neural Information Processing Systems 8*. MIT Press, Cambridge, MA.

Friedman, A., Pilon, D. J., & Gabrys, G. L. (1988). Cognitive coordinate systems for mental rotation. In *Meeting of the Psychonomic Society*, Chicago, IL.

Fries, W., Albus, K., & Creutzfeldt, O. D. (1977). Effects of interacting visual patterns on single cell responses in cat's striate cortex. *Vis. Res.*, 17:1001–1008.

Fukushima, K. & Fukushima, J. (1991). Otolith-visual interaction in the control of eye-movement produced by sinusoidal vertical linear acceleration in alert cats. *Exp. Brain Res.*, 85:36–44.

Fukushima, K. & Fukushima, J. (1992). Involvement of the interstitial nucleus of Cajal in the midbrain reticular formation in the position-related tonic component of vertical eye movement and head posture. In Berthoz, A., Graf, W., & Vidal, P. P., editors, *The Head-Neck Sensory-Motor System*, pp. 330–345. Oxford University Press, New York.

Fukushima, K., Harada, C., Fukushima, J., & Suzuki, Y. (1990). Spatial properties of vertical eye movement-related neurons in the region of the interstitial nucleus of Cajal. *Exp. Brain Res.*, 79:25–42.

Gallant, J. L., Van Essen, D. C., & Nothdurft, H. C. (1995). Two-dimensional and three-dimensional texture processing in visual cortex of the macaque monkey. In Papathomas, T. V., Chubb, C., Gorea, A.,

& Kowler, E., editors, *Early Vision and Beyond*, pp. 89–98. MIT Press, Cambridge, MA.

Gardner, H. (1985). *The Minds New Science*. Basic Books, New York, NY.

Garner, W. (1962). *Uncertainty and Structure as Psychological Concepts*. Wiley, New York, NY.

Geisler, W. S. (1984). Physical limits of acuity and hyperacuity. *J. Opt. Soc. Am. A*, 1:775–782.

Geisler, W. S. (1989). Sequential ideal-observer analysis of visual discriminations. *Psychol. Rev.*, 96:267–314.

Geisler, W. S. & Davila, K. D. (1985). Ideal discriminators in spatial vision: two-point stimuli. *J. Opt. Soc. Am. A*, 2:1483–1497.

Gennery, D. (1990). Visual tracking of known three-dimensional objects. *IJCV*, 7(3):243–270.

Georgopolous, A. P. (1990). Neural coding of the direction of reaching and a comparison with saccadic eye movements. *Cold Spring Harbour Symp. Quant. Biol.*, 55:849–859.

Georgopolous, A. P., Schwartz, A. B., & Kettner, R. E. (1986). Neuronal population coding of movement direction. *Science*, 233:1416–1419.

Gibson, J. J. (1937a). Adaptation, after-effect and contrast in the perception of tilted lines - II. simultaneous contrast and the areal restriction of the after-effect. *J. Expt. Psych.*, 20:553–569.

Gibson, J. J. (1937b). Adaptation with negative after-effect. *Psych. Rev.*, 44:222–244.

Gibson, J. J. (1950). *The Perception of the Visual World*. Houghton Mifflin, Boston, MA.

Gibson, J. J. (1966). *The Senses Considered as Perceptual Systems*. Houghton Mifflin, Boston, MA.

Gilbert, C. D. (1977). Laminar differences in receptive field properties of cells in cat primary visual cortex. *J. Physiol.*, 268:391–421.

Gilbert, C. D. & Wiesel, T. N. (1990). The influence of contextual stimuli on the orientation selectivity of cells in primary visual cortex of the cat. *Vis. Res.*, 30:1689–1701.

Gilinsky, A. S. (1967). Masking of contour-detectors in the human visual system. *Psychon. Sci.*, 8:395–396.

Glass, A. L., Holyoak, K. J., & Santa, J. L. (1979). *Cognition*. Addison-Wesley Publishing Co., Reading, MA.

Glenn, B. & Vilis, T. (1992). Violations of Listing's law after large eye and head gaze shifts. *J. Neurophysiol.*, 68:309–318.

Godaux, E., Halleux, J., & Gobert, C. (1983). Adaptive change of the vestibulo-ocular reflex in the cat: the effects of a long-term frequency-selective procedure. *Exp. Brain Res.*, 49:28–34.

Goldberg, M. E. & Bruce, C. J. (1990). Primate frontal eye fields III. Maintenance of a spatially accurate saccade signal. *J. Neurophysiol.*, 64:489–508.

Goodale, M. A. & Milner, A. D. (1992). Separate visual pathways for perception and action. *Trends in Neurosci.*, 15:20–25.

Graf, W. (1988). Motion detection in physical space and its peripheral and central representation. *Ann. New York Acad. Sci.*, 545:154–169.

Grasse, K. L. & Cynader, M. (1991). The accessory optic system in frontal-eyed animals. In Leventhal, A. G., editor, *The Neural basis of visual function*, pp. 111–139. CRC, Boca Raton.

Gregory, R. L. (1969). *Eye and Brain: the Psychology of Seeing.* McGraw Hill, New York, NY.

Gregory, R. L. (1980). Perceptions as hypotheses. *Phil. Trans. Roy. Soc. Lond. B*, 290:181–197.

Grimson, W. & Lozano-Pérez, T. (1984). Model-based recognition and localization from sparse range or tactile data. *Int. J. Robotics Res.*, 3(3):3–35.

Groh, J. M., Born, R. T., & Newsome, W. T. (1995). Microstimulation of area MT affects both saccades and smooth pursuit eye movements. *Soc. Neurosci. Abst.*, 21:281.

Gross, C. G., Desimone, R., Albright, T. D., & Schwartz, E. L. (1985). Inferior temporal cortex and pattern recognition. *Exp. Brain Res. Suppl.*, 11:179–201.

Grossberg, S. (1987). Cortical dynamics of three-dimensional form, color and brightness perception: II. binocular theory. *Perception and Psychophysics*, 41:117–158.

Grossberg, S. (1994). 3D vision and figure-ground separation by visual cortex. *Perception and Psychophysics*, 55:48–120.

Grossberg, S., Mingolla, E., & Todorovic, D. (1989). A neural network architecture for preattentive vision. *IEEE Trans. Biomed. Eng.*, 36:65–84.

Guitton, D. & Crawford, J. D. (1994). Three-dimensional constraints on coordinated eye-head gaze shifts in the monkey. *Soc. Neurosci. Abst.*, 20:1405.

Hallett, P. E. & Lightstone, A. D. (1976). Saccadic eye movements to flashed targets. *Vis. Res.*, 16:107–114.

Hamilton, D. B., Albrecht, D. G., & Geisler, W. S. (1989). Visual cortical receptive fields in monkey and cat: spatial and temporal phase transfer function. *Vis. Res.*, 29:1285–1308.

Hammond, P. (1991). Binocular phase specificity of striate cortical neurones. *Exp. Brain Res.*, 87:615–623.

Hammond, P. & Smith, A. T. (1982). On the sensitivity of complex cells in feline striate cortex to relative motion. *Exp. Brain Res.*, 47:457–460.

Harris, C. S. (1965). Perceptual adaptation to inverted, reversed, and displaced vision. *Psych. Rev.*, 72:419–444.

Harris, L. R. (1994). Visual motion caused by movements of the eye, head and body. In Smith, A. T. & Snowden, R. J., editors, *Visual Detection of Motion*, pp. 397–435. Academic Press, London.

Harris, L. R., Blakemore, C., & Donaghy, M. J. (1980). Integration of visual and auditory space in the mamalian superior colliculus. *Nature*, 288:56–59.

Harris, L. R. & Jenkin, M. (1996). Comparing judgements of linear displacement using visual and vestibular cues. *Invest. Ophthal. Vis. Sci.*, 37. (in press).

Harris, L. R. & Jenkin, M. R. (1993a). Spatial vision in humans and robots. In Harris, L. R. & Jenkin, M. R., editors, *Spatial Vision in Humans and Robots*, pp. 1–7. Cambridge University Press, New York, NY.

Harris, L. R. & Jenkin, M. R., editors (1993b). *Spatial Vision in Humans and Robots*. Cambridge University Press, New York, NY.

Harris, L. R. & Lott, L. A. (1995). Sensitivity to full-field visual movement compatible with head rotation: variations among axes of rotation. *Vis. Neurosci.*, 12:743–754.

Harris, L. R. & Mente, P. (1995). Shifting the axis of rotation of the vestibulo-ocular reflex in cats. *Neurosci. Abst.*, 21:60.11.

Harris, L. R. & Mente, P. (1996). The consequences of a channel-based system for coding head movement. *J. Vestibular Res.* (in press).

Hartridge, H. (1923). Visual discrimination and the resolving power of the eye. *J. Physiol.*, 57:52–67.

Haslwanter, T. (1995). Mathematics of 3-dimensional eye rotations. *Vis. Res.*, 35:1727–1739.

Haslwanter, T., Hepp, K., Straumann, D., Dursteller, M. R., & Hess, B. J. M. (1992). Smooth pursuit eye movements obey Listing's law in the monkey. *Exp. Brain Res.*, 87:470–472.

Hasselmo, M. E., Rolls, E. T., & Baylis, G. C. (1989a). The role of expression and identity in the face-selective responses of neurons in the temporal visual cortex of the monkey. *Behav. Brain Res.*, 32:203–218.

Hasselmo, M. E., Rolls, E. T., Baylis, G. C., & Nalwa, V. (1989b). Object-centered encoding by face-selective neurons in the cortex in the superior temporal sulcus of the monkey. *Exp. Brain Res.*, 75:417–429.

Hatfield, G. (1990). Gibsonian representations and connectionist symbol processing: Prospects for unification. *Psych. Rev.*, 52:243–252.

Hayes, P. J. (1985). Some problems and non-problems in representational theory. In Brachman, R. J. & Levesque, M. J., editors, *Readings in Knowledge Representation*. Morgan Kaufman, Los Altos, CA.

Head, H. (1920). *Studies in Neurology, Vol I*. Oxford University Press, Oxford.

Hebb, D. O. (1949). *The Organization of Behavior: a Neuropsychological Theory*. Wiley, New York, NY.

Heeger, D. J. (1987). Model for the extraction of image flow. *J. Opt. Soc. Am. A*, 4:1455–1471.

Heeger, D. J. (1991). Nonlinear model of neural responses in cat visual cortex. In Landy, M. S. & Movshon, J. A., editors, *Computational Models of Visual Processing*, pp. 119–133. MIT Press, Cambridge, MA.

Heeger, D. J. (1992a). Half-squaring in responses of cat simple cells. *Vis. Neurosci.*, 9:427–443.

Heeger, D. J. (1992b). Normalization of cell responses in cat striate cortex. *Vis. Neurosci.*, 9:181–198.

Heeger, D. J. (1993). Modeling simple cell direction selectivity with normalized, half-squared, linear operators. *J. Neurophysiol.*, 70:1885–1898.

Heggelund, P. (1986). Quantitative studies of the discharge fields of single cells in cat striate cortex. *J. Physiol. (Lond.)*, 373:277–292.

Henn, V., Hepp, K., & Vilis, T. (1989). Rapid eye movement generation in the primate: physiology, pathophysiology, and clinical implications. *Revue Neurologique (Paris)*, 145:540–545.

Hepp, K. (1994). Oculomotor control: Listing's law and all that. *Current Opinion in Neurobiology*, 4:862–868.

Hepp, K., Suzuki, J., Straumann, D., & Hess, B. J. M. (1994). On the 3-dimensional rapid eye movement generator in the monkey. In Delgado-Garcia, J. M., Godeaux, E., & Vidal, P. P., editors, *Information Processing Underlying Gaze Control*, pp. 65–74. Pergamon Press., Oxford, UK.

Hepp, K., Van Opstal, A. J., Straumann, D., Hess, B. J. M., & Henn, V. (1993). Monkey superior colliculus represents rapid eye movements in a two-dimensional motor map. *J. Neurophysiol.*, 69:965–979.

Hering, E. (1868). *Die Lehre vom Binokularin Sehen.* Engelmann, Leipzig. *The Theory of Binocular Vision* (English Translation) translated by B. Bridgeman (1977), New York, NY, Plenum.

Hering, E. (1899). Uber die Grenzen der Sehscharfe. *Der Konigl Sachs ges Wiss Math Phys Kl*, 20:16–24.

Hess, R. F. & Snowden, R. J. (1992). Temporal properties of human visual filters: Number, shapes and spatial covariation. *Vis. Res.*, 32:47–59.

Hinton, G. E. (1979). Some demonstrations of the effects of structural descriptions in mental imagery. *Cognitive Science*, 3:231–251.

Hinton, G. E. (1989). *Parallel Models of Associative Memory.* Erlbaum, Hillsdale, NJ.

Hinton, G. E. (1990). *Neuroscience and Connectionist Theory.* Erlbaum, Hillsdale, NJ.

Hinton, G. E. (1991). *Philosophy and Connectionist Theory.* Erlbaum, Hillsdale, NJ.

Hinton, G. E., Dayan, P., Frey, B. J., & Neal, R. M. (1995). The "wake-sleep" algorithm for unsupervised neural networks. *Science*, 268:1158–1161.

Hinton, G. E. & Zemel, R. S. (1994). Autoencoders, minimum description length, and Helmholtz free energy. In Cowan, J. D., Tesauro, G., & Alspector, J., editors, *Advances in Neural Information Processing Systems 6.* Morgan Kaufmann, San Mateo, CA.

Hochberg, J. & Gellman, L. (1977). The effect of landmark features on mental rotation times. *Memory and Cognition*, 5:23–26.

Hoffman, D. D. & Richards, W. A. (1984). Parts of recognition. *Cognition*, 18:65–96.

Hogben, J. H., Julesz, B., & Ross, J. (1976). Short-term memory for symmetry. *Vis. Res.*, 16:861–866.

Holyoak, K. J. & Thagard, P. (1989). Analogical mapping by constraint satisfaction. *Cognitive Science*, 13:295–355.

Hore, J., Watts, S., & Tweed, D. (1992a). Throwing in three dimensions. *Soc. Neurosci. Abs.*, 18:1055.

Hore, J., Watts, S., & Vilis, T. (1992b). Constraints on arm position when pointing in three dimensions: Donders' law and the Fick gimbal strategy. *J. Neurophysiol.*, 68:374–383.

Hornak, J., Rolls, E. T., & Wade, D. (1995). Face and voice expression identification and their association with emotional and behavioural changes in patients with frontal lobe damage. *Neuropsychologia.* in press.

Howard, I. P. (1982). *Human Visual Orientation.* Wiley, New York, NY.

Howard, I. P. (1996). Interactions with and between the spatial senses. *J. Vestib. Res.* (in press).

Howard, I. P. & Zacher, J. E. (1991). Human cyclovergence as a function of stimulus frequency and amplitude. *Exp. Brain Res.*, 85:445–450.

Hubel, D. & Wiesel, T. (1970). Stereoscopic vision in macaque monkey. *Nature*, 225:41–42.

Hubel, D. H. & Wiesel, T. N. (1962). Receptive fields, binocular interaction, and functional architecture in the cat's visual cortex. *J. Physiol. (Lond.)*, 160:106–154.

Humphreys, G. W. & Bruce, V. (1989). *Visual Cognition.* Erlbaum, Hove.

Huttenlocher, D. P. & Ullman, S. (1990). Recognizing solid objects by alignment with an image. *IJCV*, 5(2):195–212.

Imig, T. J. & Morel, A. (1983). Organization of the thalamocortical auditory system in the cat. *Ann. Rev. Neurosci.*, 6:95–120.

Jackson, M. (1989). *Michael Jackson's Malt Whisky Companion.* McGraw-Hill, Toronto, Canada.

Jay, M. F. & Sparks, D. L. (1984). Auditory receptive fields in primate superior colliculus shift with changes in eye position. *Nature*, 309:345–347.

Jay, M. F. & Sparks, D. L. (1987). Sensorimotor integration in the primate superior colliculus .2. coordinates of auditory signals. *J. Neurophysiol.*, 57:35–55.

Jenkin, H. (1987). Spatial tasks: A study of representation and transformation processes. MA Thesis, Department of Psychology, York University.

Johnson-Laird, P. N. (1980). Mental models in cognitive science. *Cognitive Science*, 4:71–115.

Johnson-Laird, P. N. (1983). *Mental Models.* Harvard University Press, Cambridge, MA.

Johnson-Laird, P. N. (1990). Mental models. In Posner, M. I., editor, *Foundations of Cognitive Science*, pp. 469–494. A Bradford Book, MIT Press, Cambridge, MA.

Jones, J. P. & Palmer, L. A. (1987). The two-dimensional spatial structure of simple receptive fields in cat striate cortex. *J. Neurophysiol.*, 58:1187–1211.

Julesz, B. (1963). Towards the automation of binocular depth perception (automap-1). In Popplewell, C. M., editor, *Proc. 1962 IFIPS Cong.* North Holland, Munich.

Julesz, B. (1971). *Foundations of Cyclopean Perception.* University of Chicago Press, Chicago, IL.

Julesz, B. (1975). Experiments in the visual perception of texture. *Scientific American*, 232(4):34–43.

Julesz, B. (1986). Texton gradients: The texton theory revisited. *Biological Cybernetics*, 54:245–251.

Julesz, B. (1991). Early vision and focal attention. *Reviews of Modern Physics*, 63:735–772.

Julesz, B. & Bergen, J. R. (1983). Textons, the fundamental elements in preattentive vision and perception of textures. *The Bell System Technical Journal*, 62:1619–1645.

Julesz, B. & Johnson, S. C. (1968). Stereograms portraying ambiguously perceivable surfaces. *Proc. Nat. Acad. Sci.*, 61:437–441.

Jürgens, R., Becker, W., & Kornhuber, H. H. (1981). Natural and drug induced variations of velocity and duration of human saccadic eye movements: evidence for a control of the neural pulse generator by local feedback. *Biological Cybernetics*, 39:87–96.

Kandel, E. R., Schwartz, J. H., & Jessell, T. M. (1994). *Principles of Neural Science*. Appleton & Lange, Norwalk, CN.

Kanizsa, G. (1976). Subjective contours. *Sci. Am.*, 234:48–52.

Kass, M., Witkin, A., & Terzopoulos, D. (1988). Snakes: Active contour models. *IJCV*, 1:321–331.

Kastner, S., Nothdurft, H.-C., & Pigarev, I. (1995). Neuronal correlates of pop-out in feline striate cortex. *Perception*, 24:S42.

Kastner, S., Nothdurft, H. C., & Pigarev, I. N. (1996). Neuronal correlates of pop-out in cat striate cortex. submitted for publication.

King, W. M. & Fuchs, A. F. (1979). Reticular control of vertical saccadic eye movements by mesencephalic burst neurons. *J. Neurophysiol.*, 42:861–876.

Klein, S. A., Casson, E., & Carney, T. (1990). Vernier acuity as line and dipole detection. *Vis. Res.*, 30:1703–1719.

Klein, S. A. & Levi, D. M. (1985). Hyperacuity thresholds of 1 second: theoretical predictions and empirical validation. *J. Opt. Soc. Am. A*, 2:1170–1190.

Klein, S. A. & Levi, D. M. (1987). Position sense of the peripheral retina. *J. Opt. Soc. Am. A*, 4:1543–1553.

Knierim, J. J. & Van Essen, D. C. (1992). Neuronal responses to static texture patterns in area V1 of the alert macaque monkey. *J. Neurophysiol.*, 67:961–980.

Knudsen, E. I., Du Lac, S., & Esterly, S. D. (1987). Computational maps in the brain. *Ann. Rev. Neurosci.*, 10:41.

Koenderink, J. & van Doorn, A. (1979). The internal representation of solid shape with respect to vision. *Biol. Cybernetics*, 32:211–216.

Koenderink, J. J. & van Doorn, A. J. (1986). Dynamic shape. *Biological Cybernetics*, 53:383–396.

Kohonen, T. (1988). *Self-Organization and Associative Memory*. Springer-Verlag, New York. 2nd Edition.

Kolers, P. A. (1972). *Aspects of Motion Perception*. Pergamon Press.

Konishi, M. (1986). Centrally synthesized maps of sensory space. *Trends Neurosci.*, 9:163–168.

Kosslyn, S. M. (1973). Scanning visual images: Some structural implications. *Perception and Psychophysics*, 14:90–94.

Kosslyn, S. M. (1975). Information representation in visual images. *Cognitive Psychology*, 7:341–370.

Kosslyn, S. M. (1976). Can imagery be distinguished from other forms of internal representation? evidence from studies of information retrieval times. *Memory & Cognition*, 4:291–297.

Kosslyn, S. M. (1980). *Image and Mind*. Harvard University Press, Cambridge, MA.

Kosslyn, S. M. (1983). *Ghosts in the Mind's Machine: Creating and Using Images in the Brain*. Norton, New York, NY.

Kosslyn, S. M. (1987). Seeing and imagining in the cerebral hemispheres: A computational approach. *Psych. Rev.*, 94:148–175.

Kosslyn, S. M., Ball, T. M., & Reiser, B. J. (1978). Visual images preserve metric spatial information: Evidence from studies of image scanning. *J. Exp. Psych.: Human Perception and Performance*, 4:47–60.

Kosslyn, S. M., Chabris, C. S., Marsolek, C. S., & Koenig, O. (1992). Categorical versus coordinate spatial relations: Computational analyses and computer simulations. *J. Exp. Psych.: Human Perception and Performance*, 18:562–577.

Kosslyn, S. M. & Schwartz, S. P. (1977). A simulation of visual imagery. *Cognitive Science*, 1:265–295.

Kosslyn, S. M. & Schwartz, S. P. (1978). Visual images as spatial representations in active memory. In Risemann, E. M. & Hanson, A. R., editors, *Vision*. Academic Press, New York NY.

Kristensen, S. & Nielsen, H. (1992). 3d scene modeling for robot navigation. *M.SC. Thesis*.

Lamdan, Y., Schwartz, J., & Wolfson, H. (1988). On recognition of 3-D objects from 2-D images. In *Proc. IEEE R&A*, pp. 1407–1413, Philadelphia, PA.

Lathan, C. E., Wall, C. W., & Harris, L. R. (1995). Human eye-movement response to z-axis linear acceleration - the effect of varying the phase-relationships between visual and vestibular inputs. *Exp. Brain. Res.*, 103:256–266.

Leonard, C. M., Rolls, E. T., Wilson, F. A. W., & Baylis, G. C. (1985). Neurons in the amygdala of the monkey with responses selective for faces. *Behav. Brain Res.*, 15:159–176.

Leonard, C. S., Simpson, J. I., & Graf, W. (1988). Spatial-organization of visual messages of the rabbits cerebellar flocculus .1. Typology of inferior olive neurons of the dorsal cap of Kooy. *J. Neurophysiol.*, 60:2073–2090.

LeVay, S. & Voigt, T. (1988). Ocular dominance and disparity coding in cat visual cortex. *Vis. Neurosci.*, 1:395–413.

Levi, D. M. & Klein, S. A. (1990). The role of separation and eccentricity in encoding position. *Vis. Res.*, 30:557–585.

Levi, D. M., Klein, S. A., & Wang, H. (1994a). Amblyopic and peripheral Vernier acuity: a test-pedestal approach. *Vis. Res.*, 34:3265–3292.

Levi, D. M. & Waugh, S. J. (1994). Spatial scale shifts in peripheral Vernier acuity. *Vis. Res.*, 34:2215–2238.

Levi, D. M. & Waugh, S. J. (1996). Position acuity with opposite contrast polarity features: evidence for a nonlinear collector mechanism for position acuity? *Vis. Res.*, 36:573–588.

Levi, D. M., Waugh, S. J., & Beard, B. L. (1994b). Spatial scale shifts in amblyopia. *Vis. Res.*, 34:3315–3333.

Levitt, H. (1971). Transformed up-down methods in psychoacoustics. *J. Opt. Soc. Am. A*, 49:467–477.

Leyton, M. (1988). A process grammar for shape. *Artificial Intelligence*, 34(2):213–247.

Li, M. (1992). Minimum description length based 2-D shape description. Technical Report CVAP114, Computational Vision and Active Perception Lab, Royal Institute of Technology, Stockholm, Sweden.

Lisberger, S. G., Miles, F. A., & Optican, L. M. (1983). Frequency-selective adaptation: evidence for channels in the vestibulo-ocular reflex? *J. Neurosci.*, 3:1234–1244.

Liu, Z., Gaska, J. P., Jacobson, L. D., & Pollen, D. A. (1992). Interneuronal interaction between members of quadrature phase and anti-phase pairs in the cat's visual cortex. *Vis. Res.*, 32:1193–1198.

Logie, R. & Denis, M., editors (1991). *Mental Images in Human Cognition*. North Holland, Amsterdam, Netherlands.

Logothetis, N. K., Pauls, J., Bulthoff, H. H., & Poggio, T. (1994). View-dependent object recognition by monkeys. *Current Biol.*, 4:401–414.

Lowe, D. (1985). *Perceptual Organization and Visual Recognition*. Kluwer Academic Publishers, Norwell, MA.

Lowe, D. (1991). Fitting parameterized three-dimensional models to images. *IEEE PAMI*, 13(5):441–450.

Luschei, E. S. & Fuchs, A. F. (1972). Activity of brain stem neurons during eye movements of alert monkeys. *J. Neurophysiol.*, 35:445–461.

Malik, J. & Perona, P. (1990). Preattentive texture discrimination with early vision mechanisms. *J. Opt. Soc. Am. A*, 7:923–932.

Malonek, D., Tootell, R. B. H., & Grinvald, A. (1994). Optical imaging reveals the functional architecture of neurons processing shape and motion in owl monkey area MT. *Proc. Roy. Soc. Lond. B*, 258:109–119.

Mandler, M. B. & Makous, W. (1984). A three-channel model of temporal frequency perception. *Vis. Res.*, 24:1881–1887.

Mani, K. & Johnson-Laird, P. N. (1982). The mental representation of spatial descriptions. *Memory and Cognition*, 10:181–187.

Marr, D. (1982). *Vision*. Freeman, San Francisco, CA.

Marr, D. & Poggio, T. (1979). A computational theory of human stereo vision. *Proc. Roy. Soc. Lond. B*, 204:301–328.

Marr, D. C. & Hildreth, E. (1980). Theory of edge detection. *Proc. Roy. Soc. (Lond.) B.*, 207:187–217.

Marroquin, J. L. (1976). Human visual perception of structure. Master's Thesis, MIT.

Marshak, W. & Sekuler, R. (1979). Mutual repulsion between moving visual targets. *Science*, 205:1399–1401.

Marslen-Wilson, W. & Tyler, L. K. (1980). The temporal structure of spoken language understanding. *Cognition*, 8:1–71.

Maske, R., Yamane, S., & Bishop, P. O. (1984). Binocular simple cells for local stereopsis: comparison of receptive field organizations for the two eyes. *Vis. Res.*, 24:1921–1929.

Mather, G. (1994). Motion detector models: Psychophysical evidence. In Smith, A. T. & Snowden, R. J., editors, *Visual Detection of Motion*, pp. 117–143. Academic Press, London, UK.

Mather, G. & Moulden, B. P. (1980). A simultaneous shift in apparent direction: Further evidence for a 'distribution-shift' model of direction coding. *Quart. J. Exp. Psych.*, 32:325–333.

Maunsell, J. H. R. & Newsome, W. T. (1987). Visual processing in monkey extrastriate cortex. *Ann. Rev. Neurosci.*, 10:363–401.

McGuiness, C. (1989). Visual imagery: The question of representation. *Irish J. Psych.*, 10:188–200.

McIlwain, J. T. (1964). Receptive fields of optic tract axons and lateral geniculate cells: Peripheral extent and barbiturate sensitivity. *J. Neurophysiol.*, 27:1154–1173.

McKee, S. P. & Nakayama, K. (1984). The detection of motion in the peripheral visual-field. *Vis. Res.*, 24:25–32.

Merzenich, M. M. & Brugge, J. F. (1993). Rpresentation of the cochlear partition on the superior temporal plane of the macaque monkey. *Brain Res.*, 50:275–296.

Metaxas, D. (1992). Physics-based modeling of nonrigid objects for vision and graphics. *Ph.D. thesis, Dept. of Computer Science, Univ. of Toronto.*

Metaxas, D. & Dickinson, S. (1993). Integration of quantitative and qualitative techniques for deformable model fitting from orthographic, perspective, and stereo projections. In *Proc. ICCV*, Berlin, Germany.

Metaxas, D. & Terzopoulos, D. (1993). Shape and nonrigid motion estimation through physics-based synthesis. *IEEE PAMI.*

Metzler, S. & Shepard, R. N. (1982). Transformational studies of the internal representations of three-dimensional objects. In Shepard, R. N. & Cooper, L., editors, *Mental images and their transformations*, pp. 25–71. MIT Press, Cambridge, MA.

Miles, F. A. & Wallman, J. (1993). *Visual Motion and its Role in the Stabilization of Gaze.* Elsevier, North Holland.

Miller, E. K. & Desimone, R. (1994). Parallel neuronal mechanisms for short-term memory. *Science*, 263:520–522.

Miller, L. E., Theeuwen, M., & Gielen, C. C. (1992). The control of arm pointing movements in three dimensions. *Exp. Brain Res.*, 90:415–426.

Minken, A. W. H., Gielen, C. C. A. M., & Van Gisbergen, J. A. M. (1995). An alternative 3d interpretation of Hering's equal-innervation law for version and vergence eye movements. *Vis. Res.*, 35:93–102.

Minsky, M. (1975). A framework for representing knowledge. In Winston, P. H., editor, *The Psychology of Computer Vision.* McGraw-Hill, New York, NY.

Misslisch, H., Tweed, D., Fetter, M., & Vilis, T. (1994). The influence of gravity on Donders' law for head movements. *Vis. Res.*, 34:3017–3025.

Mitson, L., Ono, H., & Barbieto, R. (1976). Three methods of measuring the location of the egocentre: their reliability, comparative locations and intercorrelations. *Canad. J. Psychol.*, 30:1–8.

Miyashita, Y. (1993). Inferior temporal cortex: where visual perception meets memory. *Ann. Rev. Neurosci.*, 16:245–263.

Mok, D., Ro, A., Cadera, W., Crawford, J. D., & Vilis, T. (1992). Rotation of Listing's plane during vergence. *Vis. Res.*, 32:2055–2064.

Moran, J. & Desimone, R. (1985). Selective attention gates visual processing in the extrastriate cortex. *Science*, 229:782–784.

Morgan, M. J. (1986). The detection of spatial discontinuities: Interactions between contrst and spatial contiguity. *Spatial Vision*, 1:291–303.

Morgan, M. J. (1991). Hyperacuity. In Regan, D. M., editor, *Spatial Vision*, pp. 87–113. The Macmillan Press Ltd, London.

Morgan, M. J., Adam, A., & Mollon, J. D. (1992). Dichromats detect colour-camouflaged objects that are not detected by trichromats. *Proc. Roy. Soc. Lond. B.*, 248:291–295.

Morgan, M. J. & Aiba, T. S. (1985a). Positional acuity with chromatic stimuli. *Vis. Res.*, 25:689–695.

Morgan, M. J. & Aiba, T. S. (1985b). Vernier acuity predicted from changes in the light distribution of the retinal image. *Spatial Vision*, 1:151–161.

Morgan, M. J. & Hotopf, W. H. N. (1989). Perceived diagonals in grids and lattices. *Vis. Res.*, 29:1005–1015.

Morgan, M. J. M. & Regan, D. M. (1987). Opponent model for line interval discrimination: interval and vernier performance compared. *Vis. Res.*, 27:107–118.

Moschovakis, A. K. & Highstein, S. M. (1994). The anatomy and physiology of primate neurons that control rapid eye movements. *Ann. Rev. Neurosci.*, 17:465–488.

Moulden, B. (1994). Collator units: second-stage orientational filters. In Bock, B. & Goode, J. A., editors, *Higher-Order Processing in the Visual System*, pp. 170–192. Wiley, Chichester, UK. (Ciba Foundation Symposium 184).

Mountcastle, V. B. & Powell, T. P. S. (1959). Neural mechanisms subserving cutaneous sensibility, with special reference to the role of afferent inhibition in sensory perception discriminations. *Bul. Johns Hopkins Hosp.*, 105:201–232.

Movshon, J. A., Thompson, I. D., & Tolhurst, D. J. (1978). Spatial summation in the receptive fields of simple cells in the cat's striate cortex. *J. Physiol. (Lond.)*, 283:53–77.

Müller, J. (1840). *Handbuch der Physiologie des Menschen Vol II*. Holscher, Coblentz.

Muller, R. & Greenlee, M. W. (1994). Effect of contrast and adaptation on the perception of the direction and speed of drifting gratings. *Vis. Res.*, 34:2071–2092.

Munoz, D. P., Guitton, D., & Palisson, D. (1991). Control of orienting gaze shifts by the tecto-reticulo-spinal system in the head free cat. III. Spatiotemporal characteristics of phasic motor discharges. *J. Neurophysiol.*, 66:1642–1666.

Mussap, A. J. & Levi, D. M. (1995a). Binocular processes in vernier acuity. *J. Opt. Soc. Am. A*, 12:225–233.

Mussap, A. J. & Levi, D. M. (1995b). Spatial properties of filters underlying Vernier acuity revealed by masking: Evidence for collator mechanisms. *Vis. Res.* (in press).

Mussap, A. J. & Levi, D. M. (1996). Vernier acuity with plaid masks: The role of oriented filters in vernier acuity. *Vis. Res.* (in press).

Nakayama, K. (1975). Coordination of extraocular muscles. In Bach-y-Rita, P. & Lennerstrand, G., editors, *Basic Mechanisms of Ocular Motility and Their Clinical Implications*, pp. 193–207. Pergamon, Oxford, UK.

Nakayama, K. (1983). Kinematics of normal and strabismic eyes. In Schor, C. M. & Ciuffreda, K. J., editors, *Vergence Eye Movements: Basic and Clinical Aspects*, pp. 543–564. Butterworths, Boston, MA.

Nakayama, K. & Shimojo, S. (1990a). Da Vinci stereopsis: Depth and subjective occluding contours from unpaired image points. *Vis. Res.*, 30:1811–1825.

Nakayama, K. & Shimojo, S. (1990b). Towards a neural understanding of visual surface representation. In Sejnowski, T., Kandel, E. R., Stevens, C. F., & Watson, J. D., editors, *The Brain, Cold Spring Harbor Symposium on Quantitative Biology*, volume 55, pp. 911–924. Cold Spring Harbor Laboratory, NY.

Nelson, J. I. & Frost, B. J. (1978). Orientation-selective inhibition from beyond the classic visual receptive field. *Brain Res.*, 139:359–365.

Newsome, W. T., Wurtz, R. H., Dürsteler, M. R., & Mikami, A. (1985). Deficits in visual motion processing following ibotenic acid lesions of the middle temporal visual area of the macaque monkey. *J. Neurosci.*, 5:825–840.

Nikara, T., Bishop, P. O., & Pettigrew, J. D. (1968). Analysis of retinal correspondence by studying receptive fields of binocular single units in cat striate cortex. *Exp. Brain Res.*, 6:353–372.

Nomura, M., Matsumoto, G., & Fujiwara, S. (1990). A binocular model for the simple cell. *Biol. Cybernetics*, 63:237–242.

Nothdurft, H. C. (1985a). Orientation sensitivity and texture segmentation in patterns with different line orientation. *Vis. Res.*, 25:551–560.

Nothdurft, H. C. (1985b). Sensitivity for structure gradient in texture discrimination tasks. *Vis. Res.*, 25:1957–1968.

Nothdurft, H. C. (1990). Texton segregation by associated differences in global and local luminance distribution. *Proc. Roy. Soc. Lond. B.*, 239:295–320. (erratum B 241: 249-250).

Nothdurft, H. C. (1991). Texture segmentation and pop-out from orientation contrast. *Vis. Res.*, 31:1073–1078.

Nothdurft, H. C. (1992). Feature analysis and the role of similarity in pre-attentive vision. *Percept. & Psychophys.*, 52:355–375.

Nothdurft, H. C. (1993a). The conspicuousness of orientation and motion contrast. *Spatial Vision*, 7:341–363.

Nothdurft, H. C. (1993b). The role of features in preattentive vision: Comparison of orientation, motion, and color cues. *Vis. Res.*, 33:1937–1958.

Nothdurft, H. C. (1994a). Common properties of visual segmentation. In Bock, G. A. & Goodie, J. A., editors, *Higher-Order processing in the visual system*, pp. 245–268. Wiley, Chichester, UK. (Ciba Foundation Symposium 184).

Nothdurft, H. C. (1994b). Cortical properties of preattentive vision. In Albowitz, B., Albus, K., Kuhnt, U., Nothdurft, H. C., & Wahle, P., editors, *Structural and functional organization of the neocortex*, pp. 375–384. Springer Verlag, Heidelberg, Germany.

Nothdurft, H. C. (1995). Generalized feature contrast in preattentive vision. *Perception*, 24:S22.

Nothdurft, H. C., Gallant, J. L., & Van Essen, D. C. (1992). Neural responses to texture borders in macaque area V1. *Soc. Neurosci. Abs.*, 18(2):1275.

Nothdurft, H. C. & Li, C. Y. (1985). Texture discrimination: Representation of orientation and luminance differences in cells of the cat striate cortex. *Vis. Res.*, 25:99–113.

O'Brien, V. (1958). Contour perception, illusion and reality. *J. Opt. Soc. Am. A*, 48:112–119.

Ohzawa, I., DeAngelis, G. C., & Freeman, R. D. (1990). Stereoscopic depth discrimination in the visual cortex: neurons ideally suited as disparity detectors. *Science*, 249:1037–1041.

Ohzawa, I. & Freeman, R. D. (1986a). The binocular organization of complex cells in the cat's visual cortex. *J. Neurophysiol.*, 56:243–259.

Ohzawa, I. & Freeman, R. D. (1986b). The binocular organization of simple cells in the cat's visual cortex. *J. Neurophysiol.*, 56:221–242.

Ohzawa, I. & Freeman, R. D. (1994). Monocular and binocular mechanisms of contrast gain control. In Lawton, T. B., editor, *Computational Vision Based on Neurobiology, SPIE Proc. V. 2054*, pp. 43–51.

Oja, E. (1982). A simplified neuron model as a principal component analyzer. *J. Math. Biol.*, 15:267–73.

O'Keefe, J. & Dostrovsky, J. (1971). The hippocampus as a spatial map. preliminary evidence from unit activity in the freely moving rat. *Brain Res.*, 34:171–175.

Olson, C. R. & Gettner, S. N. (1995). Object-centered direction selectivity in rhesus monkey supplementary eye field. *Soc. Neurosci. Abst.*, 21:282.

Olson, D. R. & Bialystok, E. (1983). *Spatial Cognition*. Erlbaum, Hillsdale, NJ.

Olson, R. K. & Attneave, F. (1970). What variables produce similarity grouping? *Am. J. Psych.*, 83:1–21.

Oman, C. M. (1990). Motion sickness - a synthesis and evaluation of the sensory conflict theory. *Can. J. Physiol. and Pharmacol.*, 68:294–303.

Orban, G. A., Gulyas, B., & Vogels, R. (1987). Influence of a moving textured background on direction selectivity of cat striate cortex neurons. *J. Neurophysiol.*, 57:1792–1812.

Oyster, C. W., Takahashi, E., & Collewijn, H. (1972). Direction-selective retinal ganglion cells and control of optokinetic nystagmus in the rabbit. *Vis. Res.*, 12:183–193.

Paivio, A. (1971). *Imagery and verbal processes*. Holt, Rinehart & Winston, New York, NY.

Paivio, A. (1983). The empirical case for dual coding. In Yuille, J. C., editor, *Imagery, memory and cognition: Essays in honor of Allan Paivio*, pp. 307–332. Lawrence Erlbaum Associates Inc., Hillsdale, NJ.

Paivio, A. (1986). *Mental representations: A dual coding approach*. Oxford University Press, Oxford, UK.

Paivio, A. (1991). *Images in mind: The evolution of a theory*. Harvester Wheatsheaf, Hertfordshire, UK.

Paivio, A. & Csapo, K. (1973). Picture superiority in free recall: Imagery or dual coding? *Cognitive Psychology*, 5:176–206.

Palmer, L. A. & Davis, T. L. (1981). Receptive-field structure in cat striate cortex. *J. Neurophysiol.*, 46:260–276.

Palmer, S. E. (1975). Visual perception and world knowledge: Notes on a model of sensory-cognitive interaction. In Norman, D. A. & Rumelhart, D. E., editors, *Explorations in Cognition*, pp. 279–307. W. H. Freeman and Co., San Francisco, CA.

Palmer, S. E. (1982). Symmetry, transformation and the structure of perceptual systems. In Beck, J., editor, *Organization and Representation in Perception*, pp. 95–144. Lawrence Erlbaum, Hillsdale, NJ.

Parker, A. & Hawken, M. (1985). Capabilities of monkey cortical cells in spatial-resolution tasks. *J. Opt. Soc. Am. A*, 2:1101–1114.

Parsons, L. M. & Fox, P. T. (1995). Neural basis of mental rotation. In *Soc. Neurosci. Abst.*, volume 21, p. 272.

Penfield, W. (1959). The interpretative cortex. *Science*, 129:1719–1725.

Pentland, A. (1986). Perceptual organization and the representation of natural form. *Artificial Intelligence*, 28:293–331.

Pentland, A. (1988). Automatic extraction of deformable part models. Vision Sciences TR-104, MIT Media Lab.

Pentland, A. & Sclaroff, S. (1991). Closed-form solutions for physically based shape modeling and recognition. *IEEE PAMI*, 13:715–729.

Pentland, A. P. (1985). On describing complex surface shapes. *Image and Vision Computing*, 3(4):153–162.

Perrett, D. I., Mistlin, A. J., & Chitty, A. J. (1987). Visual neurons responsive to faces. *Trends in Neurosc.*, 10:358–364.

Perrett, D. I., Rolls, E. T., & Caan, W. (1982). Visual neurones responsive to faces in the monkey temporal cortex. *Exp. Brain Res.*, 47:329–342.

Perrett, D. I., Smith, P. A. J., Mistlin, A. J., Chitty, A. J., Head, A. S., Potter, D. D., Broennimann, R., Milner, A. D., & Jeeves, M. A. (1985a). Visual analysis of body movements by neurones in the temporal cortex of the macaque monkey: a preliminary report. *Behav. Brain Res.*, 16:153–170.

Perrett, D. I., Smith, P. A. J., Potter, D. D., Mistlin, A. J., Head, A. S., Milner, A. D., & Jeeves, M. A. (1985b). Visual cells in the temporal cortex sensitive to face view and gaze direction. *Proc. Roy. Soc. Lond. B*, 223:293–317.

Pettigrew, J. D. (1972). The neurophysiology of binocular vision. *Scientific American*, August:84–95.

Pettigrew, J. D. (1979). Binocular visual processing in the owl's telencephalon. *Proc. Roy. Soc. Lond. B*, 204:435–454.

Pettigrew, J. D. & Konishi, M. (1976). Neurons selective for orientation and binocular disparity in the visual wulst of the barn owl (Tyto alba). *Science*, 193:675–678.

Pettigrew, J. D., Nikara, T., & Bishop, P. O. (1968). Responses to moving slits by single units in cat striate cortex. *Exp. Brain Res.*, 6:373–390.

Phillips, D. P. (1989). The neural coding of simple and complex sounds in the auditory cortex. In Lund, J. S., editor, *Sensory processing in the mammalian brain*, pp. 172–203. Oxford University Press, New York, NY.

Piaget, J. (1969). *The Mechanisms of Perception*. Basic Books, New York, NY. Translated by G. N. Geagrin.

Pinker, S. (1985). Visual cognition: An introduction. In Pinker, S., editor, *Visual Cognition*, pp. 1–64. MIT Press, Cambridge, MA.

Poggio, G. F. & Fischer, B. (1977). Binocular interaction and depth sensitivity in striate and prestriate cortex of behaving Rhesus monkey. *J. Neurophysiol.*, 40:1392–1405.

Poggio, G. F., Motter, B. C., Squatrito, S., & Trotter, Y. (1985). Responses of neurons in visual cortex (v1 and v2) of the alert macaque to dynamic random-dot stereograms. *Vis. Res.*, 25:397–406.

Poggio, G. F. & Talbot, W. H. (1981). Mechanisms of static and dynamic stereopsis in foveal cortex of the rhesus monkey. *J. Physiol. (Lond.)*, 315:469–492.

Poggio, T. & Edelman, S. (1990). A network that learns to recognize three-dimensional objects. *Nature*, 343:263–266.

Poggio, T. & Girosi, F. (1990a). Networks for approximation and learning. *Proc. IEEE*, 78:1481–1497.

Poggio, T. & Girosi, F. (1990b). Regularization algorithms for learning that are equivalent to multilayer networks. *Science*, 247:978–982.

Pollen, D. A. & Ronner, S. E. (1981). Phase relationships between adjacent simple cells in the visual cortex. *Science*, 212:1409–1411.

Pollen, D. A. & Ronner, S. E. (1983). Visual cortical neurons as localized spatial frequency filters. *IEEE SMC*, 13:907–916.

Pouget, A., Fisher, S. A., & Sejnowski, T. J. (1993). Egocentric spatial representation in early vision. *J. of Cognitive Neurosci.*, 5:150–161.

Powell, K. D., Quinn, K. J., Rude, S. A., Peterson, B. W., & Baker, J. F. (1991). Frequency-dependence of cat vestibuloocular reflex direction adaptation - single frequency and multifrequency rotations. *Brain Res.*, 550:137–141.

Pylyshyn, Z. W. (1973). What the mind's eye tells the mind's brain: A critique of mental imagery. *Psychological Bulletin*, 80:1–24.

Pylyshyn, Z. W. (1979). The rate of "mental rotation" of images : a test of a holistic analogue hypothesis. *Memory and Cognition*, 7:19–28.

Pylyshyn, Z. W. (1981). The imagery debate: Analogical media versus tacit knowledge. *Psych. Rev.*, 88:16–45.

Pylyshyn, Z. W. (1984). *Computation and Cognition*. MIT Press, Cambridge, MA.

Pylyshyn, Z. W. (1988). Tracking multiple independent targets: Evidence for a parallel tracking mechanism. *Spatial Vision*, 3:179–197.

Pylyshyn, Z. W. & Storm, R. (1986). *Computation and Cognition*. MIT Press, Cambridge, MA.

Quick, R. F. (1974). A vector magnitude model for contrast detection. *Kybernetik*, 16:65–67.

Radau, P., Tweed, D., & Vilis, T. (1994). Three-dimensional eye, head, and chest orientations after large gaze shifts and the underlying neural strategies. *J. Neurophysiol.*, 72:2840–2852.

Ramachandran, V. S. (1986). Capture of stereopsis and apparent motion by illusory contours. *Perception and Psychophysics*, 39:361–373.

Ramachandran, V. S. (1993). Behavioural and magentoencephalographic correlates of plasticity in the adult human brain. *Proc. Nat. Acad. Sci. USA*, 90:10413–10420.

Ramachandran, V. S., Levi, L., Stone, L., Rogers-Ramachandran, D., Schatz, A., McKinney, R., Stalcup, M., Arcilla, G., & Flippin, A. (1995). Illusions of body image: What they reveal about human nature. In *Decade of the Brain Lecture, Society for Neuroscience*, San Diego, CA.

Ramachandran, V. S., Ruskin, D., Cobb, S., Rogers-Ramachandran, D., & Tyler, C. W. (1994). On the perception of illusory contours. *Vis. Res.*, 34:3145–3152.

Raphan, T. & Cohen, B. (1985). Velocity storage and the ocular response to multidimensional vestibular stimuli. In Berthoz, A. & Melvill-Jones, G., editors, *Adaptive mechanisms in gaze control*, pp. 123–144. Elsevier, North Holland.

Reason, J. T. (1978). Motion sickness adaptation: a neural mismatch model. *J. Roy Soc. Med.*, 71:819–829.

Regan, D. (1982). Visual information channeling in normal and disordered vision. *Psych. Rev.*, 89:407–444.

Regan, D. (1989). *Human Brain Electrophysiology*. Elsevier, North Holland.

Regan, D. & Beverley, K. I. (1985). Postadaptation orientation discrimination. *J. Opt. Soc. Am. A*, 2:147–155.

Reichardt, W. (1961). Autocorrelation, a principle for the evaluation of sensory information by the central nervous system. In Rosenblith, W. A., editor, *Sensory Communication*. MIT Press, Cambridge, MA.

Rentschler, I., Hübner, M., & Caelli, T. (1988). On the discrimination of compound Gabor signals and textures. *Vis. Res.*, 28:279–291.

Rissanen, J. (1989). *Stochastic Complexity in Statistical Inquiry*. World Scientific Press, Singapore.

Robinson, D. A. (1975). Ocular control signals. In Bach-y-Rita, P. & Lennerstrand, G., editors, *Basic Mechanisms of Ocular Motility and Their Clinical Implications*, pp. 337–374. Pergamon, Oxford, UK.

Robinson, D. A. (1977). Vestibular and optokinetic symbiosis: an example of explaining by modelling. In Baker, R. & Berthoz, A., editors, *Control of Gaze by Brain Stem Neurones*, pp. 49–58. Elsevier, North Holland.

Robinson, D. A. & Zee, D. S. (1981). Theoretical considerations of the function and circuitry of various rapid eye movements. In Fuchs, A. F. & Becker, W., editors, *Progress in Oculomotor Research*, pp. 3–9. Elsevier, North-Holland, New York, NY.

Robson, J. G., DeAngelis, G. C., Ohzawa, I., & Freeman, R. D. (1991). Cross-orientation inhibition in cat cortical cells originates from within the receptive field. *Invest. Ophthal. Vis. Sci.*, 32:429.

Rock, I. (1973). *Orientation and form*. Academic Press, New York, NY.

Rock, I., Wheeler, D., & Tudor, L. (1989). Can we imagine how objects look from other viewpoints? *Cognitive Psychology*, 21:185–210.

Rolls, E. T. (1981). Responses of amygdaloid neurons in the primate. In Ben-Ari, Y., editor, *The Amygdaloid Complex*, pp. 383–393. Elsevier, Amsterdam.

Rolls, E. T. (1984). Neurons in the cortex of the temporal lobe and in the amygdala of the monkey with responses selective for faces. *Human Neurobiol.*, 3:209–222.

Rolls, E. T. (1986a). Neural systems involved in emotion in primates. In Plutchik, R. & Kellerman, H., editors, *Emotion: Theory, Research, and Experience, Volume 3, Biological Foundations of Emotion*, pp. 125–143. Academic Press, New York.

Rolls, E. T. (1986b). A theory of emotion, and its application to understanding the neural basis of emotion. In Oomura, Y., editor, *Emotions. Neural and Chemical Control*, pp. 325–344. Japan Scientific Societies Press, Tokyo.

Rolls, E. T. (1989a). Functions of neuronal networks in the hippocampus and cerebral cortex in memory. In Coterill, R. M. J., editor, *Models of Brain Function*, pp. 15–33. Cambridge University Press, Cambridge.

Rolls, E. T. (1989b). Functions of neuronal networks in the hippocampus and neocortex in memory. In Byrne, J. H. & Berry, W. O., editors, *Neural Models of Plasticity: Experimental and Theoretical Approaches*, pp. 240–265. Academic Press, San Diego, CA.

Rolls, E. T. (1989c). The representation and storage of information in neuronal networks in the primate cerebral cortex and hippocampus. In

Durbin, R., Miall, C., & Mitchison, G., editors, *The Computing Neuron*, pp. 125–159. Addison-Wesley, Wokingham, England.

Rolls, E. T. (1990). A theory of emotion, and its application to understanding the neural basis of emotion. *Cog. and Emot.*, 4:161–190.

Rolls, E. T. (1991). Neural organisation of higher visual functions. *Current Op. Neurobiol.*, 1:274–278.

Rolls, E. T. (1992a). Neurophysiological mechanisms underlying face processing within and beyond the temporal cortical visual areas. *Phil. Trans. Roy. Soc.*, 335:11–21.

Rolls, E. T. (1992b). Neurophysiology and functions of the primate amygdala. In Aggleton, J. P., editor, *The Amygdala*, pp. 143–165. Wiley-Liss, New York, NY.

Rolls, E. T. (1992c). The processing of face information in the primate temporal lobe. In Bruce, V. & Burton, M., editors, *Processing Images of Faces*, pp. 41–68. Ablex, Norwood, NJ.

Rolls, E. T. (1994). Brain mechanisms for invariant visual recognition and learning. *Behav. Proc.*, 33:113–138.

Rolls, E. T. (1995). A theory of emotion and consciousness, and its application to understanding the neural basis of emotion. In Gazzaniga, M. S., editor, *The Cognitive Neurosciences*, pp. 1091–1106. MIT Press, Cambridge, MA.

Rolls, E. T. & Baylis, G. C. (1986). Size and contrast have only small effects on the responses to faces of neurons in the cortex of the superior temporal sulcus of the monkey. *Exp. Brain. Res.*, 65:38–48.

Rolls, E. T., Baylis, G. C., & Hasselmo, M. E. (1987). The responses of neurons in the cortex in the superior temporal sulcus of the monkey to band-pass spatial frequency filtered faces. *Vis. Res.*, 27:311–326.

Rolls, E. T., Baylis, G. C., Hasselmo, M. E., & Nalwa, V. (1989). The effect of learning on the face selective responses of neurons in the cortex in the superior temporal sulcus of the monkey. *Exp. Brain Res.*, 76:153–164.

Rolls, E. T., Baylis, G. C., & Leonard, C. M. (1985). Role of low and high spatial frequencies in the face-selective responses of neurons in the cortex in the superior temporal sulcus in the Monkey. *Vis. Res.*, 25:1021–1035.

Rolls, E. T., Hornak, J., Wade, D., & McGrath, J. (1994a). Emotion-related learning in patients with social and emotional changes associated with frontal lobe damage. *J. Neurol., Neurosurg. Psychiat.*, 57:1518–1524.

Rolls, E. T. & Tovee, M. J. (1994). Processing speed in the cerebral cortex, and the neurophysiology of visual masking. *Proc. Roy. Soc. Lond. B*, 257:9–15.

Rolls, E. T. & Tovee, M. J. (1995a). The responses of single neurons in the temporal visual cortical areas of the macaque when more than one stimulus is present in the receptive field. *Exp. Brain Res.*, 103:409–420.

Rolls, E. T. & Tovee, M. J. (1995b). Sparseness of the neuronal representation of stimuli in the primate temporal visual cortex. *J. Neurophys.*, 73:713–726.

Rolls, E. T., Tovee, M. J., Purcell, D. G., Stewart, A. L., & Azzopardi, P. (1994b). The responses of neurons in the temporal cortex of primates, and face identification and detection. *Exp. Brain Res.*, 101:474–484.

Rolls, E. T., Tovee, M. J., & Ramachandran, V. S. (1993). Visual learning reflected in the responses of neurons in the temporal visual cortex of the macaque. *Soc. Neurosci. Abs.*, 19:27.

Rolls, E. T. & Treves, A. (1990). The relative advantages of sparse versus distributed encoding for associative neuronal networks in the brain. *Network*, 1:407–421.

Rolls, E. T., Treves, A., & Tovee, M. J. (1996). The representational capacity of the distributed encoding of information provided by populations of neurons in the primate temporal visual cortex. (submitted for publication).

Rumelhart, D. E., Hinton, G. E., & McClelland, J. L. (1986a). A general framework for parallel distributed processing. In Rumelhart, D. E., McClelland, J. L., & the PDP Research Group, editors, *Parallel distributed processing: Vol. 1, Foundations*, pp. 45–76. MIT Press, Cambridge, MA.

Rumelhart, D. E. & McClelland, J. L. (1986). *Parallel distributed processing: explorations in the microstructure of cognition (Vols. 1-3)*. MIT Press, Cambridge, MA.

Rumelhart, D. E., McClelland, J. L., & the PDP Research Group, editors (1986b). *Parallel distributed processing: Vol. 1, Foundations*. MIT Press, Cambridge, MA.

Sachtler, W. L. & Zaidi, Q. (1993). Effect of spatial configuration on motion aftereffects. *J. Opt. Soc. Am. A.*, 10:1433–1449.

Sacks, O. W. (1985). *The Man Who Mistook His Wife For a Hat*. Duckworth, London, UK.

Sagi, D. (1995). The psychophysics of texture segmentation. In Papathomas, T. V., Chubb, C., Gorea, A., & Kowler, E., editors, *Early Vision and Beyond*, pp. 69–78. MIT Press, Cambridge, MA.

Sagi, D. & Julesz, B. (1987). Short-range limitations on detection of feature differences. *Spatial Vision*, 2:39–49.

Saint-Marc, P., Chen, J.-S., & Medioni, G. (1991). Adaptive smoothing: A general tool for early vision. *IEEE PAMI*, 13:514–529.

Salzman, C. D. & Newsome, W. T. (1994). Neural mechanisms for forming a perceptual decision. *Science*, 264:231–237.

Saund, E. (1995). A multiple cause mixture model for unsupervised learning. *Computation*, 7.

Schiller, P. H. & Koerner, F. (1971). Discharge characteristics of single units in superior colliculus of the alert Rhesus monkey. *J. Neurophysiol.*, 34:920–936.

Schiller, P. H. & Stryker, M. (1972). Single-unit recording and stimulation in superior colliculus of the alert Rhesus monkey. *J. Neurophysiol.*, 35:915–924.

Schlag, J., Schlag-Rey, M., & Dassonville, P. (1989). Interactions between natural and electrically evoked saccades II. At what time is eye position sampled as a reference for the localization of a target? *Exp. Brain Res.*, 76:548–558.

Schnabolk, C. & Raphan, T. (1994). Modelling three-dimensional velocity-to-position transformation in oculomotor control. *J. Neurophsyiol.*, 71:623–638.

Sclar, G., Ohzawa, I., & Freeman, R. D. (1985). Contrast gain control in the kitten's visual system. *J. Neurophysiol.*, 54:668–675.

Sekuler, R. & Ganz, L. (1963). Aftereffect of seen motion with a stabilized retinal image. *Science*, 139:419–420.

Sekuler, R. & Levinson, E. (1974). Mechanisms of motion perception. *Psychologia*, 17:38–49.

Sekuler, R., Pantle, A., & Levinson, E. (1978). *Handbook of Sensory Physiology*, volume 8. Springer-Verlag, Berlin, Germany.

Seltzer, B. & Pandya, D. N. (1978). Afferent cortical connections and architectonics of the superior temporal sulcus and surrounding cortex in the rhesus monkey. *Brain Res.*, 149:1–24.

Shannon, C. E. & Weaver, W. (1949). *The Mathematical Theory of Communication*. University of Illinois Press, Urbana, IL.

Shapley, R. & Victor, J. (1986). Hyperacuity in cat retinal ganglion cells. *Science*, 231:999–1002.

Shepard, R. N. (1978). The mental image. *The American Psychologist*, 33:125–137.

Shepard, R. N. (1981). Psychophysical complementarity. In Kubovy, M. & Pomerantz, J. R., editors, *Perceptual Organization*, pp. 279–341. Lawrence Erlbaum, Hillsdale, NJ.

Shepard, R. N. & Cooper, L. (1982). *Mental Images and their transformations*. MIT Press, Cambridge, MA.

Shepard, R. N. & Metzler, J. (1971). Mental rotation of three-dimensional objects. *Science*, 171:701–703.

Shepard, R. N. & Metzler, J. (1988). Mental rotation: Effects of dimensionality of objects and types of tasks. *J. Exp. Psych.: Human Perception and Performance*, 14:3–11.

Shiffrar, M. M. & Shepard, R. N. (1991). Comparison of cube rotations around axes inclined relative to the environment or to the cube. *J. Exp. Psych.: Human Perception and Performance*, 17:44–54.

Simmen, M. W., Rolls, E. T., & Treves, A. (1995). Rapid retrieval in an autoassociative network of spiking neurons. In *Proceedings of the Computation and Neural Systems Meeting*, Monterey, CA.

Simpson, J. I., Leonard, C. S., & Soodak, R. E. (1988a). The accessory optic-system - analyzer of self-motion. *Ann. New York Acad. Sci.*, 545:170–179.

Simpson, J. I., Leonard, C. S., & Soodak, R. E. (1988b). The accessory optic-system of rabbit. 2. spatial-organization of direction selectivity. *J. Neurophysiol.*, 60:2055–2072.

Singer, W. (1993). Synchronization of cortical activity and its putative role in information processing and learning. *Ann. Rev. Physiol.*, 55:349–374.

Smith, D. V. & Travers, J. B. (1979). A metric for the breadth of tuning of gustatory neurons. *Chem. Sens.*, 4:215–229.

Smolensky, P. (1988). On the proper treatment of connectionism. *Behavioural and Brain Sciences*, 11:1–74.

Snowden, R. J. (1994). Motion processing in the primate cerebral cortex. In Smith, A. T. & Snowden, R. J., editors, *Visual Detection of Motion*, pp. 51–83. Academic Press, London, UK.

Solso, R. L. (1991). *Cognitive Psychology 3rd. Edition*. Allyn and Bacon, Boston, MA.

Somers, D. C., Nelson, S. B., & Sur, M. (1995). An emergent model of orientation selectivity in cat visual cortical simple cells. *J. Neurosci.*, 15:5448–5465.

Sparks, D. L. (1988). Neural cartography: sensory and motor maps in the superior colliculus. *Brain Behav. Evol.*, 31:49–56.

Sparks, D. L., Lee, C., & Rohrer, W. H. (1990). Population coding of the direction amplitude and velocity of saccadic eye movements by neurones in the superior colliculus. *Cold Spring Harbour Symp. Quant. Biol.*, 55:805–811.

Sparks, D. L. & Mays, L. E. (1983). Spatial localization of saccade targets I. compensation for stimulation-induced perturbations in eye position. *J. Neurophysiol.*, 49:45–63.

Sparks, D. L. & Mays, L. E. (1990). Signal transformations required for the generation of saccadic eye movements. *Ann. Rev. Neurosci.*, 13:309–336.

Stein, B. E. & Meredith, M. A. (1993). *The Merging of the Senses.* MIT Press, Cambridge, MA.

Steinbach, M. J. & Money, K. E. (1973). Eye movements of the owl. *Vis. Res.*, 13:889–891.

Stiles, W. S. (1939). The directional sensitivity of the retina and the spectral sensitivities of the rods and cones. *Proc. Roy. Soc. Lond. B*, 127:64–105.

Stiles, W. S. (1959). Color vision: The approach through increment threshold sensitivity. *Proc. Nat. Acad. Sci.s*, 45:100–114.

Stone, L. S. & Thompson, P. (1992). Human speed perception is contrast dependent. *Vis. Res.*, 32:1535–1549.

Straumann, D., Haslwanter, T., Hepp-Reymond, M. C., & Hepp, K. (1991). Listing's law for eye head and arm movements and their synergistic control. *Exp. Brain Res.*, 86:209–215.

Sutherland, N. S. (1961). Figural aftereffects and apparent size. *Quart. J. Exp. Psych.*, 13:222–228.

Swanson, W. H. & Wilson, H. R. (1985). Eccentricity dependence of contrast matching and oblique masking. *Vis. Res.*, 25:1285–1295.

Takano, Y. (1989). Perception of rotated forms: A theory of information types. *Cognitive Psychology*, 21:1–59.

Tan, H. S., Van Der Steen, J., Simpson, J. I., & Collewijn, H. (1993). Three-dimensional organization of optokinetic responses in the rabbit. *J. Neurophysiol.*, 69:303–317.

Tanaka, K., Saito, C., Fukada, Y., & Moriya, M. (1990). Integration of form, texture, and color information in the inferotemporal cortex of the macaque. In Iwai, E. & Mishkin, M., editors, *Vision, Memory and the Temporal Lobe*, pp. 101–109. Elsevier, New York, NY.

Tarr, M. J. & Pinker, S. (1989). Mental rotation and orientation-dependence in shape recognition. *Cognitive Psychology*, 21:233–282.

Terzopoulos, D. & Metaxas, D. (1991). Dynamic 3D models with local and global deformations: Deformable superquadrics. *IEEE PAMI*, 13(7):703–714.

Terzopoulos, D. & Szeliski, R. (1992). Tracking with kalman snakes. In Blake, A. & Yuille, A., editors, *Active Vision*, pp. 3–21. MIT Press.

Terzopoulos, D., Witkin, A., & Kass, M. (1987). Symmetry-seeking models and 3d object reconstruction. *IJCV*, 1:211–221.

Terzopoulos, D., Witkin, A., & Kass, M. (1988). Constraints on Deformable Models: Recovering 3D shape and nonrigid motion. *Artificial Intelligence*, 36:91–123.

Thompson, D. & Mundy, J. (1987). Model-directed object recognition on the connection machine. In *Proc. DARPA Image Understanding Workshop*, pp. 93–106, Los Angeles, CA.

Thompson, P., Stone, L. S., & Swash, S. (1996). Speed estimates from grating patches are not contrast-normalized. *Vis. Res.*, 36:667–674.

Thorpe, S. J. & Imbert, M. (1989). Biological constraints on connectionist modeling. In Pfeifer, R., Schreter, Z., & Fogelman-Soulie, F., editors, *Connectionism in Perspective*, pp. 63–92. Elsevier, Amsterdam.

Tovee, M. J. & Rolls, E. T. (1995). Information encoding in short firing rate epochs by single neurons in the primate temporal visual cortex. *Visual Cognition*, 2:35–58.

Tovee, M. J., Rolls, E. T., & Azzopardi, P. (1994). Translation invariance in the response to faces of single neurons in the temporal visual cortical areas of the alert Macaque. *J. Neurophysiol.*, 72:1049–1060.

Tovee, M. J., Rolls, E. T., Treves, A., & Bellis, R. P. (1993). Information encoding and the responses of single neurons in the primate temporal visual cortex. *J. Neurophysiol.*, 70:640–654.

Treisman, A. (1985). Preattentive processing in vision. *CVGIP*, pp. 156–177.

Treves, A. (1993). Mean-field analysis of neuronal spike dynamics. *Network*, 4:259–284.

Treves, A. & Rolls, E. T. (1991). What determines the capacity of autoassociative memories in the brain? *Network*, 2:371–397.

Treves, A. & Rolls, E. T. (1994). A computational analysis of the role of the hippocampus in memory. *Hippocampus*, 4:374–391.

Treves, A., Rolls, E. T., & Tovee, M. J. (1996). On the time required for recurrent processing in the brain. In Torre, V. & Conti, F., editors, *Neurobiology*. Plenum, New York, NY.

Tsotsos, J. K. (1990). Analysing vision at the complexity level. *Behavioral and Brain Sciences*, 13(3):423–496.

Turvey, M. T. (1973). On peripheral and central processes in vision: inferences from an information processing analysis of masking with patterned stimuli. *Psych. Rev.*, 80:1–52.

Tweed, D. (1994). Binocular coordination, stereo vision, and Listing's law. *Soc. Neurosci. Abst.*, 20:1403.

Tweed, D., Cadera, W., & Vilis, T. (1990). Computing three-dimensional eye position quaternions and eye velocity from search coil signals. *Vis. Res.*, 30:97–110.

Tweed, D., Glenn, B., & Vilis, T. (1992). A model for 3-dimensional eye-head saccades. *Soc. Neurosci. Abst.*, 18:698.

Tweed, D., Misslisch, H., & Fetter, M. (1995). Testing modesl of the oculomotor velocity-to-position transformation. *J. Neurophysiol.*, 72:1425–1429.

Tweed, D. & Vilis, T. (1987). Implications of rotational kinematics for the oculomotor system in three dimensions. *J. Neurophysiol.*, 58:832–849.

Tweed, D. & Vilis, T. (1990a). Geometric relations of eye position and velocity vectors during saccades. *Vis. Res.*, 30:111–127.

Tweed, D. & Vilis, T. (1990b). The superior colliculus and spatiotemporal translation in the saccadic system. *Neural Networks*, 3:75–86.

Tye, M. (1991). *The Imagery Debate*. MIT Press, Cambridge MA.

Tyler, C. W. (1975). Characteristics of stereomovement suppression. *Perception and Psychophysics*, 17:225–230.

Tyler, C. W. (1983). Sensory processing of binocular disparity. In Schor, C. M. & Ciuffreda, K. J., editors, *Vergence Eye Movements: Basic and Clinical Aspects*, pp. 199–296. Butterworth, Boston, MA.

Tyler, C. W. (1995). Theoretical issues in symmetry perception. *Spatial Vision*, 8:383–391.

Tyler, C. W., Barghout, L., & Kontsevich, L. L. (1994). Computational reconstruction of the mechanisms of human stereopsis. In Lawton, T. B., editor, *Computational Vision Based on Neurobiology*, pp. 52–68. Proc. SPIE 2054.

Tyler, C. W., Hardage, L., & Miller, R. T. (1995). Multiple mechanisms for the detection of mirror symmetry. *Spatial Vision*, 9:79–100.

Tyler, C. W. & Kontsevich, L. L. (1995). Mechanisms of stereoscopic processing: stereoattention and surface perception in depth reconstruction. *Perception*, 24:127–153.

Tyler, C. W. & Miller, R. H. (1994). Pattern identification by trajectory analysis in autocorrelation hyperspace. In *Proc. World Congress on Neural Networks. III*, pp. 312–316.

Ungerleider, L. G. & Mishkin, M. (1982). Two cortical visual systems. In Ingle, D. J., Goodale, M. A., & Mansfield, R. J. W., editors, *Analysis of Visual Behavior*, pp. 549–586. MIT Press, Cambridge, MA.

Uttal, W. R. (1973). *The Psychobiology of Sensory Coding*. Harper & Row, New York, NY.

Vallbo, A. B. (1989). Single fibre microneurography and sensation. In Kennard, C. & Swash, M., editors, *Hierarchies in Neurology: A Reappraisal of a Jacksonian Concept*, pp. 93–109. Springer, London.

Van Essen, D. C. & Anderson, C. H. (1990). Information processing strategies and pathways in the primate retina and visual cortex. In Zornetzer, S. F., Davis, J. L., & Lau, C., editors, *Introduction to Neural and Electronic Networks*, pp. 43–72. Academic Press, Orlando, Florida.

Van Essen, D. C. & Zeki, S. M. (1978). The topographic organization of Rhesus monkey prestriate cortex. *J. Physiol. (Lond.)*, 277:193–226.

Van Gisbergen, J. A. M., Van Opstal, A. J., & Minkin, A. W. H. (1990). Current views on the visuomotor interface of the saccadic system. In Gorea, A., Fregnae, Y., Kapoula, Z., & Findlay, J., editors, *Representations of Vision: Trends and Tacit Assumptions in Vision Research*, pp. 201–215. Cambridge University Press, Cambridge, UK.

Van Opstal, A. J., Hepp, K., Hess, B. J. M., Straumann, D., & Henn, V. (1991). Two- rather than three-dimensional representation of saccades in monkey superior colliculus. *Science*, 252:1313–1315.

Van Rijn, L. J. & Van den Berg, A. V. (1993). Binocular eye orientation during fixations: Listing's law extended to include eye vergence. *Vis. Res.*, 33:691–708.

Verghese, G., Gale, K., & Dyer, C. (1990). Real-time, parallel motion tracking of three dimensional objects from spatiotemporal sequences. In Kumar, V., Gopalakrishnan, P. S., & Kanal, L. N., editors, *Parallel Algorithms for Machine Intelligence and Vision*. Springer-Verlag, New York.

Verstraten, F. A. J. (1996). On the ancient history of the motion aftereffect direction. *Perception*. (in press).

Vilis, T., Hepp, K., Schwarz, U., & Henn, V. (1989). On the generation of vertical and torsional rapid eye movements in the monkey. *Exp. Brain Res.*, 77:1–11.

von der Malsburg, C. (1990). A neural architecture for the representation of scenes. In McGaugh, J. L., Weinberger, N. M., & Lynch, G., editors, *Brain Organization and Memory: Cells, Systems and Circuits*, pp. 356–372. Oxford University Press, New York, NY.

Von der Marlsburg, C. & Schneider, W. (1986). A neural cocktail-party processor. *Biol. Cyb.*, 54:29–40.

von Helmholtz, H. (1867). *Handbuch der Physiologischen Optik (1st edn, Vol. 3)*. Voss, Hamburg. Treatise on Physiological Optics (English Translation), translated by J. P. C. Southall (1925), Rochester, NY, *Opt. Soc. Am.*, vol. 3, pp. 44-51.

Wagner, H. & Frost, B. (1993). Disparity-sensitive cells in the owl have a characteristic disparity. *Nature*, 364:796–798.

Wagner, H. & Frost, B. (1994). Binocular responses of neurons in the barn owl's visual wulst. *J. Comp. Phys. A*, 174:661–670.

Waitzman, D. M., Ma, T. P., Optican, L. M., & Wurtz, R. H. (1991). Superior colliculus neurons mediate the dynamic characteristics of saccades. *J. Neurophysiol.*, 66:1716–1737.

Wall, C., Harris, L. R., & Lathan, C. E. (1992). Interactions between otoliths and vision revealed by the response to z-axis linear movements. *Ann. New York Acad. Sci.*, 656:898–900.

Wallis, G., Rolls, E. T., & Foldiak, P. (1993). Learning invariant responses to the natural transformations of objects. In *Int. Joint Conf. on Neural Net.*, volume 2, pp. 1087–1090.

Wang, H. & Levi, D. M. (1994). Spatial integration in position acuity. *Vis. Res.*, 34:2859–2877.

Wang, H., Levi, D. M., & Klein, S. A. (1996). Intrinsic uncertainty and integration efficiency in bisection acuity. *Vis. Res.* (in press).

Watt, R. J. & Morgan, M. J. (1984). Spatial filters and the localization of luminance changes in human vision. *Vis. Res.*, 24:1387–1397.

Watt, R. J. & Morgan, M. J. (1985). A theory of the primitive spatial code in human vision. *Vis. Res.*, 25:1661–1674.

Waugh, S. J. & Levi, D. M. (1993a). Visibility and vernier acuity for separated targets. *Vis. Res.*, 33:539–552.

Waugh, S. J. & Levi, D. M. (1993b). Visibility, luminance and vernier acuity. *Vis. Res.*, 33:527–538.

Waugh, S. J. & Levi, D. M. (1993c). Visibility, timing and vernier acuity. *Vis. Res.*, 333:505–526.

Waugh, S. J. & Levi, D. M. (1995). Spatial alignment across gaps: contributions of orientation and spatial scale. *J. Opt. Soc. Am. A*, 12:2305–2317.

Waugh, S. J., Levi, D. M., & Carney, T. (1993). Orientation, Masking and Vernier Acuity for line targets. *Vis. Res.*, 33:1619–1638.

Wehrhahn, C. & Westheimer, G. (1990). How vernier acuity depends on contrast. *Exp. Brain Res.*, 80:618–620.

Westheimer, G. (1957). Kinematics of the eye. *J. Opt. Soc. Am.*, 47:967–974.

Westheimer, G. (1975). Visual acuity and hyperacuity. *Investigative Ophthalmology*, 14:570–572.

Westheimer, G. & McKee, S. P. (1977). Spatial configurations for visual hyperacuity. *Vis. Res.*, 17:941–947.

Wetherill, G. B. & Levitt, H. (1965). Sequential estimation of points on a psychometric function. *Brit. J. Math. Stat. Psych.*, 18:1–10.

Wilkinson, F. (1986). Visual texture segmentation in cats. *Behavourial Brain Research*, 19:71–82.

Williams, G. V., Rolls, E. T., Leonard, C. M., & Stern, C. (1993). Neuronal responses in the ventral striatum of the behaving macaque. *Behav. Brain Res.*, 55:243–252.

Willis, W. D. (1985). *The pain system. The neural basis of nocieptive transmission in the mammalian nervous system.* Basel, Karger.

Wilson, F. A. W., O'Scglaidhe, S. P., & Goldman-Rakic, P. S. (1993). Dissociation of object and spatial processing domains in primate preforontal cortex. *Science*, 260:1955–1958.

Wilson, H. R. (1986). Responses of spatial mechanisms can explain hyperacuity. *Vis. Res.*, 26:453–469.

Wilson, H. R. & Bergen, J. (1979). A four-mechanism model for threshold spatial vision. *Vis. Res.*, 19:19–32.

Wilson, H. R., McFarlane, D. K., & Phillips, G. C. (1983). Spatial frequency tuning of orientation selective units estimated by oblique masking. *Vis. Res.*, 23:873–882.

Wolfe, J. M., Cave, K. R., & Franzel, S. L. (1989). Guided search: An alternative to the feature integration model for visual search. *J. Exp. Psych.: Human Perception & Performance*, 15:419–433.

Wright, M. J. & Johnston, A. (1985). The relationship of displacement thresholds for oscillating gratings to cortical magnification, spatiotemporal frequency and contrast. *Vis. Res.*, 25:187–193.

Wu, J. J., Rink, R. E., Caelli, T. M., & Gourishankar, V. (1989). Recovery of the 3D location and motion of a rigid object through camera image (an extended Kalman filter approach). In *IJCV*, volume 2, pp. 373–394.

Wurtz, R. H. & Albano, J. E. (1980). Visual-motor function of the primate superior colliculus. *Ann. Rev. Neurosci.*, 3:189–226.

Wurtz, R. H. & Mohler, C. W. (1976). Organization of monkey superior colliculus: enhanced visual response of superficial layer cells. *J. Neurophysiol.*, 39:745–765.

Wylie, D. R. & Frost, B. J. (1993). Responses of pigeon vestibulocerebellar neurons to optokinetic stimulation. 2. the 3-dimensional reference frame of rotation neurons in the flocculus. *J. Neurophysiol.*, 70:2647–2659.

Wylie, D. R., Kripalani, T., & Frost, B. J. (1993). Responses of pigeon vestibulocerebellar neurons to optokinetic stimulation .1. functional organization of neurons discriminating between translational and rotational visual flow. *J. Neurophysiol.*, 70:2632–2646.

Xerri, C., Barthelemy, J., Borel, L., & Lacour, M. (1988). Neuronal coding of linear motion in the vestibular nuclei of the alert cat. 3. dynamic characteristics of visual otolith interactions. *Exp. Brain Res.*, 70:299–309.

Yamane, S., Kaji, S., & Kawano, K. (1988). What facial features activate face neurons in the inferotemporal cortex of the monkey? *Exp. Brain Res.*, 73:209–214.

Young, J. Z. (1962). Why do we have two brains? In Mountcastle, V. B., editor, *Interhemispheric Relations and Cerebral Dominance.*, pp. 7–24. Johns Hopkins University Press, Baltimore, MD.

Young, M. P. & Yamane, S. (1992). Sparse population coding of faces in the inferotemporal cortex. *Science*, 256:1327–1331.

Yuille, J. C. & Steiger, J. H. (1982). Nonholistic processing in mental rotation: Some suggestive evidence. *Perception and Psychophysics*, 31:201–209.

Zemel, R. S. (1994). A minimum description length framework for unsupervised learning. Ph.D. Dissertation, Computer Science, University of Toronto, Canada.

Ziebell, O. & Nothdurft, H. C. (1995). Facilitated detection of pop-out targets by localised cueing. *Perception*, 24:S46.

Zipser, D. & Andersen, R. A. (1988). A back-propogation programmed network that simulates response properties of a subset of posterior parietal neurons. *Nature*, 331:679–684.

Zohary, E. & Hochstein, S. (1989). How serial is serial processing in vision? *Perception*, 18:191–200.

Index

WITHDRAWN
FROM THE LIBRARY OF
UNIVERSITY OF ULSTER